The Four Ancient Books of Wales [Black Book of Carmarthen, Book of Haneirin, Book of Taliesin, Red Book of Hergest] Containing the Cymric Poems Attributed to the Bards of the Sixth Century, by W.F. Skene

Anonymous

The Four
Ancient Books of Wales

Printed by R. Clark

FOR

EDMONSTON AND DOUGLAS, EDINBURGH.

LONDON . . . HAMILTON, ADAMS, AND CO.
CAMBRIDGE . . MACMILLAN AND CO.
DUBLIN . . . M'GLASHAN AND GILL.
GLASGOW . . . JAMES MACLEHOSE.

THE

Four Ancient Books

OF

WALES

CONTAINING

The Cymric Poems attributed to the Bards of
The Sixth Century

BY WILLIAM F. SKENE

VOLUME II.

EDINBURGH
EDMONSTON AND DOUGLAS
1868

CONTENTS OF VOLUME II.

* This number has been by mistake printed XXXII.

APPENDIX.

ILLUSTRATIONS.

NOTE AS TO THE WELSH TEXT.

THE Welsh Text was printed in 1863, after collating the text
of the poems with the original MSS., first in MS., and again
in proof. The collation, however, was to a great extent purely
mechanical. The opportunities which the Editor had of con-
sulting original MSS., contained in three different libraries, at
a distance from himself and from each other, were necessarily
so limited, both in time and in frequency, that, although the
kindness of their owners made them accessible to him as
often as was possible in the circumstances, the collation had
in consequence to be made very rapidly, and he was unable
to pause in his task to consider the meaning of the text.

Instead of preserving the text as it is usually transcribed
in such MSS., continuously, and without break either as to
sentences or metrical lines, he has arranged it in lines so far
as he could at the moment be guided by the rhyme, but he
has preserved the original punctuation, and made no conjectural emendations whatever in the text. He has printed it
exactly as he found it, even where the scribe had obviously
either mistaken the word, or written a wrong letter. Where
words in this text differ from those in the Myvyrian or other
texts, and the former is obviously a mistake, the error is that
of the writer of the original MS., and not of the Editor in
collation, as in Poem No. XXII. of the Black Book of Caer-

marthen, where "rereint" is written in the MS. for "redeint."
The words are also not always rightly divided, and it is
difficult to distinguish between U and N, the one being often
intended where the other has been printed.

As to the orthography, it may be remarked, that in old
MSS., in the mute consonants, the tenues are frequently used
where modern orthography has the mediæ, as final C and T for
G and D, and that the initial mutation only occasionally appears; but, although not expressed in the orthography, it
seems to have been understood, as G sometimes expresses the
simple sound, and at others obviously represents NG. The
letter N must also be assumed occasionally before T and D.
Initial C is often represented by K; modern F by U and V;
and W after G and A is represented in the older MSS. by U,
sometimes V, and in the Book of Taliessin and Red Book of
Hergest by a peculiar letter 6. The diphthongs AI and AU
appear as EI and EU. The diphthong EI is represented by Y.

The old English capitals represent the rubrical letters in
the original MSS.

I.

TWO POEMS

From a MS. of the hexametrical Paraphrase of the Gospels, by C. Vettius Aquilinus Juvencus, preserved in the University Library of Cambridge. Transcribed in the ninth century.

I.

POEM ON PAGE FIRST.

1. *Omnipotens auctor*
   Ti dicones adiamor
      P . . (*cut off*) . .
2. Nit arcup betid hicouid
   Canlon cetticeidin gui— haguid
      Uor — rdutou ti guirdoned
3. Dicones *pater* harimed
   Presen isabruid icunmer
      Nisacup m — arcup leder
4. Dicones *Ihesu* dielimlu
      pbetid aguirdou pendibu
      guotcapaur anmer— adu
5. Gur dicones remedau
   Elbid anguorit anguoraut
      Niguru gnim molim trinta [ut]
6. It cluis inban iciman
   Guorsed ceinmicun ucmout ran
     · · Ucatrintaut bean trident [an]

B

7. It cluis it humil inhared celmed
   Rit pucsaun mi detrintaut
      gurd.meint iconidid imolaut
8. Rit ercis o —— raut inadaut
   Presen pioubui int groisauc
      Inungueid guoled trintaut
9. Un hanied napuil heper
   Uuc nem isnem nitcouer
      Nit guorgnim molim map meir

II.

POEM ON PAGES 48, 49 AND 50.

1. Niguorcosam nemheunaur
   Henoid mitelu nit gurmaur
      Mi amfranc dam ancalaur
2. Nicanu niguardam nicusam
   Henoid cet iben med nouel
      Mi amfranc dam anpatel
3. Namercit mi nep leguenid
   Henoid is discyrr mi coueidid
      Dou nam riceus unguetid

NOTE.—These two poems are written in the Saxon character. The first has been read with great difficulty, owing to its having been transcribed on the first page of the MS., and injured and partly effaced by rubbing. The second poem has been previously but inaccurately printed, and is now for the first time correctly given. There are only two words that are doubtful. *Nicanu* in the fourth line may be read *Nicanil;* and if so, it is probably transposed, and should be placed at the end of the line, so as to correspond in rhyme with the words *nouel* and *patel*. The letter represented by *y* in *discyrr* is a peculiar letter, which may represent one of the Saxon forms for *y*, or the Irish contraction for *ui*, in which case the word will read *discuirr*.

antytaman · hid attad y
daeth rad kyulaun · llat
kyndux tra messur y ku
ynan · llas haelon odin
on tra uuan : Try uir ·
nod maux eu clod · gan ·
elgan · Mirdh Truy ath
tui · Ruy · a Ruy · trav ath
ran imdoech y doethan ·

II.

THE BLACK BOOK OF CAERMARTHEN.

A MS. of the 12th Century in the Hengwrt Collection, the Property of W. W. E. Wynne, Esq. of Peniarth, M.P.

I.

Fol. 1. a. ꟿOR truan genhẏf mor truan.
Aderẏv. am keduẏv a chaduan.
Oed llachar kẏulauar kẏulauan.
Oed ẏscuid o trẏuruẏd o trẏuan.

TALYESSIN.

Oed maelgun a uelun inimnau
Ẏ teulu rac torẏuulu nẏ thauant.

MYRTIN.

Rac deuur ineutur ẏtirran.
Rac errith. a gurrith ẏ ar welugan.
Mein winev in diheu a dẏgan.
Moch guelher ẏ niuer gan elgan.
Och oe leith maur a teith ẏ deuthan.

TALIESSIN.

Rẏs undant oet rẏchvant ẏ tarian.
Hid attad ẏ daeth rad kẏulaun.

Llas kẏndur tra messur ẏ kuẏnan.
Llas haelon o dinon tra uuan.
Trẏuir. nod maur eu clod. gan. elgan.

MIRTIN.

Truẏ athrui. ruẏ. a ruẏ. ẏ doethan.
Trav athrau imdoeth bran amelgan.
Llat dinel oe dinet. kẏulauan
Ab erbin ae uerin a wnaethan.

TALIESSIN.

Llu maelgun bu ẏscun ẏ doethan.
Aer wir kad trẏbelidiad. guaedlan.
Neu gueith arẏwderit pan
Vit ẏ deunit. o hid ẏ wuchit ẏ darperan.

MIRTIN.

Llẏavs peleidrad guaedlad guadlan.
Llẏaus. aerwir brẏv breuaul vidan.
Llẏaus ban brivher. llẏaus ban foher.
Llẏaus ev hẏmchuel in eu hẏmvan.

TALIESSIN.

Seith meib eliffer. Seith guir ban brouher.
Seith guaew nẏ ochel in eu seithran.

MYRTIN.

Seith tan. vuelin. Seith kad kẏuerbin.
Seithued kinvelin ẏ pop kinhuan.

TALIESSON.

Seith guaew gowanon. Seith loneid awon.
O guaed kinreinon ẏ dẏlanuan.

MYRTIN.

Seith ugein haelon. a aethan ẏgwllon.
Ẏg coed keliton. ẏ. daruuan.

Can ẏs mi mẏrtin guẏdi. taliessin.
Bithaud. kẏffredin. vẏ darogan.

II.

Fol. 4. a.

Breuduid a uelun neithwir. ẏsceluit ae dehoglho.
Ny ritreithir ẏ reuit. nis guibit ar nuẏgelho.
Gueithred llara llẏuiau niuer nid hoffet meiuret bro.
Neur uum ẏdan un duted a bun dec liu guanec gro.
Nid cur llauur urth dinda. ae coffa arnuẏdalho.
Guaeth. vẏgniw odiuattep. ir nep nuẏ hatnappo.
Nẏtiuuic rac dricweithred. im attrec guẏdi darffo.
Nẏ dichuenic but pedi. ẏs guell delli urth auo.
Ac imganlin adeduit. adioffrid aaduo.
Awna mẏnich enuuẏret. ordivet. aserlinho.
Nid ehalath astraetha. nẏchaffaw ae hamhevo.
Nẏ lluit renuet ẏ direid. Nẏ chenir buẏeid arffo.
Nẏ naut ucheneid rac guael. Nẏ derllit haelar nuẏbo.
Nẏ rẏ del   .   .   .

III.

Fol. 5. a.

Devs ren rimawẏ awen.   Amen fiat.
Fẏnedic. waud. fruẏthlaun. traethaud trẏbestraud heid.
Hervit urten autẏl kẏrridven ogẏrven amhad.
Amha(d)anav areith awẏrllav. ẏ cavkeineid.
Cuhelin bart. kẏmraec hart kidvrthodiad.
Kert kimuẏnas. ked kẏwtaa. nifain tinieid.
Gathẏr kẏwẏstraud. kẏvan volaud. cluttaud attad.
Kẏwrgein genhid. cor a chiwid. kẏhid kẏdneid.
Kẏwẏrgẏrn kẏvle kẏwlaun flamde kẏwvire vad.

Kenetẏl woror. kẏwrisc woscord. kẏghẏgneid.

Kẏwolv. waur. kẏwarvs mavr. kir llavr eircheid.

Kerit vẏchod. kerenhit nod clod achvbiad.

Clo kelvid. kant kalan kid. kẏnvllid greid.

Greid bleit blẏghaud. Gretẏw detẏw duraud. gnaud brand-
uriaeth.

Gur oet eitoel gorvẏreol. gordethol doeth.

Gvẏtbuil dragon. gosparth brẏthon. gosgẏman gvith.

Gnaud trẏganet. gnaud kẏhidet. gorsset metveith.

Mettvin kẏwran. marchauc mitlan. mann meidrolaeth.

Meitrid mur ior. maus pedir pedror. maur cor kẏvoeth.

Moes vreisc vreẏr. moes wirth vehir. milwir orvith.

Maer claer kẏwid. mad cathẏl kẏvid. moidit ieith.

Mas cas nognav. minhev nev frav. molav frav fraeth.

Muner uodauc. maer anhetauc. maretauc doet.

Medel visci mel vartoni. mẏnogi gvẏth.

Mẏnvinad vron. metv ton dros traeth.

Mer kertev kein. mẏwir covein. mirein anoeth.

Menestir. vẏtud. meuvet vetvd. molud esmuith.

Music a gan mal eur orian. man vahanieth.

Gveith reith rẏsset. gvich ruich rẏuet. rinuet reen.

Rec rẏsiolaw. rec a archaw. ruẏmav iurthen.

Ruthur. vthir avel. rẏnaut uvel. rẏvel vebin.

Ruteur dẏrllit. rẏchlud clodrit. rihit aden.

Rev wet paraud. rin vẏnn. wascaud. tra gwaud wobrin.

Rẏ hait itaut. rẏcheidv ẏ naut. rac caut gelin.

Rẏ. chedwis detẏf. ry chẏnis gretẏw. rac lletẏw ogẏrven.

Rac. dac. drossow. reghid brid bot. rot cuhelin.

IV.

5. a.   ƘERVIT vrten. autẏl kẏrridven. ogẏrven amhad.

Amhad anav. areith awẏrllav. ẏ cav keineid.

Cvhelin doeth. kẏmraec coeth. kẏvoeth awẏrllav.

Keluit id gan. cluir vir aedan. kẏwlavan lev.

Kert kẏwlaunder. kadeir dirper cadir wober. ẏv.
Kanholicion caffod eilon. keinon vrthav.
Cau tẏirnet. cathil kẏhidet kẏurẏsswẏv.
Campus ẏ veirch. canhẏn ae peirch. kẏwren eirch glẏv.
Cor waradred. kenetẏl noted ked kẏwetliv.
Lliwed a hun. llẏsseit eitun. llun venediv.
Llẏd am kẏwor. llog desseffor. llog porth anav.
Llvgẏrin kẏtrim. lledvegin grim. llim ẏd grim glev.
Lleuver sẏnhuir. llauer a vẏr. llvir id woriv.
Gorpo gvr gulet druẏ tagnevet het o hetiv.

V.

KYVAENAD keluit. kẏnelv o douit.
Kẏuaenad kẏnan o crist kein didan.
Ac vei gẏuerkinan am.ẏ.gẏlchin huan.
Ar gnẏuer pegor ẏssit ẏ dan mor.
Ar gnẏuer. edeinauc a oruc kẏuoethauc.
Ac vei. vei. paup. tri trẏchant tauaud.
Nẏ ellẏnt vetraethaud. kẏwoethev ẏ trindaud.
Din dẏual ẏ faud.   Nẏ eruill cospaud.
Kẏmun bid paraud. in erbin tridaud.
Bid glaf glefẏchaud. ban wanha. ẏ gnaud
Y diodrut. ẏ isscaud.
Guae ti din hewid pir doduid unbid.
Onid imwaredit. or druc digonit.
Nev duid ẏthrihit. ẏthurid. a. kerit.
Drud dẏtihenit. dẏ imtuin ar llogẏlwit.
Trvach dẏdivet. dẏ lauriav. o. vet.
Asegi athraed ẏmlith prit athẏdwet.
Dihafal dẏimteith dẏisscar ath kedimteith.
Corph diffid direid. gobuill. o. theneid.
Corph ni glivit paleueir ẏ gilit.
Pa roteiste oth rev vet. kin kẏues argel.
Pa roteiste otholud kin muill moll mud.

Ac ẏ haruetud. ac ẏ diadaud.

Ac nẏ riuelssud ẏ meint a garẏssud.

Ac itoet o wud ẏ lurv teint. dud.

Adaon i taethant ig kẏmeint offuiant.

Prit prinude chant. othriit ageugant.

Ac ẏsmortiuant. mal gossod amrant.

A ueleiste o garant asv treis tragissaut.

Nẏ phercheiste guener oth vaur etẏllter.

Ni cheuntoste pader na philgeint na gosper.

Pader priw traethaud. gobuill o nebaud

Namuin ẏ trindaud.

Ry talud istedlit tri seith pader beunit.

Affv ac nidoes. ac nithreghis. ev hoes.

Moe ẏ dinwassute merwerit. no phregeth evegil.

An deid i glethuir guerth na buost vffil.

Ni phercheiste creirev na lloc na llanev.

Nid endeueiste kiwrev beirt gouec higlev.

Ni phercheiste kiureith creaudir new kin lleith

Llẏaus aghiuieith adodute ardiareith.

Gvae vi pir imteith genhide in kẏueith.

Gvae vi pir wuuf ar dikiuolv.

Pan douthume attad oeth bichan vianuad.

Neu rimartuad oth laur kiueithad.

Arnun nincred ni nep. oth tremint. trvẏ ted.

VI.

Fol. 12. a. ꬲNEID kid im guneit. in aghen digerit.

Guir ẏv guae uinhev pir deuthoste imgotev.

Nac irofe. nac aghev. na diuet. na dechrev.

O seith lauanad. ban im se suinad.

O seith creadur pan im dodaeth ar pur.

Oet un. tan. llachar. pan im roted par.

Oetun prit daear. nym dẏhaetci alar.

Oetun guint gouchaf llei vẏnruc nom da.

Oetun nẏul ar mẏnit ẏn keissau keton hit.
Oetun blodev guit ar vinep eluit.

. Amssuinasseie douit im dodath ar deunit.

Eneid kid im guneit.

VII.

ẞAC im adneirun nev. rim waredun.
Keugant kẏwraghaum. wide kẏwisscaran.
A chiwnod senet.   A cheugant kinatlet.
A daduirein obet guẏdi hir gorwet.
Kẏwoethauc duw awet. ẏ din inẏ deheu wuchet.
A dẏadu tan ar poploet anẏlan.
Alluch a tharian. a llẏaus llẏdan.
Nẏ llettaud lle dinag. na didrif na diag.
A widẏ tagde teernas arvere.
Dẏgettaur. ẏ. tri. llv. rac drech. drem iessu.
Llu guirin guinion eiliv egilion.
Llv arall brithion. eiliv brodorion.
Tryde llv diuedit. syth leith gyweithit.
Huilant iglithuir un parthred dievil.
In vn nidaon gan dull aghimon.
Mẏnẏ mae meillon agulith ar tirion.
Mẏnẏ mae kertorion in kẏveir kẏsson.
Kein vid ev goffalon gan guledic gorchortion.
Mẏny mae ehestil am teernas uwil.
Men ẏ mae perẏw hael inẏ claer kẏueistet.
Rotiad bid beddrael. nid guael ẏ gerenhit.
A chin deginull emne eilivert vedit.
Or saul dẏmguẏtat. ar lleith dimgorbit.
Ac ew gueith dimgunelemne. dimbrodic dit.
Nis rydraeth rẏuetev kẏvoeth ruẏtev douit.

VIII.

Fol. 14. a.

TRI an reith march inis pridein.
Carnawlauc march. owein. mab vrien.
A. Bucheslum seri. march gugaun cletẏwrut.
A. Tauautir breichir. m. kadwallaun. fil. k.

TRI thom etẏstir inis pridein.
Arwul melin. march passcen fil. vrien.
A. Duhir terwenhit. m. selẏw mab kẏnan garrvin.
A. drudluid. m. rẏterch hael.

TRI gohoev etẏster inis pridein.
Guẏnev godvff. hir. march kei.
Ruthir ehon tuth blet. m. gilberd mab kadgẏffro.
A. keincaled. m. gualchmei.

TRI hoev etistir inis pridein.
Llv agor. m. karadauc.   b.
A. melẏnlas. m. kaswallaun mab belẏ.*

IX.

Fol. 15. a.

MOLI duu innechrev a diuet.
Ae kẏniw nẏ welli nẏ omet.
Vn mab meir modridaw teernet.
Meir mam crist. ergẏnan rianet.
Dẏdav ẏr heul or duẏrein ir goglet.
Dẏ eiraul ir dẏ. maur drugaret.
Ar dẏ mab iolud en karet.
Duv uchom.   Duu ragom.   Duu vet.
Ren new anrotone. ran trugaret.
Teẏrn uron. tanc ẏ romne. heb imomet
Diwẏccomne a digonhom ogamuet.

* The MS. here seems defective.

Kin mýned im guerid imiruet.

In týwill heb canvill im gorsset.

Ym gueinvod im gorod im gorwet.

Guýdi merch ac imtuin glassuet.

A chýuet a chid im agraget.

Ný chisgaw gobuýllaw om diwet.

Gulad it imne. ýsagro ýmassvet.

Mal deil ovlaen guit daduet.

Guae agaur a graun maur uerthet.

Ac onýsguataul ý riet.

Kýn gatter ew in rýred. pressen. perýgil uit inýdivet.

Ný vir drud. nid ýscrid iný timhýr.

Ný chiuid uore. ný chiueirch. nid eistet.

Ný chan wen nid eirch trugaret.

Bit chuero ý talhaur iný diwet.

Sýberuid. a maur wrid. a maret.

Meithrin corph. ý lýffeint a nadret.

Allevuod ac imtuin enviret.

Ac aghen dýdau urth gluýdet.

Ew inluth dý chinull dý chiuet.

Dýnessa heneint alled arnad.

Dý clust. di trein. di teint neud adwet.

Dý chricha croen diuisset.

Athuna heneint alluidet.

An eirolve ne inihagel. ar ren new raua trugaret.

Kintevin keinhaw amsser.   Dýar adar glas callet.

Ereidir in rich. ich iguet.

Guirt mor brithottor tiret.

Ban ganhont cogev ar blaen guit

Guiw handid muý. výllauuridet.

Tost muc amluc anhunet.

Kan ethint uý kereint in attwet.

Ym brin in týno. ininýsset

Mor impop fort itelher. rac crist guin nid oes inialet.

Oet in chuant in car in trosset

Treitau tẏ tir dẏalltudet.

Seith seint a seith ugeint. a seith cant. awant in un
orsset.

Ygid a crist guin. nẏ forthint vevẏgilet.

Rec aarchawe nim naccer. ẏ rof aduv. dagnouet.

Am bo forth. ẏ porth riet.

Crist nẏ buve trist ẏthorsset.

X.

GOGONEDAUC argluit hanpich guell.

Athuendicco de egluis. achagell.

A. kagell. ac egluis.

A. vastad. a diffuis.

A. Teir finhaun ẏssit.

Due uch guint. ac vn uch eluit.

A. ẏ risgaud ar dit.

A. Siric a perwit.

Athuendiguiste awraham pen fit.

A. vuchet tragiuit.

A. adar a guenen.

A. attpaur. adien.

Athuendiguste aron a moesen.

A. vascul a femen.

A. seithnieu a ser.

A. awir. ac ether.

A. llevreu a llẏther.

A. piscaud ẏn hẏdiruer.

A. kẏwid. agueithred.

A. tẏuvod athẏdued.

A. ẏsaul da digoned.

Athuendigaf de argluit gogoned.

Gogonedauc a. h. g.

XI.

. 18. b.

ARDUIREAUE tri trined in celi.
Yssi un athri. vned un ẏuni.
Vn guirth oe teithi. un duu diuoli.
Athuolaf uaurri maur dẏurhidri.
Dẏuolaur ẏsguir.   Dẏuolaudir ẏsmi.
Ys bud bartoni arhelv eloẏ.
Hanpich guell cristi.
Pater. & fili & spiru. domni.
        on. adonaẏ.

ARDUIREAUE dev. ẏssi vn a deu.
Yssi tri hep. ev. hep haut ẏ amhev.
Awnaeth fruith afreu afop. amriffreu.
Duu ẏ env. in deu. duẏuaul ẏ kẏffreu.
Duu ẏ env. in tri duẏuuaul. ẏ inni.
Duu ẏ env in vn.   Duu paulac annhun.

ARDUYREAUE. vn. isẏ deu ac un.
Issi tri ar nun. issi duu ẏ hun.
Aunaeth maurth a llun. a mascul a bun.
Ac nat kẏuorun bas ac anotun.
Auneth tuim ac oer. a. heul alloer.
Allẏthir. ig. cuir afflam im pabuir.
A. serch in sinhuir. a bun hẏgar huir.
Allosci. pimp kaer otẏueti. wir.

XII.

ɔl. 20. a.

YNENU domni meu ẏ. voli. maur ẏ uolaud.
Molawe douit. maur ẏ kinnit ar ẏ cardaud.
Duu anamuc.   Duu angoruc.   Duu anguaraud.
Duu angobeith. teilug pirfeith. tec ẏ purfaud.
Duu andyli.   Duu issi vry. vrenhin trindaud.

Duu abroued inẏ truẏted in ẏ trallaud.

Duu a dẏfu. oe garcharu gan vuildaud.

Guledic deduit an gunel inrit erbin dit braud.

An duch ir gulet irẏ varet. ae. werindaud.

Ym paraduis. impur kẏnnuis rac puis pechaud.

Angunel iechid irẏ penid ae pimp dirnaud.

Dolur eghirith.   Duu andiffirch ban kẏinirth cnaud.

*Din a collei bei nasprinhei diuei devaud.

Or croc crevled ẏ deuth guared ir vedissẏaud.

Kadarn bugeil Crist nid adweil. ẏ teilẏgdaud.

XIII.

ʾol. 21. a.

BRENHIN guirthvin guirth uchaw ẏssit.

Yssi pen plant adaw.

Yssi per gadeir gadarnaw.

Yssi hael diwael diweirhaw.

Yssi haul uraul gurhaw.

A cliwir. issi owir id pridaw.

Y Duv maur. ẏ duv llaur llariaw.

Y duv guin guengert aganaw.

Ynẏ wuẏw. ẏ duv indin digerit. ordevnit ẏ diallaw.

O pechu a pechuis adaw.

O pechaud kin braud prẏderaw.

Erbin oed ẏ dit. ẏ del paup oe

Bet inẏ devret in devraw.

Mal ẏ bv ban fv oreuhaw.

In vn llv ir vn lle teccaw.

Hid impen vn brin erbin ev barnv.

Or teulv teilẏghaw.

Teilẏgdaud wascaud. osgort nav grad new.

Vẏ Dewis kinvllaud.

* The handwriting changes here and becomes smaller. Hitherto the letters have been large, and each page contains only twelve lines ; but the scribe,
finding it necessary to economise space, puts sixteen lines in a page. Though
the letters are smaller, it seems to have been written by the same hand.

Vẏ Devs domenvs menaud.

Vẏ bardeir. ẏ Beirt ẏ uedissiaud.

Vẏ maurhidic nen. vẏ perchen.

Vẏ parch. kin tẏwarch. Kin tẏwaud.

Amgadu ẏ traethu traethaud.

Yth voli kin tewi tawaud.

Ac im cow. valioff. adiwaud

Urth ẏ gureic. ẏ am dreic vffẏldaud.

Ban dẏwu guas duv diwarnaud

Attav. ir imbrav ae briaud.

Rotesew dirneid. kin dirnaud.

A bilwis o bilion. ẏ gnaud.

Canẏdoet hagen higaff. ẏ rotion. a rothei o nebaud.

Gvnaeth duv trvgar gardaud.

In evr coeth kẏvoeth. ẏ trindaud.

Y mas maeistaud. ẏ mae moliduv.

Adwin ẏ coti. A. diwad pechaud.

Wid. weti. Adiwin kelv brad keli.

Culuit argluit new nav kanmaul attad.

Guenglad vad veidroli.

Guenvlit rit rieitun voli.

Gwingar kar gvar guironet kedwi.

Nẏ chedwis eva irawallen per barauẏs duv.

Vrthi. am ẏ cham nẏchimv ahi.

Guẏth golev a orev erni.

Rẏv duted edmic. ogẏllestic guisc. A guiscvis imdeni.

Periw new a peris idi. imperuet ẏchiwoeth ẏ noethi.

Ac eil guirth. awnaeth ehalaeth argluit a ergliw ẏ voli.

Ban winnvis gochel ẏ deli.

Sew fort ẏffoes iti.

Inẏtoet aradur in eredic tir

Herwit guir in gueini. Y diwaud ẏ trindaud keli.

Ew ae mam dinam daun owri.

Agur guin. Turr guir gwẏdi nẏ.

A dav ẏ geissav in guesti.

Ar owris ẏ winiti.

· A gueleiste gureic a mab genti.

A diwed tithev irolev guironet.

Mẏ thomet in gweti.

Jn gueled in mẏned hebti.

Y rander arad duv erni.

Ar huni ẏ doeth digiwoeth gwerin.   Llin kain kaderthi.

Toriw anwar enwir ev hinni.

Turr keisseid ẏ keissav keli.

Y diwod vn gurthwn gurtharab.   Vrth ẏ gvr aweli.

A gueleiste dinion din. gowri.

In mẏned hebod heb drossi.

Gueleis ban llẏuneis ẏllentir

Deguch a weluch ẏ medi.

Sew awnaethant plant kai

Y Vrth ẏ medel ẏm chueli.

Druẏ eiroled meir mari

Oe gvẏbod guẏbv duv oheni.

Yt oet inẏ diffrid. ẏ. gidahi.

Ysprid glan a gleindid indi.

XIV.

b. 23.   *ADWIN caer ẏssit ar lan llẏant.

Adwin ẏd rotir ẏ pauper ẏ chwant.

Gogẏwarch de gwinet boed tev wẏant.

Gwaewaur rrin.   Rei adarwant.

Dẏv merchir. gueleisse guir ẏg cvinowant.

Dẏv iev bv. ir. guarth. it adcorssant.

Ad oet brẏger coch. ac och ar dant.

Oet llutedic guir guinet.   Dit ẏ deuthant.

* The handwriting here changes and becomes much smaller; the two following pieces, though in the same hand with those that follow, seem to have
been subsequently inserted in a blank page.

Ac am kewin llech vaelvẏ kẏlchuẏ wriwant.

Cuẏtin ẏ can keiwin llv o carant.

XV.

Fol. 23. b. DINAS maon duv daffar. pendevic adwin adviar.

    Asich heul. agulich edar.

DINAS maon cas vnbin teernet. kẏmẏnad kad degin.

    Asich heul agulich. mervin.

DINAS maon gulad adav. amdiffin duv amdanav.

    Asich heul agulich. nẏnhav

MAD dodes ẏ mortuit. ar merchin march lluid.

    Kadeirdeur am diwurn. asich heul agulich maelgun.

XVI.

Fol. 24. a. ⓒWIN ẏ bid hi ẏ vedwen in diffrin guẏ.

A sirch ẏ chegev pop vn. pop dvẏ.

Ac auit pan vo. ẏ gad in ardudvẏ.

A chimrevan biv am rid vochnvẏ.

A pheleidir a gaur inẏ ganhvẏ.

Ac edwin imonban gluedichuẏ.

Ar gueisson gleisson ẏsca(win) tra vodi.

Ar dillad rution in ev roti.

ⓒWIN ẏ bid hi ẏ vedwen. ẏm pimlumon.

A wil ban vit ban baran eilon.

Ac awil. ẏ. freigc in lluricogion.

Ac am gewin iraeluid bvid balawon.

A mineich in vynich in varchogion.

ⓒWIN ẏ bid hi ẏ veduen ẏ guarthaw dinvẏthuẏ.

A vibid ban vo ẏgad in ardudwẏ.

Ar peleidir kẏchuin amedrẏwuẏ.

A. phont ar taw. ac arall ar tawuẏ.

Ac arall amwall amdwẏlan gwẏ.

c

Ar saer ae gunelwẏ. bid ẏ env garvẏ.

Ar benẏgaul mon ae. guledẏchuẏ.

Guraget dan ẏ gint. guir ẏg kẏstvẏ.

Dedwẏtach no mi ae harhowe.

Amser kadwaladir. kert aganhwi.

XVII.

Fol. 24. b.   **A**FALLEN peren per ẏchageu.

Puwaur maur weirrauc enwauc invev.

Ami disgoganave rac perchen machrev.

In diffrin machavuẏ merchẏrdit crev.

Goruolet ẏ loegẏr gorgochlawnev.

Oian a parchellan dẏdau dẏwiev.

Gorvolet ẏ gimrẏ goruaur gadev.

In amuin kẏminaud clefẏtaud clev.

Aer o Saesson. ar onn verev.

A guarwẏaur pelre ac ev pennev.

A mi disgoganafe gwir heb gev.

Dyrchafaud maban in advan y dehev.

AFALLEN peren pren hẏduf glas.

Pvwaur ẏ chagev hẏ ae chein wanas.

Ami dysgoganafe kad am dias.

Penguern kẏwetẏrn metẏ hatas. *

AWALLEN peren. a pren melin.

A. tẏw in hal art. heb art inychilchin.

Ami discoganwe kad im prẏdin.

In amvin ev terwin aguir dulin.

Seith log. ẏ deuant dros lẏdan lin.

A seith cant. dros mor ẏ oreskin.

* The following lines are added, at the bottom of the page, in the same
hand, but with fainter ink :—

Ac am gylch kyminawd kymyn leas
Eingyl gan pendeuic eryri eri attkas.

Or saul ẏ deuant. nẏdant ẏ kenhin.
Namuin seith lledwac gwẏdi ev llettkiut.

AWALLEN peren. Atẏf tra run.
Kẏmaeth lissvne inẏ bon. ir bot ẏ wun.
Amẏscud. ar wẏ isguit. amdet ar wẏdun.
Ac ẏg coed. keliton ẏ kisceisse vẏhun.
Oian a perchellan. pir puẏllutte hun.
Andaude adar dẏwir ev hẏmevtun.
Teernet dros mor adav dẏv. llun.
Guin ev bid ve kẏmri or arowun.

AWALLEN peren atif in llanerch.
Y hangert ae hargel rac riev rẏderch.
Amsathir inẏbon. maon ẏnẏchilch.
Oet aclav vt vt dulloet diheueirch.
Nu nẏm cari guendit ac nimeneirch.
Oef kas gan gwassauc guaessaf rydirch.
Rẏrewineis ẏ mab ae merch.
Aghev aduc paup. pa rac nam kẏueirch.
A. guẏdi guendolev nep riev impeirch.
Nẏm gogaun guarvẏ. nym goffvẏ gorterch.
Ac igueith arẏwderit. oet eur. wẏgorthorch
Kin buẏf. aelav hetiv gan eiliv eleirch.

AFALLEN peren. blodev essplit.
Atiff in argel in argoẏdit.
Chuetlev a giklev ir inechrev dit.
Rẏssorri guassauc guaessaf. meufit
Duẏweith atheirgueith. pedeirgueith in vn. dit.
Och iessu. na dẏffv wẏnihenit.
Kẏn dẏffod ar willave lleith mab guendit.

*A*FALLEN peren atiff ar lan. afon.
Inẏ llurv. nẏ lluit maer. arẏchlaer aeron.
Trafu vm puẏll. wastad. am buiad inibon.
A. bun wen warius. vn weinus vanon
Dec inlinet adev ugein inẏ gein anetwon
It vif inẏmteith gan willeith agwillon.
Guẏdi da diogan aditan kertorion.
Nv nev nam guẏ. guall. gan wẏlleith a guẏllon.
Nv nev nachẏscafe ergrinaf. wẏnragon.
Vẏ argluit guendolev ambrorrẏv brodorion.
Guẏdi porthi heint a hoed am cẏlch coed keliton.
Buẏf guas guinwẏdic. gan guledic gorchortion,

*A*FALLEN peren blodev essplit.
Atẏf igwerid ag hiid ẏ guit.
Disgogan hwimleian hwetil adiwit.
Id lathennaur gan brid gurhid erwit.
Rac dreigev arderchev. riev rẏbit.
Goruit grat wehin din digrefit.
Rac maban hvan heolit arweit.
Saesson ardiwreit beirt ar kinit.

*A*FALLEN peren a pren fion
Attif ẏ dan gel ẏg coed keliton.
Kid keisseer ofer vit heruit ẏ haton.
Inẏ del kadwaladir oe kinadil kadwaon.
Y erir tẏwi a teiwi affon.
A dyuod grande o aranwinion.
A guneuthur guar. o. willt. o gwallt hirion.

*A*FALLEN peren a pren fion.
Attif. ẏ dan gel ẏg coed keliton.
Kid keisser ofervit herwit. ẏ hafon.
Yn ẏ del kadwaladir oe kinadẏl. rid reon.

Kinan inẏ erbin ef kẏchwin ar saesson.
Kimrẏ a orvit kein bid endragon.
Kaffaud paub ẏ teithi. llauen vi bri brẏthon.
Kenhittor kirrn eluch. kathil hetuch a hinon.

XVIII.

ᏰIAN a parchellan. a parchell dedwit.*
Nachlat dẏredcir ẏmpen minit.
Clat in lle argel in arcoedit.
Rac erwis ritech hael ruẏfadur fit.
Ami disgoganafe a gwir uit.
Hid in aber taradir rac trausev prẏdein
Kimrẏ oll inẏeu kẏfluit.
Llẏuelin ẏ env o eissillit
Gwinet gur digorbit.

27. a. ᏰIAN a parchellan. oet reid mẏned
Rac. kinẏtion mordei bei llafassed.
Rac diuod erlid arnamne ac ingueled.
Ac or diaghune. nẏ chumune in lluted.
Ami disgoganafe. rac ton navfed.
Rac vnic bariffvin gvehin dived.
Dirchafaud llogaud tud ir llettcred.
Yn tẏmhir gurthtir a guẏstuiled.
In ẏ del kinan iti oechin gueled.
Nẏ bit attcor bith ar ẏ threfred.

ᏰIAN a parchellan nẏhaut kisscaff.
Rac godurt ẏ galar ẏssit arnaf.
Deg mlinet a deu ugein ẏd. portheise poen
Y struc aorhoen yssit arnaf.
Oes imi gan iessv gaffv guaessaf

The first stanza is written in a different hand at the end of the previous

Brenhinoet newoet achoet uchaf.

Nẏmad rianed oplant adaw.

Ar nẏ creddoe ẏdovit indit diwethaf.

Yd welese gnendolev in perthic riev.

In cẏnull preitev o pop eithaw.

Ydan vẏguerid rut nv neud araf.

Pen teernet goglet llaret mvẏhaw.

ⓄIAN aparchellan oet reid gweti.

Rac offin pimp penaeth o nortmandi.

Ar pimhed in mẏned dros mor heli.

Y oreskin iwerton tirion trewi.

Ef gunahaud rẏuel a difissci.

Ac arfev coch. ac och indi.

Ac winttuẏ in dihev adoant o heni.

Ac. awnant enrẏdet ar bet.   Dewi.

Ami disgoganafe bid divisci.

O ẏmlat mab a thad gulad ae guẏbi.

A mẏned ẏ loegruis diffuis trewi.

Ac nabo guared bith ẏ nortmandi.

ⓄIAN a parchellan.   Nauit hunauc.

Rẏdibit attamne chuetil dẏfridauc.

Penaetheu bẏchein anudonauc.

Meiri mangaled am pen keinhauc.

Pan diffon. dros mor guir eneichauc.

Kad meirch. ẏ danuitt ve dev wẏnepauc.

Deuwlaen. ar euguaev anoleithauc.

Erti heb medi ẏmbid dẏhetauc.

Guell bet. no buhet pop ẏghenauc.

Cirrn ar ẏ guraget pedrẏfanhauc.

Affanvont ve corforion meibon eidauc.

Y bit bore taer. rac kaer sallauc.

ƠIAN a parchellan. a parchell dẏhet.
Run dẏuueid huimleian chuetẏl enrẏuet.
Ami discoganaue haf guithlonet.
Kẏwrug brodorẏon brad o winet.
Ban diholer taguistil inhir o tir guinet.
Dẏbit seith ganllog o ẏnt gan wint goglet
Ac in aber dev eu kinatlet.

ƠIAN a parchellan a parchell guin.
Rẏmdẏwod huimleian chuetil am echrin.
Pan bebillo lloegir in tir ethlin.
A guneuthur dẏganhuẏ dinas degin.
O g*(——) lloegir a llẏuelin
Aduit mab arwarr. (——) kẏchuin.
Ban sorro deinoel mab dunaud deinwin.
Ad vit frangc ar ffo fort nẏ ofin.
In aber dulas. gvanas guehin.
Cochuet inev kẏlwet. ẏn ev kilchin.

ƠIAN a parchellan hoian hoiev.
Bei ẏchenauc duv gunai. ẏmchuelev.
ẏ (——) ll ẏssẏ. wiv. bitaud mev.
Ar hun ẏssẏ (—) keissed intev.

ƠIAN a parchellan neud dit golev.
Andaude leis adar duffẏr dẏar leissev.
An hit ni bluitinet a hir diev.
Ariev enwir edwi fruẏtheu.
Ac escib. lluch lladron differch llannev.
Amẏneich a obrin beich o bechodev.

---

* The line within brackets marks a hole in the parchment caused by the green capitals having eat into it.

ⓄIAN a parchellan llim ẏ vinet.
Kẏuuelẏ anwinud panelhute ẏ oruet.
Bẏchan awir rẏderch hael heno ẏ ar ẏ wlet.
A portheise neithuir o anhunet.
Eiri hid impen clun. gan cun callet.
Pibonvẏ imblev. blin wẏ rẏsset.
Rẏ dibit div maur dit guithlonet.
Kẏwrug glẏu powis achlas guinet.
A chivod hirell oe hir orwet.
Y amvin ae elin terwin guinet.
Ac onẏmbit gan vẏ ri ran trugaret.
Guae wi ban imbv. trv vẏ diwet.

ⓄIAN a parchan.   Nẏ bit kẏwun.
Ban kẏhuin llu aer o kaer wẏrtin.
Y harduẏ dev kenev. in kẏwrenhin.
O hil ris aerllut. aer llẏf bitin.
Ban llather ẏ Saesson ẏ kimerev trin.
Guin ev. bid vẏ kimri. kimrvẏ. werin.

ⓄIAN a parchellan. a parchell guin gvis.
Nachuste hun bore. nachlat im prisc.
Rac dẏuod.   Rẏderch hael ae cvn kẏfruẏs.
Kin caffael o honautte ẏ coed reddaud. dẏchuis.

ⓄIAN a parchellan a parchell guin.
Bei guelud a weleis o treis degin.
Nẏchẏscute hun bore. nẏ chlatude brin.*
Ban eistetho saesson inẏ sarffren.
A chirchu o pell castell gollwin.
A tuit dillad hoev a gloev dullin.

* On the margin—
    Ny chirchud differch o diffuis lin.

ⓒIAN a parchellan andaude ẏ naur
Ban dottint. ve guir guinet ev gueith maur.
Llaffnev in ertirn kirn a ganhaur.
Briuhaud llurugev rac llun waewaur.*
Ami disgoganaue. deu priodaur.
A luniont tegnevet o nef hid laur.
Kẏnan kadwaladir.   Kẏmri penbaladir.
Bitaud ev kinatil aedmẏccaur.
A chiureithau gulad. a chistutia gwad.
Allv alle(——)divahaur.
An bi ni inaeth guared guẏ(——)aeth
Neb o haelonaeth nididolaur.

ⓒIAN a parchellan.   Nud glas minit.
Tenev vẏllen imi nẏd llonit.
Lluid ẏv. vẏbleit nim treit guendit.
Ban diffont guir. brineirch ir guarth luit.
Kimri a oruit kein bid ev dit.

ⓒIAN a parchellan. a parchell gawi.
Na chlat de redkir nac iste. wiuuẏ.
Nac achar waes. nachar. warvẏ.
A chussil arotafe ẏ wenabuẏ.
Nauid ieuangc serchauc sẏberv warruẏ.
Ami discoganafe gueith machavvi.
Aduit geloraur rut in riv didmuẏ.
O kiwranc ẏ kẏnvrein bron reinon kifrvi.
Advit bore och. acoch ofuy.
Arth o deheubarth a dirchafuẏ.
Rẏllettaud ẏ wir ew tra thir mẏnvẏ.

The following lines are written in the same hand on the margin :—
Ban diffon nortmin. yar llidan lin
Advit imurchrin ina gan vitinaur.
Agorescin pridein y uiron yswein
Ar vall o lundein adyattavr. ami

Guini bid hi guendit ae harovẏ
Ban vo pendewic dẏued ae guledichuẏ.

ᴔIAN a parchellan neud blodeu drein.
Gorlas kein minit eliut neud kin.
Ami discoganaue kad coed lluiuein.
A geloraur rirtion rac ruthir owein.
Ban gunelhont meiriev datlev bichein.
Anudon abrad gulad veibonin.
A phan del kadualadir ẏ orescin
Mon dileaur saeson o tirion prẏdein.

ᴔIAN a parchellan maur erissi
A uit impridein ac nim dorbi.
Ban diffon brodorion o amtiret.
Mon. ẏ holi brithon brithuid dẏbi.
Dirchafaud dreic faud fau isperi
Gurt kẏuan uaran o lan teiwi.
Gunahaud am dẏued diguiẏsci.
Bit itau inaelau eilon indi.

ᴔIAN a parchellan. Mor enrẏuet.
Na bit un enhid ẏ bid munvet.
Pelled son saeson seil kẏnriss.
Ar brithon haelon hil kẏmuẏet.
A mi discoganaue kindiguet.
Brithon dros saesson brithuir ae met.
Ac ina indaune daun goruolet.
Guidi bod inhir inhuir. vridet.

ᴔIAN a parchellan andaude ireilon
A groar adar kir kaer reon.
Vn ẏssun aroun minit maon
Y edrich drichumauc drich serchogion.

Ami discoganawe kad ar ẏ ton.
A chad machavvẏ. a chad avon.
A chad corsmochno. a chad minron.
A chad kẏminaud. a chad caerlleon.
A chad abergweith. a chad ieithion.
A phan vo diwed tir terwin. ẏ. eilon.
Maban dirchavaud mad. ẏ vrẏthon.

OIAN a parchellan.   Bẏdan a vit.
Mor truan ẏ. dẏuod. ac ew dẏbit.
Morẏnion moelon. guraget revit.
Karant nẏ pharchant eu kerenhit.
Rvit nẏ kẏwriut. vrth ẏ gilit.
Escẏp agkẏueith diffeith difid.

OIAN a parchellan bichan brẏchni.
Andaude leis adar mẏr. maur ev hinni.
Kertorion allan heb ran teithi.
Kẏn safont inẏ drvs this nẏs deupi.
Rymdivod gwẏllan o pell ẏmi.
Teernet en rẏuet ev kiniweti.
Gwitil a brithon a romani.
Avvnahont dẏhet a divẏsci.
Ac ẏ kẏwenv dẏwiev divod iti.
Ac imlat in taer am dvẏlan tẏwi.

OIAN a parchellan. bẏchan breichvras.
Andav de leis adar mor maur eu dias.
Kertorion allan heb ran vrdas.
Gurthwnaud espid a brid gan gwas.
Heb cadvid. vẏnep heb ran vrdas.
Ban. vo. dev broder. deu itas am tir.
Megittor oc ev guir. vẏ. hir alanas.

KOIAN a parchellan.   Nẏm dawe kingid.
O clẏbod lleis adar duwir dẏar ev grid.
Tenev gvallt vẏ pen. vẏ llen nẏd clid.
Dolit vẏ iscubaur. nẏd maur vẏ id.
Vẏ craun haw ami nid imverid.
Kẏn iscar aduv ditaul kẏvid.
Ami discoganawe kin. gorffen bid.
Gwraget heb gvilet. gwir heb gurhid.

KOIAN a parchellan a parchell rẏmi.
Tenev vyllen nid llonit ẏmi
Yr gueith arẏwderit mi nẏm dorbi.
Kẏnduguitei awir ẏ lavr. allẏr. enlli.
Ami discoganawe gvẏdi henri.
Breenhin na breenhin brithwẏd dẏbi.
Ban vo pont. ar. taw ac arall ar tẏwi.
Y dav ẏ dẏved rẏvel iti.

XIX.

ENGLYNNIONN Y BEDEV.

Fol. 32. a. BETEV ae gulich ẏ glav.*
Gvir nẏ ortẏwnassint vẏ dignav.
Kerwid. a chivrid a chav.
EBETEV ae tut gvitwal.
Ny lesseint heb ẏmtial.
Gurẏen. morien. a morial.
EBETEV ae gulich kauad.
Gvẏr. nẏ lesseint in lledrad.
Gwen. a gurien. a guriad.
BET tedei tad awen. ẏg godir brin
Aren. ẏnẏdvna ton tolo.
Bet dilan llan bevno.

* This poem is written in a different hand and in paler ink.

BET keri cletifhir. ẏ godir hen
   Egluis. ẏnẏ diffuis graeande.
   Tarv torment. ẏmẏnwent corbre.
BET seithennin sinhuir vann.
   Y rug kaer kenedir a glann.
   Mor mauridic a kinran.
EN aber gwenoli. ẏ mae
   Bet prẏderi ẏnẏ terw tonnev tir.
   Yg karrauc bet gwallauc hir.
BET gwalchmei ẏm perẏton.
   Ir diliv. ẏ dẏneton.
   In llan padarn bet kinon.
BET gurgwaud urtin
   In uchel tẏtin. inisel gwelitin.
   Bet kẏnon mab clẏtno idin.
BET run mab pẏd in ergrid
   Avon. in oervil ig gverid.
   Bet kinon in reon rid.
PIEV ẏ bet ẏdan ẏ brin.
   Bet gur gurt ẏg kẏniscin.
   Bet kinon mab clẏtno idin.
BET mab osvran ẏg camlan.
   Gvẏdi llaver kẏwlavan.
   Bet bedwir in alld trẏvan.
BET owen ab urien im pedrẏal
   Bid. dan gverid llan morvael.
   In abererch riderch hael.
GWYDI gurum a choch a chein.
   A goruẏtaur maur minrein.
   In llan helet bet. owein.
GWYDI gweli a gwaedlan.
   A gviscav seirch a meirch cann.
   Neud ew hun bet kintilan.
PIEV ẏ bet da ẏ cẏstlun.

A wnai ar loegir. lv kigrun.

Bet gwen ab llẏuarch hen hun.

PIEV ẏ bet in ẏr amgant.

    Ae tut mor a goror nant.

    Bet meigen mab run rviw cant.

PIEV ẏ bet inẏ rinis

    Ae tut mor a goror gwris.

    Bet meigen mab run rvif llis.

ES cul ẏ bet ac ẏs hir.

    In llurv llẏaus amhir.

    Bet meigen ab run ruẏw gwir.

TRI. bet tri bodauc inarterchauc

    Brin. ẏm pant gwinn. gvinionauc.

    Mor. a meilir. a madauc.

BET madauc mur egluc.

    Yg kẏwluc kinhen. vir vrien.

    Gorev. mab ẏ guẏn. o winllẏuc.

BET mor maurhidic diessic

    Unben. post kinhen kinteic.

    Mab peredur penwetic.

BET meilir maluinauc saluvodauc

    Sinhvir. fisscad fuir fodiauc.

    Mab ẏ bruin o bricheinauc.

PIEV ẏ bet in rid vaen ked.

    Ae pen gan ẏ ranvaered.

    Bet. run mab alun diwed.

BET alun dẏwed ẏnẏ drewred

    Drav. nẏ kiliei o caled.

    Mab meigen. mad pan aned.

BET llia gvitel in argel

    Ardudwẏ. dan ẏ gvellt ae gvevel.

    Bet epint inẏffrin gewel.

BET dẏwel mab erbin ig gwestedin.

    Caeav. nẏ bitei gur ẏ breinhin.

Divei nẏ ochelei trin.

*BET gurgi gvẏchit a guindodit

Lev. a bet llaur llu ouit.

Yg guarthaw guanas guẏr ẏssit.

E BETEU hir ẏg guanas

Nẏ chauas ae dioes.

Pvẏ vẏnt vẏ pvẏ eu neges.

TEULU oeth ac anoeth a dẏuu

Y noeth ẏ eu gur ẏ eu guas.

Ae ceisso vẏ clated guanas

BET llvch llaueghin ar certenhin

Avon pen saeson suẏt erbin

Nẏ bitei drimis heb drin.

EBETEU ẏn hir vẏnẏt.

Yn llvẏr ẏ guẏr lluossit.

Bet gvrẏen gvrhẏd enguavt. allvẏtauc uab lliwelit.

Pieu ẏr bet ẏnẏmẏnẏt

A lẏviasei luossit.

Bet fẏrnuael hael ab hẏvlẏt.

PIEU ir bet hun bet eitivlch

Hir. ig gurthtir pennant turch.

Mab arthan gẏwlauan gẏuulch.

BET llev llaugẏfes ẏ dan achles

Mor ẏnẏ bu ẏ gẏwnes.

·   Gur oet hvnnv guir ẏ neb nẏ rotes.

BET beidauc rut ẏn amgant riv

Lẏvnav. bet lluoscar ẏg keri

Ac ẏn rẏd britu bet omni.

PELL ẏ vẏsci ac argut

Guerẏd machave ae cut.

Hirguẏnion hẏsset beidauc rut.

PELL ẏ vẏsci ac anau

Guerẏd machave arnau.

* The handwriting changes here.

Beidauc rut ẏv hun ab emer llẏdau.

BET unpen o pridein ẏn lleutir

Guẏnnassed ẏn ẏda lliv ẏn llẏchur.

Ig kelli uriauael bet gẏrthmul.

EBET ẏn ẏstẏuacheu

Ymae paup ẏnẏ amheu.

Bet gurtheẏrn gurtheneu.

*KIAN a ud ẏn diffeith cund

Drav otuch pen bet alltud.

Bet kindilic mab corknud.

NEUM duc. i. elffin.

Y prowi vẏ bartrin.

Gessevin vch kinran.

Bet ruvaun ruẏvenit ran.

NEUM duc. i. elffin

Y browi vẏ martrin.

Vch kinran gessevin.

Bet ruwaun ryievanc daerin.

BET ẏ march. bet ẏ guẏthur.

Bet ẏ gugaun cletẏfrut.

Anoeth bid bet ẏ arthur.

BET elchwith ẏs gulich glav.

Maes meuetauc ẏdanav.

Dẏliei kẏnon ẏno ẏ kiniav.

PIEV. ẏ bet. hun. bet hun a hun.

Gowin ẏmi. mi ae gun.

Bet ew. bet etew oet hun,

A bet eidal tal ẏscvn.

EITEW ac eidal diessic

Alltudion kanavon cẏlchuẏ drei.

Mekid meibon meigen meirch mei.

PIEV y bet hun. bet bruẏno

Hir hẏdir ẏwir inẏ bro.

* The handwriting of the first part of this poem is here resumed.

Parth ẏ dvei nẏ bitei fo.
PIEV ẏ bet hun nid
   Aral guẏthuch urth ervid.
   Trath lathei chvarchei vrthid.
BET silit dẏval inedrẏwuẏ le.
   Bet llemenic in llan elvẏ.
   Yg guernin bre bet eilinvẏ.
BET milur mirein gnaud kelein
   Oelav. kin bu. tav. ẏ dan mein.
   Llachar mab run ẏg clun kein.
BET talan. talẏrth
   Yg kinhen teir cad.
   Kẏmẏnad pen pop nẏrth.
   Hẏget a goret ẏ pirth.
BET elissner abner. inẏwinder.
   Daear diarchar dibrẏder.
   Pen llv wu tra wu ẏ amser.
BET gur gurch ẏ var.
   Llachar llẏv niver. in aber duwir dẏar.
   Ynẏ gvna tavne toniar
PIEV ẏ bet ẏnẏ ridev.
   Bet ruẏw ẏv hunnv mab rigenev.
   Gur a digonei da ar ẏ arwev.
PIEV ẏ bet hun bet breint.
   Y rug llewin ae lledneint.
   Bet gur guae. ẏ isscereint.
PIEV ẏ bet ẏn llethir. ẏ brin.
   Llauer nẏs guir ae gowin.
   Bet ẏ coel mab kinvelin.
BET deheveint ar cleveint awon.
   Yg gurthtir mathauarn.
   Y stifful kedwir cadarn.
BET aron mab diwinvin.

Inhir gwennle.

Nẏ dodeilew ar ladron.

Nẏ rotei gwir ẏ alon.

BET taw logev. mab llut. inẏtrewrut

Trav. mal ẏ mae inẏ kẏstut.

Ae clathei caffei but.

PIEV ẏ bet ar lan rẏddnant.

Run. ẏ. env radev keucant.

Ri oet ew. Riogan ae gvant.

OET ef kẏfnẏssen ẏ holi

Galanaş. guawrut grut aten.

Achen bvir but bet bradwen.

PIEV ẏ bet pedrival.

Ae pedwar mein amẏtal.

Bet madauc marchauc dẏwal.

EN eiwonit elvit tir.

Ymae gur hẏduf hir.

Lleas paup pan rẏdighir.

ETRI bet ẏg kewin kelvi.

Awen ae divaud imi.

Bet kinon garv ẏ duẏael.

Bet kinvael. bet kinveli.

BET llvid lledneis. ig kemeistir.

Kin boed hirtuw ẏ eis.

Dẏgirchei tarv trin ino treis.

BET siaun sẏberv in hirerw.

Minit. ẏrug ẏ gverid ae derv.

Chuerthinauc braucbrid chuerv.

PIEV ẏ bet ẏnẏ clidur.

Tra wu nẏ bv eitilur.

Bet ebediv am maelur.

PIEV ẏ bet inẏ rallt. trav.

Gelin ẏ lauer ẏ lav.

Tarv trin trugaret itav.

*Y BEDDEU ẏnẏ morua

 Ys bẏchan aẏ haelewẏ.

 Ymae sanauc sẏberw vun.

 Y mae run rẏuel aswẏ.

 Ymae earrwen verch hennin

 Y mae lledin allẏwẏ.

BET hennin henben ẏn aelwẏt

 Dinorben. bet airgwl ẏn dẏuet

 Yn rẏt gẏnan gẏhoret.

GOGYUARCH pob diara

 Pieu ẏr ьedgor ẏssẏ ẏma.

 Bet einẏaьn ab cunedda

 Cwl ẏm prẏdein ẏ ddiua.

PIEU ẏr bed ẏnẏ maes mawr.

 Balch ẏ law ar ẏ lafnawr.

 Bet beli ab benlli gawr.

XX.

KYGOGION. ELAETH AE CANT.

Fol. 35. b. †**C**ANTREGHIS wiguisc amhoen.

O amrẏues neus adwaen.

Nẏm gunaho douit duẏ poen.

Nẏ gvnaho dowit duẏ poen

Ar din amẏdic ae awar.

Direid new. direid daear.

Daearaul pechodaul imẏoel aduv.

A deweint. duhuned.

A gothuẏ crist nachisced.

Nachisced mab. din. ẏr dioteiveint

Mab duv. a duhuned pilgeint.

Ew keiff new a chirreiveint.

---

* What follows is in a different hand, and, from the orthography, more modern.

† The older hand is here resumed.

Rẏrreiweint a geiff a goffaho

Duv ac nistirmẏcco.

A new ẏ nos ẏ tragho.

Otreinc mab din heb imdiwin

A duv. am awnel o pechaud.

Nẏ mad aeth eneid inẏ gnaud.

Nẏ naud ẏ direid imioli

A duv. inerbin dit kẏnhi.

Nẏ thebic drud ẏ treghi.

    Cantreghis.

XXI.

ELAETH AGANT.

HEB coffav duv daun diffrid

Gwirion ac egilion hevid

Gormot o cam syberwid.

Guae ae gunel heb kel imbit.

Nẏcharaw alaw ol difod

Bressuil. pop pressent ẏshawod.

Din wuẏf itav. eitav clod

Yduv gorev im gorvod.

Caraw voli pedẏr avedir tagtew

Iaun. ae pelltaun. ẏgid ac ew

Im pop ieith obeith atew.

Llara cloduaur, hael porthaur new.

Y duv ẏ harchaw arch roti

Argluit. ẏn argledir eloẏ.

Im eneid rac ẏ poeni.

Naut oll ẏr holl merthẏri.

Y duv ẏ harchaw arch aton

Dihev rac poenev gelinion.

Y. menid. o pleid cofion.

Naut meir gwiri ar gueriton.

Y duv. ẏ. harchaw arch hewid
Kẏwiaun can dichaun vẏniffrid.
Y. meneid rac poen enbid.
Naut cristonogion ẏ bid.
Y duv. ẏ. harchaw arch giwreint·
Bresswil inprissur pop pilgeint.
Y meneid rac poein oweint.
Naut duire ẏ rolre seint.

Heb coffav duv.

XXII.

GEREINT FIL ERBIN.

36. a.   RAC gereint gelin kẏstut.
Y gueleise meirch can crimrut.
A gwidẏ gaur garv achlut.
Rac Gereint gelin dihad.
Gueleise meirch crimrut o kad.
Aguẏdi gaur garu puẏllad.
Rac Gereint gelin ormes.
Gueleis meirch can eu crees.
Aguẏdi gaur garv achles.
En llogborth ẏ gueleise vrcheint.
Ageloraur mvẏ nomeint.
Aguir rut rac ruthir gereint.
En llogporth ẏ gueleise giminad.
Guirigrid aguaed am iad.
Rac gereint vaur mab ẏ tad.
En llogporth gueleise gottoev.
A guir nẏ gilint rac gvaev.
Ac ẏ ved gvin o guẏdir gloev.
En llogporth ẏ gueleise arwev
Guir a guẏar in dinev.
A gvẏdi gaur garv atnev.

En llogporth ẏ gueleise. ẏ arthur
Guir deur kẏmẏnint adur.
Ameraudur llẏwiaudir llawur
En llogporth ẏ llas ẏ gereint.
Guir. deur o odir diwneint.
Achin rillethid ve. llatẏsseint.
Oet re rereint dan vortuid
Gereint garhirion graun guenith.
Rution ruthir eririon blith.
Oet re rerent dan vortuid
Gereint. garhirion graun ae bv.
Rution ruthir eriron dv.
Oet re rereint dan mortuid
Gereint. garhirion graun boloch.
Rution ruthir eriron coch.
Oet re rereint dan mortuid
Gereint. garhirion graun wehin.
Rution ruthir eririon gvinn.
Oet re rereint dan vortuid
Gereint. garhirion grat hit.
Turuf goteith ar diffeith mẏnit.
Oet re rereint. dan vortuid
Gereint garhirion gran anchvant.
Blaur blaen eu raun in ariant.
Oet re rereint dan mortuid.
Gereint. garhirion. graun adas.
Rution ruthir erẏrion glas.
Oet re rereint dan mortuid
Gereint. garhirion graun cu buẏd
Rution ruthir eririon llvid.
Ban aned gereint oet a gored
Pirth new. rotei crist a arched
Prid mircin prẏdein wogoned.

XXIII.

. a.

DUV in kẏmhorth in nerth in porth in canhorthuẏ.
Y valch teeirn dinas unbin degin adwi.
Hẏwel welmor. kimrẏ oror kẏghor arvẏ.
Terruin trochiad. torwoet ueitad vab goronvẏ.
Godrut y var. gurt in trẏdar gvae rẏcothvẏ.
Pedridauc heuL muẏhaw ẏ treuL vchel kẏlchwy.
Tir brẏcheinauc. dẏ iaun priaud. paup ae gwelhvẏ.

DEV rẏdadlas am luith eurgvas euas lẏvuẏ.
Ergig anchvant. guent. gulad morgant. Dyffrin mẏnvy.
Gvhir penrin ẏstradvi brin. tẏwin. warvẏ.
Dẏued dvẏcaun. kerediciaun. kiflaun owuẏ.
A meironit ac ewionit. ac ardudvẏ.
A llein drav. ac aberffrav. a. dẏganhvẏ.
Ros rowẏnniauc. ran arderchauc. rugil ẏg gortuẏ.
Tegigil (—)al. edeirnaun ial arial arlvẏ.
Rẏuel ebruit. a diffrin cluit. a nant convẏ.
Powis enwauc. a chẏueilauc ac avo mvẏ.
Dẏffrin hawren. keri dẏgen. kẏven venvẏ.
Elwael buellt. maelenit guell. pell ẏ treithvẏ.
Teir rac ẏnis. ar teir inis. ar tramordvẏ.
Hẏuel guledic. vt gveith vutic. id ẏ guẏstlvẏ.

Y THARKIVEIR ar pennic penn. o. plant nevuẏ.
Goruir edwin. guraul breenhin. dilẏwin denvẏ.
Dreic angerdaul turvf moroet maur. meint achupvẏ.
Rẏwiscuis llaur am ẏ vẏssaur eur amaervẏ.
Bei na chaned. ẏ. tẏernet anhvẏet rvẏ.
Or saul pennaeth ageis inaeth. arvaeth camrvẏ.
Hẏdir y kẏmhell. hẏwel env opelL guell ẏv noc vẏ.
Diprẏderant di ẏscarant. rac. ẏ dibvẏ.
Dihev ittunt. trallaud kẏstut. achur kẏstvẏ.

Gwerin werid. gwedẏ clevid crid a chymvẏ.
Ny dav metic hid orphen bid. hid ẏ nottvẏ.
Hẏuel haelaf. vaur eilassaw gorescẏnhvẏ.
Caffaud hẏuel urth ẏ hoewet. wẏ rẏbuchvẏ.

Y rẏ puched ẏ colowin ked. clod pedrẏdant.
Rẏuel dẏwal vrien haval. arial vẏtheint.
Gurisc gueilgi dowẏn. kẏvid hehowin colofẏn milcant.
Llugirn deudor. lluoet agor. gur. bangor breint.
Prẏdus perchen priodaur ben. pen pop kinweint.
Gorev breenhin ar gollewin. hid in llundein.
Haelaw lariaw. levaf teccaf. o adaw plant.
Gwerlig haeton gvaut verdidon vaton vetveint.
Goruir menic mur gwerennic gurhid gormant.
Terruin am tir. ri reith kẏwir. o hil morgant.
O morccanhvc o rieinvc radev rvẏtheint.
O teernon kẏwrid leon. galon reibeint
Vn vid veneid ẏ ellẏspp bid. gelleist porthant.
Hoethil hir ac ew. a chein ẏ atew trvi artuniant.
Vrten arnav. rad ac anaw. affav a phlant.

XXIV.

ASSUYNAW naut duv diamehv
Y daun aedonẏauc wiffinnhev.
Ar dẏ guir erir aerev.
Ar dẏ gulad guledic dehev.
Assuinaf archaf eirchad
Ym gelwir. naut kẏuir kẏgwastad.
Ar dẏdrissev aer. drussad.
Ar didrissaur gvaur gwenvlad.
Assuinaw archaw arch vaur
Y periw a peris new allaur.
Naut rac dẏuar car kertaur.
Ar dẏpirth ar diporthaur.

Assuinaf naut haut haelon
Deheuparth diheuporth kertorion.
Athturuf othtarianogion.
Athtorẏf oth teern meibon.
Assuinaf ẏ chnaut nacheluch.
Ychporth. can perthin attreguch.
Gostecwir llis gosteguch.
Gostec. beirt bart aglẏwuch.
Assuinaf haut naut haelvonet.
Worsset. nẏth orsseiw teernet.
Ar dẏ torif corẏf kẏwrisset
Ar dẏ teulu teilug met.
Met cuin ev gwiraud met kirn
Ae gwallav. ae gwellig in eurdirn.
Agloev ẏ ved in edirn.
Agliv deur. aglev teeirn.
Teern weilch pridein prẏdaw
Ych priwgert. ẏch priwclod adigaw.
Ych. bart ẏch beirnad vẏtaw.
Ych porth perthin ẏv ataf.
Attep aganaw ar canhuẏw.
Vẏ argluit. ergliv. wi. can dothuif.
Lleissaun lliw llev gliv glevrvit.
Laessa divar di bart wif.
Viw kertaur imruw. ruisc. morkimlaut
Gurt. ruis firt kvit kert. vahaut.
Assuinasserv herv hirvlaut.
Assuinaf ar wut naw. naut.
Assuinaw naut duv diamhev. ẏ daun.

XXV.

Fol. 40. a. *ĦERA vom kẏd keredd. goned kẏdimẏteith.
Bid pẏrfeẏth in gueithred.

* This short poem is written in the same more modern hand with the stanzas at the end of the Englynnonn y bedev.

Keýssun ý minared drvi fit

A. crevit. acred. kýd credwit

Douit. drvi kereirhýt. fit.

Maur penýd meith peunýt.

Eneid pan im kenerchýt.

Pa divet ae bet ambit.

XXVI.

Fol. 41. a.

* 𝕯V dý uarch du dý capan.

Du dý pen du duhunan.

Ia du ae ti ýscolan.

Mi iscolan ýscolheic

Yscawin ý puill iscodic.

Guae. ný baut agaut guledic.

O losci ecluis. allat buch iscol.

Allývir rod ý voti.

Vý penhid. ýstrum kýnhi.

Creaudir ý creadurev. perthidev

Muýhaw. kýrraw de imi výgev.

Ath vradaste. am tuýllas ýnnev.

Bluýtin llaun im rýdoded.

Ym. bangor ar paul cored.

Edrich de poen imý gan mor prýued.

Bei ýscuýpun arvn.

Mor amluc guint. ý vlaen bric guit fallum.

Arav vneuthume bith nýs gunaun.†

* The handwriting of the early part of the MS. is here resumed.

† The following stanza is added in a smaller hand :—

    Creaudir y creaduriev perthidev muythaw.

    Matev imvygev. athuradaste am tuyllas yuheu.

    Bluytin llaun ymrydodid. ym bangor ar paul

    Cored. edrich de poen imi gan mor pryued.

XXVII.

. 41. b.

KYNTAW geir adẏwedaw.
Y bore ban kẏuodaw.
Croes crist in wissc ẏmdanaw.
Arhelv uẏ ren ẏ guiscav
Hetiu. un trev a glẏuaw.
Nid ew wẏ duu niscredaw.
Guiscaw ẏmdanaw inberch.
Nẏ credaw coel canẏd kerch.
Y gur am creuẏse am nerth.
Ymae vimrid ardebed.
Arowun ar mor wẏned.
Etẏl butic bitaud ked.
Ymae vẏmrid ar kighor.
Arowun mẏned. ar mor.
Etẏl butic bẏtaud ior.
Dẏrcheuid bran ẏ hasgell.
Arowun mẏned. impell.
Etẏl butic bitaud guell.
Dẏrcheuid bran ẏ hadein.
Arowun mẏned ruvein.
Etil butic bẏtaud kein.
Ystarnde wineu fruin guin.
Redec hiraethauc raun rin.
Ren new. oet reid duu genhin.
Ystarnde winev birr ẏ blev.
Ruit ẏgniw. rẏgig. otew.
Mẏnẏd vo truin. ẏduit trev.
Ystarnde winev hir ẏ neid.
Ruit ẏg nẏw rẏgig. woteid.
Nẏ lut ar lev trev direid.
Trum kẏduod daear. tev deil dris.
Chuerv vuelin met melis.

Ren new ruitade vẏ neges.

O eissillit guledic. a gueith

Wtic. wosprid. aphedir pen pop ieith.

Sanffreid suẏnade in imdeith.

Heul eirioled arouned

Argluit. crist kelẏ. colowin ked.

Dẏwẏccviff wẏm pechaud am gueithred.*

𝕸𝕸I aego winneis ẏ offereid

Bid. ae hesgip ae higneid

Ba beth orev rac eneid.

Pader a buẏeid a bendiceid

Creto. ae canho rac eneid.

Hid wraud goreu gortẏwneid.

Yscẏthrich fort a delhich ti. allunhich tagneuet.

Nẏthvi tranc ar trugaret.

Ro vẏd. ẏ. newẏnauc. a dillad ẏ noeth.

A chenich golẏchuid.

O kẏuil dieuil dothuid.

Sẏberu asegur dolur ar eu knaud.

Guerth mẏned dros uessur.

Ystir nithiau nẏ bo pur.

Rẏhun a rẏuetudaud. ariwiraud

O vet. a rietillter. o gẏnaud.

Llẏna chuec chuerv erbin. braud.

Anudon am tir. abrad argluid.

A diuanv llaugar.

Dit braud bitaud ediwar.

O kẏuodi pilgeint adeueint

Torrwin pisc tuth eleirch

Tonn. trybelid areith.

Duv y din a denvin kedimdeith.

Gorwin blaen perthen.   Kein gywrev

Adar. hir dit bann cogev.

Trugar daffar duv orev.

Duhunau. ac ẏ meitunav. ar seint.
Id keiff. pop cristaun. kẏrreiueint.

XXVIII.

Fol. 43. a. **G**VLEDIC ar bennic erbin attad.
Er barch o kẏuarch. o. kẏuaenad.
Ynigabil barabil ar ẏ parad.
Vẏ kert ith kirpuill. kanuill kangulad.
Can vid priodaur.
Canuid meidrad maur.
Canuid kighoraur guaur goleuad.
Canuid bron proffuid. canuid inad.
Canuid riev hael. canuid. rotiad.
Canuid. athro im. namethrẏad.
Oth. vann. oth varan. oth virein gulad.
Nam ditaul oth. wt. vt echeiad.
Nam gwellic ẏmplic impled dirad.
Nam gollug oth lav. guallus trewad.
Nam ellug gan llu du digarad.

GWLEDIC arbennic. ban geneise.
O. honaud. nid ower traethaud imi ar a trecheis.
Nid eissev. wẏ kerd. ẏg kein ewreis.
Nid eissẏwed ked men ẏ keweis.
Nid ew ẏm crevis dews diffleis.
Yr guneuthur. amhuill na thuill. na threis.
Nid ew duhunaur a handeneis.
Nid ew rotir new. ir neb nvẏ keis.
Nid rvẏ o awit awenẏt eis.
Nid rvẏ o obruẏ a obrẏneis.
Nid porthi rẏuic rẏuegeis im bron.
Nid porthi penid. rẏ vetẏleis.
In adaud wẏ ren rẏdamvneis.
Rẏdid imeneid. reid rẏ ioles.

XXIX.

BENDITH ẏ wenwas. ir dec diẏrnas.
Breisc ton. bron ehalaeth.
Duv. ẏ env in nvfin impop ieith.
Dẏllit enweir meir rẏmaeth.
Mad devthoste ẏg corffolaeth.
Llẏna mab gowri gobeith.
A dẏlivas idas ẏ leith.
Bu drvi. vewil. athuẏllvriaeth.
In hudaul gvar guassanaeth ẏ argluit.
Bu hẏwit. ac. nẏ bu doeth.
Ac hid vraud. nẏ vn ẏ arvaeth.
Kẏffei bart pridit. ar ẏssit.
In eluit.   Ar hallt ar echuit.
Ar graean. ar mir. ar sir sẏweditiaeth.
Beirnad rodiad llara llau fraeth.
Mui ẏ dinwas sune. gunaune eddwaeth.
Kẏuoethev. ri. nisrdraeth.
Maur duv hetiv. moli dẏvr daaeth.

BENDITH nautorẏw new. ir keluit
Creaudir. kẏuothauc duu douit.
Aperis lleuver lleuenit.
Hael. vẏnver heul in dit.
Eil kanuill cristaun. a leuich uch eigaun.
Lloer vilioet vilenhit.
Athrẏdit rẏuet. ẏv merwerit
Mor. cv threia. cud echwit.*
Cv da. cvd ẏnida. cv. treigil. cv threwna.
Pa hid. a. nev cud vit.
Y pen ẏ seith mlinet.

* On the margin, in a small hand —
        Digones perw. pedwerit
        Yvet. redecauc duwyr chwit.

Y duc ren ẏ risset.
Y dadwet. ẏnẏduit.
Jolune ara beir. kẏvoethauc
Duu vab meir a peris new ac eluit.
Pan deuthoste ẏ passc diwedit.
O vffern. awu ran iti. bv rit.
Ren new rẏphrinomne digerenhit.

XXX.

Fol. 45. a.

IGYM awel llum brin.
Anhaut caffael clid.
Llicrid rid reuhid llin.
Rẏseiw gur arvn conin.
Ton trathon toid tu tir.
Goruchel guaetev rac bron banev
Bre breit allan or seuir.
Oer lle. lluch rac brẏthuch
Gaeaw. crin caun calaw truch.
Kedic awel. coed inibluch.
Oer guelẏ pisscaud ẏgkisscaud
Iaen. cul hit caun barẏwhaud.
Birr diuedit guit gvẏrhaud.
Ottid eirẏ guin ẏ cnes.
Nida kedwir oe neges.
Oer llinnev eu llẏu heb tes.
Ottid eirẏ guin. aren.
Segur ẏscuid ar iscuit hen.
Rẏuaur guint reuhid dien.
Ottid eirẏ ar warthaw rev.
Gosgupid gint blaen guit tev.
Kadir ẏscuid ar ẏscuit glev.
Ottid eirẏ tohid istrad.
Diurẏssintvẏ keduir ẏ cad.
Mi nidaw. anaw nim gad.

Ottid eirỳ o dv riv.
Karcharaur goruit cul biv.
Nid annuỳd hawdit hetiv.
Ottid eirỳ. guin goror
Mỳnit. llum guit llog ar mor.
— Meccid llvwỳr llauer kỳghor.
Eurtirn am cirn. cirn am duir.
Oer llỳri lluchedic auir bir
Diwedit blaen gvit gvir.
Gvenin igogaur guan gaur
Adar.   dit duilith.
Kỳssulwin kewin brin coch gwaur.
Guenin igodo. oer agdo
Rid. reuid rev pan vo.
Ir nep goleith. lleith dỳppo.
Guenin igkeithiv gwirdiv
Mor crin calaw caled riv.
Oer divlit. ỳr eluit hetiv.
Guenin ig clidur rac gulỳbur
Gaeaw. glas cunlleit cev ewur.
Dric weuet llỳvrder ar gur.
Hir nos llum ros lluid riv.
Glas glan guilan in emriv.
Garv mir glau auit hetiv.
Sich guint gulip hint.
Kinuedauc diffrint.
Oer callet cul hit
Llỳwin awon hinon uit.
Driccin imỳnit avonit
Igniw. gulichid lliw llaur trewit.
Neud gueilgi gueled ir eluit.
Nid vid iscolheic. nid vid eleic
Unben. nỳth eluir in dit reid.
Och gindilic. na buost gureic.

Kirchid carv crum tal cum
Clid. briuhid. ia. brooet llum.
Rydieigc glev o lauer trum.
Bronureith breith bron.
Breith bron bronureith.
Briuhid talglan. gan
Garn carv culgrum cam.
Goruchel awel guaet. vanu.
Breit guir or seuir allan.
Kalangaeaw gurim gordugor
Blaen gruc. goreuynauc ton mor.
Bir dit deruhid ych kighor.
O kiscaud yscuid ac aral
Goruit. a guir deur diarchar.
Tec nos. y. ffissccau escar.
Kinteic guint creilum
Coed. crin caun caru iscun.
Pelis enuir pa tir hun.
Kin ottei eiry hid inaruul
Melin. nim gunaei artu awirtul.
Towissune lv y brin. tytul.
Can medrit morruit. y rodwit
A rid a riv eiry adiguit.
Pelis pan vid kyvarwit.
Nim guna pryder im prydein
Heno kyrchu bro priw uchei.
Y ar can kanlin owein.
Kin imtuin ariw eu ac yscuid
Arnad. diffreidad kad kynuid.
Pelis pa tir. ythuaguid.
Y gur a rithao duv. o rigaeth
Carchar. rut y par o penaeth
Owein. reged am ryvaeth.
Can ethiv ruiw in.

E

Rodwit iwerit a teulu na fouch.

Guẏdi. met meuil na vẏnuch.

Y bore gan las ẏ dit

Ban kirchuid mug maur treuit.

Nẏd oet uagaud meirch mechit.

Nim guna lleuenit llad.

Or chuetleu amdiallad.

Mechit golo guit arnad.

Kẏuaruuan amcavall.

Kelein ariuar ar wall

Kiwranc run ar drud arall.

Canisfonogion mugc. alataut mechit.

Druduas nis amgiffre dit.

Periw new pereiste imi dẏuit.

Gwir. igrid. rid rewittor.

Oeruelauc tonn. brith bron mor.

Ren rothid. duv. in. kighor.

Mechit mab llẏwarch. dihawarch

Vnben. glvẏstec llenn lliwalarch.

Kẏntaw. a ffruincluẏmus march.

XXXII.

Fol. 47. b.   PA gur ẏv ẏ porthaur.

Gleuluid gauaeluaur.

Pa gur ae gouin.

Arthur. a chei guin.

Pa imda genhid.

Guir gorev im bid.

Ym tẏ nẏ doi.

Onẏsguaredi.

Mi ae guardi.

Athi ae gueli.

Vẏthneint elei.

Assivẏon ell tri.

Mabon am mýdron.
Guas uthir pen dragon.
Kýsceint. mab. banon.
A guin godýbrion.
Oet rinn vý gueisson
In amuin ev detvon.
Manawidan ab llýr.
Oet duis ý cusil.
Neustuc manauid
Eis tull o trýwruid.
A mabon am melld.
Maglei guaed ar guelld.
Ac anguas edeinauc.
A lluch. llauýnnauc.
Oetin diffreidauc
Ar eidin cýminauc.
Argluit ae llochei
Mý nei ýmtiwýgei.
Kei ae heiriolei.
Trae llathei pop tri.
Pan colled kelli.
Caffad cuelli. aseirolei.
Kei hid trae kýmýnhei.
Arthur ced huarhei.
Y guaed gouerei.
In neuat awarnach
In imlat ew agurach.
Ew a guant pen palach.
In atodev. dissethach.
Ym minit eidin.
Amuc. a. chinbin.
Pop cant id cuitin.
Id cvitin. pop cant.
Rac beduir bedrýdant.

Ar traethev trýwruid.
In amvin a garv luid.
Oet guýchir ý annuýd.
O detýw ac ýscuid.
Oet guaget bragad
Vrth. kei ig kad.
Oet cletýw ighad.
Oe lav diguistlad.
Oet hýneiw guastad
Ar lleg ar lles gulad.
Beduir. a bridlav.
Nau cant guarandau.
Chuechant ý eirthau.
A talei ý ortinav.
Gueisson am buýint.
Oet guell banuitint.
Rac riev emreis.
Gueleise. kei ar uris.
Preitev gorthowis.
Oet gur hir in ewnis.
Oet trum ý dial.
Oet tost ý cýnial.
Pan ýuei o wual
Y uei urth peduar.
Yg kad pandelhei.
Vrth cant idlathei.
Ný bei duv ae digonhei.
Oet diheit aghev kei.
Kei guin allachev.
Digonint we kadev
Kin gloes glas verev.
Y guarthaw ýstaw in gun.
Kei a guant nav guiton.
Kei win aaeth von
Y dilein lleuon.

Y iscuid oet mẏnud

Erbin cath paluc.

. Pan gogiueirch tud.

Puẏ guant cath paluc.

Nau ugein kinlluc.

A cuẏtei in ẏ buẏd.

Nau ugein kinran. a.º

XXXII.

1. 49. a.   †Meinoeth kiclev lew heid.

Pen gethin pell ban dẏgneid.

Onẏ lochir llaur nẏffeid.

AN is coegauc issi moreurauc

Ahin in emil llis guallauc.

Minnev bitaw golvdauc.

Boed emendiceid ir guit.

Attinvis ẏ ligad. in ẏ wit.

Gwallauc ab lleinauc argluit.

Boed emendiceid ir guit dv.

Attinnuis ẏ ligad oe ttv.

Guallauc ab lleinnauc pen llv.

Boed emendiceid ir guit guenn.

Attinvis ẏ ligad. oe penn.

G. ab lleinauc unben.

Boed emendiceid ir guit glas.

Attinwis ẏ ligad in guas.

G. mab lleẏnnauc vrtas.‡

* The MS. is here again defective.
† The handwriting changes, and what follows is in the same hand
as the Hoianau.
‡ On margin, in a small handwriting —
Nid aeth neb auei envauc.
In gorlluro idaeth gvallauc
Yvalaen yr veiriauc.
Nid aeth nep auei edmic
Ir gorllùro id aeth meuric
Ar kewin y gureic in tri diblic.

XXXIII.

Fol. 49. a.

MARV trin anvidin blaut.
Ar benic llu llid anhaut.
Dinam eiroes am oes naut.
Ygan gur gurt ẏ kinnit.
Arbennic llv llid owit.
Athvit naut canẏserchit.
Canis naut im arotit.
Mor verth ẏ thogẏuechit.
Guaur llv pẏ dv pandoit.
Ban deuaw o kad a chiminad
Maur ac aessaur in aghad.
Briuint penaur peleidrad.
Ath kiuarchaw hv ẏscun
Gur. ae iscuid in aghen.
Pebir gur pan iv dẏechen.
Caringrun wimarch kad trablut.
Hud im gelwire guin mab nud.
Gorterch creurdilad merch lut.
Canisti guin gur kiwir.
Racod nẏ rẏimgelir.
Minnev guitnev garanhir.
Nim gade gan kẏulauaret
Athi. urthi fruin ẏdwet.
Dẏwris im trum tawuẏ anet.
Nid ẏ tawue nessaw alawaraw
Urthid. nam vin ẏ tawue eithaw.
Erir mor terruin treiaw.
Yscithreid vẏ modruẏ eur kẏwruẏ
Cann. ẏ gan wẏauarvẏ.
Gueleis aer rac kaer wantvẏ.
Rac mantvẏ llv a weleis
Aessaur brilluid. torrhid eis.
Mẏgedaul. kein a dẏgei treis.

Gwin ab nut but. bitinaur.

Kint ẏsirthei kadoet rac carnetaur

Dẏ ueirch. no bruẏn briw ẏ laur.

Ystec vẏ ki ac istrun.

Ac ẏssew. orev or cvn.

Dormach oet hunnv afv ẏ maelgun.

Dormach truinrut ba ssillit

Arnaw canissam giffredit.

Dẏ gruidir ar wibir winit.

Mi awum inẏ lle llas guendolev.

Mab keidav colowin kertev.

Ban rẏerhint brein ar crev.

Mi awum in lle llas bran.

Mab ẏwerit clod lẏdan.

Ban rẏerint brein garthan.

Mi awum lle llas llachev.

Mab arthur uthir ig kertev.

Ban rẏreint brein ar crev.

Mi awum lle las meuric.

Mab karreian clod edmic.

Ban rẏreeint brein ar cic.

Nẏ buum lle llas gwallauc

Mab goholheth teithiauc.

Attwod lloegir mab lleẏnnac.

Mi awum lle llas milvir

Pridein. or duẏrein ir goglet.

Mi. wi. wiw. vintev. ẏ. bet.

Mi awum lle llas milguir

Bridein or duẏrein ir dehev.

Mi. wi. wiv. vintev. ẏ aghev.

XXXIV.

. 49. b.   **K**YD karhwine morva. cassaue mor

Pẏr toei wanec carrec camhur.

Glev diwal hẏgar hael huẏscur.

Yscinvaen beirt bit butic clẏdur.

Goruc clod heilin benffic awirtul.

Hid braud parahaud ẏ ertiwul.

Kẏd carhiuwe morua cassaaue ton.

Digones ton treis oer cleis ẏ ron.

Ew kuẏnhiw inẏ wuiw in hervit hon.

Gweith heinẏw golchiw ar winvẏwron.

Kid ẏ lleinv keudaud nis beirv calon.

Ac inllvrv kẏheic kiniod ẏ ron.

Yssim edivar oe negessev.

Ban wrissuis pebrur pell ẏ aghev.

Glev diwal kẏweithit ẏd vam in dev.

Menic it arwet duwir dalennev.

Fechid diristan othiwod.

Mi nẏthervill imchod.

Omparth guertheisse march irod.

Dial kẏheic amoet blis.

Am ẏ kẏwrev ẏ melis.

Och corr dẏ sorrde ẏmi bv ewnis.

XXXV.

ARCHAUC agirch ẏ dinas

Ae cun gwinion ae cirn bras.

Nẏthadwaen. mi rẏthwelas.

Marchauch a kirch ir aber.

Y ar march cadarn kad fer.

Dabre genhiw nẏm gwatter.

Mi nẏd aw ina in aur.

Gotev gueith ẏ godriccaur.

Elhid bendith new. a. llaur.

Ygur nim guelas beunit.

Ytebic ẏgur deduit.

Ba hid eidẏ aphandoit.

Ban deuaw o caer seon
O imlat ac itewon.
Itaw caer lev a gwidion.
Dabrede genhiw ir dinas
Athuit met ara phellas.
Ac eur coeth ar diwanas.
Mi nẏd adwaen ẏ gurhẏ
Ametev tan a gveli.
Tec achuec ẏ diwedi.
Dabre genhiw imtino
Athuit guin gorẏsgelhor.
Vgnach ẏw. vẏheno mab mẏdno.
Vgnach bendith ithorsset
Athvo rad ac enrẏdet.
Taliessin viw inhev talaw itti dẏ gulet.
Taliessin penhaw or guir.
Beitad ẏg kert ẏkẏuergir.
Tric ima hid dẏv merch.
Vgnach mvihaw ẏ alaw.
Athvo. rad ẏ gulad pennhaw.
Nẏ haetaw kabil nẏ thrigiaw.

XXXVI.

MARUNAD MADAUC MAB MAREDUT.

KYNTELV PRIDIT MAUR AE CANT.

Fol. 52. a.

ᏩODURẎW o glẏuaw. ar claur
Maelenit. mur eluit eluan gaur.
Teulv Madauc mad anhaur.
Mal teulv. bann benlli gaur.
Godurẏw a glẏuaw. ar claur ieithon.
Hir. hẏdir ẏ wir ar saesson.
Teulv madauc mur galon.
Mal turuw. tormenhoet kinon.
Godurẏw a glivaw. godor drein

Waewaur guae loegir in dit kein.

Teulv madauc mur prẏdein.

Yn lluithauc. in llithiav brein.

Godurẏw a gliuaw. ar claur llavur.

Rei. rẏuelclod dissegur.

Teulv madauc mur eglur.

Mal gavr torẏw teulu arthur.

Godurẏw a glẏaw. ar claur vagv

Glẏv. gloev madauc bẏeiwu.

Trinva kẏva kinẏtu.

Trẏdit tri diweir teulv.

XXXVII.

MARUNAD MADAUC FIL MAREDUT.

Fol. 52. b.   KYWARCHAW im ri. rad wobeith.

Kẏwarchaw kẏwercheise canweith.

Y prowi prẏdv. opriwieith.

Eurgert. ẏm argluit kedẏmteith.

Y cvinav madauc. metweith

Y alar. ae alon ẏmpob ieith.

Dor ẏscor iscvid canhimteith.

Tarian in aerwan. in evrweith.

Turuw gruc ẏg gotuc goteith.

Tariw escar ẏ iscuid in dileith.

Rwẏ. mirt kẏrt. kertorion. wobeith.

Rut. dilut diletẏw kedimteith.

Rẏ gelwid. madauc. kin noe leith.

Ruid galon. ẏ. vogion diffeith.

Rvit attaw attep vẏgobeith.

Rit. wisscoet. wessgvin canhimteith.

Rut on gir.   Bran vab llir lledieith.

Ruit ẏ clod includav anreith.

Rvt woauc vaon nẏ oleith.

Rad wastad gwistlon canhimteith.

Llawin arẏrad. ig kad ig cvnlleith.*

Llav escud. dan iscvd calchwreith.

Llev powis peues diobeith.

Haul owin. gur nẏ minn mabweith.

Hvil ẏscvn ẏscvid pedeirieith.†

Hael madauc. veuder anhẏweith.

Can derẏv. darfv am ocleith.

Can daeraud. darw kedẏmteith.

Oet beirtcar. bart clvm di ledieith.

Oet cadarn agor. dẏwinmor diffeith.

Oet hir ẏ truited. oed hẏged higar.

Oet llawar guẏar. oe kẏwarweith.

Oet buelin blas. gwanas gwaedreith,

Oet eurllev. o aer llin kadieith.

Oet diwarn kadarn kedẏmteith unbin.

Oet dirn in heirn. haearn ẏ talheith.

Ae diwet ẏspo. canbv. ẏ leith.

Ydiwin ẏ cam kẏmeint ẏ affeith.

Yg goleuder seint. ig goleudeith.

Yg goleuad rad. ridid perfeith.

XXXVIII.

Fol. 53. b. ‡SEITHENHIN sawde allan.

Ac edrẏchuirde varanres

Mor. maes guitnev rẏtoes.

Boed emendiceid ẏ morvin

Aehellẏgaut guẏdi cvin.

Finaun wenestir mor terruin.

* On margin —
    Llawin gviar a gar. o kidweith

† On margin —
    Hil teirn in heirn henveith

‡ What follows is in the same handwriting as No. 24.

Boed emendiceid ẏ vachteith.

Ae. golligaut guẏdi gueith.

Finaun wenestir mor diffeith

Diaspad vererid ẏ ar vann caer.

Hid ar duu ẏ dodir.

Gnaud guẏdi traha trangc hir.

Diaspad mererid. ẏ ar van kaer

Hetiv. hid ar duu ẏ dadoluch.

Gnaud guẏdi traha attreguch.

Diaspad mererid am gorchuit

Heno. ac nimhaut gorlluit

G.   g.   traha tramguit.

Diaspad mererid ẏ ar gwinev

Kadir keadaul duv ae gorev.

Gnaud guẏdi gormot eissev.

Diaspad mererid. am kẏmhell

Heno ẏ urth nẏistauell.

Gnaud guẏdi traha trangc pell.

Bet seithenhin sẏnhuir vann

Rug kaer kenedir a glan.

Mor maurhidic a kinran.

XXXIX.

ENWEV. MEIBON. LLYWARCH HEN.

Fol. 54. a. * ЖЖEC ẏd gan ir adaren ar perwit pren.

Vch. pen gwen. kin ẏ olo dan

Tẏwarch briw ei calch hen.

Goreu trẏwir in ev gulad

Y amdiffin ev — treuad.

Eithir. ac erthir. ac argad.

Tri meib llẏwarch. tri aghimen.

Kad. tri cheimad awlawen.

---

* The handwriting again changes to the same handwriting as
that of Nos. 36 and 37.

Llev. ac arav. ac vrien.
Handid haus imachuisson
Oe adav ar lan awon.
Y gid allvewur. lluydon.
Tarv trin ryuel adun.
Cledir kad kanvill. o. giriun.
Ren new ruy a endeid hun.
Gorev try wir y dan new
Y amdiffin euhadew
Pill. a seliw. a sandew.
Y bore gan las y dit.
Ban kirchuid mug maur trevit.
Nid oed vagaud meirch mechit.
Kywarvan am cavall.
Kelein ar wiar ar wall.
Kyvranc run. ar drud arall.
Diaspad a dodir ygwarthaw lluc.
Vynit. o. duch pen bet kinlluc
Meu gerit. mi ae goruc.
Ottid eiry tohid istrad.
Dwrissint kedwir y cad.
Mi nyd aw anaw nimgad.
Ny duid ti yscoleic. nid vid eleic
Vnben nithelwir in dit reid.
Och kindilic na buost gureic.
Pell otima aber llyv.
Pellach yn duy kyuetliw.
Talan teleiste deigir imi hetiv.

III.

THE BOOK OF ANEURIN.

A MS. OF THE LATTER PART OF THE 13TH OR THE BEGINNING
OF THE 14TH CENTURIES, THE PROPERTY OF SIR THOMAS
PHILLIPPS, BARONET, OF MIDDLE HILL.

HWN YW E GODODIN.

ANEIRIN AE CANT.

GREDYF gwr oed gwas
Gwrhẏt am dias.
Meirch mwth mẏngvras.
A dan vordwẏt megẏr was.
Ysgwẏt ẏsgauẏn lledan
Ar bedrein mein vuan.
Kledẏuawr glas glan
Ethẏ eur aphan.
Nẏ bi ef a vi
Cas e rof a thi.
Gwell gwneif a thi
Ar wawt dẏ uoli.
Kẏnt ẏ waet elawr
Nogẏt ẏ neithẏawr.
Kẏnt ẏ vwẏt ẏ vrein
Noc ẏ argẏurein.
Ku kẏueillt ewein.

Facsimile of a Page from the Book of Aneurin.

Kwl ẏ uot a dan vrein.
Marth ẏm pa vro
Llad un mab marro.

KAYAWC kẏnhorawc men ẏ delhei.
Diffun ẏmlaen bun med a dalhei
Twll tal ẏ rodawr ene klẏwei
Awr. nẏ rodei nawd meint dilẏnei.
Ni chilẏei o gamhawn enẏ verei
Waet mal brwẏn gomẏnei gwẏr nẏt echei.
Nẏs adrawd gododin ar llawr mordei.
Rac pebẏll madawc pan atcorẏei
Namen un gwr o gant enẏ delhei.

KAEAWC kẏnnivẏat kẏwlat erwẏt.
Ruthẏr erẏr en ebẏr pan llithẏwẏt.
E amot a vu not a gatwẏt.
Gwell a wnaeth e aruaeth nẏ gilẏwẏt.
Rac bedin ododin odechwẏt.
Hẏder gẏmhell ar vreithel vanawẏt
Nẏ nodi nac ẏsgeth nac ẏsgwẏt.
Nẏ ellir anet rẏ vaethpwẏt
Rac ergẏt catvannan catwẏt.

KAEAWC kẏnhorawc bleid e maran.
Gwevrawr godiwawr torchawr am rann.
Bu gwevrawr gwerthvawr gwerth gwin vann.
Ef gwrthodes gwrẏs gwẏar disgrein.
Ket dẏffei wẏned a gogled e rann.
O gussẏl mab ẏsgẏrran
Ysgwẏdawr angkẏuan.

KAEAWC kẏnhorawc aruawc eg gawr
Kẏn no diw e gwr gwrd eg gwẏawr.

Kẏnran en racwan rac bẏdinawr
Kwẏdei pẏm pẏmwnt rac ẏ lafnawr.
O wẏr deivẏr a brennẏch dẏchiawr.
Ugein cant eu diuant en un awr.
Kẏnt ẏ gic e vleid nogẏt e neithẏawr.
Kẏnt e vud e vran nogẏt e allawr.
Kẏn noe argẏurein e waet e lawr.
Gwerth med eg kẏnted gan lliwedawr.
Hẏueid hir ermẏgir tra vo kerdawr.

GWYR a aeth ododin chwerthin ognaw.
Chwerw en trin a llain en emdullẏaw.
Bẏrr vlẏned en hed ẏd ẏnt endaw.
Mab botgat gwnaeth gwẏnnẏeith gwreith e law.
Ket elwẏnt e lanneu e benẏdẏaw.
A hen a ẏeueing a hẏdẏr allaw.
Dadẏl diheu angheu ẏ eu treidaw.

GWYR a aeth ododin chwerthin wanar.
Disgẏnnẏeis em bedin trin diachar.
Wẏ lledi a llavnawr heb vawr drẏdar
Colovẏn glẏw reithuẏw rodi arwar.

GWYR a aeth gatraeth oed fraeth eu llu.
Glasved eu hancwẏn a gwenwẏn vu.
Trẏchant trwẏ beirẏant en cattau.
A gwedẏ elwch tawelwch vu.
Ket elwẏnt e lanneu e benẏdu.
Dadẏl dieu agheu ẏ eu treidu.

GWYR a aeth gatraeth vaduaeth uedwn.
Fẏrẏf frwẏthlawn oed caın nas kẏmhwẏllwn.
E am lavnawr coch gorvawr gwrmwn.
Dwẏs dengẏn ed emledẏn aergwn.

Ar deulu brenneẏch beẏch barnasswn.
Dilẏw dẏn en vẏw nẏs adawsswn.
Kẏueillt a golleis diffleis oedwn.
Rugẏl en emwrthrẏn rẏnn riadwn.
Nẏ mennws gwrawl gwadawl chwegrwn.
Maban ẏ gian o vaen gwẏnngwn.

GWYR a aeth gatraeth gan wawr
Trauodẏnt en hed eu hovnawr.
Milcant a thrẏchant a emdaflawr.
Gwẏarllẏt gwẏnnodẏnt waewawr.
Ef gorsaf ẏng gwrẏaf. eg gwrẏawr.
Rac gosgord mẏnẏdawc mwẏnvawr.

GWYR a aeth gatraeth gan wawr
Dẏgẏmẏrrws eu hoet eu hanẏanawr.
Med evẏnt melẏn melẏs maglawr.
Blwẏdẏn bu llewẏn llawer kerdawr.
Coch eu cledẏuawr na phurawr
Eu llain. gwẏngalch a phedrẏollt bennawr
Rac gosgord mẏnẏdawc mwẏnvawr.

GWYR a aeth gatraeth gan dẏd.
Neus goreu o gadeu gewilid.
Wẏ gwnaethant en geugant gelorwẏd.
A llavnawr llawn annawd em bedẏd.
Goreu ẏw hwnn kẏn kẏstlwn kerennẏd.
Enueint creu ac angeu oe hennẏd.
Rac bedin ododin pan vudẏd
Neus goreu deu bwẏllẏat neirthẏat gwẏchẏd.

GWR a aeth gatraeth gan dẏd.
Ne llewes ef vedgwẏn veinoethẏd.
Bu truan gẏuatcan gẏvluẏd.

F

E neges ef or drachwres drenghidẏd.
Nẏ chrẏssiws gatraeth
Mawr mor ehelaeth
 E aruaeth uch arwẏt.
Nẏ bu mor gẏffor
O eidẏn ẏsgor
 A esgarei oswẏd
Tutuwlch hir ech e dir ae dreuẏd.
Ef lladei Saesson seithuet dẏd.
Perheit ẏ wrhẏt en wrvẏd
Ae govein gan e gein gẏweithẏd.
Pan dẏvu dutvwlch dut nerthẏd.
Oed gwaetlan gwẏaluan vab kilẏd.

ⓢWR a aeth gatraeth gan wawr.
Wẏneb udẏn ẏsgorva ẏsgwẏdawr.
Crei kẏrchẏnt kẏnnullẏnt reiawr.
En gẏnnan mal taran twrẏf aessawr.
Gwr gorvẏnt gwr etvẏnt gwr llawr.
Ef rwẏgei. a chethrei. a chethrawr.
Od uch lled lladei a llavnawr.
En gẏstud heẏrn dur arbennawr.
E mordei ẏstẏngei a dẏledawr.
Rac erthgi erthẏchei vẏdinawr.

ⓟ vreithẏell gatraeth pan adrodir.
Maon dẏchiorant eu hoet bu hir.
Edẏrn diedẏrn amẏgẏn dir.
A meibẏon godebawc gwerin enwir.
Dẏforthẏnt lẏnwẏssawr gelorawr hir.
Bu tru a dẏnghetven anghen gẏwir.
A dẏngwt ẏ dutvwlch a chẏvwlch hir.
Ket ẏvein ved gloẏw wrth leu babir
Ket vei da e vlas ẏ gas bu hir.

BLAEN echeching gaer glaer ewgei.
Gwŷr gweirŷd gwanar ae dilŷnei.
Blaen ar e bludue dŷgollouit vual
Ene vwŷnvawr vordei.
Blaen gwirawt vragawt. ef dŷbŷdei.
Blaen eur a phorphor kein as mŷgei.
Blaen edŷstrawr pasc ae gwaredei.
Gwrthlef ac euo brŷt ae derllŷdei.
Blaen erwŷre gawr buduawr drei.
Arth en llwrw bŷth hwŷr e techei.

ANAWR gŷnhoruan
Huan arwŷran.
Gwledic gwd gŷffgein
Nef enŷs brŷdein.
Garw rŷt rac rŷnn ;
Aes elwrw budŷn.
Bual oed arwŷnn
Eg kŷnted eidŷn.
Erchŷd rŷodres.
E ved medwawt
Yuei win gwirawt.
Oed eruit uedel.
Yuei win gouel.
A erueid en arued.
Aer gennin vedel.
Aer adan glaer.
Kenŷn keuit aer.
Aer seirchŷawc
Aer edenawc.
Nŷt oed dirŷf ŷt ŷsgwŷt
Gan waŷwawr plŷmnwŷt.
Kwŷdŷn gŷuoedŷon ;
Eg cat blŷmnwŷt

Diessic e dias.
Divevýl as talas.
Hudid e wýllýas.
Kýn bu clawr glas
Bed gwruelling vreisc.

MEITHI etmýgant
Tri llwrý nouant.
Pýmwnt a phýmcant.
Trýchwn a thrýchant.
Tri si chatvarchawc ;
Eidýn euruchawc.
Tri llu llurugawc ;
Tri eur deýrn dorchawc.
Tri marchawc dýwal ;
Tri chat gýhaual.
Tri chýsneit kýsnar ;
Chwerw fýsgýnt esgar.
Tri en drin en drwm.
Llew lledýnt blwm ;
Eur e gat gýngrwn.
Tri theýrn maon ;
A dývu o vrýthon.
Kýnri a chenon.
Kýnrein o aeron.
Gogýuerchi ýn hon
Deivýr diuerogýon.
A dývu o vrýthon
Wr well no chýnon
Sarph seri alon.

GVEIS ý win a med e mordei.
Mawr meint e vehýr
Yg kýuaruot gwýr.

Bwýt e erýr erýsmýgei.
Pan grýssýei gýdýwal kýfdwýreei.
Awr gan wýrd wawr kýui dodei.
Aessawr dellt ambellt a adawei.
Pareu rýnn rwýgýat dýgýmmýnei.
E gat blaen bragat briwei
Mab sývno ; sýwýedýd ae gwýdýei.
   A werthws e eneit
    Er wýneb grýbwýllýeit ;
A llavýn lliveit lladei.
Lledessit ac athrwýs ac affrei ;
Er amot aruot aruaethei.
   Ermýgei galaned
    O wýr gwýchýr gwned
Em blaen gwýned gwanei.

EVEIS ý win a med e mordei
Can ýueis disgýnneis rann fin. fawt ut
Nýt didrachýwed colwed drut.
Pan disgýnnei bawb ti disgýnnvt
Ys deupo gwaeanat gwerth na phechut.
Pressent adrawd oed vreichýawr drut.

GWYR a aeth gatraeth buant enwawc.
Gwin a med o eur vu eu gwirawt.
Blwýdýn en erbýn urdýn deuawt.
Trýwýr a thri ugeint a thrýchant eurdorchawc.
Or sawl ýt grýssýassant uch gormant wirawt
Ný diengis namýn tri o wrhýdri fossawt.
Deu gatki aeron a chenon daýrawt
A minheu om gwaetfreu gwerth vý gwennwawt.

UYG car ýng wirwar nýn gogýffrawt
O neb oný bei o gwýn dragon ducawt.

Nẏ didolit ẏng kẏnted o ved gwirawt.
Ef gwnaei ar beithing peithẏng aruodẏawc.
Ef disgrein eg cat disgrein en aelawt.
Neus adrawd gododin gwedẏ fossawt
Pan vei no llivẏeu llẏmach nebawt.

ARYF angkẏnnull agkẏman dull agkẏsgoget.
Trachẏwed vawr treiglessẏd llawr lloegrwẏs giwet.
    Heessit eis ẏgkẏnnor eis ẏg cat uereu.
        Goruc wẏr lludw
        A gwraged gwẏdw
          Kẏnnoe angheu.
        Greit vab hoewgir
        Ac ẏsberi
          Y beri creu.

ARWR ẏ dwẏ ẏsgwẏd adan
E dalvrith. ac eil tith orwẏdan.
Bu trẏdar en aerure bu tan.
Bu ehut e waewawr bu huan ;
Bu bwẏt brein bu bud e vran.
A chẏn edewit en rẏdon
Gan wlith erẏr tith tirẏon.
Ac o du gwasgar gwanec tu bronn.
Beird bẏt barnant wẏr o gallon.
Diebẏrth e gerth e gẏnghẏr ;
Diua oed e gẏnrein gan wẏr.
A chẏnn e olo a dan eleirch
Vre ; ẏtoed wrẏt ene arch.
Gorgolches e greu ẏ seirch
Budvan vab bleidvan dihavarch.

CAM e adaw heb gof camb ehelaeth.
Nẏt adawei adwẏ ẏr adwrẏaeth.

Nẏt edewis e lẏs les kerdorẏon prẏdein
Diw calan ẏonawr ene aruaeth.
Nẏt erdit e dir kevei diffeith.
Dra chas anias dreic ehelaeth.
Dragon ẏg gwẏar gwedẏ gwinvaeth
Gwenabwẏ vab gwenn ; gẏnhen gatraeth.

BU gwir mal ẏ meud e gatlew.
Nẏ deliis meirch neb marchlew
Heessit waẏwawr ẏ glẏw.
Y ar llemenic llwẏbẏr dew.
Kenẏ vaket am vẏrn am borth ;
Dẏwal ẏ gledẏual emborth.
Heessẏt onn o bedrẏollt ẏ law ;
Y ar veinnẏell vẏgedorth.
Yt rannei rẏgu e rẏwin ;
Yt ladei a llauẏn vreith o eithin.
Val pan vel medel ar vreithin
E gwnaei varchlew waetlin.

MESSAC anuonawc o barth deheu.
Tebic mor lliant ẏ deuodeu.
   O wẏled a llarẏed
     Achein ẏuet med ;
Men ẏth glawd e offer e bwẏth madeu.
Nẏ bu hẏll dihẏll na heu diheu.
Seinnẏessẏt e gledẏf ẏm penn mameu
Mur greit oed moleit ef mab gwẏdneu.

KEREDIC caradwẏ e glot.
Achubei gwarchatwei not.
Lletvegin is tawel kẏn dẏuot
E dyd gowẏchẏd ẏ wẏbot.

Ys deupo car kẏrd kẏvnot
Y wlat nef adef atnabot.

KEREDIC caradwẏ gẏnran.
Keimẏat ẏg cat gouaran.
Ysgwẏt eur crwẏdẏr cadlan ;
Gwaewawr uswẏd agkẏuan.
Kledẏual dẏwal diwan.
Mal gwr catwei wẏaluan.
Kẏnn kẏsdud daear hẏnn affan
O daffar diffẏnnei e vann.
Ys deupo kẏnnwẏs ẏg kẏman.
Can drindawt en vndawt gẏuan.

PAN grẏssẏei garadawc ẏ gat ;
Mal baed coet trẏchwn trẏchẏat.
Tarw bedin en trin gomẏnẏat ;
Ef llithẏei wẏdgwn oe anghat.
Ys vẏn tẏst ewein vab eulat.
A gwrẏen. a gwẏnn a gwrẏat.
O gatraeth o gẏmẏnat.
O vrẏnn hẏdwn kẏnn caffat.
Gwedẏ med gloew ar anghat
Nẏ weles vrun e dat.

GWYR a grẏssẏassant buant gẏtneit.
Hoedẏl vẏrrẏon medwon uch med hidleit.
Gosgord vẏnẏdawc enwawc en reit.
Gwerth eu gwled o ved vu eu heneit.
Caradawc amadawc pẏll ac ẏeuan ;
Gwgawn a gwiawn. gwẏnn a chẏnvan.
Peredur arueu dur ; gwawrdur ac aedan.
Achubẏat eng gawr ẏsgwẏdawr angkẏman.

A chet lledessÿnt wÿ lladassan ;
Neb ÿ eu tÿmhÿr nÿt atcorsan.

GWYR a grÿssÿassant buant gÿtvaeth.
Blwÿdÿn od uch med mawr eu haruaeth.
Mor dru eu hadrawd wÿ. angawr hiraeth.
Gwenwÿn eu hadlam nÿt mab mam ae maeth.
Mor hir eu hetlit ac eu hetgÿllaeth
En ol gwÿr pebÿr temÿr gwinvaeth.
Gwlÿget gododin en erbÿn fraeth.
Ancwÿn mÿnÿdawc enwawc e gwnaeth.
A phrit er prÿnu breithÿell gatraeth.

GWYR a aeth gatraeth ÿg cat ÿg gawr.
Nerth meirch a gwrÿmseirch ac ÿsgwÿdawr.
Peleidÿr ar gÿchwÿn allÿm waewawr.
A llurugeu claer a chledÿuawr.
Ragorei tÿllei trwÿ vÿdinawr.
Kwÿdei bÿm pÿmwnt rac ÿ lavnawr.
Ruuawn hir ef rodei eur e allawr.
A chet a choelvein kein ÿ gerdawr.

DY wnaethpwÿt neuad mor orchÿnnan.
Mor vawr mor oruawr ÿ gÿvlavan.
Dÿrllÿdut medut morÿen tan.
Nÿ thraethei na wnelei kenon kelein.
Un seirchÿawc saphwÿawc son edlÿdan.
Seinnÿessit e gledÿf em penn garthan.
Noc ac esgÿc cariec vÿr vawr ÿ chÿhadvan.
Nÿ mwÿ gÿsgogit wit uab peithan.

DY wnaethpwÿt neuad mor anvonawc
Onÿ bei vorÿen eil caradawc.
Nÿ diengis en trwm elwrw mÿnawc.

Dýwal dýwalach no mab ferawc.
Fer ẏ law faglei fowẏs varchawc.
Glew dias dinas e lu ovnawc.
Rac bedin ododin bu gwasgarawc.
Y gẏlchwẏ dan ẏ gẏmwẏ bu adeuawc.
Yn dẏd gwẏth bu ẏstwẏth neu bwẏth atveillẏawc.
Dẏrllẏdei vedgẏrn eillt mẏnẏdawc.

AY wnaethpwẏt neuad mor diessic
No chẏnon larẏ vronn geinnẏon wledic.
Nẏt ef eistedei en tal lleithic.
E neb a wanei nẏt atwenit.
Raclẏm e waewawr ;
Calch drei tẏllei vẏdinawr.
Rac vuan ẏ veirch ; rac rẏgiawr ;
En dẏd gwẏth atwẏth oed e lavnawr.
Pan grẏssẏei gẏnon gan wẏrd wawr.

DISGYNSIT en trwm ẏg kessevin.
Ef diodes gormes ef dodes fin.
Ergẏr gwaẏw rieu rẏvel chwerthin.
Hut effẏt ẏ wrhẏt e lwrẏ elfin.
Eithinẏn uoleit mur greit tarw trin.

DISGYNSIT en trwm ẏg kesseuin.
Gwerth med ẏg kẏnted a gwirawt win
Heẏessẏt ẏ lavnawr rwg dwẏ vẏdin.
Arderchawc varchawc rac gododin.
Eithinẏn uoleit mur greit tarw trin.

DISGYNSIT en trwm rac alauoed wẏrein.
Wẏre llu llaes ẏsgwẏdawr.
Ysgwẏt vriw rac biw beli bloedvawr.
Nar od uch gwẏar fin festinẏawr.

An deliit kẏnllwẏt ẏ ar gẏnghorawr.
Gorwẏd gwareus rith riu ẏch eurdorchawr.
Twrch goruc amot emlaen ẏstre ẏstrẏwẏawr.
Teilingdeith gwrthẏat gawr.
An gelwit e nef bit athledhawr.
Emẏt ef krennit e gat waewawr.
Catvannan er a clut clotvawr.
No chẏnhennit na bei llu idaw llawr.

𝔄M drẏnni drẏlaw drẏlenn.
Am lwẏas am diffwẏs dẏwarchen.
Am gwẏdaw gwallt e ar benn.
Y am wẏr erẏr gwẏdẏen.
Gwẏduc neus amuc ac waẏw
Ardullẏat diwẏllẏat e berchen.
Amuc morẏen gwenwawt
Mirdẏn. a chẏvrannv penn
Prif eg werẏt. ac an nerth ac am hen ;
Trẏwẏr ẏr bod bun bratwen.
Deudec gwenabwẏ vab gwenn.

𝔄M drẏnni drẏlaw drẏlenn.
Gweinẏdẏawr ẏsgwẏdawr ẏg gweithẏen.
En arẏal cledẏual am benn.
En lloegẏr drẏchẏon rac trẏchant unben.
A dalwẏ mwng bleid heb prenn.
En e law ; gnawt gwẏchnawt enẏ lenn.
O gẏurang gwẏth ac asgen.
Trenghis nẏ dienghis bratwen.

𝔈UR ar vur caer krẏsgrwẏdẏat
Aer cret tẏ͵na thaer aer vlodẏat.
Un ara ae leissẏar
Ar gatwẏt adar brwẏdrẏar

Sẏll o virein neus adrawd a vo mwẏ
O damweinnẏeit llwẏ
Od amluch lliuanat.
Neus adrawd auo mwẏ
En awr blẏgeint
Na bei kẏnhawal kẏnheilweing.

PAN vuost di kẏnnivẏn clot
En amwẏn tẏwẏssen. gordirot
O haedot en gelwit redẏrch gwẏr not.
Oed dor diachor diachor din drei
Oed mẏnut wrth olut ae kẏrchei.
Oed dinas e vedin ae cretei.
Nẏ elwit gwinwit men na bei

KET bei cann wr en vntẏ
Atwen ovalon kenẏ.
Penn ; gwẏr tal being a delẏ.

MYT wẏf vẏnawc blin
Nẏ dialaf vẏ ordin.
Nẏ chwardaf ẏ chwerthin
A dan droet ronin.
Ystẏnnawc vẏg glin
A bundat ẏ en tẏ deẏerẏn.
Cadwẏn heẏernin
Am ben vẏn deulin
O ved o vuelin.
O gatraeth werin.
Mi na vi aneirin.
Ys gwẏr talẏessin
Ovec kẏwrenhin.
Neu cheing e ododin
Kẏnn gwawr dẏd dilin.

GOROLED gogled gwr ae goruc.
Llarẏ vronn haeladon nẏ essẏllut.
Nẏt emda daear nẏt emduc
Mam ; mor eirẏan gadarn haearn gaduc.
O nerth e kledẏf claer e hamuc.
O garchar an war daear em duc.
O gẏvle angheu o anghar dut
Keneu vab llẏwarch dihauarch drut.

BYT ef borthi gwarth gorsed
Senẏllt. ae lestri llawn med ;
Godolei gledẏf e gared.
Godolei lemein e rẏuel.
Dẏfforthsei lẏnwẏssawr oe vreẏch.
Rac bedin ododin a breennẏch.
Gnawt ene neuad vẏthmeirch
Gwẏar a gwrẏmseirch.
Keingẏell hirẏell oe law.
Ac en elẏd brẏssẏaw.
Gwen ac ẏmhẏrdwen hẏrdbeit.
Disserch a serch ar tro
Gwẏr nẏt oedẏn drẏch draet fo.
Heilẏn achubẏat pob bro.

LLECH leutu tut leudvre
    Gododin ẏstre.
Ystre ragno ar ẏ anghat.
Angat gẏnghor e leuuer cat.
    Cangen gaerwẏs
    Keui drillẏwẏs.
Tẏmor dẏmhestẏl tẏmhestẏl dẏmor.
E beri restẏr rac riallu.
O dindẏwẏt ẏn dẏvu
    Wẏt ẏn dẏwovu.

Dwẏs ẏd wodẏn

Llẏm ẏt wenẏn.

Llwẏr genẏn llu.

Ysgwẏt rugẏn

Rac tarw trin

   Y dal vriw vu.

ERKRYN e alon ar af

Erẏ brwẏdrin trin tra chuar.

Kwr e vankeirw

Am gwr e vanncarw.

Bẏssed brẏch briwant barr.

Am bwẏll am disteir am distar.

Am bwẏll am rodic am rẏchward.

Ys bro ẏs brẏs treullẏawt rẏs en riwdrec.

Nẏ hu wẏ nẏ gaffo e neges.

Nẏt anghwẏ a wanwẏ odiwes.

NY mat wanpwẏt ẏsgwẏt

Ar gẏnwal carnwẏt.

Nẏ mat dodes ẏ vordwẏt

Ar vreichir mein-llwẏt.

Gell e baladẏr gell

Gellach e obell.

Y mae dẏ wr ene gell

En cnoi anghell

Bwch bud oe law idaw

Poet ẏmbell.

DA ẏ doeth adonwẏ atwen.

Ym adawssut wenn heli bratwen.

Gwnelut. lladut. llosgut.

No morẏen nẏ waeth wnelut.

Nẏ delẏeist nac eithaf na chẏnhor.

Ysgwn drem dibennor.
Nẏ weleist e morchwẏd mawr marchogẏon
Wẏnedin nẏ rodin nawd ẏ Saesson.

GODODIN gomẏnaf dẏ blegẏt.
Tẏnoeu dra thrumein drum essẏth.
Gwas chwant ẏ arẏant heb emwẏt.
O gussẏl mab dwẏwei dẏ wrhẏt.
Nẏt oed gẏnghor wann.
Wael ẏ rac tan veithin.
O lẏchwr ẏ lẏchwr luch bin.
Luchdor ẏ borfor berẏerin.
Llad gwaws. gwan maws mur trin
Anẏsgarat vu ẏ nat ac aneirin.

KYWYREIN ketwẏr kẏwrennin
E gatraeth gwerin fraeth fẏsgẏolin.
Gwerth med ẏg kẏnted a gwirawt win.
Heẏessit e lavnawr rwng dwẏ vedin.
Arderchauc varchawc rac gododin
Eithinẏn voleit mur greit tarw trin.

KYWYREIN ketwẏr kẏwrenhin.
Gwlat atvel gochlẏwer eu dilin.
Dẏgoglawd tonn bevẏr berẏerin.
Men ẏd ẏnt eilẏassaf elein.
O brei vrẏch nẏ welẏch weẏelin.
Nẏ chemẏd haed ud a gordin.
Nẏ phẏrth mevẏl morẏal eu dilin.
Llavẏn durawt barawt e waetlin.

KYWYREIN ketwẏr kẏwrenhin.
Gwlat atvel gochlẏwer eu dilin.

Ef lladawd a chẏmawn allain
A charnedawr tra gogẏhwc gwẏr trin.

KYWYREIN ketwẏr hẏuaruuant.
Y gẏt en vn vrẏt ẏt gẏrchassant.
Bẏrr eu hoedẏl. hir eu hoet ar eu carant.
Seith gẏmeint o loegrwẏs a ladassant.
O gẏvrẏssed gwraged gwẏth a wnaethant.
Llawer mam ae deigẏr ar ẏ hamrant.

RY wnaethpwẏt neuad mor dianaf
Lew ; mor hael baran llew llwẏbẏr vwẏhaf.
A chẏnon larẏvronn adon deccaf.
Dinas ẏ dias ar llet eithaf.
Dor angor bedin bud eilẏassaf.
Or sawl a weleis ac awelav
Ymẏt ; en emdwẏn arẏf grẏt gwrẏt gwrẏaf.
Ef lladei oswẏd a llavẏn llẏmaf.
Mal brwẏn ẏt gwẏdẏnt rac ẏ adaf.
Mab klẏtno clot hir canaf
Ytẏ or ; clot heb or heb eithaf.

WINVEITH a medweith
Dẏgodolẏn. gwnlleith
Mam hwrreith
    Eidol enẏal.
Ermẏgei rac vre
Rac bronn budugre
Breein dwẏre   ·
    Wẏbẏr ẏsgẏnnẏal.
Kẏnrein en kwẏdaw
Val glas heit arnaw ;
    Heb giliaw gẏhaual.
Sẏnnwẏr ẏstwẏr ẏstemel ;

Y ar weillẏon gwebẏl
   Ac ardemẏl gledẏual.
Blaen ancwẏn anhun
Hediw an dihun ;
   Mam reidun rwẏf trẏdar.

  WINVEITH a medweith
Yd aethant. e genhẏn
Llurugogẏon nẏs gwn lleith lletkẏnt.
Cẏn llwẏded eu lleas dẏdaruu.
Rac catraeth oed fraeth eu llu.
O osgord vẏnẏdawc wawr dru.
O drẏchant namen vn gwr nẏ dẏuu.

  WINVEITH a medveith ẏt grẏssẏassant.
Gwẏr en reit moleit eneit dichwant.
Gloew dull ẏ am drull ẏt gẏtvaethant.
Gwin a med amall a amucsant.
O osgord vẏnẏdawc am dwẏf atveillẏawc ;
A rwẏf a golleis om gwir garant.
O drẏchan riallu ẏt grẏssẏassant
Gatraeth ; tru namen vn gwr nẏt atcorsant.

  KV bẏdei ẏg kẏwẏrein pressent mal pel
Ar ẏ e hu bẏdei. ene uei atre.
Hut amuc ododin
O win a med en dieding
Yng ẏstrẏng ẏstre.
Ac adan gatvannan cochre
Veirch marchawc godrud emore.

  ANGOR dewr daen
Sarph seri raen
Sengi wrẏmgaen

Emlaen bedin.
Arth arwẏnawl drussẏat dreissẏawr
Sengi waewawr
En dẏd cadẏawr.
   Yg clawd gwernin.
Eil nedic nar ;
Neus duc drwẏ var.
Gwled ẏ adar
   O drẏdar drin.
Kẏwir ẏth elwir oth enwir weithret ;
Ractaf rwẏuẏadur mur catuilet
Merin a madẏein mat ẏth anet.

𝔄RDYLEDAWC canu kẏman caffat.
Ketwẏr am gatraeth a wnaeth brithret.
Brithwẏ a wẏar sathar sanget.
Sengi wit gwned bual am dal med.
A chalaned kẏuirẏnged.
Nẏt adrawd kibno wede kẏffro cat ;
Ket bei kẏmun keui daẏret.

𝔄RDYLEDAWC canu kẏman ovri.
Twrẏf tan atharan arẏuerthi.
Gwrhẏt arderchawc varchawc mẏsgi.
Ruduedel rẏuel a eiduni.
Gwr gwned divudẏawc dimẏngẏei
Y gat. or meint gwlat ẏd ẏ klẏwi.
Ae ẏsgwẏt ẏsgwẏt ar ẏ ẏsgwẏd. hut arolli
Waẏw mal gwin gloew o wẏdẏr lestri.
Arẏant am ẏued eur dẏlẏi.
Gwinvaeth oed waetnerth vab llẏwri.

𝔄RDYLEDAWC canu claer orchẏrdon.
A gwedẏ dẏrreith dẏlleinw aeron.

Dimcones lovlen benn erýron.
Llwýt; ef gorevvwýt ý ýsgýlvýon.
Or a aeth gatraeth o eur dorchogýon.
Ar neges mýnýdawc mýnawc maon.
Ný doeth en diwarth o barth vrýthon.
Ododin wr bell well no chýnon.

ARDYLEDAWC canu keman kýwreint.
Llawen llogell být bu didichwant.
Hu mýnnei eng kýlch být; eidol anant.
Yr eur a meirch mawr; a med medweint.
Namen ene delei o výt hoffeint.
Kýndilic aeron wýr enouant.

ARDYLEDAWC canu claer orchýrdon.
Ar neges mýnýdawc mýnawc maon.
A merch eudaf hir dreis gwananhon.
Oed porfor gwisgýadur dir amdrýchýon.

DYFFORTHES meiwýr molut nýuet.
Baran tan terýd ban gýnneuet.
Duw mawrth gwisgýassant eu gwrým dudet.
Diw merchýr perideint eu calch doet.
Divýeu bu diheu eu diuoet.
Diw gwener. calaned amdýget.
Diw sadwrn bu divwrn eu kýt weithret.
Diw sul eu llavneu rud amdýget.
Diw llun hýt benn clun gwaetlun gwelet.
Neus adrawd gododin gwedý lludet.
Rac pebýll madawc pan atcorýet
Namen vn gwr o gant ene delhet.

MOCH dwýreawc ý more.
Kýnnif aber. rac ýstre

Bu bwlch bu twlch tande.
Mal twrch ẏ tẏwẏsseist vre.
Bu golut mẏnut bu lle.
Bu gwẏar gweilch gwrẏmde.

ꟿOCH dwẏreawc ẏ meitin.
O gẏnnu aber rac fin.
O dẏwẏs ẏn tẏwẏs ẏn dẏlin.
Rac cant ef gwant gesseuin.
Oed garw ẏ gwnaewch chwi waetliu.
Mal ẏuet med drwẏ chwerthin.
Oed llew ẏ lladewch chwi dẏnin.
Cledẏual dẏwal fẏsgẏolin.
Oed mor diachor ẏt ladei
Esgar ; gwr haual en ẏ bei.

ᴅISGYNNWYS en affwẏs dra phenn.
Nẏ deliit kẏwẏt kẏwrennin benn.
Disgiawr breint vu e lad ar gangen.
Kẏnnedẏf ẏ ewein esgẏnnv ar ẏstre
Ystwng kẏn gorot goreu gangen.
Dilud dẏleẏn cathleu dilen.
Llẏwẏ llẏvroded rwẏch ac asgen.
Anglas asswẏdeu lovlen.
Dẏfforthes ae law luric wehẏn.
Dẏmgwallaw gwledic dal ;
Oe brid brennẏal.
Eidol adoer crei grannawr gwẏnn
Dẏsgiawr pan vei ; bun barn benn.
Perchen meirch
A gwrẏmseirch
Ac ẏsgwẏdawr ẏaen.
Gẏuoet a gẏuergẏr esgẏn disgẏn.

AER dẏwẏs rẏ dẏwẏs rẏvel.
Gwlat gord garei gwrd uedel.
Gwrdwerẏt gwaet am irved ;
Seirchẏawr am ẏ rud ẏt ued.
Seingẏat am seirch seirch seingẏat.
Ardelw lleith dẏgiawr lludet.
Peleidẏr en eis en dechreu cat.
Hẏnt am oleu bu godeu beleidrẏal.

KEINT amnat amdina dẏ gell
Ac ẏstauell ẏtuẏdei. dẏrllẏdei
Med melẏs ; maglawr
Gwrẏs. aergẏnlẏs gan wawr.
Ket lwẏs lloegrwẏs lliwedawr.
Rẏ benẏt ar hẏt ẏd attawr.
Eillt wẏned klẏwer e arderched.
Gwananhon bẏt ved.
Savwẏ cadavwẏ gwẏned.
Tarw bedin treis trin ; teẏrned.
Kẏn kẏwesc daear kẏn gorwed ;
But orfun gododin bed.

BEDIN ordẏvnat en agerw.
Mẏnawc lluẏdawc llaw chwerw.
Bu doeth a choeth a sẏberw.
Nẏt oed ef wrth gẏued gochwerw.
Mudẏn geinnẏon ar ẏ helw.
Nẏt oed ar lles bro pob delw.
An gelwir mor a chẏnnwr. ẏmplẏmnwẏt
Yn trẏvrwẏt peleidẏr. peleidẏr gogẏmwẏt
Goglẏssur heẏrn lliveit llawr en assed.
Sẏchẏn ẏg gorun en trẏdar ;
Gwr frwẏthlawn flamdur rac esgar.

DYFFORTHES cat veirch a chat seirch.
Greulet ar gatraeth cochre
Mac blaenwÿd bedin dinus
Aergi gwÿth gwarth vre.
An gelwir nÿ faw glaer fwÿre.
Echadaf heidÿn haearnde.

MYNAWC gododin traeth e annor.
Mÿnawc am rann kwÿnhÿator.
Rac eidÿn arÿal flam nÿt atcor.
Ef dodes e dilis ÿg kÿnhor.
Ef dodes rac trin tewdor.
En arÿal ar dÿwal disgÿnnwÿs.
Can llewes porthes mawrbwÿs.
O osgord vÿnÿdawc nÿ diangwÿs
Namen vn arÿf amdiffrÿf amdiffwÿs.

O GOLLET morÿet nÿ bu aessawr
Dÿfforthÿn traeth ÿ ennÿn llawr.
Rÿ duc oe lovlen glas lavnawr.
Peleidÿr pwÿs preiglÿn benn periglawr.
Y ar orwÿd erchlas penn wedawr
Trindÿgwÿd trwch trach ÿ lavnawr.
Pan orvÿd oe gat nÿ bu foawr.
An dÿrllÿs molet med melÿs maglawr.

GWELEIS ÿ dull o benn tir adoÿn.
Aberth am goelkerth a disgÿnnÿn.
Gweleis oed kenevin ar dref redegein.
A gwÿr nwÿthÿon rÿ gollessÿn.
Gweleis gwÿr dullÿawr gan awr adevÿn
A phenn dÿvÿnwal a breÿch brein ae cnoÿn.

MAT vudic ẏsgavẏnwẏn asgwrn aduaon.
Ae lassawc tebedawc tra mordwẏ alon.
Gwrawl amdẏvrwẏs goruawr ẏ lu.
Gwrẏt vronn gwrvan gwanan arnaw.
Y gẏnnedẏf disgẏnnu rac naw riallu.
Yg gwẏd gwaed a gwlat. a gordiẏnaw ;
Caraf vẏ vudic lleithic a vu anaw.
Kẏndilic aeron kenhan lew.

CARASSWN disgẏnnu ẏg catraeth gessevin.
Gwert med ẏg kẏnted a gwirawt win.
Carasswn neu chablwẏs ar llain.
Kẏn bu e leas oe las uffin.
Carasswn eil clot dẏfforthes gwaetlin.
Ef dodes e gledẏf ẏg goethin.
Neus adrawd gwrhẏt rac gododẏn
Na bei mab keidẏaw clot vn gwr trin.

TRUAN ẏw gennẏf gwedẏ lludet.
Godef gloes angheu trwẏ angkẏffret.
Ac eil trwm truan gennẏf vẏ gwelet.
Dẏgwẏdaw an gwẏr nẏ penn o draet.
Ac ucheneit hir ac eilẏwet ;
En ol gwẏr pebẏr temẏr tudwet.
Ruvawn a gwgawn gwiawn a gwlẏget.
Gwẏr gorsaf gwrẏaf gwrd ẏg calet.
Ys deupo eu heneit wẏ wedẏ trinet.
Kẏnnwẏs ẏg wlat nef adef avneuet.

EF gwrthodes tres tra gwẏar llẏnn.
Ef lladei val dewrdull nẏt echẏn.
Tavloẏw ac ẏsgeth tavlet wẏdrin.
A med rac teẏrned tavlei vedin.
Menit ẏ gẏnghor men na llcveri

Lliaws ac vei anwaws nẏt edewẏt.
Rac ruthẏr bwẏllẏadeu a chledẏvawr
Llẏveit handit gwelir llavar llew.

ꝑORTHLOED vedin
Porthloed lain.
A llu racwed
En ragẏrwed
En dẏd gwned
Yg kẏvrẏssed.
Buant gwẏchawc
Gwede meddawt
A med ẏuet
Nẏ bu waret
An gorwẏlam
Enẏd frwẏthlam.
Pan adroder torret ergẏr
O veirch a gwẏr tẏngir tẏnget.

ꝑAN ẏm dẏvẏd lliaws prẏder
Prẏderaf fun.
Fun en ardec
Arẏal redec.
Ar hẏnt wẏlaw.
Ku kẏstudẏwn.
Ku carasswn
    Kelleic faw.
Ac argoedwẏs
Guae gordẏvnwẏs
    Y emdullẏaw.
Ef dadodes ar lluẏd pwẏs ar lles rieu.
    Ar dilẏvẏn goet
    Ar diliw hoet
        Yr kẏvedeu.

Kẏvedwogant ef an dẏduc ar dan adloẏw
 Ac ar groen gwẏnn. gosgroẏw
 Gereint rac deheu gawr a dodet.
 Lluch gwẏnn gwẏnndwll ar ẏsgwẏt
 Y or ẏspar llarẏ ẏor.
 Molut mẏnut mor.
 Gogwneif heissẏllut
 Gwgẏnei gereint
 Hael mẏnawc oedut.

DIANNOT e glot e glutvan.
Diachor angor ẏg kẏman.
Diechẏr erẏr gwẏr govaran.
Trinodef eidef oed eirẏan.
Ragorei veirch racvuan.
En trin lletvegin gwin o bann.
Kẏn glasved a glassu eu rann.
Bu gwr gwled od uch med mẏgẏr o bann.

DIENHYT ẏ bob llawr llanwet
E hual amhaual afneuet.
Twll tall e rodawr
Cas ohir gwẏthawc
Rẏwonẏawc diffreidẏeit.
Eil gweith gelwideint amalet.
Yg cat veirch a seirch greulet.
Bedin agkẏsgoget ẏt vẏd cat vorẏon ;
Cochro llan ban rẏ godhet.
Trwm en trin a llavẏn ẏt lladei
Garw ; rẏbud o gat dẏdẏgei.
Cann calan a darmerthei
Ef gwenit a dan vab ervei.
Ef gwenit adan dwrch trahauc.
Un ricin a morwẏn a mẏnawc.

A phan oed mab teẏrn teithiawc
Yng gwẏndẏt gwaed glẏt gwaredawc.
Kẏn golo gwerẏt ar rud
Llarẏ ; hael etvẏnt digẏthrud.
O glot a chet echiawc ;
Neut bed garthwẏs hir o dir rẏwouẏawc.

PEIS dinogat e vreith vreith.
O grwẏn balaot ban wreith.
Chwit chwit chwidogeith.
Gochanwn gochenẏn wẏthgeith.
Pan elei dẏ dat tẏ e helẏa ;
Llath ar ẏ ẏsgwẏd llorẏ enẏ llaw.
Ef gelwi gwn gogẏhwc.
Giff gaff. dhalẏ dhalẏ dhwc dhwc.
Eff lledi bẏsc ẏng corwc.
Mal ban llad. llew llẏwẏwc.
Pan elei dẏ dat tẏ e vẏnẏd.
Dẏdẏgei ef penn ẏwrch pen gwẏthwch penn hẏd.
Penn grugẏar vreith o venẏd.
Penn pẏsc o raẏadẏr derwennẏd.
Or sawl ẏt gẏrhaedei dẏ dat tẏ ae gicwein
O wẏthwch a llewẏn a llwẏuein.
Nẏt anghei oll nẏ uei oradein.

PEUM dodẏw angkẏvwng o angkẏuarch
Nẏm daw nẏm dẏvẏd a uo trẏmach.
Nẏ magwẏt ẏn neuad a vei lewach
Noc ef ; nac ẏng cat a vei wastadach.
Ac ar rẏt benclwẏt pennawt oed e veirch ;
Pellẏnic e glot pellws e galch.
A chẏn golo gweir hir a dan dẏwarch ;
Dẏrllẏdei vedgẏrn vn mab feruarch.

*GUELEYS ẏ dull o bentir a doẏn
Aberthach coelkerth a emdẏgẏn.
Gueleẏs ẏ deu oc eu tre re rẏ gwẏdẏn.
O eir nwẏthon rẏ godessẏn.
Gueleẏs ẏ wẏr tẏlluawr gan waur a doẏn
A phenn dẏuẏnwal vrẏch brein ae knoẏn.

GODODIN gomẏnnaf oth blegẏt.
Yg gwẏd cant en arẏal en emwẏt.
A guarchan mab dwẏwei da wrhẏt
Poet gno en vn tẏno treissẏt.
Er pan want maws mvr trin.
Er pan aeth daear ar aneirin.
Mi neut ẏsgaras nat a gododin.

LLECH llefdir arẏf gardith tith ragon
Tec ware rac gododin ẏstre anhon.
Rẏ duc diwẏll o win bebẏll ar lles tẏmẏr
Tẏmor tẏmestẏl tra merin llestẏr.
Tra merin llu. llu meithlẏon.
Kein gadrawt rwẏd rac riallu
O dindẏwẏt en dẏuuwẏt ẏn dẏvuu.
Ysgwẏt rugẏn rac doleu trin tal vriw vu.

DIHENYD ẏ bop llaur llanwet
Y haual amhal afneuet
Twll tal ẏ rodauc
Cas ohir gwẏchauc
Rẏwẏnẏauc diffret.
Eil with gwelẏdeint amalet
Y gat veirch ae seirch greulet
Bit en anẏsgoget bit get

* What follows is written in a different hand, and the capital
letters are no longer illuminated.

Uoron gwýchýrolýon pan rý godet.
Trwm en trin allain ýt ladei
Gwaro rýbud o gat dýdýgei
Gant. can ýg calan darmerthei.
Ef gwenit a dan vab uruei.
Ef gwenit a dan dwrch trahauc.
Un riein a morwýn a menauc
A chan oed mab brenhin teithiauc.
Ud gwýndýt gwaet kilýd gwaredawc.
Kýn golo gwerýt ar grud hael etvýnt
Doeth dýgýrchet ý get ae glot ae echiauc
Uot bed gorthýn hir o orthir rýwýnauc.

AM drýnni drýlav drýlen
Am lwýs am diffwýs dýwarchen
Trihue baruaut dreis dili plec hen
Atguuc emorem ae guiau hem
Hancai ureuer urag denn
At gwýr a gwýdýl a phrýdein
At gu kelein rein rud guen
Deheuec gwenauwý mab gwen.

AM ginýav drýlav drýlen
Trým dwýs tra diffwýs dýwarchen
Kemp e lumen. arwr baruaut asgell
Vreith edrých eidýn a breithell
Goruchýd ý lav loflen
Ar gýnt a gwýdýl a phrýden.
A chýnýho mwng bleid heb prenn
Ený law gnavt gwýchlaut ene lenn.
Prýtwýf ný bei marw morem
Deheuec gwenabwý. mab gwenn.

EMAN EDECHREU GORCHAN TUTWULCH.

* ARYF angkÿnnull angkÿman dull ; twrÿf en agwed.
Erac menwed. erac mawrwed. erac matÿed.
Pan ÿstÿernn gwern e am gam gÿrn. e am gamgled.
E uoli ri. alluawr. peithliw racwed.
Yd i gweles ; ar hual tres tardei galled.
Dÿgochwiawr a chloi a phor ; a pherth a pher ;
A rud uorua ac ÿ morua. ac ewÿonÿdd
A gwÿnheidÿd kein edrÿssed.
Trÿbedawt rawt rac ÿ devawt ; eil dal rossed.
Tarÿaneu bann am dal hen banu bÿ edrÿssed.
Bleid e vÿwÿt oed bleidÿat rÿt enÿ dewred.
Pubell peleidÿr pevÿr prÿt neidÿr. o lwch nadred.
Welÿd ÿd wÿt gwelÿdon rwÿt riein gared.
Carut vreidvÿw carwn dÿ vÿw ; vut heÿwred.
Camhwrawc darw kwÿnaf dÿ varw. carut dÿhed.
Baran mor ÿgkÿnhorÿf gwÿr. ÿ am gatpwll.
Ymwan bran ÿg kÿnwÿt.
Tardei donn gÿvrÿngon gowÿdawc bÿt.
Ef gwrthodes ar llwÿth peues ; ar lles pedÿt
Petwar lliwet. petwar milet miledawr bÿt.
Aessawr ÿn nellt allavÿn eg wallt. un o bedror
Gwr gwÿllÿas. o gÿrn glas med meitin
Gwr teithiawr o blith porfor porthloed bedin.
Breeÿth tutvwlch baranret dost. benongwaed gwin.
Yr med a fawrÿf ÿd aethant aerÿf dros eu hawfin.
Gwÿalvan weith er cadw kÿvreith bu kÿvÿewin.
Kÿnan kenon teithvÿw o von. ar vreint gorllin.
Tutvwlch kÿvwlch a oreu vwlch ar vann caereu.

* What follows is in the same handwriting with the first part of
the Gododin.

Gan výnýdawc bu atveillÿawc eu gwirodeu.

Blwÿdÿn hiraeth er gwÿr gatraeth am maeth ÿs meu.

Eu llavneu dur eu med en bur eu haualeu.

Arÿf angkÿnnvll angkÿman dull twrÿf neus kigleu.

AC E VELLY E TERVYNA WEITHYON
EDECHREU GWARCHAN ADEBON.

RY phell gwÿd aval o avall.

Nÿ chÿnnÿd dÿual o dÿvall.

Nÿ bÿd ehovÿn noeth en ÿsgall ;

Pawb pan rÿ dÿngir ÿt ball.

Agarwn ÿ ef carei anreithgar.

Nÿ bÿd marw dwÿweith ;

Nÿt amsud ÿ vud eareith.

Nÿ cheri gÿfofni gÿvÿeith.

Emis emwÿthwas amwÿn.

Am swrn am gorn kuhelÿn.

En adef tangdef collit.

Adef led buost lew en dÿd mit.

Kudvÿt keissÿessÿt keissÿadon ;

Mein uchel medel e alon.

Dÿ ven ar warchan Adebon

E VELLY E TERVYNA GARCHAN ADEBON.
EMA WEITHYON E DECHREU GORCHAN
KYNVELYN.

PEI mi brÿtwn

Pei mi ganwn ;

Tardei warchan gorchegin.

Gweilging torch trÿchdrwÿt

Trÿchethin trÿchinfwrth.

Kÿrchessit en avon

Kynn noe geinnyon.
Tyllei garn gaffon ;
Rac carneu riwrhon.
Ryveluodogyon.
Esgyrn vyrr vyrrvach varchogyon.
Tyllei ylvach
Gwryt govurthyach.
Ryt gwynn rae eingyl
Yawn llad. yawn vriwyn vriwyal.
Rac canhwynawl cann.
Lluc yr duc dyvel
Disgynnyal alel.
Y bob dewr dy sel.
Trwy hoel trwy hemin ;
Trwy gibellawr a gemin.
Ac eur ar dhrein
A galar dwvyn dyvyd ;
Y wynnassed velyn.
E greu oe gylchyn ;
Keledic ewyn.
Med mygyr melyn.
Eil creu oe gylchyn ;
Rac cadeu kynvelyn.
Kynvelyn gasnar
Ysgwn bryffwn bar.
Goborthyat adar
Ar denin dwyar.
Dyrreith grad voryon ;
Adan vordwyt haelon.
Kyvret kerd wyllyon ;
Ar welling diryon.
Teyrn tut anaw
Ysmeu e gwynaw ;
Eny vwyf y dyd taw.

Gomẏnẏat gelẏn ;

Ehangsett ervẏn.

Gochawn kẏrd keinmẏn ;

Yw gwarchan kẏnvelẏn.

Gorchan kẏnvelẏn kẏlchwẏ wẏlat ;

Etvẏn gwr gwned gwẏned e wlat.

Dẏchiannawr dewr dẏchianat.

Eidẏn gaer gleissẏon glaer

Kẏverthrẏnneit.

Kein dẏ en rud enẏs gwerth

Ruduolawt ved meirch

Eithinẏn neut ẏnt blennẏd.

Gwarchan kẏnvelẏn ar ododin

Neus goruc o dẏn dogẏn gẏmhwẏlleit.

E waẏw drwn oreureit am rodes

Poet ẏr lles ẏw eneit.

Etmẏgir e vab tecvann ;

Wrth rif ac wrth rann wẏr catvan

Colovẏn greit.

Pan vẏrẏwẏt arveu

Tros benn cat vleidẏeu

Buan deu en dẏd reit.

Trẏ wẏr a thrivgeint a thrẏchant

I vreithẏell gatraeth ẏd aethant.

Or sawl ẏt grẏssẏassant

Uch med menestri ; namẏn tri nẏt atcorsant.

Kẏnon a chadreith a chatlew o gatnant.

A minheu oni creu dẏchiorant.

Mab coel kerth vẏgwerth ẏ a wnaethant ;

O eur pur a dur ac arẏant.

Evnẏvet nẏt nodet e cawssant ;

Gwarchan kẏrd kẏnvelẏn kẏvnovant.

EMAN E TERVYNA GWARCHAN KYNVELYN.

*Canu vn caniawc a dal pob awdyl or Gododin herwyd breint yng kerd amrysson. Tri chanu a thriugeint a thrychant adal pob vn or gwarchaneu. Sef a chaws yn am goffan ene gorchaneu riuedi e gwyr a aethant e gatraeth. Noc a dele gwr mynet y emnid heb arveu. ny dele bard mynet e amrysson heb e gerd vonn. Eman weithyon edechreu gwarchan Maelderw. Talyessin ae cant ac awdel breint idaw. Keiment ac eodleu e Gododin oll ei dri gwarchan yng kerd amrysson.

DOLEU deu ebŷr am gaer.
Ymduhun am galch am glaer.
Gwibde a doer adwŷaer.
Clodrŷd keissidŷd kŷsgut.
Brithwe arwe arwrut.
Ruthŷr anorthwe a uebir.
Adwŷ adodet nŷ debit.
Odef ŷnŷas dof ŷ wrŷt.
Dŷgwgei en arŷf en esgut.
Hu tei en wlŷd elwit.
Gwr a ret pan dŷchelwit.
Kŷwelŷ krŷmdŷ krŷmdwŷn.
Kŷueiliw nac eiliw etvrwŷn
Nac emniel dŷ dŷwal a therwŷn.
Tervŷn torret tec teithŷawl
Nŷt aruedauc e uolawt.
Diffrŷderas ŷ vrascawt.
Molawt rin rŷmidhin rŷmenon.

* This rubric, with the Gwarchan Maelderw which follows, is the same handwriting with the last part of the Gododin. Both seem to be additions made by a different hand to the original MS.

H

Dẏssẏllei trech tra manon.

Disgleirẏawr ac archawr tal achon

Ar rud dhreic fud pharaon.

Kẏueillẏawr en awel adawaon.

Trengsẏd a gwẏdei neb ae eneu

Y ar orthur teith teth a thedẏt.

Menit a osgord mavr mur onwẏd.

Ar vor ni dheli.

Na chẏngwẏd gil na chẏngor

Gordibleu eneit talachor

Nẏt mwẏ rẏ uudẏt ẏ esgor.

Esgor eidin rac dor.

Kenan kein mur e ragor.

Gossodes ef gledẏf ar glawd meiwẏr.

Budic e ren enẏ

Annavd wledic.

Y gẏnnwithic

Kẏnlas kẏnweis

Dwnẏn dẏvẏnveis.

Kẏchuech nẏ chwẏd kẏchwerw

Kẏchvenẏches

Kẏchwenẏchwẏ enlli weles.

A lenwis miran mir edles.

Ar ẏstre gan vore godemles.

Hu tei idware ẏngorvẏnt

Gwẏr goruẏnnaf rẏ annet.

En llwrw rwẏdheu rẏ gollet.

Collwẏd. medwẏd menwẏt.

Gogled run ren rẏ dẏnnit.

Gorthew am dẏchuel dẏchuelit.

Gorwẏd mwẏ galwant no melwit.

Am rwẏd am rẏ ẏstoflit.

Ystofflit llib llain.

Blin blaen blen blenwẏd.

Trybedavt ẏ wledic e rwng drem dremrud
Dremrẏt nẏ welet ẏ odeu dhogẏn rẏd.
Nẏ welet ẏ odeu dhogẏn fẏd
Mor eredic dar digerẏd.
Kentaf digonir canwelw
Kẏnnwẏthic lleithic llwẏrdelw
Kẏn ẏ olo gouudelw
Taf gwr mavr ẏ wael mælderw.
Delwat dieirẏdaf ẏ errẏ par ar delw
Rwẏsc rwẏf bre
Rẏmun gwlat rẏmun rẏmdẏre.
Ysgavl dhisgẏnnẏawd wlawd gẏnire
Nac ẏsgawt ẏ redec rẏ gre.
Godiweud godiwes gwlat vre.
Nẏ odiweud o vevẏl veint gwre.

Da dẏvot adonwẏ adonwẏ am adaussut.
    A wnelei vratwen gwnelut lladut llosgut
    Nẏ chetweist nac erthaf na chẏnnor
    Ysgwn tref dẏ beuwel. nẏ weleis or mor
    Bwẏr mor marchauc avei waeth no odgur.
Trẏcan eurdorch a grẏssẏassant
    En amwẏn breithell bu edrẏwant
    Ket rẏlade hwẏ wẏ ladassant
    Ahẏt orfen bẏt etmẏc vẏdant.
    Ac or sawl a aẏtham o gẏt garant.
    Tru namẏn un gur nẏt englẏssant.
Trẏcant eurdorchauc
    Gwned gar guaenauc
    Trẏchan trahaavc
    Kẏuun kẏuarvavc
    Trẏchan meirch godrud
    A grẏssẏws ganthud
    Trẏchwn a thrẏchant

Tru nẏt atcorsant.
Dẏwal ẏg cat kẏniwng ẏgkeni.

Yg kẏvrang nẏt oed dang as gwnehei
Yn dẏd gwẏth nẏt ef weith gocheli.
Baran baed oed bleidic mab eli.
Ervessit gwin gwẏdẏr lestri llawn ;
Ac en dẏd camavn camp a wneei
Y ar aruul cann kẏnn oe dreghi.
Calaned cochwed ae deui.

Pwẏs blaen rẏdre ferei ẏ gadeu
Drẏll kedẏr cat
Kein crẏsgwẏdẏat.
Brẏt am gorlew
Diechwith lam
Y orwẏlam
Nat rẏ gigleu
Ef gwneei gwẏr llẏdw
A gwraged gwẏdw
Kẏnn oe agheu.
Breint mab bleidgi
Rac ẏsberi
Y beri greu.

Kein guodeo e celẏo erẏ vẏhẏr
O hanav ar a fẏsgut
Af eirẏangut.
Pan esgẏnnei baub ti disgẏnnvt.
Cenei gwin gwaet meirw meint a wanut.
Teir blẏned a phedeir
Tutet en vavr ẏtuaer
Asgẏmmẏrr hut
Ath uodi gwas nẏm gwerth na thechut
Pressent kẏuadraud oed breichẏaul glut.

Pan gẏrchei ẏg kẏwlat e glot oed anvonavc
Ef dilẏdei win gwr eurdorchauc

Ef rodei gloẏwdull glan ẏ gwẏchiauc
Ardwẏei cann wr arwr mẏnauc.
Anvonavc eissẏllut alltut marchauc
Un maban e gian o dra bannauc
Nẏ sathravt gododin ar glavr fossaut.
Pan vei no llif llẏmach nebaut.
Angor deor dain sarff sarffwẏ graen
   Anẏsgoget vaen. blaen bedin arall
   Arlwẏ treis tra chẏnnivẏn.
   Rwẏ gobwrẏ gordwẏlain.
   Enwir ẏt elwir oth gẏwir werthret.
   Restor rwẏfẏadur. mvr pob kẏnẏeith.
   Tutvwlch treissic aer caer o dileith.
Angor deor dain sarph saffwẏ grain. blaen bediu
   Enwir ẏt elwir oth gẏwir gverit.
   Kewir. ẏth elwir oth kẏwir werthret.
   Rector rwẏvẏadur mur pob kiwet.
   Merẏn mab madẏeith mat ẏth anet.
Aches guolouẏ glasvleid duuẏr dias dull.
   Angor deor dain anẏsgoc vaen ein blaen bedin
   Let rud leuir a meirch a gwẏr rac gododin
   Re cw gẏuarch kẏwuẏrein
   Bard kemre tot tarth rac garth merin.
Scwẏt dan wodef. nẏ ẏstẏngei
   Rac neb wẏneb cared erẏthuaccei
   Dirẏeit o eirch meirch ẏg kẏndor
   Aur gwrẏavr hein gwaewawr kelin creudei.
   Pan wanet ẏg kẏueillt ef gwanei
   Ereill nẏt oed amevẏl ẏt a dẏccei.
   Dẏvit en cadwrẏt kein asmẏccei
   Pan dẏdut kẏhuran clotuan mordei.
Geu ath diwedus tutleo
   Na deliis meirch neb marchlew
   Kenẏ vaccet am bẏrth amporth

Oed cadarn e gledẏual ẏnẏorth
Ur rwẏ ẏsgeinnẏei ẏ onn o bedrẏholl
Llav ẏ ar vein erch mẏgedorth.
Ardwẏnef adef eidun gwalat.
Gwae ni rac galar ac avar gwastat.
Pan doethan deon o dineidin
Parth deetholwẏl pob doeth wlat.
Yg kẏwrẏssed a lloegẏr lluẏd amhat.
Nav ugeint am bob vn am beithẏnat.
Ardemẏl meirch a seirch a seric dillat
Ardwẏei waetnerth e gerth or gat.
O osgord mẏnẏdauc pan grẏssẏassant.
Gloew dull e am drull ẏt gẏnuaethant.
O ancwẏn mẏnẏdauc handit tristlavn vẏ nirẏt.
Rwg e rẏgolleis ẏ om gwir garant
O drẏchan curdorchauc a grẏssẏws gatraeth
Tru namen vn gwr nẏt anghassant.
Gosgord gododin e ar ravn rin.
Meirch eiliv eleirch a seirch gwehin.
Ac ẏg kẏnnor llu lliwet disgiu
En amwẏn called a med eidin.
O gussẏl mẏnẏdawc
Trossassei ẏsgwẏdawr.
Kwẏdassei lafnavr
Ar grannaur gwin.
Wẏ ceri gon gwẏlaes disgin.
Nẏ phorthassan warth wẏr nẏ thechẏu.
Neut erẏueis ẏ ued ar ẏg kerdet
Gwinuaeth rac catraeth ẏn un gwaret
Pan ladhei ac lavnawr ẏnẏsgoget
Yn daẏr nẏt oed wael men ẏt welet
Nẏt oed hẏll ẏdellẏll en emwaret.
Atwẏthic scẏndauc madauc eluet.
Pan dec ẏ cẏuarchant nẏt oed hoedẏl dianc

Dialgur aruon cẏrchei eur ceinẏo arurchẏat
Urẏthon browẏs meirch cẏnon.
Leech leud ud tut leu ure
Gododin stre stre
Ancat ancat cẏngor cẏngor
Temestẏl tramerẏn lestẏr tramerẏn lu
Heidilẏaun lu meidlẏaun let lin lu
O dindẏwẏt en dẏowu
Saiẏt grugẏn irac tarẏf trun tal briv bu.
Eur ar mur caer crisguitat
Dair caret na hair air mlodẏat
Un S saxa secisiar argounduit
Adar bro unal pelloid nuirein
Nẏs adraud auo bẏv o dam gueinieit
Liu o dam lun luch liuanat
Nẏs adraud a uo bin in dit pleinueit
Na bei cinaual cinelueit.
Dim guoru ediu o adam neimin
Un huc an guoloet guoreu edlinet
Em ladaut lu maur i guert i adraut.
Ladaut map niuthon o eurdorchogẏon
Cant o deẏrnet hit pan grimbuiller bu
Guell prit pan aeth canwẏr ẏ gatraeth
Ord eilth gur guinuaeth callon ehelaeth
Oed gur luit einim oed luric teinim
Ord girth oed cuall ar geuin e gauall
Nẏ wisguis imil i mil luit heinim
I guaiu ae ẏscuit nac gledẏf nae gẏllell
No neim ab nuithon gur auei well.
Tra merin iodeo trileo
Yg caat tri guaid (franc) fraidus leo
Bribon a guoreu bar deo
Gnaut iar fisiolin am diffin gododin
Im blain trin terhid rei

Gnaut i lluru alan buan bithei
Gnaut rac teulu deor em discinhei
Gnaut mab golistan cen nei bei
Guledic i tat indeuit a lauarei
Ganut ar les minidauc scuitaur trei
Guaurud rac ut eidin uruei.
Ni forthint ueiri molut muet
 Rac trin riallu trin orthoret
 Tebihic tan terÿd drui cinneuet.
 Diu maurth guisgassant eu cein duhet
 Diu merchÿr bu guero eu cit unet
 Diu ÿeu cennadeu amodet
 Diu guener calanet a ciuriuet
 Diu sadurn bu dedurnn eu cit gueithret
 Diu sul laueneu rud a at ranhet.
 Diu llun hÿt benn clun guaet lunguelet
 Nÿs adraud Gododin guedÿ lludet
 Hir rac pebÿll madauc pan atcorhet.
Disgÿnsit in trum in alauoed dwÿrem
 Cintebic e celeo erit migam
 Guannannon guirth med gurÿt mui hiam
 Ac guich fodiauc guichauc inham
 Eithinin uoleit map bodu at aın.
Guir gormant aethant cennin
 Gwinweith a medweith oedÿn
 O ancwÿn mÿnÿdauc
 Anthuem cim inruinauc
 O goll gur gunet rin
 Mal taran nem tarhei scuÿtaur
 Rac rÿnnaud eithinin.
Moch aruireith i meitit pan cis
 Cenerein i midin odouis
 In towÿs inilin
 Rac cant em guant ceseuin

Oed mor guanauc idinin
Mal inet med neu win
Oed mor diachar
Yt wanei esgar
Uid att guanar gurthẏn
Moch aruireit i more
Icinim apherẏm rac stre
Bu ciuarch gueir guiat
Igcin or or cat
Ciueillt ar garat
Init gene
Buguolut minut bu lee
Bu guanar gueilging gwrẏmde.
Guelet e lauanaur en liwet
In ciuamuin gal galet
Rac godurẏf ẏ aessaur godechet
Techin rac eidin vre uruiet
Meint a gaffeilau nẏt atcorẏet
O hanau cuir oed arnav ac canet
Cin dinnẏauc calc drei pan griniec griniei
Nit atwanei ri guanei ri guanet
Oed menẏch gwedẏ cwẏn i escar
Icimlian oed guennin hic caraitet
A chin i olo atan titguet daiar
Dirlishei etar med met.
Huitreuit clair cinteiluuat
Claer cleu na clair
Air uener sehic am sut
Seic sic sac adleo gogẏuurd gogẏmrat
Edili edili ni puillẏat
Nẏs adraud gododin in dit pleigbeit
Na bei cinhaual citeluat.
Llafnaur let rud laim cinach lud
Guron guorut ẏ maran laim gur leidẏat

Laguen udat stadal vleidiat bleid ciman
Luarth teulu laur in ladu
Cinoidalu ni bu guan
Enuir ith elwir od gwir guereit
Rector liuidur mur pob kẏvẏeith
Tutvwlch treissic hair caer godileit.
Kẏuaruu ac ac erodu leidiat lu
— ero nẏ bu ac cihoit ac i hero ni bu
Hero ciued guec guero
Gnissint gueuilon ar e helo
Nit oed ar les bro bot ero
Ni cilias taro trin let un ero
Traus ẏ achaus liuir delo
Ef guant tra trigant echassaf
Ef ladhei auet ac eithaf
Oid guiu e mlaen llu llarahaf
Godolei o heit meirch e gaẏaf
Gochore brein du ar uur
Caer cein bei ef arthur
Rug ciuin uerthi ig disur
Ig kunnor guernor guaur
Erdẏledam canu icinon cigueren
In guauth ac cin bu diuant dileit aeron
Riuesit i loflen ar pen erirhon
Luit em rannuit guoreu buit i igluion
Ar les minidauc marchauc maon
Em dodes itu ar guaiu galon
Ar gatraeth oed fraith eurdorchogẏon
Wẏ guenuit lledint seuiogion
Oed ech en temẏr treis canaon
Oed odit imit o barth urẏthon
Gododin o bell guell no chenon
Erdiledaf canu ciman cafa
In cetwir am gatraeth ri guanaid britret

Britgue ad guiar sathar sanget
Segit guid gunet dial am dal med
O galanet ciuei riget
Nis adraud cipno gwedi kÿffro cat
Ceuei cimun idau ciui daeret.
Llithÿessit adar ada am edismicaf
Edeuuniat eithuuat aruhicat efguisgus
Aur ig cinnor gaur ig cin uaran odeiuiniet
Ballauc tal gellauc cat tridid engiriaul
Erlinaut gaur arth arwÿnaul ar guigiat
Guor vlodiat riallu erigliriat
Hir lu cein bu gipno mab guengat.
Erdiledaf canu ciman ci guerunit
Llawen llogell bit budit
Dit di.*

* Seems unfinished.

IV.

THE BOOK OF TALIESSIN.

A MS. OF THE BEGINNING OF THE 14TH CENTURY, IN THE HENGWRT COLLECTION, THE PROPERTY OF W. W. E. WYNNE, ESQ. OF PENIARTH, M. P.

I.

Fol. 1. a.   *Gan ieỽyd gan elestron.
Ry ganhymdeith achỽysson.
Blỽydyn yg kaer ofanhon.
ỽyf hen ỽyf newyd. ỽyf gỽion.
ỽyf llỽyr ỽyf synỽyr keinon.
Dy gofi dyhen vrython.
Gỽydyl kyl diuerogyon.
Medut medỽon.
ỽyf bard ny rifafi eillon.
ỽyf syỽ llyỽ ỽyf syỽ amrysson.
Syhei arahei. arahei nys medei.
Si ffradyr yn y fradri.
Pos beirdein bronrein a dyfei.
A deuhont uch medlestri.
A ganhont gam vardoni.
A geissont gyfarỽs nys deubi.

* The MS. as it at present exists, is defective, a leaf being apparently wanting both at the beginning and at the end. It therefore begins in the middle of a poem. A complete copy of this poem will be found in the Red Book of Hergest.

lan . uilhin nyt eban . kyfrog mor aglan . neu
goroyf gwaeclan . aruab cant kynvan . rud em
hyg kychoy . eur vy yscoytroy . ny ganet ynadyr
anu yn gorky namyn goronvy odoleu edryvy .
hyr dywnn vy myffaor . pell na bum heuffaor .
Treigleis ympyn llaor kyn bum lleenaor . Trei
gleis kylchynet kyfceu cant ynys . cant
caer athrugys . derdydon doethur . darogenuch
y arthur . yffit yffyd gynt . neur iu ergehynit .
ac vn aderyo o yftyr dilyo . dchrift ycwctao . ddyd
braot racllao . eurem yn euryll . ini hudoyf berth
yll ac vydyf drychyll o eryinef fferyll . eo ab gur
yfaithaf ymixn yfiyyp . leu valiellin .
ab aden . py dyduc agheu bytu no cheftuen .
kyffefin ym byt atu etflywoyt . meneich aleit pyr
nam dywbert . pyr nam erxtryt . vn aor nam herly
nyt . py datoyreith miec . pyt echeuis dao . py ffyn
haon adioc uch argel tywy lloc . pan yo kalaf cant .
pan yo nof lloenxan . arall ny chanlyoyt dyyfcoyt
allan . Pan yo gofaran toroф tonneu oth lan .
yn dial dylan . dy dahaed attan . pan yo mor trom
maen . pan yo mor llym draen . Ddofti poy gwell
aevon ae y vlaen . py peift ptroyroog dyn acan
nyyt . Poy gwell yadoyt ac ieuaut aelloyt . Ao
oft u peth oyt ptu bychyn kyfcoyt . de corff ae e
nert . de argel canhbyt . eiledyd belnyd pyrnam

Heb gyfreith heb reith heb rodi.
A goedy hynny digoni.
Brithuyt abyt dyuysci.
Nac eruyn ti hedoch nyth vi.
Ren nef rymawyr dy wedi.
Rac ygres rym goares dy voli.
Ri Rex gle am gogyfarch yn geluyd.
A weleisti dñs fortis.
Darogan dofyn dñi
Budyant uffern.
Hic nemo in per pgenie.
Ef dillygoys ythoryf dñs uirtutu.
Kaeth naot kynnulloys estis iste est.
Achyn buasson asvmsei
Arnaf. boyf derwyn y duv diheu.
Achyn mynhoyf derwyn creu.
Achyn del ewynurio ar vyggeneu.
Achyn vyg hyfalle ar y llathen preu.
Poet ym heneit ydagyfedeu.
Abreid om dyweit llythyr llyfreu.
Kystud dygyn goedy goely agheu.
Ar saol agigluen vymbardgyfreu.
Ry prynoynt wlat nef adef goreu.

II.

MARVNAT Y VIL VEIB.

Fol. 1. a. ARCHAF wedi yr trindaot.
Ren am rothoyr dyvolaot.
O ryret pressent periglaot.
An goeith an reith goyth gogyffraot.
Yd edryfynt seint sef kiodaot.
Rex nef boyf ffraeth o honaot.
Kyn yscar vy eneit am knavt.
Rymawyr ym pa ym pechaot.

ALy eirolet rac ried.
Bydѵyf or trindaѵt trugared.
Iolaf rybechaf eluȳd gѵaed.
Naѵ rad nef nestic toruoed.
A decuet seint seic seithoed.
Gѵrhydrych ryfyd ieithoed.
Morheic mat gynnyd kyhoed.
Nifer awyl Duѵ trychoed.
Yn nef yn dayar yn diwed.
Yn yg yn ehag yn ygwed.
Ygcorff yn eneit yn hagwed.
Pell pѵyll rac rihyd racwed.
Athiolaf wledic wlat hed.
Poet ym heneit ym buched.
Yn tragywyd ygkynted
Yn gѵas nef nym gomed.

EBESTYL a merthyri.
Gѵerydon gѵedwon gofri.
A selyf Duѵ a serui.
Glan ieith glan teith dyteithi.
Ac yn duun glas dyfyd imi.
Hyt pan rychatѵyf vynteithi.
Nifer auuant glan lѵys
Gradeu eur golofneu eglѵys.
Ar meint traethadur a traethѵys
Sywedyd llyfreu llѵyrlѵys.
Rac gѵerin digarat disѵys.
Boet ym heneit y amdiffynnѵys.

NIFER a uuant yn aghyffret
Uffern. oer gѵerin gѵaretret.
Hyt pymhoes byt.
Hyt pan dillygѵys Crist keithiwet.

O dὐfyn ueis affὐys abret.

Meint dyduc Duὐ trὐy nodet.

Dὐy vil veib o plant llia.

A bimatu et infra.

A ledeint yr amistra

Edris ertri kila.

Deccraὐn rachel gὐelsit pla.

Dybi ierosolima.

PIFER seint amorica.

Anifer yn dull toronia.

A thorsi trachaer roma.

A poli ac alexandria.

A garanὐys ac indra.

Tres partes diuicia.

Asicia affrica europa.

PIFER seint capharnaὐm. marituen anaim

A zabulon a cisuen a ninifen a neptalim.

In dubriactus a zorim.

Yndi y proffὐydὐys Crist vab meir verch ioachim.

O artemhyl pen echen pan ym.

PIFER seint erechalde.

Clot pell castell marie.

Nat attorroed syloe

Eclie retunde

Phalatie cesarie.

Amanion amabute.

A dyffrynoed bersabe.

A chyncret gὐyr cartasine.

A reithuoryon retὐnde.

Ieithoed groec a efrei

A lladin gὐyr llacharte.

ꝺIFER seint enugynyeit.
Deꝺrwyr echeurin eu pleit.
Rac rihyd rꝺýsc uoleit.
Ketwyr neb cu kyneircheit.
Yn yg yn ehag ym pop reit.
Bꝺynt dinas in corff ac yn heneit.

ꝺIFER seint sicomorialis
A deproffani ynys.
Ar meint glan a vendigꝺys
Dꝺfyr gꝺin gꝺyr al distryꝺys.
Ac eiraꝺl ei urdaꝺl pꝺys.
Dan syr seint ryseilꝺys.

ꝺIFER seint a deily goror.
Effectus re inferior.
A superare superior.
Ac armonim a thyfor.
A dyffryn enor a segor.
A chartago maꝺr a minor.
Ac ynys gꝺyr terwyn mor.

ꝺIFER seint ynys prydein.
Ac iwerdon adꝺyn ran.
Toruoed gꝺeithredoed mirein.
A gredis a gꝺeinis y genhyn.

ꝺIFER seint sened anchwant.
O Duw dewin darogant.
Ympop ieith ym prydant.
Ygkylch eluyd y buant.
Ar meint doethur a darogan
Crist achyn dybei dybuant.

NIFER seint oriente.
A chyfundaϭt kiϭdaϭt iude.
Ieithoed groec ac efrei.
A lladin gϭyr llacharte.

SEITH vgeint seith vgeint seith cant o seint
A seith mil a seith dec vgeint
Nouember nifer aduunant.
Trϭy verthyri mat doethant.
Pymthec vgeint seint a uuant.
A their mil morialis plant.
Hijs decembris uch carant.
Tra phen Jessu dichiorant.

DEUDEG mil yny gyman
A gredϭys trϭy lef ieuan.
Golychan gobrynant van.
Yn nefoed nys digofant.

DAϭ mil seint a aruolles
Bedyd a chrefyd achyffes.
Yr goleith poen poploed gϭres.
Vffern oer y hachles.
Os dofyd ryndigones.
Trϭy pen pedyr perit anlles.

QUI venerunt angli
In natale dñi
Mediai nocte in laudem
Cum pastoribus in bethleem.
Niuem angli de celo
Cum michaele archanglo
Qui precedunt precelio
Erga animas in mundo.

I

Am niuem angeli.

Precedunt confirmati.

Vnistrati baptizati.

Usque in diem iudicii.

Quando fuit Christus crucifixus ut sibi

Ipsi placuisset. venissent ibi in aʋxilium.

Plusquam duodecim legiones angelorum

Toto orbe terrarum.

Jesus Christus uidentem in agonia in mundo.

Vt sint nostri auxilium

Duodecim milia miliantem

Ante tribunal stantem.

Qui laudantie laudantium

Tues mores rex regum.

DIFER auu ac auyd

Vch nef is nef meint yssyd.

Ar meint a gredʋys ygkywyd.

A gredis trʋy ewyllis dofyd.

Meint ar lit trʋy yrodyd.

Trugar duʋ dygerenhyd.

An bʋyr gʋar anwar gʋledic.

Nyth godʋyf kyn bʋyf diennic.

Tost yt gʋyn pop colledic.

Ffest yd haʋl eissywedic.

Ny reha bryt ryodic.

O ryret pressent pan ʋyf dic.

Traethaf pan vydaf yggro

O ossymdeith osepio

A ryfyr o merthyr elo.

Yn edryfynt seint segerno.

O eir pechaʋt pan ymbo.

Dim uch dim meint am clyho.

III.

Buarch Beird.

Fol. 3. a.   EDYMPEILLI oet ympỽyllat.
Y veird brython prydest ofer.
Ymryorsseu ymryorsed.
Digaỽn gofal y gofangord.
Ỽyf eissygpren kyfyg ar gerd.
Buarth beird ar nys gỽypo.
Pymtheg mil drostaỽ
Yny gymhỽyssaỽ.
Ỽyf kerdolyat. Ỽyf keinyat claer.
Ỽyf dur ỽyf dryỽ
Ỽyf saer ỽyf syỽ.
Ỽyf sarff ỽyf serch yd ymgestaf.
Nyt ỽyf vard syn yn aryfreidaỽ.
Pan gan keinyeit canu ygkof.
Nyt ef wnafut ỽy ryfed vchon.
Handit ami eu herbyniaỽ.
Mal aruoll dillat heb laỽ.
Val ymsaỽd yn llyn heb naỽ.
Tyrui aches ehofyn ygrad
Uchel ygỽaed mordỽyt trefyd.
Creic am wanec. ỽrth vaỽr trefnat.
An clut yscrut escar nodyat.
Creic pen perchen pen anygnat.
Yn gỽna medut meddaỽt medyd.
Ỽyf kell ỽyf dell ỽyf datweirllet.
Ỽyf logell kerd ỽyf lle ynnyet.
Karaf y gorỽyd a goreil clyt.
A bard a bryt ny pryn yret.
Nyt ef caraf amryssonyat.
A geibyl keluyd ny meued med.

Madѡs mynet yr ymdiot
A cheluydeit am geluydyt.
Achamclwm kystѡm kywlat.
Bugeil brooed porthoed neirthyat.
Mal ymdeith heb troet y gat.
Eri vynnei ymdeith heb troet.
Eri vagei kneuha heb goet.
Mal keissaѡ bẏdueid yg gruc.
Mal peireint aureith ynuut.
Mal gosgord lluyd heb pen.
Mal porthi anclut ar ken.
Mal grynniaѡ tyndei o vro.
Mal haedu awyr a bach.
Mal eirach a gѡaet yscall.
Mal gѡneuthur goleu y dall
Mal docni dillat ynoeth.
Mal tannu engѡyn ar traeth.
Mal porthi pyscaѡt ar laeth.
Mal toi neuad a deil.
Mal lladu llyry a gѡyeil.
Mal todi dyfet rac geir.
Ѡyf bard neuad. Ѡyf kyѡ kadeir.
Digonaf y veird llafar llesteir.
Kyn vy argyѡrein ym garѡ gyfloc.
Ryprynhom ni an llocyth tydi vab meir.

IV.

Aduvyneu Taliessin.

Fol. 3. b.   ATUYN rin rypenyt i ryret.
Arall atѡyn pan vyd Duѡ dymgѡaret.
Atѡyn kyfed nѡy gomed gogyffret.
Arall atѡyn y am kyrn kyfyfet.
Atѡyn nud ud bleid naf.

Arall at6yn hael g6yl golystaf.
At6yn aeron yn amser kynhaeaf.
Arall at6yn g6enith ar galaf.
At6yn heul yn eh6ybyr yn n6yfre.
Arall at6yn rythalh6yr aede.
At6yn march mygvras mangre.
Arall at6yn dil6y6h6e.
At6yn chwant ac ar̷yant amaer6y.
Ar. at. dyvor6yn modr6y.
At6. eryr ar lan llyr pan llanh6y.
Ar. at. g6ylein yn g6ar6y.
At6yn march ac eurgalch gylch6y.
Ar. at. adu6yn yn ad6y.
At. eyna6n medit ẏ lia6s.
Ar. at. kerda6r hael hygna6s.
At. mei y gogeu ac ea6s.
Ar. at. pan vyd hinha6s.
At6. reith a pherpheith neithia6r.
Ar. at. kyfl6yn a garha6r.
At. bryt 6rth penyt perigla6r.
Ar. at. dyd6yn y alla6r.
At. med ygkynted y gerda6r.
Ar. at. am terwyn toryf va6r.
At. cleiric catholic yn egl6ys.
Ar. at. enefyd yn neuad6ys.
At. pl6yf kymr6yd6y atowys.
Ar. at. yn amser parad6ys.
At. lloer llewycha6t yn eluyd.
Ar. at. pan vyd da dymgofyd.
At. haf ac araff hirdyd.
Ar. at. a threida6 o geryd.
At. blodeu ar warthaf perwyd.
Ar. at. a chrea6dyr kerenhyd.
At. didryf ewic ac elein.

Ar. at. ewyna6c am harchuein.
At. lluarth pan ll6yd y genhin.
Ar. at. katawarth yn egin.
At. edystystyr ygkebystyr lletrin.
Ar. at. kyweithas a brenhin.
At. gle6 n6y goleith gogywec.
Ar. at. ellein gymraec.
At. gruc pan vyd ehoec.
Ar. at. morua ywarthec.
At. tymp. pan dyn lloe llaeth.
Ar. at. ewyna6c marchogaeth.
Ac ys imi at6yn nyt g6aeth.
A that bual 6rth tal medueith.
At. pysc yny lyn llywÿa6t.
Arall at. y oreil6 gwaryha6t.
At. geir a lefeir y trinda6t.
Ar. at. rypenyt y pecha6t.
Adu6yn haf or adu6ynda6t.
Kerenhyd a dofyd dydbra6t.

V.

Fol. 4. b.

DEUS du6 delwat.
G6ledic g6aed neirthyat.
Crist Jessu g6yliat.
R6ysc rihyd amnat.
Aduelach kaffat.
Nym g6nel heb ranned.
Moli dy trugared.
Nÿ dyfu yma.
G6ledic dy gynna.
Nÿ dyfu nÿ dyfyd.
Neb kystal a douyd
Nÿ ganet yn dyd pl6y6.
Neb kystal a Du6.

Nac nyt adef.
Neb kystal ac ef.
Vch nef is nef.
Nyt gvledic namyn ef.
Vch mor is mor.
Ef an crevys.
Pan dyffo devs.
Ef an gwnaho mavr trvs.
Dyd bravt yn echwrys.
Kennadeu o drvs.
Gvynt a mor. a than.
Lluchet a tharyan.
Eiryf. ab gvengan.
Llvyth byt yg griduan.
Ergelavr. dygetavr llavhethan.
Ergelhavr mor a syr.
Pan discynho pater.
Y dadyl ae nifer.
A chyrn gopetror.
Ac ennynnu mor.
Llvyth byt lloscetavr.
Hyny uvynt marwavr.
Lloscavt ynyal ran
Rac y vavr varan.
Ef tynho aches
Rac y varanres.
Diffurn dyd reges.
Gvae ae harhoes.
Ef tardho talavr.
Terdit nef y lavr.
Gvynt rud dygetavr.
Ech y gadvynavr.
Neu byt mor wastat
Mal pan great.

Seith pedyr ae dywaʋt.
Dayar diwarnaʋt.
Dywaʋt duʋ sadʋrn
Dayar yn vn ffʋrn.
Sadʋrn vore rʋyd.
In gʋnaho ny culʋyd.
Tir bydaʋt tywyd.
Gʋynt y todo gʋyd.
Ebryn pop dyhed.
Pan losco mynyded.
Atuyd triganed
A chyrn rac rihed.
Kyfoethaʋc ae henuyn.
Mor. a tir. a llyn.
Atuyd cryn dygryn.
A dayar gychwyn.
Ac uch pop mehyn.
A marʋ mein uudyn.
Eryf argelʋch.
Ac enȳnnu llʋch
Ton aghyolʋch.
Taryan ymrythʋch.
Teithȳaʋc afar.
Ac eryf trʋy alar.
Ac enynnu trʋy var
Rwg nef a dayar.
Pan dyffo trindaʋt
Ymaes maestaʋt.
Llu nef ymdanaʋ.
Llʋyth llydan attaʋ.
Kyrd a cherdoryon
A chathleu egylyon.
Drychafant o vedeu.
Eirant o dechreu.

Eirant kѵu coet.
Ar gymeint adoet.
A rewinẏѵys mor.
A wnant maѵr gaѵr.
Pryt pan dyffo
Ef ae gѵahano.
Y saѵl a uo meu.
Ymchoelant o deheu.
A digonѵy kamwed.
Ymchaelent y perthgled.
Ponyt erlys dy gyfreu.
A lefeir dy eneu
Dy vynet yn du hynt yn nauheu
Yn tywyll heb leuuereu.
Ac ym oed y ereu.
Ac ym oed i ieitheu.
Ac ym oed i ganwlat
Ac eu cant lloneit.
Canuet gѵlat pressent.
Nẏ bum heb gatwent.
Oed mynych kyfar chwerѵ
Y rof eim kefynderѵ.
Oed mynych kyrys cѵydat
Y rof y am kywlat.
Oed mynych kyflafan.
Y rofi ar truan.
Am goryѵ hѵn vyth.
Nym gѵnaei dyn byth.
Am gyrrѵys ygcroc
A wydѵn yn oc.
Am gyrrѵys ym pren.
Dipynѵys vympen.
Tafaѵ ti vyn deutroet.
Mor tru eu hadoet.

Taua6 dyr boenet.
Escyrn vyn traet.
Taua6 dy vyn d6y vreich
Ny ny dybyd eu beich.
Taua6 dy vyn d6y ysc6yd.
Handit mor dyuyd.
Taua6 dyr cethron
Ymy 6n vyg callon.
Taua6 dy gethra6t.
Y r6g vyn deu lygat.
Taua6 yr da allat
Coron drein ym iat.
Taua6 dy oestru
A wanp6yt vyn tu.
Teu ẏ6 chitheu.
Mal yr y6ch lla6 deheu.
I6ch nẏ byd madeu
Vy gwan a bereu.
A wledic ny wydyein.
Pan oed ti a grogein.
G6ledic nef g6ledic pop tut
Nẏ wydein ni grist tut vyhut.
Bei ath 6ybydein.
Crist athathechein.
Nyt aruollir g6at
Gan l6yth eissyfflat.
Digonsa6chi anuat
Yn erbyn dofydyat.
Can mil egylyon
Yssyd imi yn tyston.
A doeth ym kyrcha6
G6edy vyg croga6.
Ygcroc yn greulet.
Myhun ym g6aret.

Yn nefoed bu cryt.

Pan ẏm crogyssit.

Pan orelwisk eli

Dy culỽyd vch keli.

A chenỽch deu ieuan

Ragof y deu gynran.

A deu lyfyr yn ach llaỽ

Yn eu darlleaỽ.

Nys deubi ryrys

Rygossỽy rygossys.

Ac aỽch bi wynnyeith

Gỽerth aỽch ynuyt areith.

Kayator y dyleith

Arnaỽch y vffern lleith

Crist Jessu uchel ryseilas trychamil blỽydyned

Er pan yttyỽ ym buched.

Ac eil mil kyn croc.

Yt lewychi enoc.

Neu nyt atwen drut

Meint eu heissillut.

Gỽlat pressent yth ermut.

A chyt aỽch bei odit.

Trychan mil blỽydyned namyn vn

Oricodit buched tragywyd.

VI.

ARYMES PRYDEIN VAVR.

Fol. 6. a. DYGOGAN awen dygobryssyn.

Maraned a meued ahed genhyn.

A phennaeth ehelaeth affraeth vnbyn.

Agỽedy dyhed anhed ympop mehyn.

Gỽyr gỽychyr yntrydar kasnar degyn.

Escut yggofut ryhyt diffyn.

Gỽaethyl gỽyr hyt gaer weir gỽasgaraỽt allmyn.
Gỽnahaỽnt goruoled gỽedy gỽehyn.
A chymot kymry agỽyr dulyn.
Gỽydyl iwerdon mon aphrydyn.
Cornyỽ achludỽys eu kynnỽys genhyn.
Atporyon uyd brython pan dyorfyn.
Pell dygoganher amser dybydyn.
Teyrned abonhed eu gorescyn.
Gỽyr gogled ygkynted yn eu kylchyn.
Ymperued eu racwed ydiscynnyn.

ᴰYSGOGAN myrdin kyferuyd hyn.
Yn aber perydon meiryon mechteyrn.
A chyny bei vn reith lleith a gỽynyn.
O vn ewyllis bryt yd ymỽrth uynnyn.
Meiryon eu tretheu dychynnullyn.
Igketoed kymry nat oed a telhyn.
Yssyd ỽr dylyedaỽc alefeir hyn.
Nỷ dyffei atalei ygkeithiwet.
Mab meir maỽr a eir pryt na thardet.
Rac pennaeth saesson ac eu hoffed.
Pell bỽynt kychmyn ỷ ỽrtheyrn gỽyned.
Ef gyrhaỽt allmyn y alltuded.
Nys arhaedỽy neb nys dioes dayar.
Ny wydynt py treiglynt ympop aber.
Pan prynassant danet trỽy fflet called.
Gan hors ahegys oed yng eu ryssed.
Eu kynnyd bu yỽrthym yn an uonhed.
Gỽedỷ rin dilein keith ym ynuer.
Dechymyd meddaỽ maỽr wiraỽt o ved.
Dechymyd aghen agheu llawer.
Decymyd anaeleu dagreu gỽraged.
Dychyfroy etgyllaeth pennaeth lletfer.
Dechymyd tristid byt aryher.

Pan uyd kechmyn danet an teyrned.
Gúrthottit trindaút dyrnaút a búyller.
Y dilein gúlat vrython a saesson yn anhed.
Poet kynt eu reges yn alltuded.
No mynet kymry yn diffroed

ᎷᎯᏴ meir maúr a eir pryt nas terdyn.
Kymry rac goeir breyr ac vnbyn.
Kyneircheit kyneilweit vnreith cúynnyn.
Vn gor vn gyghor vn eissor ynt.
Nyt oed yr maúred nas lleferynt.
Namyn yr hepcor goeir nas kymodynt.
Yd duú adewi ydymorchymynynt.
Talet gúrthodet flet y allmyn.
Gúnaent úy aneireu eisseu trefdyn.
Kymry a saesson kyferuydyn
Y amlan ymtreulaú ac ymúrthry ir.
O diruaúr vydinaúr pan ymprofyn.
Ac am allt lafnaúr a gaúr a gryn.
Ac am gúy geir kyfyrgeir y am peurllyn.
Alluman adaú agarú discyn.
A mal balaon saesson syrthyn.
Kymry kynyrcheit kyfun dullyn.
Blaen úrth von granwynyon kyfýng oedyn.
Meiryon ygwerth eu gan yn eu creinhyn.
Eu bydin ygúaetlin yn eu kylchýn.
Ereill ar eu traet trúy goet kilhyn.
Trúy uúrch ý dinas fforas ffohýn.
Ryfel heb dychwel y tir prydyn.
Attor trúy laú gyghor mal morllithryn.
Meiryon kaer geri difri cúynant.
Rei y dyffryn abryn nys dirwadant.
Y aber peryddon ný mat doethant.
Anaeleu tretheu dychynullant.

Naᵥ vgein canhᵥr y discynnant.
Maᵥr watwar namyn petwar nyt atcorant.
Dyhed ẏ eu gᵥraged a dywedant.
Eu crysseu yn llaᵥn creu aorolchant.
Kymry kyneïrcheit eneit dichwant.
Gᵥyr deheu eu tretheu a amygant.
Llym llifeit llafnaᵥr llᵥyr ẏ lladant.
Nẏ byd ẏ vedyc mᵥynor awnaant.
Bydinoed katwaladyr kadyr ẏ deuant.
Rydrychafᵥynt kymry kat awnant.
Lleith anoleith rydygyrchassant.
Yg gorffen eu tretheu agheu aᵥdant.
Ereill arosceill ryplanhassant.
Oes oesseu eu tretheu nys escorant.
Ygkoet ymaes ym bryn.
Canhᵥyll yn tywyll a gerd genhyn.
Kynan yn rac wan ympop discyn.
Saesson rac brython gᵥae agenyn.
Katwaladyr yn baladyr gan y unbyn.
Trᵥy synhᵥyr yn llᵥyr yn eu dychlyn.
Pan syrthᵥynt eu clas dros eu herchwyn.
Ygcustud a chreu rud ar rud allmyn.
Yggorffen pop agreith anreith degyn.
Seis ar hynt hyt gaerwynt kynt pᵥy kynt techyn.
Gᵥyn eu byt ᵥy gymry pan adrodynt.
Ryn gᵥaraᵥt y trindaᵥt or trallaᵥt gynt.
Na chrynet dyfet na glyᵥyssyg
Nys gᵥnaho molaᵥt meiryon mechteyrn.
Na chynhoryon saesson keffyn ebryn.
Nys gᵥnaᵥ medut meddaᵥt genhyn.
Heb talet o dynget meint a geffyn.
O ymdifeit veibon ac ereill rẏn.
Trᵥy eiryaᵥl dewi a seint prydeyn.
Hyt ffrᵥt arlego ffohaᵥr allan.

DYSGOGAN awen dydaỼ y dyd.
Pan dyffo i wys y vn gỼssyl.
Vn cor vn gyghor alloegyr lloscit.
Yr gobeith anneiraỼ ar yn prydaỼ luyd.
A cherd aralluro a ffo beunyd.
Ny Ỽyr kud ym da cỼd a cỼd vyd.
DychyrchỼynt gyfarch mal arth o vynyd.
Y talu gỼynyeith gỼaet eu hennyd.
Atvi peleitral dyfal dillyd.
Nyt arbettỼy car corff y gilyd.
Atui pen gaflaỼ heb emennyd.
Atui gỼraged gỼedỼ a meirch gỼeilyd.
Atui o bein vthyr rac ruthyr ketwyr.
A lliaỼs llaỼ amhar kyn gỼascar lluyd.
Kennadeu agheu dychyferwyd.
Pan safhỼynt galaned Ỽrth eu hennyd.
Ef dialaỼr y treith ar gỼerth beunyd.
Ar mynych gennadeu ar geu luyd.

DYGORFU kymry trỼy kyfergyr.
Yn gyweir gyteir gỼtson gytffyd.
Dygorfu kymry y peri kat.
A llỼyth lliaỼs gỼlat agynnullant.
A lluman glan dewi adrychafant.
YtywysaỼ gỼydyl trỼy lieingant.
A gynhen dulyn genhyn y safant.
Pan dyffont yr gad nyt ymwadant.
Gofynnant yr saesson py geissyssant.
PỼy meint eu dylyet or wlat a dalyant.
CỼ mae eu herỼ pan seilyassant.
CỼ mae eu kenedloed py vro pan doethant.
Yr amser gỼrtheyrn genhyn y sathrant.
Ny cheffir o wir rantir ankarant.
Neu vreint an seint pyr y saghyssant.

Neu 6rtheu dewi pyr y toryassant.
Ym getwynt gymry pan ymwelant.
Nyt ahont allmyn or nen y safant.
Hyt pan talhont seith weith g6erth digonsant.
Ac agheu diheu y g6erth eu cam.
Ef talha6r o ana6r garma6n garant.
Y pedeir blyned ar pedwar cant.
G6yr g6ychyr g6allt hiryon ergyr dofyd.
A dehol saesson o iwerdon dybyd.
Dybi o lego lyghes rewyd.
Rewinya6t y gat r6ycca6t lluyd.
Dybi o alclut g6yr drut diweir.
Y dihol o prydein virein luyd.
Dybi o lyda6 pryda6 gyweithyd.
Ketwyr y ar katueirch ny pheirch eu hennyd.
Saesson o pop parth y g6arth ae deubyd.
Ry treghis eu hoes nys oes eluyd
Dyderpi agheu yr du gyweithyd.
Clefyt a dyllid ac ang6eryt.
G6edy eur ac aryant a chann6yned
Boet perth eu diffeith ygwerth eu drycffyd.
Boet mor boet agor eu kussulwyr
Boet creu boet agheu eu kyweithyd.
Kynan a chatwaladyr kadyr yn lluyd.
Etmycca6r hyt vra6t ffa6t ae deubyd.
Deu vnben degyn d6ys eu kussyl.
Deu oresgyn saesson o pleid dofyd.
Deu hael deu geda6l g6lat warthegyd.
Deu diarchar bara6t vn ffa6t vn ffyd.
Deu erchwyna6t prydein mirein luyd.
Deu arth nys g6na g6arth kyfarth beunyd.
Dysgogan derwydon meint a deruyd.
O vyna6 hyt lyda6 yn eu lla6 yt vyd.
O dyued hyt danet 6y bieiuyd.

O waʋl hyt weryt hyt eu hebyr.
Lettataʋt eu pennaeth tros yr echʋyd.
Attor ar gynhon saeson nybyd.
Atchwelʋynt ʋydyl ar eu hennyd.
Rydrychafʋynt gymry kadyr gyweithyd.
Bydinoed am gʋrʋf othʋrʋf milwyr.
A theyrned deʋs rygedʋys eu ffyd.
I wis ẏ pop llyghes tres a deruyd.
A chymot kynan gan y gilyd.
Ni alwaʋr gynhon yn gynifwyr
Namyn kechmyn katwaladyr ae gyfnewitwyr.
Eil kymro llawen llafar auyd.
Am ynys gymʋyeit heit a deruyd.
Pan safhʋynt galaned ʋrth eu hennyd.
Hyt yn aber santwic sʋynedic vyd.
Allmyn ar gychwẏn i alltudyd.
Ol ʋrth ol attor ar eu hennyd.
Saesson ʋrth agor ar vor peunyd.
Kymry generaʋl hyt vraʋt goruyd.
Na cheissʋynt lyfraʋr nac agaʋr brydyd.
Arymes yr ynys hon namyn hyn ny byd.
Iolʋn i ri a greʋys nef ac eluyd.
Poet tywyssaʋc dewi yr kynifwyr.
Yn yr yg gelli kaer am duʋ yssyd.
Ny threinc ny dieinc nyt ardispyd.
Ny ʋiʋ ny wellyc ny phlyc ny chryd.

VII.

ANGAR KYFYNDAʋT.

ıl. 9. a. **B**ARD yman ymae neu cheint aganho.
Kanet pan darffo.
Sywedyd yn yt uo.
Haelon am nacco.

K

Nys deubi arotho.
Trѵy ieith taliessin.
Bu dyd emellin.
Kian pan darfu.
Lliaѵs y gyfolu.
By lleith bit areith auacdu.
Neus duc yn geluyd.
Kyuren argywyd.
Gѵiaѵn a leferyd.
A dѵfyn dyfyd.
Gѵnaei o varѵ vyѵ.
Ac aghyfoeth yѵ.
Gѵneynt eu peiron.
Av erwynt heb tan.
Gѵneynt eu delideu.
Yn oes oesseu.
Dydѵyth dydyccaѵt
O dyfynwedyd gѵaѵt.
Neut angar kyfyndaѵt.
Pѵy ychynefaѵt.
Kymeint kerd kiѵdaѵt
A delis aѵch tafaѵt.
Pyr na threthѵch traethaѵt.
Llat uch llyn llathraѵt.
Penillyach paѵb
Dybydaf yna gnaѵt.
Dѵfyn dyfu ygnaѵt.
Neur dodyѵ ystygnaѵt.
Trydyd par ygnat.
Trѵgein mlyned
Yt portheisilaѵrwed.
Yn dѵfyr kaѵ a chiwed.
Yn eluyd tired.
Kanweis am dioed.

Kant rihyd odynoed.
Kan y6 yd aethant.
Kan y6 y doethant.
Kan eilewyd y gant.
Ac ef ae darogant.
Lladon verch liant.
Oed bychan ychwant
Y eur ac aryant.
P6yr by6 ae diadas
G6aet ẏar wynwas.
Odit traethator
Ma6r molhator.
Mit6yf taliessin.
Ry phrydaf y ia6n lliu
Para6t hyt ffiu
Ygkynel6 elphin.
Neur deirẏg het
O rif eur dylyet.
Pan gassat nẏ charat.
Anudon a brat.
Nu ny chwennych vat
Tr6y gogyuec an g6a6t.
A gogyfarch6y bra6t
6rthyf ny g6ybyd neba6t.
Doethur prif geluyd.
Disp6ylla6t sywedyd.
Am 6yth am edry6yth
Am doleu dynwedyd.
Am g6yr g6a6t geluyd.
Kerd6n du6 yssyd
Tr6y ieith talhayarn.
Bedyd bu dyd varn.
A varn6ys teithi
Angerd vardoni.

Ef ae rin rodes
Awen aghymes.
Seith vgein ogyruen
Yssyd yn awen.
Uyth vgein o pop vgein e uyd yn vn.
Yn annufyn y diuyth.
Yn annufyn y goruyth.
Yn annufyn is eluyd.
Yn awyr uch eluyd
Y mae ae guybyd.
Py tristit yssyd
Guell no llewenyd.
Gogun dedyf radeu.
Awen pan deffreu.
Am geluyd taleu.
Am detwyd dieu.
Am buched ara.
Am oesseu yscorua.
Am haual teyrned. py hyt eu kygwara.
Am gyhaual ydynt truy weryt.
Maurhydic. sywyd pan dygyfrensit
Awel uchel gyt.
Pan vyd gohoyu bryt
Pan vyd mor hyfryt.
Pan yu gurd echen.
Pan echreuyt uchel.
Neu heul pan dodir.
Pan yu toi tir.
Toi tir puy meint.
Pan tynhit guytheint.
Gwytheint pan tynnit.
Pan yu guyrd gueryt.
Gueryt pan yu guyrd.
Puy echenis kyrd.

Kyrd póy echenis.
Ystir póy ystyryóys.
Ystyryóyt yn llyfreu
Pet wynt pet ffreu.
Pet ffreu pet wynt.
Pet auon ar hynt.
Pet auon yd ynt.
Dayar póy y llet.
Neu póy y theóhet.
Gogón tróս llafnaór
Am rud am laór.
Gogón atrefnaór
Róg nef a llaór
Pan atsein aduant.
Pan ergyr diuant.
Pan lewych aryant.
Pan vyd tywyll nant.
Anadyl pan yó du.
Pan yó creu a uu.
Buch pan yó bannaóc.
Góreic pan yó serchaóc.
Llaeth pan yó góyn.
Pan yó glas kelyn.
Pan yó baruaót myn.
Yn lliaós mehyn.
Pan yó baruaót.
Pan yó keu efór.
Pan yó medó colóyn.
Pan yó lledyf ordóyn.
Pan yó brith iyrchwyn.
Pan yó hallt halóyn
Córóf pan yó ystern.
Pan yó lletrud góern.
Pan yó góyrd llinos.

Pan yꝟ rud egroes.

Neu wreic ae dioes.

Pan dygynnu noa.

Py datweir yssyd yn eur lliant.

Ny ꝟyr neb pan rudir y bron huan.

Lliꝟ yn erkynan newyd

Anahaꝟr ydꝟyn.

Tant telyn py gꝟyn.

Coc py gꝟyn py gan.

Py geidꝟ y didan.

Py dydꝟc garthan

Gereint ac arman.

Py dydꝟc glein.

O erddygnaꝟt vein

Pan yꝟ per erwein.

Pan yꝟ gꝟyrliꝟ brein.

Talhayarn yssyd

Mꝟyhaf y sywedyd.

Pꝟy amgyffraꝟd gꝟyd

O aches amot dyd.

Gogꝟn da a drꝟc

Cꝟda cꝟd amewenir mꝟc

Maꝟr meint gogyhꝟc.

Kaꝟc pꝟy ae dylifas.

Pꝟy gꝟaꝟr gorffennas.

Pꝟy abregethas.

Eli ac eneas.

Gogꝟn gogeu haf.

A uydant y gayaf.

Awen aganaf.

O dꝟfyn ys dygaf.

Auon kyt beryt.

Gogꝟn y gꝟrhyt.

Gogꝟn pan dyucinꝟ.

Gogͧn pan dyleinͧ.
Gogͧn pan dillyd.
Gogͧn pan wescryd.
Gogͧn py pegor
Yssyd y dan vor.
Gogͧn eu heissor
Paͧb yny oscord.
Pet gygloyt yn dyd
Pet dyd ymblͧydyn.
Pet paladyr ygkat.
Pet dos ygkawat.
Atuͧyn y trannaͧt.
Gͧaͧt nͧy mefyl gogyffraͧt
Aches gvyd gͧydyon.
Gogͧn i nebaͧt
Py lenwis auon
Ar pobyl pharaon.
Py dydͧc rͧynnon
Baran achͧysson.
Py yscaͧl odef
Pan drychafafͧyt nef.
Pͧy uu fforch hͧyl
O dayar hyt awyr.
Pet byssed am peir
Am vn am nedeir
Pͧy enͧ y deueir.
Ny eing yn vn peir.
Pan yͧ ḿor meddͧhaͧt.
Pan yͧ du pyscaͧt.
Moruͧyt uyd eu cnaͧt.
Hyd pan yͧmedysc.
Pan yͧ gannaͧc pysc.
Pan yͧ du troet alarch gͧyn.
Pedrydaͧc gͧaeͧ llym.

Llƿyth nef nyt ystyg.

Py pedeir tywarchen.

Nẏ wys eu gorffen.

Py voch neu py grƿydyr hyd.

Ath gyfarchaf vargat vard.

Gƿr yth gynnyd escyrn nyƿl.

Cƿdynt deu rayadyr gƿynt.

Traethattor vygofec.

Yn efrei yn efroec.

Yn efroec yn efrei.

Laudatu Laudate Jessu.

Eil gƿeith ym rithat.

Bum glas gleissat.

Bum ki bum hyd.

Bum iƿrch ymynyd.

Bum kyff bum raƿ

Bum bƿell yn llaƿ.

Bum ebill yggefel

Blƿydyn ahanher.

Bum keilyaƿc brithƿyn

Ar ieir yn eidin.

Bum amƿs ar re.

Bum tarƿ toste.

Bum bƿch melinaƿr.

Mal ymaethaƿr.

Bum gronyn erkennis.

Ef tyfƿys ymryn.

A mettaƿr am dottaƿr.

Yn sawell ymgyrraƿr.

Ymrygiaƿr o laƿ.

ƿrth vyg godeidaƿ.

Am haruolles yar.

Grafrud grib escar.

Gorffowysseis naƿ nos

Ynẏ chroth yn was.
Bum aeduedic
Bum llat rac gѵledic.
Bum marѵ bum byѵ.
Keig ydym ediѵ
Bum y arwad aѵt.
Y rac daѵ bum taѵt.
Am eil kyghores gres
Grafrud am rodes.
Odit traethattor
Maѵr molhator.
Mitѵyf taliesin
Ryphrydaf iaѵnllin.
Parahaѵt hyt ffin.
Ygkynnelѵ elphin.

VIII.

KAT GODEU.

11. a.

BUM yn lliaѵs rith
Kyn bum disgyfrith.
Bum cledyf culurith.
Credaf pan writh.
Bum deigyr yn awyr.
Bum serwaѵ sẏr.
Bum geir yn llythyr.
Bum llyfyr ym prifder.
Bum llugyrn lleufer
Blѵydyn a hanher.
Bum pont ar triger.
Ar trugein aber.
Bum hynt bum eryr.
Bum corѵc ymyr.
Bum darwed yn llat.
Bum das ygkawat.

Bum cledyf yn aghat.
Bum yscỽyt ygkat.
Bum tant yn telyn
Lletrithaỽc naỽ blỽydyn.
Yn dỽfyr yn ewyn.
Bum yspỽg yn tan.
Bum gỽyd yngỽarthan.
Nyt mi ỽyf ny gan
Keint yr yn bychan.
Keint ygkat godeu bric.
Rac prydein wledic.
Gỽeint veirch canholic.
Llyghessoed meuedic.
Gỽeint mil maỽrein.
Arnaỽ yd oed canpen.
A chat er dygnaỽt.
Dan von y tauaỽt.
A chat arall yssyd
Yn y wegilyd.
Llyffan du gaflaỽ.
Cant ewin arnaỽ.
Neidyr vreith gribaỽc.
Cant eneit trỽy bechaỽt
Aboenir yny chnaỽt.
Bum ygkaer uefenhit.
Yt gryssynt wellt agỽyd.
Kenynt gerdoryon
Kryssÿnt katuaon.
Datỽyrein y vrythron
A oreu gỽytÿon.
Gelwyssit ar neifon.
Ar grist o achỽysson.
Hyt pan y gỽarettei
Y ren rỽy digonsei.

As atteb૯ys dofyd
Tr૯y ieith ac eluyd.
Rith૯ch rieda૯c wyd.
Ganta૯ yn lluyd.
A r૯ystra૯ peblic.
Kat arlla૯ annefic.
Pan s૯ynh૯yt godeu.
Y gobeith an godeu.
Dygottorynt godeu
O pedrydant tanheu.
K૯ydynt am aereu.
Trych૯n trymdieu.
Dyar gardei bun.
Tardei am atgun.
Blaen llin blaen bun.
Budyant buch anhun
Nyn g૯nei emellun.
G૯aet g૯yr hyt an clun.
M૯yhaf teir aryfgryt.
A chweris ymbyt.
Ac vn a dery૯
O ystyr dily૯.
A christ y crocca૯
A dyd bra૯t rac lla૯.
G૯ern blaen llin
A want gysseuin.
Helyc a cherdin.
Buant h૯yr yr vydin.
Eirinwyd yspin.
Anwhant o dynin.
Keri kywrenhin.
G૯rthrychyat g૯rthrin.
Ffuonwyd eithyt.
Erbyn llu o ge૯ryt.

Auanwyd gŵneithyt.
Ny goreu emwyt.
Yr amgelŵch bywyt.
Ryswyd a gŵyduŵyt.
Ac eido yr y bryt.
Mor eithin yr gryt.
Siryan seuyssit
Bedŵ yr y vaŵr vryt.
Bu hŵyr gŵiscyssit.
Nyt yr y lyfyrder.
Namyn yr y vaŵred.
Auron delis bryt.
Allmyr uch allfryt.
Ffenitwyd ygkynted.
Kadeir gygwrysed.
Omi goreu ardyrched
Rac bron teyrned.
Llŵyf yr y varanhed.
Nyt oscoes troetued.
Ef laddei a pherued
Ac eithaf a diwed.
Collwyd bernyssit
Eiryf dy aryfgryt.
Gŵyros gŵyn y vyt.
Tarŵ trin teyrn byt.
Moraŵc a moryt.
Ffawyd ffynyessit.
Kelyn glessyssit
Bu ef y gŵrhyt.
Yspydat amnat.
Heint ech y aghat.
Gŵiwyd gorthorat.
Gorthoryssit ygat.
Redyn anreithat.

Banadyl rac bragat
Yn rychua briwat.
Eithin ny bu vat.
Yr hynny g૯erinat.
Gruc budyd amnat.
Dy werin s૯ynat.
Hyd g૯yr erlynyat.
Der૯ buana૯r.
Racda૯ crynei nef alla૯r.
Glelyn gle૯ drussia૯r
Y en૯ ym peulla૯r.
Clafuswyd kygres.
Kymra૯ arodes.
G૯rthodi g૯rthodes
Ereill o tylles.
Per goreu gormes
Ym plyml૯yt maes.
Goroutha૯c kywyd
Aches veilon. wyd.
Kastan kewilyd.
G૯rthryat fenwyd.
Hantit du muchyd.
Handit cr૯m mynyd.
Handit kyl coetdyd.
Handit kynt' myr ma૯r.
Er pan gigleu yr a૯r.
An deilas blaen bed૯.
An datrith dated૯.
An maglas blaen der૯.
O warchan maelder૯.
Wherthina૯c tu creic.
Ner nyt ystereic.
Nyt o vam athat.
Pan ym digonat.

Am creu am creat.
O naᵹrith llafanat.
O ffrᵹyth o ffrᵹytheu.
O ffrᵹyth duᵹ dechreu.
O vriallu a blodeu bre.
O vlaᵹt gᵹyd a godeu.
O prid o pridret.
Pan ym digonet
O vlaᵹt danat
O dᵹfyr ton naᵹvet.
Am sᵹynᵹys i vath.
Kyn bum diaeret.
Am sᵹynᵹys i wytyon
Maᵹnut o brython.
O eurwys o ewron
O euron o vodron
O pymp pumhᵹnt keluydon.
Arthaᵹon eil math
Pan ymdygyaed.
Amsᵹynᵹys i wledic.
Pan vei let loscedic.
Am sᵹynᵹys sywydon
Sýwyt kyn byt.
Pan vei genhyf y vot
Pan vei veint byt.
Hard bard bud an gnaᵹt
Ar waᵹt y tuedaf a traetho tauaᵹt.
Gᵹaryeis yn llychᵹr.
Kysceis ym porffor.
Neu bum yn yscor
Gan dylan eil mor.
Ygkylchet ymperued
Rᵹg deulin teyrned.
Yn deu wayᵹ anchwant

O nef pan doethant.
Yn annꝺfyn llifereint
Ꝺrth urꝺydrin dybydant
Petwar vgeint cant.
A gꝺeint yr eu whant.
Nyt ynt hyn nyt ynt ieu
No mi yn eu bareu.
Aryal canhꝺr a geni paꝺb o naꝺ cant
Oed genhyf inheu.
Ygcledyf brith gꝺaet
Bri am darwed
O douyd o golo lle yd oed.
O dof yt las baed.
Ef gꝺrith ef datwrith.
Ef gꝺrith ieithoed.
Llachar y enꝺ llaꝺffer.
Lluch llywei nifer.
Ys ceinynt yn ufel.
O dof yn uchel.
Bum neidyr vreith y mryn.
Bum gꝺiber yn llyn.
Bum ser gan gynbyn.
Bum bꝺystuer hyn.
Vyg. cassul am kaꝺc.
Armaaf nyt yn drꝺc.
Petwar vgeint mꝺc
Ar paꝺb a dydꝺc
Pymp pemhꝺnt aghell
A ymtal am kyllel.
Whech march melynell.
Canweith yssyd well.
Vy march melyngan
Kyfret a gꝺylan.
Mihun nyt eban.

Kyfróg mor a glan.
Neu goróyf góaetlan.
Arnaó cant kynran.
Rud em vyg kychóy.
Eur vy yscóytróy.
Ny ganet yn adóy.
A uu ym gowy
Namyn goronóy
O doleu edryóy.
Hir wynn vy myssaór.
Pell na bum heussaór.
Treigleis y myón llaór
Kyn bum lleenaór.
Treigleis kylchyneis
Kysceis cant ynys.
Cant caer a thrugys.
Derwydon doethur.
Darogenóch ý arthur.
Yssit yssyd gynt.
Neur mi ergenhynt.
Ac vn aderyó
O ystyr dilyó.
A christ y croccaó.
A dyd braót racllaó.
Eurein yn euryll.
Mi hudóyf berthyll
Ac óydyf drythyll
O erymes fferyll

IX.

MAB GYFREU TALIESSIN.

Fol. 13. a.

KYFARCHAF ym ren
Y ystyrgaó awen.

Py dyduc aghen
Kyn no cherituen.
Kyssefin ym byt
A uu eissywyt.
Meneich aleit
Pyrnam dyweit.
Pyr nam eisgyt
Vn aʋr nam herlynyt.
Py datʋyreith mʋc
Pyt echenis drʋc.
Py ffynhaʋn a diʋc
Uch argel tywyllʋc.
Pan yʋ kalaf cann.
Pan yʋ nos lloergan.
Arall ny chanhʋyt
Dyyscʋyt allan.
Pan yʋ gofaran
Tʋrʋf tonneu ʋrth lan.
Yn dial dylan.
Dydahaed attan.
Pan yʋ mor trʋm maen.
Pan yʋ mor llym draen.
Aʋdosti pʋy gʋell
Ae von al y vlaen.
Py peris parʋyt
Rʋg dyn ac annʋyt.
Pʋy gʋell y adʋyt
Ae ieuanc ae llʋyt.
A ʋdostti peth ʋyt
Pan vych yn kyscʋyt.
Ae corff ae eneit.
Ae argel canhʋyt.
Eilewyd keluyd
Pyr nam dywedyd.

L

A ỽdosti cỽd uyd
Nos yn arhos dyd.
A ỽdosti arwyd.
Pet deilen yssyd.
Py drychefis mynyd
Kyn rewinyaỽ eluyd.
Py gynheil magỽyr
Dayar yn bresỽyl.
Eneit pỽy gỽynaỽr
Pỽy gỽelas ef pỽy gỽyr.
Ryfedaf yn llyfreu
Nas gỽdant yn diheu.
Eneit pỽy y hadneu
Pỽy pryt y haelodeu.
Py parth pan dineu
Ry wynt a ryffreu
Ryfel anygnaỽt.
Pechadur periglaỽt.
Ryfedaf ar waỽt
Pan uu y gỽadaỽt.
Py goreu medd daỽt
O ved a bragaỽt.
Py goryỽ y ffaỽt
Amỽyn duỽ trindaỽt.
Pyr y traethỽn i traythaỽt.
Namyn o honaỽt.
Py peris keinhaỽc
O aryant rodavt.
Pan yỽ mor redegaỽc.
Karr mor eithiaỽc.
Agheu seilyaỽc
Ympop gỽlat ys rannaỽc.
Agheu uch an pen
Ys lledan y lenn.

Vch nef noe nen.

Hynaf uyd dyn pan anher

Aieu ieu pop amser.

Yssit a pryderer

Or bressent haed.

Goedy anreufed

Pyr yn gona ni byrhoedled.

Digaon llaoryded

Kywestoch a bed.

Ar gor an gonaeth

Or wlat goerthefin.

Boet ef an duo an duoch

Attao or diwed.

X.

DARONOY.

l. 13. b.

Dvo differth nefoy

Rac llano llet ofroy.

Kyntaf attarroy.

Atreis dros vordoy.

Py pren a vo moy ;

No get daronoy.

Nyt oy am nodoy

Am gylch balch nefoy.

Yssit rin yssyd uoy

Goaor goyr goronoy.

Odit ae goypoy.

Hutlath vathonoy.

Ygkoet pan tyfoy.

Ffroytheu noy kymroy.

Ar lan goyllyonoy.

Kynan ae kaffoy

Pryt pan wledychoy.

Dedeuant etwaeth
Tros trei athros traeth.
Pedeir prif pennaeth.
Ar pymhet nyt góaeth.
Góyr górd ehelaeth
Ar prydein aruaeth.
Góraged a ui ffraeth.
Eillon a ui kaeth
Ryferthóy hiraeth
Med a marchogaeth.
Dedeuho dóy rein.
Góedó a góryaóc vein
Heyrn eu hadein.
Ar wyr yn goryein.
Dydeuho kynrein
O am tir rufein.
Eu kerd a gygein
Eu góaót ayscein.
Anan deró a drein.
Ar gerd yt gygein.
Ki ẏ tynnu.
March y rynnyaó.
Eidon y wan. hóch y tyruu.
Pymhet llódyn góyn a wnaeth Jessu.
O wisc adaf y ymtrau.
Góyduet coet kein eu syllu.
Hyt yt uuant a hyt yt uu.
Pan wnel kymry kamualhau.
Keir aralluro póy karonu
Llemeis i lam o lam eglóc.
Keóssit da nyr gaho dróc.
Megedorth run yssef a óc.
Róg kaer rian a chaer ryóc
Róg dineidẏn. a dineidóc

Eglur dremynt a wyl gol6c.
Rac ryna6t tan dychyfr6ym6c.
An ren du6 an ry am6c.

XI.

14. a. &N en6 g6ledic nef goluda6c.
Y drefynt biewyd gyneil uoa6c.
Eiric y rethgreu rieda6c.
Rieu ryfelgar ge6herua6c.
Ef differth adu6yn llan lleena6c.
Torhyt vn h6ch ard6ya6c.
Hir dychyferuydein.
O brydein gofein.
O berth ma6 ac eidin.
Nẏ chymeryn kyuerbyn.
Kyweith kyweithyd clytwyn.
Digon6yf digones lyghes.
O beleidyr o bleigheit prenwres.
Prenyal y6 y pa6b y trachwres.
Aghyfnent o gadeu digones
G6alla6c g6ell g6yd u6yt noc arthles.
Kat yr agathes o achles
G6a6t gogna6 y brot digones.
Kat ymro vretr6yn tr6y wres
Ma6r tan. meidra6l y6 y trachwres.
Kat yr ae kymr6y kanhon.
Kat kat crynei yn aeron.
Kat yn arddunyon ac aeron
Eidywet. eilywet y veibon.
Kat ygcoet beit boet ron dyd.
Ny medylyeisti dy alon.
Kat yn rac uyda6l amabon.
Nyt atra6d adura6t achubyon.
Kat y gwensteri ac estygi lloygyr.

Safɣaɣc yn aɣner.
Kat yn ros terra gan waɣr.
Oed hyɣst gɣragaɣn eguraɣn.
Yn dechreu yghenyat y geiraɣr.
O rieu o ryfel ry diffaɣt.
Gɣyr a digaɣn godei gɣarthegaɣc.
Haeardur a hyfeid a gɣallaɣc.
Ac owein mon maelgynig deuaɣt.
A wnaɣ peithwyr gorweidaɣc.
Ym pen coet cledyfein.
Atuyd kalaned gɣein.
A brein ar disperaɣt.
Ym prydein yn eidiɲ yn adeueaɣc.
Yggafran yn aduaɲ brecheinaɣc.
Yn erbyn yɲ yscɣn gaenaɣc.
Ny wyl gɣr ny welas gɣallaɣc.

XII.

Fol. 14. b. Kɢ ENNADEU am dodynt mor ynt anuonaɣc.
Dygaɣn ymlletcynt meint vygkeud aɣt.
Gnaɣt rɣyf yn heli beli wiraɣt.
Gnaɣt yscɣyt yscaɣn argefyn yscaɣit.
Gnaɣt gɣyth ag adɣyth o yspydaɣt
Gaer. a naɣcant maer maer marɣhaɣt.
Atvyd mei ar venei crei gyflogaɣt.
Atvyd mɣy ar gonɣy creith gɣynyeith gɣnahaɣt.
Adoerlleith dyrreith anaɣ baraɣt.
O heyrn erchwyrn edyru dyrnaɣt.
Tri dillyn diachor droch drymluaɣc.
Teir llyghes yn aches arymes kyn braɣt.
Tri diwedyd kat am dri phriaɣt
Gɣlat. gɣnahaɣt bat betraɣt.

Tri o pop tri. tri phechaʋt.

Ac eryri vre varnhaʋt.

Llu o seis. eil o ynt. trydyd dygnaʋt.

Ygkymry yd erhy gʋraged gʋeddaʋt.

Rac baran kynan tan tardaʋt.

Katwaladyr ae cʋyn.

Briʋhaʋt bre a brʋyn.

Gʋellt a tho tei. ty tandaʋt.

Atvyd ryfedaʋt.

Gʋr gan verch y vraʋt.

Dyfynhyn duraʋt

Olin anaraʋt.

O honaw y tyfhaʋt

Coch kattybrudawt.

Nyt arbet nanaʋt.

Nachefyn derʋ na braʋt.

ʋrth lef corn kadʋr

Naʋ cant ynafyrdʋl

O bedrydant dygnaʋt.

Dygorelwi lesni o laswaʋt.

Efret ʋrth a gaʋd ygendaʋt.

XIII.

KADEIR TALIESSIN. XXIIII.

Fol. 15. a.   𝕸YDʋYF merweryd.

Molaʋt duʋ dofyd.

Llʋrʋ kyfranc kywyd.

Kyfreu dyfynwedyd.

Bard bron sywedyd.

Pan atleferyd.

Awen cʋdechuyd.

Ar veinnyoeth veinyd.

Beird llafar lluc de.

Eu gvavt nym gre.
Ar ystrat ar ystre.
Ystryv mavr mire.
Nyt mi vyf kerd uut.
Gogyfarch veird tut.
Ryt ebrvydaf drut.
Rytalmaf ehut.
Ryduhunaf dremut.
Teyrn terwyn wolut.
Nyt mi vyf kerd vas.
Gogyfarch veird treis.
Bath vadavl idas.
Dofyn eigyavn adas.
Pvy am ledwis kas.
Kamp ympop noethas.
Pan yv dien gvlith.
Allat gvenith.
A gvlit gvenyn.
Aglut ac ystor.
Ac elyv tra mor.
Ac eur biben llev.
A llen aryant gviv.
A rud em a gravn.
Ac ewyn eigyawn.
Py dyfrys ffynhavn
Bervr byryr davn.
Py gyssyllt gverin
Brecci boned llyn.
Allvyth lloer wehyn.
Lledyf lloned verlyn.
A sywyon synhvyr.
A sewyd am loer.
A gofrvy gved gvyr.
Gvrth awel awyr.

A mall amerin.

A góadaól tra merin.

A choróc góytrin.

Ar lla🤍 pererin.

A phybyr a phyc.

Ac vrdaól segyrffyc.

A llyseu medyc.

Lle allóyr venffyc.

Abeird ablodeu.

A gudic bertheu.

A briallu a briódeiL

A blaen góyd godeu.

A mall ameuued.

A mynych adneued.

A góin tal kibed.

O rufein hyt rossed.

A dófyn dófyr echóyd.

Daón y lif dofyd.

Neu pren puraór vyd.

Ffróythlaón y gynnyd.

Rei ias berwidyd.

Oduch peir pumóyd.

A góiaón auon.

A gofróy hinon.

A mel a meillon.

A medgyrn medwon

Adóyn y dragon.

Daón y derwydon.

XIV.

Fol. 16. a. 𝕲OLYCHAFI gulóyd arglóyd pop echen.

Arbenhic toruoed yghyoed am orden.

Keint yn yspydaót uch góiraót aflawen.

Keint rac meibon llyr in ebyr henuelen.

Gŵeleis treis trydar ac auar ac aghen.
Yt lethrynt lafnaŵr ar pennaŵr disgowen
Keint rac ŵd clotleu yn doleu hafren.
Rac brochuael powys a garŵys vy awen.
Keint yn aduŵyn rodle ym more rac ŵryen.
Yn ewyd am antraet gŵaet ar dien.
Neut amuc yggkadeir opeir kerritwen.
Handit ryd vyn tafaŵt yn adaŵt gŵaŵt ogyrwen.
Gŵaŵt ogyrwen uferen rŵy digones
Arnunt a llefrith a gŵlith a mes.
Ystyryeim yn llŵyr kyn clŵyr cyffes.
Dyfot yn diheu agheu nessnes.
Ac am tired enlli dybi dylles.
Dyrchaŵr llogaŵr ar glaŵr aches.
A galwn arygŵr an digones.
An nothŵy rac gŵyth llŵyth aghes.
Pan alwer ynys von tiryon vaes.
Gŵyn eu byt ŵy gŵleidon saesson artres.
Dodŵyf deganhŵy y amrysson.
A maelgŵn uŵyhaf y achŵysson.
Ellygeis vy arglŵyd yggŵyd deon.
Elphin pendefic ryhodigyon.
Yssit imi teir kadeir kyweir kysson.
Ac ẏt vraŵt parahaŵt gan gerdoryon.
Bum ygkat godeu gan lleu agŵydyon.
Vy arithŵys gŵyd eluyd ac elestron.
Bum y gan vran yn iwerdon.
Gŵeleis pan ladŵyt mordŵyt tyllon.
Kigleu gyfarfot am gerdolyon.
A gŵydyl diefyl diferogyon.
O penren ŵleth hyt luch reon.
Kymry yn ŵnvryt gŵrhyt ŵryon.
Gŵret dy gymry ygkymelri.
Teir kenedyl gŵythlaŵn o iawn teithi.

Gůydyl abrython aromani.
A wnahon dyhed adyuysci.
Ac am teruyn prydein kein y threfi.
Keint rac teyrned uch med lestri.
Ygkeinẏon deon im aedyrodi.
An důy pen sywet ket ryferthi.
Ys kyweir vyg kadeir ygkaer sidi.
Nys plaůd neb heint a heneint a uo yndi.
Ys gůyr manaůyt aphryderi.
Teir oryan y am tan a gan recdi.
Ac am y banneu ffrydyeu gůeilgi.
Ar ffynnhaůn ffrůythlaůn yssydd o duchti.
Ys whegach nor gůin gůyn y llyn yndi.
Agwedy ath iolaf oruchaf kyn gůeryt
          Gorot kymot. athi.

XV.

KADEIR TEYRNON. ccc.

ol. 16. b.

AREITH awdyl eglur.
Awen tra messur.
Am gůr deu aůdur.
O echen aladwr.
Ae ffonsa ae ffur.
Ae reom rechtur.
Ae ri růyfyadur.
Ae rif yscrythur.
Ae goch gochlessur
Ae ergyr dros uur.
Ae kadeir gymessur.
Ym plith goscord uur.
Neus duc o gaůr nur.
Meirch gůelů gostrodur.
Teyrnon henur.

Heilyn pascadur.
Treded dofyn doethur.
Y vendigaѵ arthur.
Arthur vendigan
Ar gerd gyfaenat.
Arѵyneb ygkat.
Arnaѵ bystylat.
Pѵy y tri chynweissat.
A werchetwis gѵlat.
Pѵy y tri chyfarѵyd
A getwis arѵyd.
A daѵ ѵrth awyd.
Erbyn eu harglѵyd.
Ban rinwed rotwyd.
Ban vyd hyn hoywed.
Ban corn kerdetrѵyd.
Ban biѵ ѵrth echѵyd.
Ban gѵir pan disgleir.
Bannach pan lefeir.
Ban pan doeth o peir.
Ogyrwen awen teir.
Bum mynaѵc mynweir.
Ygkorn ym nedeir.
Ny dyly kadeir.
Ni gatwo vyggeir.
Kadeir gynif glaer.
Awen huaѵdyl haer.
Pѵy enѵ y teir kaer.
Rѵg lliant a llaer.
Nys gѵyr ny vo taer
Eissylut eu maer.
Pedeir kaer yssyd.
Ym prydein powyssed
Rieu merweryd.

Am nyt vo nyt vyd.

Nyt vyd am nyt vo

Llyghessa/r a vo.

Tohit g/anec tra gro.

Tir dylan dirbo.

Nac eillt nac ado.

Na bryn na thyno.

Na rynna/d godo.

Rac g/ynt pan sorho.

Kadeir teyrnon.

Keluyd r/y katwo.

Keissitor ygno.

Keissitor kedic.

Ket/yr colledic.

Tebygafi dull dic.

O diua pendeuic

O dull diuynnic.

O leon luryc.

Dyrchafa/t g/ledic.

Am terwyn hen enwic.

Breuha/t braga/t bric.

Breua/l eissoric.

Oric a merin

Am teruyn chwhefrin.

Ieithoed edein.

Aches ffyscyolin

Mord/yeit merin.

O plant saraphin.

Dogyn d/fyn diwerin.

Dillygein elphin.

XVI.

KADEIR KERRITUEN. CCC.

REN rymaϭyr titheu.
Kerreifant om karedeu.
Yn deweint ym pyl geineu.
Llewychaϭt vy lleufereu.
Mynaϭc hoedyl minaϭc ap lleu.
A weleis i yma gynheu.
Diwed yn llechued lleu.
Bu gϭrd y hϭrd ygkadeu.
Auacdu vy mab inheu.
Detwyd douyd rϭy goreu.
Ygkyfamrysson kerdeu.
Oed gϭell y synhϭyr nor veu.
Keluydaf gϭr a gigleu.
Gϭydyon ap don dygynuertheu.
A hudϭys gϭreic a vlodeu.
A dydϭc moch o deheu.
Kan bu idaϭ disgoreu.
Drut ymẏt a gϭryt pletheu.
A rithϭys gorϭydaϭt
Y ar plagaϭt
Lys. ac enwerys kyfrϭyeu.
Pan varnher y kadeireu.
Arbenhic vdun y veu.
Vygkadeir am peir am deduon.
Am areith tryadyl gadeir gysson.
Rym gelwir kyfrϭys yn llys don.
Mi ac euronϭẏ ac euron.
Gϭeleis ymlad taer yn nant ffrangcon.
Duϭ sul pryt pylgeint.
Rϭg ϭytheint a gϭydyon.
Dyf ieu yn geugant yd aethant vou.

Y geissaᘁ yscut a hudolyon.

Aran rot drem clot tra gᘁaᘁr hinon.

Mᘁyhaf gᘁarth y marth o parth brython.

Dybrys am ylys efuys afon.

Afon ae hechrys gᘁrys gᘁrth terra.

Gᘁenᘁyn y chynbyt kylchbyt eda.

Nyt ᘁy dyweit geu llyfreu beda.

Kadeir getwided yssyd yma.

A hyt vraᘁt paraᘁt yn europa.

An rothᘁy y trindaᘁt.

Trugared dydbraᘁt

Kein gardaᘁt gan wyrda.

XVII.

KANU YGᘁYNT. CCC. ATAL.

17. b.   ᗞECHYMIC pᘁy yᘁ.

Creadt kyn dilyᘁ.

Creadur kadarn

Heb gic heb ascᘁrn.

Heb ᘁytheu heb waet.

Heb pen aheb traet.

Ny byd hyn ny byd ieu.

No get y dechreu.

Ny daᘁ oe odeu

Yr ofyn nac agheu.

Ny dioes eisseu

Gan greaduryeu.

Maᘁr Duᘁ mor wynneu

Ban daᘁ o dechreu.

Maᘁr y verth ideu

Y gᘁr ae goreu.

Ef ymaes ef ygkoet

Heb laᘁ a heb troet.

Heb heneint heb hoet.
Heb eidigaf adoet.
Ac ef yn gyfoet
A phymhoes pymhoet.
A heuyd yssyd hyn
Pet pemhўnt ulўydyn.
Ac ef yn gyflet.
Ac ўyneb tytwet.
Ac ef nẏ anet.
Ac ef nẏ welet.
Ef ar vor ef ar tir
Nẏ wyl nẏ welir.
Ef yn aghyўir
Nẏ daў pan vynnir.
Ef ar tir ef ar vor
Ef yn anhebcor.
Ef yn diachor
Ef yn dieissor.
Ef o pedeiror
Ni byd ўrth gyghor
Ef kychwyn agor
O duch maen mynuor.
Ef llafar ef mut.
Ef yn anuynut.
Ef yn ўrd ef yn drut.
Pan tremyn trostut.
Ef mut ef llafar.
Ef yn ordear.
Mўyhaf y vanyar
Ar ўyneb dayar.
Ef yn da ef yn drўc.
Ef yn aneglўc.
Ef yn anamlўc
Kanys gўyl golўc.

Ef yn dróc ef yn da.
Ef hónt ef yma.
Ef a antrefna
Ni dióc awna.
Oc ef yn dibech
Ef yn wlyp ef yn sych.
Ef a daóyn vyných.
O wres heul ac oeruel lloer.
Lloer yn anlles
Handit llei y góres.
Vu gór ae goreu.
Yr holl greaduryeu.
Ef bieu dechreu.
A diwed diheu.
Nyt kerdaór keluyd.
Ny mohóy dofyd.
Nyt kywir keinyat.
Ny molhóy y tat.
Ny naót vyd aradyr.
Heb heyrn heb hat
Ny bu oleuat.
Kyn ile creat.
Ny byd effeirat.
Ny bendicco auyrllat.
Ny óybyd anygnat.
Y seith lauanat.
Deg ólat darmerthat.
Yn e gylaór wlat.
Decuet digarat.
Digaróys eu tat.
Digaru kawat
Yn róy rewinyat.
Llucuffer llygrat.
Eissor eissyflat

M

Seith seren yssyd.

O seithnaῦn dofyd.

Seon sywedyd.

A ῦyr eu defnyd

Marca mercedus.

Ola olimus

Luna lafurus.

Jubiter. venerus.

O heul o hydyruer

Yt gyrch lloer lleufer.

Nyt cof yn ofer.

Nyt croc nẏ creter.

An tat an pater.

An kar an kymer.

Yn ren nẏn ranher

Gan lu llucuffer.

XVIII.

KYCHWEDYL am dodyῦ o galchuynyd.

Gῦarth yn deheubarth anreith clotryd.

Da aryd ẏ leu dywaled y vedyd.

Llaῦn yῦ y ystrat lawen gynnyd.

Llara llued peblet llara arall vro.

Kat gormes tra trachwres bro.

Odit o gymry ae llafaro.

Dyfet dygyrchet biῦ mab idno.

Ac nẏ llefessit neb ny do.

Yr talu can mu yrof vn llo.

Goleith dy yscarant amgant dy vro.

Mal tan tῦym tarth yn yt vo.

Pan gyrch assam ni trῦydet ar tir gῦydno.

Oed kelein veinwen rῦg grayan a gro.

Pan ymchoeles echῦyd o gludῦys vro.

Nyt efrefῦys buch ῦrth ẏ llo.

Gogyfarch vabon o arall vro
Kat. pan amuc owein biѵ y vro.
Kat yn ryt alclut. kat ynygwen.
Kat yg gossulѵyt abann udun.
Kat rac rodawys eirѵyn drych.
Gѵaywaѵr a du a lleullenyn.
Kat tuman llachar derlyѵ derlin.
Yscѵydaѵr yn llaѵ garthan yggryn.
A welei vabon ar ranwen reidaѵl.
Rac biѵ reget y kymyscyn.
Ony bei ac adaned yd ehettyn.
Rac mabon heb galaned vy nyt eyn.
O gyfarfot discyn a chychwyn kat.
Gѵlat vabon gѵehenyt anoleithat.
Ban disgynnѵys owein rac biѵ y tat.
Tardei galch achѵyr ac yspydat.
Nyt yscafael ẏ neb dѵyn biѵ moel.
Kyt es clѵch rac gѵyr rein rudyon.
Rac pedrydan dande
Rac kadarn gyfѵyre.
Rac gѵyar ar gnaѵt.
Rac afar ystaenaѵt.
Kychwedyl am dodyѵ
O leutired deheu.
Traeth rieu goleu haelon.
Nyth y ogyfeirch o chwynogyon.
Am ryt or am gѵern y gatuaon.
Ban berit kat ri rѵyf dragon.
Billt na owillt biѵ rac mabon.
O gyfaruot gѵrgun.
Bu kalaned ned rei yn run.
Bu llewenyd dybyd y vrein.
Ban ymadraѵd gѵyr gѵedy nuchien
Kat. nyt ef dieghis yscѵyt owein.

Yscỽyt uolch ỽrthyat ygkat trablud.
Ni reei warthec heb ỽyneb rud.
Rudyon beuder biỽ a maỽr y rat.
Gỽyar gorgolchel gỽarthyf iat.
Ac ar ỽyneb gỽyn yd yr gaffat.
Eurobell greulet genem dullyat
Preid wenhỽys iolin. preid daresteinat.
Preid rac taerurỽydyr taer gyffestraỽn.
Preid pen gyfylchi. keig ar yscỽydaỽr.
Maỽr discreinaỽr llafnaỽr am iat.
Kat y rac owein maỽr. maỽr o irat.
Meindyd kỽydynt ỽy wyr yn amỽyn gỽlat.
Pan discynnỽys owein rac gỽenwlat.
Yr echỽys gorerefein bud oe tat.

XIX.

Kanu y med.   XXIIII.

Fol. 19. b.   GOLYCHAF wledic pendiuic pop wa.
Gỽr agynheil ynef arglỽyd pop tra.
Gỽr a wnaeth y dỽfyr ẏ baỽb yn da.
Gỽr a wnaeth pop llat ac ae llỽyda.
Medhet maelgỽn mon ac an medwa.
Ae vedgorn ewyn gỽerlyn gỽymha.
As kynnull gỽenyn ac nẏs mỽynha.
Med hidleit moleit molut ẏ pop tra.
Lleaỽs creadur a vac terra.
A wnaeth duỽ ẏ dyn yr ẏ donha.
Rei drut rei mut ef ae mỽynha.
Rei gỽyllt rei dof douyd ae gỽna.
Yn dillig vdunt yn dillat yda.
Yn uỽyt yn diaỽt hyt vraỽt yt parha
Golychafi wledic pendefic gỽlat hed.
Y dillỽg elphin o alltuted.

Y gẃr am rodes y gẃin ar cẃrẃf ar med.
Ar meirch maẃr modur mirein eu gẃed.
Am rothẃy etwa mal diwed.
Trẃy vod duẃ y ryd trẃy enryded.
Pump pemhẃnt kalan ygkyman hed.
Elffinaẃc varchaẃc medhẃyrdy ogled.

XX.

KANU Y CẂRẂF. XXIIII.

Fol. 19. b.

ẂEITHI etmynt
Gẃr a gatẃynt gẃynt.
Pan del yrihyd.
Goruloedaẃc eluyd.
Menhyt yn tragywyd.
Ys tidi a uedyd.
Dylif deweint a dyd.
Dyd ymamogaẃr.
Nos ym orffowyssaẃr.
Maswed auolhaẃr.
Y ẃrth wledic maẃr.
Maẃr duẃ digones.
Heul haf ae rywres.
Ac ef digones.
Bud coet amaes.
Galwetaẃr yraches
Ar eilic aghymes.
Galwettaẃr pop neges.
Deus dymgẃares.
Achyn dybydyn
Llẃyth byt yr vnbryn.
Nẏ ellynt ronyn
Heb gyfoeth mechteyrn.
Ef ae taẃd yn llyn

Hyny vo eginyn.
Ef ae taʋd weith arall.
Hyny vo yn vall.
Dreuhaʋc dyderuyd.
Dysgofac yr eluyd.
Golchettaʋr ẏ lestri.
Bit groyʋ y vrecci.
A phan vo anawell.
Dydyccaʋr o gell.
Dydyccaʋr rac rieu.
Ykein gyfedeu.
Nys gʋrthryn pop deu.
Y mel ae goreu.
Duʋ etuynt ynof.
Yd vyd yn y vod
Llaryaf yʋ trindaʋt.
Gorʋyth medʋ medʋhaʋt.
O vynut pyscaʋt
O meint y godrefi.
Grayan mor heli.
Kyn traeth reuerthi.
Grayan mor heli :
Y dan tywaʋt.
Am kud y ar teithiaʋc.
Mi hun am gʋaraʋt.
Ny digonir nebaʋt.
Heb gyfoeth y trindaʋt.

ꟲEITHI etmygant.
Yn tryffin garant
Gallaʋc gallʋgyd. anchwant
Sybʋll symaduant.
Ban erdifel tanc.
Neu nos cʋt dyuyd.

Kwd dirgel rac dyd.
A ỽyr kerd geluyd.
Py gel kallonyd.
Am dyro amde.
Or parth pan dỽyre.
Py dyduc llyỽ gayaf.
Py gyt dechreu lle.
Yn dewis echiaỽc.
Ffus. ffons ffodiaỽc.
Ef duhun hunaỽc.
Ef gobryn karaỽc.
Kymry kaernedaỽc.
Ytat garadaỽc.
Dear meneiuon.
Dear mynaỽc mon.
Maỽr erch anudon.
Gỽenhỽys gỽallthiryon.
Am gaer ỽyragon.
Pỽy a tal y keinon.
Ae maelgỽn o von.
Ae dyfyd o aeron.
Ae coel ae kanaỽon.
Ai gỽrwedỽ ae veibon.
Nyt anchward y alon.
O ynyr ỽystlon.
Ef kyrch kerdoryon.
Se syberỽ seon.
Neur dierueis i rin.
Ymordei vffin.
Ymorhred gododin.
Ys ceirurith kyfrenhin.
Bran bore dewin.
Ỽyf kerdenhin hen.
Ỽyf kyfreu lawen.

Athra6 ydygen.

Meu mola6t vrẏen.

Eirẏan eirẏoes.

Llymina6c llumoes.

Ruduedel au6ys.

Rudyn ae llẏnvys.

Kat yn hardnen6ys.

Ynyr ae briwys.

Kant kalan kynn6ys.

Kant car amyn6ys.

Gweleis wyr gorua6r.

A dygyrchynt a6r.

G6eleis waet ar lla6r.

Rac ruthyr cledyfa6r.

Glessynt escyll g6a6r.

Escorynt vy waywa6r.

Trychant kalan kyman clotua6r.

Ynyr ar tir yn wir cocha6r.

XXI.

Fol. 20. b.   ARCHAF y wen y du6 pl6yf escori.

Perchen nef alla6r p6yll ua6r wofri.

Adu6yn gaer yssyd ar gla6r g6eilgi.

Bit lawen ygkalan eiryan yri.

Ac amser pan wna mor ma6r 6rhydri.

Ys gna6t gorun beird uch med lestri.

Dydybyd g6anec ar vrys dybrys idi.

Ada6 h6ynt y werlas o glas ffichti.

Ac am b6yf o de6s dros vygwedi.

Pan gatt6yf amot kymot athi.

Adu6yn gaer yssyd ar llydan llyn.

Dinas diachor mor ae chylchyn.

Gogyfarch ty prydein k6d gygein hyn.

Blaen llyn ap erbin boet teu voyn.

Bu goscor a bu kerd yn eil mehyn.
Ac eryr uch ỽybyr allỽybyr granwyn.
Rac vd felyc nac escar gychwyn.
Clot wascar a gỽanar yd ymdullyn.
Aduỽyn gaer yssydd ar ton naỽuet.
Aduỽyn eu gỽerin yn ymwaret.
Nẏ wnant eu dỽyn uyt trỽy veuylhaet.
Nyt ef eu defaỽt bot yn galet.
Nẏ llafaraf eu ar vyntrỽydet.
Noc eillon deutraeth gỽell kaeth dyfet.
Kyweithyd o ryd wled waretret.
Kynnỽys rỽg pop deu goreu kiwet.
Aduỽyn gaer yssydd ae gỽna kyman.
Medut a molut ac adar bann.
Llyfyn y cherdeu yn y chalan.
Am arglỽyd hywyd heỽr eiran.
Kyny vynet yn y adỽyt yn deruin llan.
Ef am rodes med a gỽin o wydrin ban.
Aduỽyn gaer yssyd yn yr eglan.
Atuỽyn y rodir y paỽb ẏ ran.
Atwen yn dinbych gorwen gỽylan.
Kyweithyd wleidud ud erlyssan.
Oed ef vyn defaỽt i nos galan.
Lledyfaỽt y gan ri ryfel eiran.
Allen lliỽ ehoec a medu prein.
Hyny uỽyf tauaỽt ar ỽeird prydein.
Aduỽyn gaer yssydd ae kyffrỽy kedeu.
Oed meu y rydeu adewissỽn.
Nẏ lafarafi deith reith ryscatỽn.
Nẏ dyly kelenic nẏ ỽyppo hỽn.
Yscriuen brydein bryder briffỽn.
Yn yt wna tonneu eu hymgyffrỽn.
Pereit hyt pell y gell atreidỽn
Aduỽyn gaer yssyd yn ardỽyrein.

Gochaᵹn y medut y molut gofrein.

Adufᵹyn areu hor escor gynfrein.

Godef gᵹrych dymbi hir ẏhadein.

Dychyrch bar karrec crec mor ednein.

Llit ymyᵹn tyghet treidet trath amein.

A bleidut gorllᵹyt goreu affein.

Dimpyner o duch llat pᵹy llad cofein.

Bendith c ulᵹyd nef gytlef afein.

Arnyn gᵹnel yn vrowyr gorᵹyr owein.

Aduᵹyn gaer yssyd ar lan lliant.

Aduᵹyn yt rodir y paᵹb ẏchwant.

Gogyfarch ti vynet boet teu uᵹyant.

Gᵹaywaᵹr ryn rein a derllyssant.

Duᵹ merchyr gᵹelẏs wyr ygkyfnofant.

Dyfieu bu gᵹartheu a amugant.

Ac yd oed vriger·coch ac och ardant.

Oed lludued vyned dyd y doethant.

Ac am gefyn llech vaelᵹy kylchᵹy vriwant.

Cᵹydyn ygan gefyn llu o garant.

XXII.

PLAEU YR REIFFT. X. C.

Fol. 21. b. EFREI etuyl ar veib israel

Vchel enuryt.

Kyt rif dilyn

Rydyn esseyn.

Rygadᵹys duᵹ dial

Ar plᵹyf pharaonus.

Dec pla poeni

Kyn eu bodi.

Ymor affᵹys.

Kyssefinpla pyscaᵹt difa.

Dignaᵹt annᵹyt.

Eilpla llyffeint lluossaᵤc.
Lleᵤssynt ffronoed.
Tei a threfneu
Athyleeu
Achelleu bᵤyt.
Tryded gᵤydbet
Gᵤychyr gohoget gᵤalatᵤyt.
Petwar iccwr
Cur am ystyr edynogyon.
Eil kyguhaes
Ffrᵤyth coet a maes
Cuᵤt kylyon.
Pymhet bᵤystnon.
Ar holl vibnon
Egiption.
Belsit milet
O trᵤm allet
Deritolyon.
Chwechet heb eu.
Chwyssic crugeu
Creitheu moryon.
Seithuet taryan
Kynllysc athan
A glaᵤ kynᵤyt.
Gᵤynt gordiberth.
Ar deil a gᵤyd.
ᵤythuet lloscus.
Llydan eu clust.
Blodeu kyfys.
Naᵤuet aruthyr
Diuedlaᵤc vthyr
Doniaᵤc nofus.
Du tywyllᵤc
Drem aneglᵤc

Egiptius.
Dec veinyoeth
Móyhaf góynyeith
Ar plóyf kynrein.
Crist iessu christ ioni grein.
Hut ynt clydór.
Chwechant milór
Milet efrei.

XXIII.

TRAÚSGANU KYNAN

GARWYN. M. BROCH.

Fol. 22. a.

KYNAN kat diffret
Amarllofeis ket.
Kanyt geu gofyget.
Górthelgón trefbret.
Kant goróyd kyfret
Aryant eu tudet.
Cant lleng ehoec
O vn ovaen gyffret.
Cant armell ym arffet
A phympónt cathet.
Cledyf góein karrec
Dyrngell góell honeb.
Cant kynan kaffat.
Kas anwelet
Katellig ystret.
Kat anyscoget.
Kat ar óy kyrchet.
Góaywaór ebrifet.
Góenhóys aladet.
A lafyn góyarlet.
Kat y mon maór tec.

Eglyt amolet.

Tra menei mynet

Gᴕorᴕyd a gᴕorgret.

Kat ygcruc dẏmet.

Aercol ar gerdet.

Nac ny rywelet.

Y biᴕ rac ffriᴕ neb.

Mab brochuael brolet.

Eidywet eidunet.

Kernyᴕ kyfarchet.

Ny maᴕl ieu tyghet.

Dystᴕc aghyffret

Ynyd am iolet.

Mygkynnelᴕ o gynan.

Kadeu ergynnan.

Aeleu fflam lydan.

Kyfᴕyrein maᴕrtan.

Kat yg wlat brachan.

Katlan godaran.

Tegyrned truan.

Crinyt rac kynan.

Lluryc yn ymwan.

Eissor llyᴕ heechan.

Kyngen kymangan

Nerthi ath wlat lydan.

Kigleu ymdidan.

Paᴕb yny gochvan.

Kylch byt goch gᴕochuan.

Keithynt dy gynan.

XXIV.

LATH MOESSEN.

Fol. 22. b.   🅶 pop aduer y torof uroder dychyfaeraᴕt.

Bud adefic. y grist gᴕledic dogyn volaᴕt.

Dẏ b6yth du6 kein. yn arffet meir y heissora6t.
Hynt g6iryoned kyfla6n rihed kynnel6 o hona6t.
G6yeil.iesse dy pobyl ïude. dychyfaera6t.
Hu gelwir lleu o luch aleho yr eu pecha6t.
Deheu reen mynyd adien m6yn kyfunda6t.
Yn ran eluyd yn temhyl selyf seil o gyffra6t.
Gofunet g6as colofyn dias ffest fflemycha6t.
Parad6ys dr6s. bugeil de6s duun g6ledycha6t.
Neu rygigleu gan proff6ydeu lleena6c.
Geni iessu a rydarfu. hyt y uuched.
A uei uuched y pop ried b6yt para6t.
Kyn perissit bei mi pryt6n peri6la6t.
Ry duc claer nyt. dayar a yspeida6t.
Ar vor diff6ys pan disgynn6ys dy amgyffra6t.
G6lat prioda6r nys duc m6ynua6r bei im oho hona6t.
Meint dy godet boet imdy rat. g6yeil iesse
Arat iessu llathyr y blodeu.
Ma6r g6yrth yn y vryt o du6 donyeu.
Ef oed ygnat. ygnat oed ef. dewin diheu.
G6r y cussyl i pop vfyd rac geu.
Ef yssyd gafael clayar nifer toeu.
Cunlleith y luyd deheu.
Y mal bẏde6in dilit o lu lloneit.
Hubyd y g6rth vn mab meir moli reen.
Huarwas g6as o du6 treidas pet wyr pet g6iryon.
Dy rac afael kyfoet coet kyfla6n.
Lledyssit gein o arffet iessu.
Rud ny popon moch y dyscat .
O rodi rat rex meibon.
Newyd ana6 nẏ ma6r glywant dynyadon.
Guir y rat g6as porthẏant heb 6r adon.
Dyg6erthydyd pop vchis rac derwydon.
Nudris nẏ widyn llarychwel g6elet mabon.
Dydugant thus ac eur delus o ethiopia.

O duꝟ gorden a duꝟ reen rex meneifon.
Herot gystic nẏ bu godic. y geleudon.
Dy poenedic gꝟallat peues perchen meibon.
Pan aeth dofyd parth pan dillyd
Nilus habed. ryduc herot. annꝟyt gayafaꝟl.
Kyflaꝟn vonhed. ygkaer nazared
Nyt aeth peues perchen anaꝟ.
Byt adebryat hu bꝟyf yth rat tut gorchordeon.
Geni douyd dyduc perchen lleg egylyon.

XXV.

ꝮORRIT anuyndaꝟl
Tuth iaꝟl dan yscaꝟl.
Ef iolen o duch llaꝟr
Tan tanhꝟytin gꝟaꝟr
Uch awel uchel
Uch no phop nyfel.
Maꝟr y anyfel.
Nẏ thric y gofel
No neithaꝟr llyr.
Llyr llꝟybyr y tebyr
Dy var ygkynebyr
Gꝟaꝟr gꝟen gꝟrthuchyr.
Ꝯrth waꝟr ꝯrth wrys
Ꝯrth pop heuelis.
Ꝯrth heuelis nꝟython
Ꝯrth pedyr afaon.
Ardꝟyreafi a varn gꝟrys
Kadarn trydar dꝟfyn y gas.
Nyt mi gꝟr llꝟfyr llꝟyt
Crꝟybyr ꝯrth clꝟyt.
Hut vyn deu garant.
Deu dich uar dichwant
Om llaꝟ yth laꝟ dyt dꝟy dim.

Trithri nodet

Atcor ar henet.

Amarch mayaѶc.

A march genethaѶc.

A march karadaѶc.

KymrѶy teithiaѶc.

A march gѶythur.

A march gѶardur.

A march arthur.

Ehofyn rodi cur.

A march taliessin.

A march lleu letuegin.

A phebyr llei llѶynin.

A grei march cunin.

Kornan kyneiwaѶc

A wyd awydaѶc.

Du moreod enwaѶc.

March brѶyn bro bradaѶc.

Ar tri carn aflaѶc.

Nyt ant hynt hilaѶ.

Kethin march keidaѶ.

Carn avarn arnaѶ.

YscѶydurith yscodic.

GorѶyd llemenic.

March ryderch rydic.

LlѶyt lliѶ elleic.

A llamrei llaѶn elwic.

Affroenuoll gѶyrenhic

March sadyrnin.

A march custenhin.

Ac ereill yn trin

Rac tir all gѶin.

Henwyn mat dyduc.

Kychwedyl o hiraduc.

Bum hŵch bum bŵch
Bum syŵ bum sŵch.
Bum bann bum banhŵch.
Bum gaŵr ym rythŵch.
Bum llif yn eirth
Bum ton yn egheirth.
Bum yscafyn ysceinat dilyŵ.
Bum kath pennrith ar tri phren.
Bum pell. bum pen.
Gafyr ar yscaŵ pren.
Bum garan gŵala gŵelet golŵc.
Tragŵres milet moryal.
Katwent kenedyl da.
Or yssyd is awyr gŵedy kassolŵn.
Nyt byŵ ormod meint am gŵyr. *

XXVI.

Fol. 24. a. Y gofeissvys byt. Bu deu tec arwlat gŵledychyssit.
Bu haelhaf berthaf or ryanet.
Bu terŵyn gŵenŵyn gŵae y gywlat.
Ef torres ar dar teir gŵeith ygkat.
Ac ef ny vyd corgŵyd y wlat dar plufaŵr
Pebyr pell athrechŵys coet gyrth y godiwaŵd
Alexander. yn hual eurin gŵae a garcharer
Ny phell garcharŵyt. agheu dybu
Ac lle ef kafas ergyr o lu
Neb kynnoc ef ny darchaŵd
Myued bed berthrŵyd or adŵyndaŵt
Hael alexander ae kymerth yna.
Gŵlat syr a siryoel a gŵlat syria
A gŵlat dinifdra. a gŵlat dinitra.

---

* A leaf of the MS. appears to be wanting between this and the following
poem, but there is some indication that the leaf had been taken out at the
time the MS. was written.

N

Gỽlat pers a mers a gỽlat y kanna.
Ac ynyssed pleth a phletheppa.
A chiỽdaỽt babilon ac agascia
Maỽr a gỽlat galldarus bychan y da.
Hyt yd ymduc y tir tywarch yna
Ac yt wnahont eu bryt ỽrth eu helya
Y wedant gỽystlon y europa.
Ac anreithaỽ gỽladoed gỽyssy oed terra.
Gỽythyr gỽenynt wraged gordynt yma.
Bron loscedigyon gỽyled gỽastra.
O gadeu afor pan atrodet
Digonynt brein gỽneint pen brithret
Y milwyr mageidaỽn pan attrodet.
Neu wlat yth weisson ti pan diffydet.
Ny byd yth escor escor lludet.
Rac gofal yr hual ac agalet
Milcant riallu a uu varỽ rac sychet.
Eu geu gogỽilleu ar eu milet.
As gỽenỽynỽys y was kyn noe trefret.
Kyn no hyn bei gỽell digonet.
Ym harglỽyd gỽlatlỽyd gỽlat gogonet.
Vn wlat ior oror goreu ystlyned.
Diwyccỽyf digonỽyf poet genhyt ty gyffret.
Ar saỽl am clyỽ poet meu eu hunet.
Digonỽynt ỽy vod duỽ kyn gỽisc tytwet.

XXVII.

AR claỽr eluyd y gystedlyd ny ryanet.
Teir person duỽ. vn mab adỽyn terỽyn trinet.
Mab yr dỽydit. mab yr dyndit. vn mab ryued.
Mab duỽ dinas. mab gỽen meirgỽas. mat gỽas gỽelet.
Maỽr y orden. maỽr duỽ reen ran gogonet.
O hil ade ac abrahe yn ryanet.
O hil dofyd dogyn dỽfynwedyd llu ryanet.

Dẏduc o eir deill abydeir o pop aelet.
Pobyl ginhiaѵc. goec gamwedaѵc salѵ amnẏned.
Rydrychafom erbyn trindaѵt gѵedy gѵaret.
Croes crist yn glaer. lluryc llachar rac pop aelat.
Rac pop anuaѵs poet yn dilis dinas diffret.

XXVIII.

24. b.

     RYFEDAF na chiaѵr
Adef nef y laѵr
O dyfot rѵyf gaѵr
Alexander maѵr.
Alexander magidaѵr.
Heѵys hayarndaѵn
Cledyfal anwogaѵn.
Aeth dan eigẏaѵn.
Dan eigaѵn eithyd
Y geisiaѵ keluydyt.
A geisso keluydyt
Bit o iewin y vryt.
Eithyd oduch gѵynt.
Rѵg deu grifft ar hynt
Y welet dremynt.
Dremynt aweles
Pressent nẏ chymes.
Gѵeles ryfedaѵt.
Gorllin gan pyscaѵt.
A eidunѵys y ny vryt.
A gafas or byt.
A heuyt oe diwed
Gan duѵ trugared.

XXIX.

25. a.

     AD duѵ meidat duѵ dofydat dewin trugar.
Maѵr enwerys pan ym nodeist i trѵy tonyar.

Toruoed moessen gѡledic reen gѡae eu hescar.

Ys arganfu perif aelu reglyt y par.

Ac y voraѡc a orugost newyd y par.

Neur dineuѡy trѡy ryferthѡy a uaѡd adar.

Adrycheif heul hyt gollewein y bu dayar.

Ti a nodyd a rygeryd o pop karchar.

Namyn toruoed teryd eu gaѡr trѡm eu dear.

A naѡd ninheu rac adѡydeu uffern anwar.

Ad duѡ meidat duѡ dofydat dewin trugar.

Ys teu ti wlat nef. ys ѡrth tagnef it y kerẏ.

Nyt oes ludet nac eissywet yth wlat dofyd.

Nẏ pherir neb ny byd escar neb ẏѡ gilyd.

Mi a wẏdẏon beis deallѡn rac kewilyd.

Karu o honaѡt y lan trindaѡt o neb keluyd.

Beird ach gogan. ѡynt acharan yn tragywyd.

Nẏ bu agѡael y rodeist israel. yn llaѡ dauyd.

Alexander keffei llaѡer nifer y wyr.

Nyt ef nerthas onẏ chafas dy gerenhyd.

Ae vẏdinoed ae vaѡr gadeu ae gamluyd.

Pan doethant yr dayar buant dear eu dihenyd.

Selyf ygnat a gennis gѡlat. bu gѡell noc yd.

Mab teyrnon. bu gnaѡt berthon oe gyweithyd.

Iago feibon a uu verthon ar eu heluyd.

A dygymuant arannyssant trѡy eir dofyd.

Auel wirẏon a uu lѡydon a gymyrth ffyd.

Y vraѡt kaim bu diwerin drѡc y gussyl.

Aser a soyѡ yn awyr loyѡ eu kyweithyd.

Seren agel a dѡyn nifer rac eu milwyr.

A llath voessen ef ae toruoed ar eu heluyd.

Rudech dalen vd eilladem vd ei genhym.

Llafar amut a doeth a drut as diwygyd.

Gѡledic cѡd vn cѡd dirperyan dihenyd.

Molaf inheu pressѡyl toruoed adef menwyt.

Molaf inheu adaѡt goreu goreilenѡ byt.

Prif teyrnas a duc ionas o perued kyt.

Ki6da6t niniuen bu g6r llawen pregethyssit.

Riein tra mor bu kysca6t ior yscoryssit.

Ac auaria meir merch anna ma6r y phenyt.

Yr dy haeled a thrugared vechteyrn byt.

An b6ym ninheu ynef kaereu kynn6ys genhyt.

XXX.

Fol. 25. b. ⑥OLYCHAF wledic pendeuic g6lat ri.

Py ledas y pennaeth dros traeth muudi.

Bu kyweir karchar gweir ygkaer sidi.

Tr6y ebostol p6yll a phryderi.

Neb kyn noc ef nyt aeth idi.

Yr gad6yn tromlas kywirwas ae ketwi.

A rac preideu ann6fyn tost yt geni.

Ac yt ura6t paraha6t yn bard wedi.

Tri lloneit prytwen yd aetham ni idi.

Nam seith ny dyrreith o gaer sidi.

Neut 6yf glot geinmyn cerd o chlywir.

Igkaer pedryuan pedyr y chwelyt.

Ygkynneir or peir pan leferit.

O anadyl na6 mor6yn gochyneuit.

Neu peir pen ann6fyn p6y y vynut.

G6rym am y oror a mererit.

Ny beir6 b6yt ll6fyr ny rytyghit.

Cledyf lluch llea6c ida6 rydyrchit.

Ac yn lla6 lemina6c yd edewit.

A rac dr6s porth vffern llugyrn lloscit.

A phan aetham ni gan arthur trafferth lethrit.

Namyn seith ny dyrreith o gaer vedwit.

Neut 6yf glot geinmyn kerd glywana6r.

Igkaer pedryfan ynys pybyrdor.

Ech6yd a muchyd kymysgetor.

G6in gloy6 eu g6ira6t rac eu gorgord.

Tri lloneit prytwen yd aetham ni ar vor.

Namyn seith ny dyrreith o gaer rigor.

Ni obrynafi lawyr llen llywyadur

Tra chaer wydyr ny welsynt úrhyt arthur.

Tri vgeint canhúr a seui ar y mur.

Oed anhaúd ymadraúd ae gwylyadur.

Tri lloneit prytwen yd aeth gan arthur.

Namyn seith ny dyrreith o gaer golud.

Ny obrynaf y lawyr llaes eu kylchúy.

Ny údant úy py dyd peridyd púy.

Py aúr y meindyd y ganet cúy.

Púy gúnaeth ar nyt aeth doleu defúy.

Ny údant úy yr ych brych bras y penrúy.

Seith vgein kygúng yny aerúy.

A phan aetham ni gan arthir auyrdol gofúy.

Namyn seith ny dyrreith o gaer vandúy.

Ny obrynaf y lawyr llaes eu goheu.

Ny údant py dyd peridýd pen.

Py aúr y meindyd y ganet perchen.

Py vil a gatwant aryant y pen.

Pan aetham ni gan arthur afyrdúl gynhen.

Namyn seith ny dyrreith a gaer ochren.

Myneich dychnut val cunin cor.

O gyfranc udyd ae gúidan hor.

Ae vn hynt gúynt ae vn dúfyr mor.

Ae vn ufel tan túrúf diachor.

Myneych dychnut val bleidaúr.

O gyfranc udyd ae gúydyanhaúr

Ny údant pan yscar deweint a gúaúr.

Neu úynt púy hynt púy y rynnaúd.

Py va diua py tir a plaúd.

Bet sant yn diuant a bet allaúr.

Golychaf y wledic pendefic maúr.

Na búyf trist crist am gúadaúl.

XXXI

26. b.

ARŮYRE gŮyr katraeth gan dyd.
Am wledic gŮeith uudic gŮarthegyd.
Vryen hŮn anwaŮt eineuyd.
Kyfedeily teyrned ae gofyn
Ryfelgar. rŮysc enwir rŮyf bedyd.
GŮyr prÿdein adŮythein yn lluyd.
GŮen ystrat ystadyl kat kynygyd.
Ny nodes na maes na choedyd
Tut achles dyormes pan dyuyd.
Mal tonnaŮr tost eu gaŮr dros eluyd.
GŮelais wyr gŮychyr yn lluyd.
A gŮedÿ boregat briŮgic.
Gweleis i tŮrŮf teirffin traghedic.
GŮaed gohoyŮ gofaran gochlywid
Yn amŮyn gŮen ystrat y gŮelit
Gofur hag agŮyr llaŮr lludedic.
Yn drŮs ryt gŮeleis ÿ wyr lletrudÿon.
Eiryf dillŮg y rac blaŮyr gofedon.
Vnynt tanc gan aethant golludyon.
LlaŮ ygcroes gryt y gro garanwynyon.
KyfedŮynt y gynrein kyŮyn don.
GŮanecaŮr gollychynt raŮn eu kaffon.
GŮeleis i wyr gospeithic gospylat.
A gŮyar a uaglei ar dillat.
A dulliaŮ diaflym dŮys Ůrth kat
Kat gŮortho ny buffo pan pŮyllatt
GlyŮ reget reuedaf i pan ueidat.
GŮeleis i ran reodic am vryen.
Pan amŮyth ae alon. yn llech wen
Galystem. y Ůytheint oed llafyn
AessaŮr gŮyr goborthit Ůrth aghen.
Awyd kat a diffo eurwyn.

Ac yny vallⱱyf y hen
Ym dygyn agheu aghen.
Ny bydif yn dirwen.
Na molⱱyf i vryen.

XXXII.

VRYEN yr echⱱyd.
Haelaf dyn bedyd.
Lliaⱱs a rodyd
Y dynyon eluyd.
Mal y kynnullyd
Yt wesceryd.
Llawen beird bedyd
Tra vo dy uuchyd.
Ys mⱱy llewenyd
Gan clotuan clotryd.
Ys mⱱy gogonyant
Vot vryen ae plant.
Ac ef yn arbennic
Yn oruchel wledic.
Yn dinas pellennic.
Yn keimyat kynteic
Lloegrⱱys ae gⱱydant
Pan ymadrodant.
Agheu a gaⱱssant.
A mynych godyant.
Llosci eu trefret
Adⱱyn eu tudet
Ac eunⱱnc collet
A maⱱr aghyffret
Heb gaffel gⱱaret.
Rac vryen reget.
Reget diffreidyat
Clot ior agor gⱱlat

Vy mod yssd arnat.
O pop erclywat
Dỽys dy peleitrat.
Pan erclywat kat.
Kat pan y kyrchynt
Gỽnyeith awneit
Tan yn tei kyn dyd
Rac vd yr echỽyd.
Yr echỽyd teccaf
Ae dynyon haelhaf.
Gnaỽt eigyl heb waessaf.
Am teyru gleỽhaf.
Gleỽhaf eissyllyd
Tydi goreu yssyd.
Or a uu ac auyd
Nyth oes kystedlyd.
Pan dremher arnaỽ
Ys ehalaeth y braỽ.
Gnaỽt gỽyled ym danaỽ
Am teyrn gocnaỽ.
Am danaỽ gỽyled.
A lliaỽs maranhed
Eu teyrn gogled
Arbenhic teyrned.
Ac yn y vallỽyf hen
Ym dygyn agheu aghen.
Ni bydif ym dirwen
Na molỽyfi vryen.

XXXIII.

Fol. 27. b.

ᗄGGORFFOWYS
Can rychedỽys
Parch ach vinnỽys.
A med meuedỽys.

Meuedɥys med
Y oruoled
A chein tired
Imi yn ryfed.
Aryfed maɥr
Ac eur ac aɥr.
Ac aɥr achet
Achyfriuet
Achyfriuyant.
A rodi chwant.
Chwant oe rodi
Yr vy llochi.
Yt lad yt gryc
Yt vac yt vyc.
Yt vyc yt vac
Yt lad yn rac.
Racwed rothit
Y veird y byt.
Byt yn geugant
Itti yt wedant
ɥrth dy ewyllis.
Duɥ ryth peris
Rieu ygnis
Rac ofyn dybris.
Annogyat kat
Diffreidyat gɥlat.
Gvlat diffreidyat.
Kat annogyat.
Gnaɥt am danat
Tɥrɥf pystylat.
Pystalat tɥrɥf
Ac yuet cɥrɥf.
Kɥrɥf oe yfet
A chein trefret

A chein tudet
Imi ryanllofet.
Llȯyfenyd van.
Ac eirch achlan
Yn vn trygan
Maȯr a bychan
Taliessin gan
Tidi ae didan.
Ys tidi goreu
Or a gigleu
Y ȯrd lideu.
Molaf inheu
Dy weithredeu.
Ac yny vallȯyf hen
Ym dygyn agheu aghen.
Ni bydif ym dirwen
Na molȯyf vryen.

XXXIV.

. 28. a.

AR vn blyned
Vn yn darwed
Gȯin a mȧll a med
A gȯrhyt diassed
Ac eilewyd gorot.
A heit am vereu
Ae pen ffuneu
Ae tec gȯydua eu
Ei paȯb oe wyt
Dyfynt ymplymnȯyt.
Ae varch y danaȯ
Yg godeu gȯeith mynaȯ.
A chwanec anaȯ
Bud am li am laȯ.
ȯyth vgein vn lliȯ

O loi a biʋ.
Biʋ blith ac ychen
A phop kein agen
Ny bydʋn lawen
Bei lleas vryen.
Ys cu kyn eithyd
Yeis kygryn kygryt.
A briger meu olchet
Ac elor y dyget
A gran gʋy ar llet
Am waet gʋyr gonodet.
A gʋr bʋrr bythic.
A uei wedʋy wreic
Am ys gʋin ffeleic
Am ys gʋin mynyc gyltʋn.
Am sorth am porth am pen
Kyn na phar kyfʋyrein.
Kymaran tauaʋ
Gʋas y drʋs gʋarandaʋ
Py trʋst ae dayar a gryn
Ae mor a dugyn.
Dy gʋynyc ychyngar ʋrth y pedyt.
Ossit vch ymryn
Neut vryen ae gryn.
Ossit uch ym pant
Neut vryen ae gʋant.
Ossit vch y mynyd
Neud vryen a oruyd.
Ossit vch yn riʋ
Neut vryen ae briʋ.
Ossit vch ygclaʋd
Neut vryen a blaʋd.
Vch nynt vch as
Vch ympop kamas.

Nac vn treѵ na deu

Ny naѵd y rac eu.

Ny bydei ar newyn

A phreideu yn y gylchyn.

Gorgoryaѵc gorllassaѵc gorlassar.

Eil agheu oed y par.

Yn llad y escar.

Ac yny vallѵyfi hen

Ym dygyn agheu aghen.

Ni bydif ym dyrwen.

Na molѵyf vryen.

XXXV.

GѵEITH ARGOET LLѵYFEIN. KANU VRYEN.

Fol. 28. b.   BORE Duѵ sadѵrn kat uaѵr a uu.

Or pan dѵyre heul hyt pan gynnu.

Dygryssѵys flamdѵyn yn petwar llu.

Godeu a reget y ymdullu.

Dyuѵy o argoet hyt ar vynyd.

Ny cheffynt eiryos hyt yr vndyd.

Atorelwis flamdѵyn vaѵr trebystaѵt.

A dodynt yggѵystlon a ynt paraѵt.

Ys attebѵys. owein dѵyrein ffossaѵt.

Nyt dodynt nyt ydynt nyt ynt paraѵt.

A cheneu vab coel bydei kymѵyaѵc.

Leѵ kyn astalei oѵystyl nebaѵt.

Atorelѵis vryen vd yr echѵyd.

O byd ymgyfaruot am garenhyd.

Dyrchafѵn eidoed oduch mynyd.

Ac amporthѵn ѵyneb oduch emyl.

A gyrchafѵn peleidyr oduch pen gѵyr.

A chyrchѵn fflamdѵyn yn y luyd.

A lladѵn ac ef ae gyweithyd.

A rac góeith argoet llóyfein
Bu llawer kelein.
Rudei vrein rac ryfel góyr.
A góerin a grÿssóys gan einewyd.
Arinaf y blóydyn nat óy kynnyd.
Ac yny vallóyf y hen
Ym dygyn agheu aghen.
Ny bydif ym dyrwen
Na molóyf vryen.

XXXVI.

Fol. 29. a. ARDÓYRE reget rysed rieu.
Neu ti rygosteis kyn bóyf teu.
Gnissynt kat lafnaór a chat vereu.
Gnissynt wyr ydan kylchóyaór. lleeu
Goóy góyn góylein ymathren
Ny mat vróytióyt. ri nÿ mat geu
Yd ymarmerth góledic órth kymryeu.
Nys gyrr neges y geissaton
Gochaón marchaóc móth molut góryon.
O dreic dylaó adaó doethaó don.
Yn y doeth vlph yn treis ar y alon.
Hyny doeth vryen yn edyd yn aeron.
Ny bu kyfergyryat ny bu gynnóys.
Talgynaót vryen y rac powys
Ny bu hyfrót brót echen gyrróys
Hyueid a gododin a lleu towys.
Deór yn emnyned a theith góyduóys
Diueuyl dydóyn ygóaet góyden.
A weles llóyuenyd. vdyd kygryn.
Yn eidoed kyhoed yn eil mehyn
Kat yn ryt alclut kat ym ynuer.
Kat gellaór breóyn. kat hireurur.
Kat ym prysc katleu kat yn aberioed

Y dygyfranc a dur breuer ma6r
Kat glutuein g6eith pen coet
Ll6yth llithya6c cun ar ormant g6aet.
Atueila6 g6yn gouchyr kyt mynan
Eigyl edyl g6rthryt.
Lletrud a gyfranc ac vlph yn ryt
G6ell ganher g6ledic pyr y ganet y vd.
Prydein pen perchen broestla6n y vd.
Nyt ymduc dillat na glas na ga6r
Na choch nac ehoec vyc mor lla6r.
Nyt ardodes y vord6yt dros vael maela6r
Veirch o genedyl vrych mor greidia6l.
Haf ydan ayaf ac araf yn lla6.
A ryt a rotwyd eu har6yla6.
A g6est y dan geird ac ymd6yra6.
Ac hyt orffen byt edrywyt ka6.
Gofydin goyscub. dyha6l am del6
Dile6r am leuuereu. neu vi erthycheis
Yneis rac h6yd peleidyr ar ysc6yd.
Ysc6yt yn lla6 godeu a reget yn ymdullya6.
Neu vi a weleis 6r yn buartha6.
Sarff soned virein segidyd la6r.
Neu vi gog6n ryfel yd argolla6r.
Ar meint a goll6yf y argolla6r.
Neu vi neu ym gor6yth medu medlyn
Gan hyfeid hy6r hy6st dilyn
Neu vi neu yscenhedeis kysca6t g6eithen
Dithrych6ys vy rieu radeu lawen
G6asca g6lat da. 6rth uru6yn.
Ac yny vall6yf y hen
Ym dygyn agheu aghen.
Ny bydif ym dirwen
Na mol6yf vryen.

XXXVII.

YSPEIL TALIESSIN. KANU VRYEN.

Fol. 29. b.

ЄG gỿrhyt gogyfeirch yntrafferth
Gỿaetỿf awellỿyf ynkerth
Wir. gỿeleis i rac neb nym gỿeles
Pop annỿyl. ef diwyl y neges.
Gỿeleis i pasc am leu am lys.
Gỿeleis i deil o dy fyn adowys.
Gỿeleis i keig kyhafal y blodeu.
Neur welcis vd haelhaf y dedueu.
Gỿeleis i lyỿ katraeth tra maeu
Bit vy nar nỿyhachar kymryeu
Gỿerth vy nat maỿr uyd y uud y radeu
Pen maon milwyr amde.
Preid lydan pren onhyt yỿ vy awen gỿen
Yscỿydaỿr y rac glyỿ gloyỿ glasgỿen
Gleỿ ryhaỿt gleỿhaf vn yỿ vryen.
Nym gorseif gỿarthegyd. gordear
Goryaỿc gorlassaỿc gorlassar goriag a gordỿyre.
Pop rei sag dileỿ du merwyd y mordei
Vd tra blaỿd yn yd eloth vod.
Vared melynaỿr yn neuad
Maranhedaỿc. diffreidaỿc yn aeron.
Maỿr y wyn y anyant. ac eilon
Maỿr dyfal ial am y alon.
Maỿr gỿrneth ystlyned ẏ vrython.
Mal rot tanhỿydin dros eluyd.
Mal ton teithiaỿc llỿyfenyd.
Mal kathyl kyfliỿ gỿen a gỿeithen.
Val mor mỿynuaỿr yỿ vryen.
Vn y egin echangryt gỿaỿr.
Vn yỿ rieu rỿyfyadur a dyaỿr.
Vn yỿ maon meirch mỿth miledaỿr.

Dechreu mei ympowys bydmaỽr.
Vn yỽ yn deuỽy pan ofỽy y werin.
Eryr tir tuhir tythremyn.
Adunsỽn y ar orỽyd ffysciolin
Tut ynyeil gỽerth yspeil taliessin.
Vn yỽ gỽrys gỽrs llaỽr a gorỽyd.
Vn yỽ breyr benffyc y arglwyd.
Vn yỽ hydgre hyd yn diuant.
Vn yỽ bleid banadlaỽc anchwant.
Vn yỽ gỽlat vab eginyr.
Ac ỽnwed a vnsỽn katua ketwyr
Vnsỽn y drỽc yieaian.
A cheneu a nud hael a hirwlat y danaỽ.
Ac os it ytỽydif ym gỽen.
Ef gỽneif beird byt yn llawen.
Kyn mynhỽyf meirỽ meib gỽyden
Gỽaladyr gỽaed gỽenwlat ỽryen.

XXXVIII.

l. 30. a.

EN enỽ gỽledic nef gorchordyon.
Rychanaut rychỽynant y dragon.
Gỽrthodes gogyfres gỽelydon
Lliaỽs run a nudd anỽython.
Ny golychaf an gnaỽt beird o vrython.
Ryfed hael o sywyd sywedyd.
Vn lle rygethlyd rygethlic
Rydysyfaf rychanaf y wledic.
Yny wlat yd oed ergrynic
Nym gỽnel nys gỽnaf ec newic
Anhaỽd diollỽg aỽdloed
Ny diffyc y wledic ny omed.
O edrych aỽdyl trỽm teyrned
Yn y uyỽ nys deubyd bud bed.
Ny dygonont hoffed oe buchynt.

O

Kaletach yr arteith hael hynt.
Toryf pressennaѵl tra phrydein
Tra phryder rygohoyѵ rylyccraѵr
Rylyccrer. rytharnaѵr rybarnaѵr.
Rybarn paѵb y gѵr banher
Ae ninat yn ygnat ac eluet.
Nyr y gѵr dilaѵ y daeret
Gѵas greit a gѵrhyt gotraet.
Er eichaѵc gѵallaѵc yn llywet.
Hѵyrwedaѵc gѵallaѵc artebet.
Ny ofyn y neb a wnech ud
Neut ym vd nac neut ych darwerther
Teѵued yn diwed haf.
Nys kynnyd namyn chwech.
Chwechach it gynan o hynnyd
Chwedlaѵc trѵydedaѵc traeth dyd.
Terned y gѵned nѵys med mat
Tebic heul haf huenyd soned gan mѵyhaf
Kenhaf gan doeth y gan llu eilassaf
Bint bydi derwyt bryt haf pryt mab
Lleenaѵc lliaѵc. hamgѵrѵl gѵnn
Gѵaѵl gѵnn gѵres. tarth gѵres gwres tarth
Tragynnis yd eghis heb warth.
Cleda cledifa cledifarch.
Nyt am tyrr y lu yledrat.
Nyt amescut y gaѵ y kywlat.
Tyllynt tal yscѵydaѵr rac talen y veirch.
O march trѵst moryal. rith car riallu
Gѵynaѵc ri gѵystlant gѵeiryd goludaѵc
O gaer glut hyt gaer garadaѵc.
Ystadyl tir penprys a gѵallaѵc
Teyrned teѵrn tagѵedaѵc.

XXXIX.

DADOLÚCH VRYEN.

LLEU uyd echassaf
Mi nyѵ dirmygaf.
Vryen a gyrchaf.
Idaѵ yt ganaf.
Pan del vygwaessaf.
Kynnѵys a gaffaf.
Ar parth goreuhaf.
Y dan eilassaf.
Nyt maѵr ym daѵr
Byth gѵeheleith awelaf.
Nyt af attadunt ganthunt ny bydaf.
Ny chyrchafi gogled
Ar mei teyrned.
Kyn pei am lawered
Y gѵnelѵn gyghѵystled.
Nyt reit im hoffed.
Vryen nym gomed.
Llwyfenyd tired
Ys meu eu reufed.
Ys meu y gѵyled.
Ys meu y llared.
Ys meu y deliden
Ae gorefrasseu
Med o uualeu
A da dieisseu
Gan teyrn goreu.
Haelaf rygigleu.
Teyrned pop ieith
It oll ydynt geith.
Ragot yt gѵynir ys dir dyoleith.

Kyt ef mynassỽn
Gỽeyhelu henỽn.
Nyt oed well a gerỽn.
Kyn ysgỽybydỽn.
Weithon ygỽelaf
Y meint a gaffaf.
Namyn y duỽ vchaf
Nys dioferaf.
Dy teyrn veibon
Haelaf dynedon.
Ỽy kanan eu hyscyrron
Yn tired eu galon.
Ac yn y vallỽyfi hen
Ym dygyn agheu aghen
Ny bydaf ym dirwen
Na molỽyfi vryen.

XL.

MARỼNAT EROF.

Fol. 31. a.

YMCHOELES eluyd
Val nos yn dyd.
O dyfot clotryd
Ercỽlff pen bedyd.
Ercỽlff a dywedei.
Agheu nas riuei.
Yscỽydaỽr y mordei
Arnaỽ a torrei.
Ercỽlf sywessyd
Ermin lloergegyd.
Pedeir colofyn kyhyt
Rudeur ar eu hyt.
Colofneu ercỽlf
Nys arueid bygỽl.

Bygúl nys beidei.
Gres heul nys gadei.
Nyt aeth neb is nef
Hyt yd aeth ef.
Ercúlf mur ffossaút.
As amdut tywaút.
As rodúy trindaút
Trugared dyd braút
Yn vndaút heb eisseu.

XLI.

☥ADAÚC mur menwyt.
Madaúc kyn bu bed.
Bu dinas edryssed.
O gamp a chymúed.
Mab vthyr kyn lleas
Oe laú dy úystlas.
Dybu erof greulaún.
Llewenyd anwogaún.
Tristyt anwogaún.
A oryú erof greulaún.
Brattau iessu
Ac ef yn credu.
Dayar yn crynu
Ac eluyd yn gardu.
A chyscoc ar ybyt
A bedyd ar gryt
Llam anwogaún
A oryú erof creulaún.
Mynet yn y trefyn
Ym plith oer gethern
Hyt yg waelaút vffern.

XLII.

MARƲNAT CORROI M. DAYRY.

Fol. 31. b.   DY ffynhaƲn lydan dylleinƲ aches.
DydaƲ dyhebcyr dy bris dybrys.
MarƲnat corroy am kyffroes.
Oer deni gƲr garƲ y anƲyteu.
A oed voy y drwc nys maƲr gicleu
Mab dayry dalei lyƲ ar vor deheu
Dathyl oed y glot kyn noe adneu.
Dy ffynhaƲn lydan delleinƲ nonneu.
DydaƲ dyhebcyr dybrys dybreu.
MarƲnat corroy genhyf inheu.
Oer deni.
Dy ffynhawn lydan dylleinƲ dyllyr.
Dy saeth dychyrch traeth diuƲg dybyr.
GƲr a werescyn maƲr y varanres.
A wedy mynaƲ mynet trefyd.
A —ant Ʋy ffres ffra wynyonyd.
Tra uu uudugere bore dugraƲr.
Chwedleu am gƲydir owir hytlaƲr.
Kyfranc corroi a chocholyn.
LliaƲs eu teruysc am eu teruyn.
Tardei pen amwern gwerin goaduƲyn.
Kaer y sy gulƲyd ny gƲyd ny grin.
GƲyn y vyt yr eneit ae harobryn.

XLIII.

MARƲNAT DYLAN EIL TON.
TAL. AE CANT.

Fol. 32. a.   VN duƲ uchaf dewin doethaf mƲyhaf aued
Py delis maes pƲy ae sƲynas ynllaƲ trahael.
Neu gynt noc ef. pƲy uu tagnef ar redyf gefel.

Gᴕrthrif gᴕastraᴕt gᴕenᴕyn awnaeth gᴕeith gᴕythloned.
Gᴕanu dylan. adᴕythic lann. treis yn hytyruer.
Ton iwerdon. a thon vanaᴕ. a thon ogled.
A thon prydein toruoed virein yn petweïred.
Golychafi tat duᴕ douydat gᴕlat heb omed.
Creaᴕdyr celi an kynnᴕys ni yn trugared.

XLIV.

Marᴕnat owein.

Fol. 32. a. **E**NEIT owein ap vryen. gobᴕyllit y ren oe reit.
Reget ud ae cud tromlas. nyt oed vas y gywydeit.
Iscell kerdglyt cloduaᴕr escyll gaᴕr gᴕayawaᴕr llifeit.
Cany cheffir kystedlyd. y vd llewenyd llatreit.
Medel galon geueilat. eissillut y tat ae teit.
Pan ladaᴕd owein fflamdᴕyn. nyt oed uᴕy noc et
        kysceit.
Kyscit lloegyr llydau nifer a leuuer yn eu llygeit.
A rei ny ffoynt hayach. a oedynt ach no reit
Owein ae cospes yn drut mal cnut. yn dylut deueit.
Gᴕr gᴕiᴕ uch y amliᴕ seirch. a rodei veirch y eircheit.
Kyt as cronyei mal calet. ny rannet rac y eneit
Eneit o. ap Vryen.

XLV.

Fol. 32. b. **E**CHRYS ynys gᴕaᴕt hu ynys gᴕrys gobetror.
Mon mat goge gᴕrhyt eruei. menei y dor.
Lleweis wiraᴕt gᴕin a bragaᴕt gan vraᴕt escor.
Teyrn wofrᴕy diwed pop rᴕyf rewinetor.
Tristlaᴕn deon yr archaedon kan rychior.
Nyt uu nyt vi ygkymelri y gyfeissor.
Pan doeth aedon. o wlat wytyon seon teᴕdor.
Gᴕenᴕyn pyr doeth pedeir pennoeth meinoeth tymhor
Kᴕydynt kyfoet ny bu clyt coet gᴕynt ygohor.

Math ac euuyd. hutᵥyt geluyd ryd eluinor.

Y myᵥ gᵥytyon ac amaethon. at oed kyghor.

Tᵥll tal y rodaᵥc ffyryf ffodiaᵥc. ffyryf diachor.

Katarn gygres y varanres ny bu werthuor.

Katarn gyfed ym pop gorsed gᵥnelit y vod.

Cu kynaethᵥy hyt tra uᵥyf uyᵥ kyr bᵥylletor.

Am bᵥyfi gan grist. hyt na bᵥyf trist ran ebostol.

Hael archaedon gan egylyon. cynᵥyssetor.

Ꞓ CHRYS ynys gᵥaᵥt huynys gᵥrys gochyma.

Y rac budwas. kymry dinas. aros ara.

Draganaᵥl ben priodaᵥr perchen ymretonia.

Difa gᵥledic or bendefic ae tu terra.

Pedeir morᵥyn wedy eu cᵥyn dygnaᵥt eu tra.

Erdygnaᵥt wir ar vor heb ar tir hir eu trefra.

Oe wironyn na digonyn dim gofettra.

Kerydus ᵥyf na chyrbᵥyllᵥyf am rywnel da.

Y lᵥrᵥ lywy pᵥy gᵥahardᵥy pᵥy attrefna.

Y lᵥrᵥ aedon pᵥy gynheil mon mᵥyn gowala.

Am bᵥyfi gan grist hyt na bᵥyf trist o drᵥc o da.

Ran trugared y wlat ried buched gyfa.

XLVI

Fol. 33. a.

ꝳ YDᵥYF taliessin deryd

Gᵥaᵥt godolaf vedyd.

Bedyd rᵥyd rifeden eidolyd.

Kyfrᵥnc allt ac allt ac echᵥyd.

Ergrynaᵥr cunedaf creisseryd.

Ygkaer weir achaer liwelyd.

Ergrynaᵥt kyfatᵥt kyfergyr.

Kyfanwanec tan tra myr

Ton. llu paᵥt gleᵥ y gilyd.

Kan kafas y wheluch eluyd.

Mal vcheneit gᵥynt ᵥrth onwyd.

Kefynderchyn y gón y gyfyl
Kyfachetwyn a choelyn kerenhyd.
Góiscant veird kywrein kanonhyd.
Maró cunedaf a góynaf a góynit.
Cóynitor teódor teódun diarchar.
Dychyfal dychyfun dyfynveis.
Dyfyngleis dychyfun.
Ymadraód códedaód caletlóm.
Kaletach órth elyn noc ascórn.
Ys kynyal cunedaf kyn kywys
A thytwet. y óyneb a gatwet
Kanweith cyn bu lleith dorglóyt.
Dychludent wyr bryneich ym pymlóyt.
Ef canet rac y ofyn ae arsóyt oergerdet.
Kyn bu dayr dogyn y dóet.
Heit haual am óydwal gónebróyt.
Góeinaó góaeth llyfred noc adóyt.
Adoet hun dimyaó a góynaf
Am lys am grys cunedaf
Am ryaflaó hallt am hydyruer mor.
Am breid afórn a ballaf.
Góaót veird a ogon a ogaf.
Ac ereill arefon arifaf.
Ryfedaór yn erulaód a naó cant goróyd.
Kyn kymun cuneda.
Rymafei bió blith yr haf.
Rymafei edystraót y gayaf.
Rymafei win gloyó ac oleó.
Rymafei torof keith rac vntreó.
Ef dyfal o gressur o gyfleó góeladur.
Pennadur pryt lleó lludóy uedei gywlat
Rac mab edern kyn edyrn anaeleó.
Ef dywal diarchar diedig.
Am ryfreu agheu dychyfyg.

Ef goborthi aes yman regoraͷl
Gͷir gͷraͷl oed y vnbyn.
Dymhun a chyfatam a thal gͷin
Kamda. diua hun o goelig.

XLVII.

DYGOGAN awen dygobryssyn.
Maranhed ameuued a hed genhyn.
A phennaeth ehalaeth a ffraeth vnbyn.
A gͷedy dyhed anhed ym pop mehyn.
Seith meib o veli dyrchafyssyn.
Kaswallͷn alludd a chestudyn.
Diwed plo coll iago o tir prydͷn.
Gͷlat uerͷ dyderuyd hyt valaon.
Lluddedic eu hoelyon ym deithic eu hafͷyn.
Gͷlat wehyn vargotyon.
Kollaͷt kymry oll eu haelder.
Ynrygystlyned o pennaeth weisson.
Rydybyd llyminaͷc
A uyd gͷr chwannaͷc
   Y werescyn mon
A rewinyaͷ gͷyned.
Oe heithaf oe pherued.
Oe dechreu oe diwed.
   A chymryt y gͷystlon.
Ystic y ͷyneb
Nyt estͷg y neb
   Na chymry na saesson.
Dydaͷ gͷr o gͷd
A wna kyfamrud.
   A chat y gynhon.
Arall a dyfyd
Pellenaͷc y luyd
   Llewenyd y vrython.

XLVIII.

MARŵNAT VTHYR PEN.

Fol. 34. a.

ĦEU vi luossaŵc yntrydar.
Ny pheidŵn rŵg deulu heb ŵyar.
Neu vi a elwir gorlassar.
Vygwreys bu enuys ym hescar.
Neu vi tywyssaŵc yn tywyll
Am rithŵy am dŵy pen kawell.
Neu vi eil kawyl yn ardu.
Ny pheidŵn heb ŵyar rŵg deulu.
Neu via amuc vy achlessur.
Yn difant a charant casnur.
Neur ordyfneis i waet am ŵythur.
Cledyfal hydyr rac meibon caŵrnur.
Neu vi araunŵys vy echlessur.
Naŵuetran yg gŵrhyt arthur.
Neu vi a torreis cant kaer.
Neu vi aledeis cant maer.
Neu vi arodeis cant llen.
Neu vi aledeis cant pen.
Neu vi arodeis i henpen.
Cledyfaŵr goruaŵr gyghallen.
Neu vi oreu terenhyd
Hayarndor edeithor penmynyd.
Ym gŵeduit ym gofit. hydyr oed gyhir.
Nyt oed vyt ny bei fy eissillyd.
Midŵyf bard moladŵy yghywreint.
Poet y gan vrein ac eryr ac ŵytheint.
Auacdu ae deubu y gymeint.
Pan ymbyrth petrywyr rŵg dŵy geint.
Drigyaŵ y nef oed ef vychwant.
Rac eryr rac ofyn amheirant.
ŵyf bard ac ŵyf telynaŵr.

Ỽyf pibyd ac Ỽyf crythaỼr.
Seith vgein kerdaỼr dygoruaỼr
Gyghallen. bu kalch vri vriniat.
Hu escyll edeinat.
Dy vab dy veirdnat
Dy veir dewndat.
Vyn tauaỼt y traethu vy marỼnat.
Handit o meinat gỼrth glodyat
Byt pryt prydein huyscein ymhỼyllat.
GỼledic nef ygkennadeu nam doat.

XLIX.

Fol. 34. b.

KEIN gyfedỼch
Y am deulỼch
  LlỼch am pleit.
Pleit am gaer.
Kaer yn ehaer
  Ry yscrifyat
Virein ffo racdaỼ.
Ar lleg kaỼ
  MỼyedic uein
Dreic amgyffreu.
O duch lleeu
  Llestreu llat.
Llat yn eurgyrn.
Eurgyrn yn llaỼ.
  LlaỼ yn ysci.
Ysci ymodrydaf
Uur ythiolaf
  Budic veli
Amhanogan. ri
RygeidỼ y teithi.
Ynys vel veli
TeithiaỼc oed idi.

Pymp pennaeth dimbi

O ỽydyl ffichti

O pechadur kadeithi

O genedyl ysci.

Pymp. ereill dymgoi

O nordmyn mandi.

Whechet ryfedri.

O heu hyt vedi.

Seithuet o heni

Y weryt dros li.

Ỽythuet lin x a dyui

Nyt llỽyded escori.

Gynt gỽaed venni.

Galwaỽr eryri

Anhaỽd ỿ deui.

Iolỽn eloi

Pan ynbo gan geli

Adef nef dimbi.

L.

Fol. 34. b.

RYDYRCHAFỽy duỽ ar plỽyf brython

Arỽyd lleỽenyd lluyd o von.

Kyfryssed gỽyned brys gorchordyon.

Ffaỽ claer o pop aer kaffael gỽystlon.

Powys dybydant dỽys ygkyfleudon.

Gỽyr goruyn gorynt ar eu deduon.

Deulu yd aut bydant gysson.

Yn vn redyf vn eir kyweir kymon.

Kyfranant yn iaỽn keredigiaỽn vaon.

Pan welych wyr ryn am lyn aeron.

Pan vo trỽm tywi a theiui auon.

Ỽy gỽnant aer ar vrys am lys lonyon.

A geunis adewis yn orllỽython.

Nỿ nothỽy dinass oed rac yr ỽython.

Dynclut. dyn maerut dyn daryfoɲ.

Nyt oed lᴠyr degyn dyn riedon

Pan dyfu gatwallaᴠn

Dros eigyaᴠn iwerdon.

Yd atrefnᴠys nefᴠy yn ardnefon.

Keinyadon moch clyᴠyf eu gofalon.

Marchaᴠc lu mor taer am gaer llion.

A dial idwal ar aranwynẏon.

A gᴠare pelre a phen saesson.

Ys trabludyo y gath vreith ae haghyfieithon.

O ryt ar taradyr hyt ym porth ᴠygyr y moɲ.

Ieuanc didᴠynas dinas maon.

Or pan amygir mel a meillon.

Gadent eu hamrydar ae hamrysson.

Nyt diᴠystyl godi dic ᴠrth alon.

Rydyrchafᴠy duᴠ ar plᴠyf brython.

LI.

TRINDAᴠT tragywyd

A oreu eluyd.

A gᴠedy eluyd

Adaf yn geluyd.

A gᴠedy adaf.

Day goreu eua.

Yr israel bendigeit

A oreu murgreit.

Gᴠrd y gyrbᴠylleit.

Glan y gywydeit.

Deudec tref yr israel dᴠyrein gywychafael.

Deudec meib yr israel a oreu duᴠ hael.

Deudec meib yr israel buant gytuaeth.

Deudec du dinam. teir mam ae maeth.

Vn gᴠr ae creᴠys creaᴠdyr ae gᴠnaeth.

Mal y gᴠna a vynho a uo pennaeth.

Deudeg meib yr israel a wnaeth culꝺyd.
Mal y gꝺna a vynho a uo arglꝺyd.
Deudec meib yr israel a wnaeth dofyd.
Mal y gꝺna a vynho a vo keluyd.
Deudec meib yr israel dymgofu
O ganhat iessu.
Ac vn tat ae bu
Atheir mam udu.
O nadu y doeth rat
Ac eissydyd mat.
A meir mat great.
A christ vy nerthat.
Arglꝺyd pop gꝺenwlat.
A alwaf a eilꝺ pop ryd.
Hu bo vyg hynnyd.
Genhyt gerenhyd.

LII.

GꝺAꝺT LUD Y MAꝺR.

Fol. 35. b.

KATHYL goreu gogant
ꝺyth nifer nodant.
Duꝺ llun dybydant
Peithiaꝺc ydant.
Duꝺ maꝺrth y trannant.
Gꝺyth yn yscarant.
Duꝺ merchyr medant
Ryodres rychwant.
Duꝺ ieu escorant
Eidyolyd anchwant.
Duꝺ gꝺener dyd gormant.
Yg waet gꝺyr gonofant.
Duꝺ sadꝺrn .   .   .   .

Duÿ sul yn geugant
Diheu dybydant.
Pymp llong a phym cant
Oranant oniant
O brithi brithoi
Nuoes nuedi
Brithi brithanhai.
Sychedi edi euroi
Eil coet cogni
Antared dÿmbi.
Paÿb y adonai
Ar weryt pÿmpai.
Darofum darogan
Gÿaed hir rac gorman.
Hir kyhoed kyghan.
Katwaladyr a chynan.
Byt budyd bychan.
Difa gÿres huan.
Dysgogan deruyd
Auu auudyd.
Ÿybyr geironyd
Kerd aÿn y genhyd.
Ÿylhaÿt eil echÿyd
Yn torroed mynyd.
Ban beu llaÿn hyd.
Brython ar gyghyr.
Y vrython dymbi
Gÿaet gÿned ofri.
Guedy eur ac eurynni.
Diffeith moni a lleenni.
Ac eryri anhed yndi.
Dyscogan perffeith
Anhed ym diffeith.
Kymry pedeir ieith.

Symudant eu hareith.
Yt y vi y uuch y uuch vreith
A wnaho góynyeith.
Meindyd brefaót.
Meinoeth beróhaót.
Ar tir beróhodaór
Yn llogoed yssadaór.
Kathyl góae canhator
Kylch prydein amgor.
Dedeuant vn gyghor
Y órthot góarthmor.
Boet góir vennhryt
Dragóynaól byt.
Dolóys dolhóyc kyt
Dolaethóy eithyt.
Kynran llaón yt
Gyfarch kynut
Heb eppa heb henuonha.
Heb ofur byt.
Byt auyd diffeith dyreit.
Kogeu tyghettor.
Hoyówed tróy groywed.
Góyr bychein bron otóyllyd.
Toruennhaól tuth iolyd.
Hóedyd ar vedyd
Ny wan cyllellaór cledyfaór meiwyr.
Nyt oed udu y puchyssón
Anaó angerdaól trefdyn.
Ac y wyr kared creudyn.
Kymry eigyl góydyl prydyn.
Kymry kyfret ac ascen.
Dygedaór góydueirch ar llyn.
Gogled o wenóynuyd o hermyn.
O echlur caslur caslyn.

P

O echen adaf henyn.
Dygedaŵr trydŵ y gychwyn
Branes o goscord gŵyrein.
Meryd milet seithin
Ar vor agor ar cristin.
Vch o vor vch o vynyd.
Vch o vor ynyal ebryn.
Coet maes tyno abryn.
Pop araŵt heb erglyŵaŵ nebaŵt
O vynaŵc o pop mehyn.
Yt vi brithret
A lliaŵs gyniret.
A gofut am wehyn.
Dialeu trŵy hoyŵ gredeu bressŵÿlo
Godi creaŵdyr kyfoethaŵc duŵ vrdin.
Pell amser kyn no dyd braŵt
Y daŵ diwarnaŵt.
A dŵyrein darlleaŵr
Teruyn tiryon tir iwerdon.
Y prydein yna y daŵ datŵyrein.
Brython o vonhed rufein.
Ambi barnodyd o aghygres dieu.
Dysgogan sywedydyon
Ygŵlat y colledigyon.
Dysgogan deruydon
Tra mor tra brython.
Haf ny byd hinon.
Bythaŵt breu breyryon.
Ae deubyd o gŵanfret
Tra merin tat ket.
Mil ym braŵt prydein vrdin.
Ac yam gyffŵn kyffin.
Na chŵyaf ygoglyt gŵern
Gŵerin gŵaelotwed uffern.

Ergrynaf kyllestric kaen
Gan wledic gꝺlat anorffen.

LIII.

Fol. 36. b.

Y̶N wir dymbi romani kar.
Odit o vab dyn arall y par.
Rac daꝺ ryglyꝺhaꝺr maꝺ gyfagar
A bydin a gꝺaetlin ar y escar.
A thriganed kyrn a gꝺerin trygar.
Ry thrychynt rygyrchynt ygcledyfar.
Brein ac eryron gollychant ꝺyar.
Arllꝺybyr gꝺrit arth gꝺrys diarchar.
Ardyrched katwaladyr lluch allachar.
Ar ꝺyneb bydinaꝺr broed ynyal.

Y̶N wir dymbi dydranoueu.
Gofunet dysgogan ygkynechreu.
Blꝺydyned budic rossed rihyd reitheu.
Gayaf gyt llyry llym llywit llogeu.
Keithiaꝺn eilyassaf mynut ryffreu.
Prit myr ryuerthꝺy ar warr tonneu.
Elyrch dymdygyrch tani o glaꝺr balcheu.
Arth a lleꝺderllys oleu bylleu.
Ef dibyn y teruyn o rud vereu.
Rꝺy keissut kystud rybud rageu.
Rac y varanres ae vaꝺr vedeu.
Credeu cꝺydynt tyrch torrynt toruoed taleu.
Y kynnif katwaladyr clot lathyr leu.
Dydyrchafꝺy dreic o parth deheu.
Gan was rydad las yn dyd dyfieu.

Y̶N wir dymbi hael hyꝺred.
Tyruaꝺt molut maꝺr edryssed.
Llꝺybyr teꝺ lluossaꝺc llydan y wed.

Hyt pan uwynt seith ieith y ri góyned
Hyt pan traghóy traghaót trydar.
Ri eidun duhun duded.
Treis ar eigyl a hynt i alltuted.
Tróy vor llithrant eu heissilled.

YN wir dymbi teithiaóc mon.
Ffaó dreic diffredyat y popyl brython.
Pen lluyd perchyd llurygogyon.
Dófyn darogan dewin drywon.
Pebyllyaónt ar tren a tharanhon.
Gorllechant gordyfynt y geissaó mon.
Pell debet by hyt o iwerdon.
Tec ffaó dillygyaó kessarogyon.

DYSGOGAN delwat o agarat dyhed.
Gogón pan perit kat arwinued.
Arth o deheubarth yn kyfarth góyned
Yn amóyn rihyd ryfed rossed.
Y cheiric altirat y darinerthed.
Gayaf kelenic yn lleu tired.
Kyfleóynt aessaór yggaór ygcled.
Y gynnif katwaladyr ar ior góyned.

YN wir dydeuhaór dyderbi hyn.
Lloegyr oll ymellun eu meuoed genhyn.
Góelet artebet y góyr brychwyn.
Róng saeth vereu a hayarn góyn.
Galóhaór ar vor. góaywaór aegrýn.
Nuchaónt yn eigaón tra llydan lyn.
Hallt ac yn yssed vyd eu budyn.

YN wir dymbi dy dra hafren.
Vrthenedic prydein brenhin gorden.

Llary lywyd lluyd lliaỽs y echen.
Teyrnas kyfadas cas o iaen.
Gỽerin byt yn wir bydaỽnt lawen. `
Medhaỽnt ar peiron berthwyr echen.
Fflemychaỽt hirell ty uch hafren.
Bydhaỽt kymry kynnull yn discowen.
Y kynnif katwaladyr bythit llawen.
Peneri cerdoryon clot y gỽeithen.

Y̆N wir dedeuhaỽr
Ae lu ae longaỽr
Ae taryf yscỽytaỽr
Ae newityaỽ gỽaywaỽr.
A gỽedy gỽychyr aỽr
Y uod ef gỽnelaỽr
Kylch prydein bo
Flemychit ygno.
Dreic nyt ymgelho
Yr meint y do.
Nyt yscaỽn iolet
Gorescyn dyuet.
Dydyccaỽt ynwet
Tra merin reget.
Perif perchen ket.
Gỽledychaỽt yn eluet.
Hael hydyr y dylif.
Goruaỽr y gynnif.
Ỽrth awyryohif
Katwaladyr gỽeith heinif.

LIV.

YMARWAR LLUD BYCHAN.

Fol. 37. b.   EN enỽ duỽ trindaỽt kardaỽt kyfrỽys.
Llỽyth lliaỽs anuaỽs eu henwerys.

Dy gorescynnan prydein prif van ynys.

Gẃyr gẃlat yr ascia a gẃlat gafis.

Pobyl pẃyllat enwir eu tir ny wys.

Famen gowyreis herwyd maris.

Amlaes eu peisseu pẃy eu heuelis.

A phẃyllat dyvyner ober efnis.

Europin arafin arafanis.

Cristyaẃn difryt diryd dilis.

Kyn ymarwar llud a llefelis.

Dysgogettaẃr perchen y wen ynys

Rac pennaeth o rufein kein y echrys

Nyt rys nyt kyfrẃys ri rẃyf y areith.

Arywelei aryweleis o aghyfyeith.

Dullator petrygẃern llugyrn ymdeith.

Rac ryuonic kynran baran godeith.

Rytalas mab grat rẃyf y areith

Kymry ny danhyal ryfel ar geith.

Pryderaf pẃyllaf pẃy y hymdeith.

Brythonic yniwis dydyrchefis.

LV.

KANU Y BYT MAẂR.

Fol. 38. a.

ᏀVOLYCHAF vyn tat.

Vyn duẃ vyn neirthat.

A dodes trẃy vy iat

Eneit ym pẃyllat.

Am goruc yn gẃylat.

Vy scith llafanat.

O tan a dayar.

A dẃfyr ac awyr.

A nyẃl a blodeu

A gẃynt godeheu.

Eil synhẃyr pwyllat

Ym poylloys vyn tat.
Vn yo a rynnyaf.
A deu a tynaf.
A thri a waedaf.
A phetwar a vlassaaf.
A phymp a welaf.
A chwech a glywaf.
A seith a arogleuaf.
Ac a agdiwedaf.
Seith awyr ysyd
O duch sywedyd.
A their ran y myr
Mor ynt amrygyr.
Mor uaor a ryfed
Y byt nat vn wed.
Ry goruc duo vry
Ary planete.
Ry goruc sola.
Ry goruc luna.
Ry goruc marca
Y marcarucia.
Ry goruc venus.
Ry goruc venerus.
Ry goruc seuerus.
A seithued saturnus.
Ry goruc duo da.
Pymp goregys terra
Pa hyt yt para.
Vn yssyd oer.
A deu yssyd oer.
Ar trydyd yssyd wres
A dyofac anlles.
Petweryd paradoys
Goerin a gynnoys.

Pymhet artymheraᴠd
A pyrth y vedyssaᴠt.
Yn tri yt rannat
Yn amgan pᴠyllat.
Vn yᴠyr asia.
Deu yᴠyr affrica.
Tri yᴠ europa.
Bedyd gygwara.
Hyt vrodic yt para.
Pan varnher pop tra
Ry goruc vy awen
Y voli vyren.
Mydᴠy taliessin
Areith lif dewin
Parahaᴠt hyt fin
Yg kynnelᴠ elphin.

LVI.

Kanu y byt bychan.

Fol. 38. b.

KEIN geneis kanaf.
Byt vndyd mᴠyhaf.
Lliaᴠs a bᴠyllaf
Ac a bryderaf.
Kyfarchaf y veird byt.
Pryt nam dyweid
Py gynheil y byt.
Na syrch yn eissywyt.
Neur byt bei syrchei.
Py ar yt gᴠydei.
Pᴠy ae gogynhalei.
Byt mor yᴠ aduant.
Pan syrch yn diuant
Etwa yn geugant.

Byt mor yꞮ ryfed.

Na syrch yn vnwed.

Byt mor yꞮ odit

Mor vaꞮr yt sethrit

Johannes. Matheus.

Lucas. a Marcus.

ꞯy a gynheil y byt

TrꞮy rat yr yspryt.*

* This poem ends on the last page of the MS., and then follows the beginning of another poem, which is nearly illegible, only à few words being distinct.
The title is DAROGAN KAT (WALADYR), and it commences with the words
Merch lꞮc mꞮch mis. As mentioned in a former note, the last leaf, containing the continuation of this poem, is awanting.

V.

THE RED BOOK OF HERGEST.

A MS. TRANSCRIBED AT DIFFERENT PERIODS FROM THE EARLY
PART OF THE 14TH TO THE MIDDLE OF THE 15TH CEN-
TURIES, AND PRESERVED IN THE LIBRARY OF JESUS COL-
LEGE, OXFORD. THE PART OF THE MS. CONTAINING THE
FOLLOWING POEMS TRANSCRIBED IN THE LATTER PART
OF THE 14TH CENTURY.

I.

KYUOESSI MYRDIN AGUENDYD YCHUAER.*

Col. 577.

DEUTHUM i attat y atraôd
Yguadaeth y gogled y gennyf.
Syô pob tut traethôyt ôrthyf.

Yr gôeith arderyd ac erydon
Gwendyd ar meint dybyd arnaf
Eneichiat kyued kwd af.

Kyuarchaf ym llallogan
Vyrdin gôr doeth darogenyd
Kan hepcoryd o honaf.
Pari an bun ganthaô.

* This and the following poem are written in the same handwriting with
that of a chronicle (Col. 516) which terminates with the year 1318.

Ny dyly yr neb y amser hennadu an
ucel. y bennaeth yvllab hoithel. ys bar
gooyein ny villvys. ny bro nes y baradvys.
nyt gwaeth urd odynn noc urd oeylbys.
Kyfuarchaf ym ychyeru vraot aczdeis
ygrdor gein. pvy thledych thedy vargotyen.
Albpoyn ahanner y uerver vrehyeyeit.
eubocs adiutyrrer. diuenkir pob dibyder.
Cann vyt thedy maeith achanon kurilleith.
tiruged dub yth eneit. pvy thledych the
dy vrehyr yeit. Dyrchauawt willic ogud.
nyt achatuo y deurud. kynan y ron kym
ry bieiuvo. kyuarchaf ethechlyfsur byt.
ym dytthet ynchirerpan. pvy thledych.
thedy kynan. Gwr pellennic o oramyr.
toeuant gaereu vierthyr. dythedynt vren
hin o vrehyr. kyuarchaf oechlyfsur byt
hau gwbst y vthyn. pvy thledych thedy vee
hyr. Dysgoganaf seruen ikyun. ken
nat gwaetat vygbydthyn. gleb gadaru gar
char gylch thyn. treiglawt vro vradabc

Yn gerd gadauael aui koel.
Kymry yỽ bi. kyuarth auel
Rỽyd yỽ arỽyd ryderch hael.

Kanys ryderch bieu ffaỽ.
A chymry oll y danaỽ.
Neu gỽedy ynteu kỽdaỽ.

Ryderch hael gymynat gelyn
Gỽan teỽ y wan ac hy.
Dyd gỽynwyd ynryt tawy.

Ryderch hael dan yspeit gelyn.
Dinas beird bro glyt
Kỽd. aa ef ỿt a yr ryt. *o/*

Mi aedyweit y wendyd.
Kan amkyueirch yngeluyd.
Na byd ryderch hael drennyd.

Kyuarchaf ym clotleỽ llallaỽc.
Anuynnaỽc ynlluyd.
Neu wedy ryderch pỽy vyd.

O leas gỽendoleu y gỽaetfreu arderyd
Handỽyf o eithur.
Morgant uaỽr uab sadyrnin.

Kyuarchaf ym clotleỽ llallaỽc
Kerglyt. kyt lliant.
Pỽy wledych wedy morgant.

O leas gỽendoleu y gỽaetfreu arderyd
A synny paham ym keugỽaladyr.
Gỽaet gỽlat y uryen.

Kyfli6 dy benn ac aryen
Gaeaf. g6ares du6 dy anghen.
P6y wledych wedy uryen.

Digones douyd digued
Arnaf claf 6yf or diwed.
Maelg6n hir ar dir g6yned.

Oys gar ymbra6t. yt vych
Vygkalon. dr6c vy hoen am ryd drych
Neu wedy maelg6n p6y wledych.

Run y en6 rugyl y ffossa6t.
Ygkynnor bydin br6ydra6t.
G6ae brydein or diwarna6t.

Kann 6yt kedymdeit achanon
Kunlleith. athal wa6r aborth6n.
Kwda g6yned g6edy run.

Run y en6 ryuel o vri.
A oganaf y dyderbi.
G6endyn g6lat yn anghat veli.

Kyfuarchaf ym clotle6 llalla6c.
Anvynna6c ygkyni.
P6y wledych wedi beli.

Cannethy6 uym p6yll gan wyllyon mynyd.
Amyhun ynagro.
Wedy beli y uab ef iago.

Cann ethy6 dy b6yll gan wyllyon mynyd
A thyhun yn agro.
P6y wledych wedy iago.

AmgÓrth gyuarch ym brytuan.
Y gyuedeu neut eban
GÓedy iago y uab ef katuan.

Y kerdeu rydraethassam
O dyuot clot bodrydan.
PÓy wledych wedy katuan.

GÓlat kadwallaÓn Óryt maÓr.
Pedryuael byt. ryglywawr
DygÓydit penn eigyl y laÓr.
A byt byt y hetmyccaÓr.

O welet dy rud mor greulaÓn
Y daÓ ym bryt neut annogaÓn.
PÓy wledych uedy kadwallaÓn.

GÓr hir yn kadÓ kynnadyl.
A phrydein yn Ón paladyr.
Goreu mab kymro kalwalaÓdyr.

Am gÓrth gyuarch yn glaear.
Y gynnedueu neut abar.
Wedy katwalaÓdyr. Idwal.

Ath gyfuarchaf yn glaear.
Clotleu goreu dyn dayar.
PÓy wledych wedy idwal.

GÓledychaÓt wedy idwal
Yn llÓrÓ dyuynnyn diarchar
YsgÓydwyn hoÓel uab kadwal.

Kyfuarchaf ym clotleu llellaÓc.

Anuynnaỽc yd ryuel.
Pỽy wledych wedy howel.

Mi aedywedaf y glot o vri.
Gỽendyd kynn esgar athi.
Gỽedy hoỽel rodri.

Kynan y mon a ui
Nyt achatuo y deithi.
A chyngalwer mab rodri.
Mab kealedigan vi.

Kyfuarchaf o echlyssur byt.
Am dyweit ychwaryan.
Pỽy wledych wedy kynan.

O leas gwendoleu yg gwaetfreu
Arderyd. digoni o vraỽ.
Meruin vrych o dir manaỽ.

Kyfuarchaf ym clot ovri.
Vraỽt kerdoleu oreudyn.
Pỽy wledych uedi meruin.

Dywedỽyf nyt o drycaỽr.
Ormes brydein pryderaỽr.
Wedy meruyn rodri maỽr.

Kyuarchaf ym clotleu llallaỽc
Anuynnaỽc yn dyd gaỽr.
Pỽy wledych wedy mab rodri maỽr.

Ar lann konỽy kymỽy duỽ merchyr
Etmyckaỽr y dauaỽt.
Arbennic aryen anaraỽt.

Kyfuarchaf ym clotleu llallaѵc.
Annvynnaѵc yn dyd gwaѵt.
Pѵy wledych wedy anaraѵt

ᴅESSAF yѵ nes y amser
Kennadeu ansel.
Y bennaeth yn llaѵ howel.

Ys bargodyein ny bissѵys.
Ny byd nes y baradѵys.
Nyt gѵaeth urd oᴄdynn noc urd o eglѵys.

Kyfuarchaf ym ychyein
Vraѵt a weleis ygclot gein.
Pѵy wledych wedy bargotyein.

Blѵydyn a hanner y ueruer
Vrehyryeit. eu hoes a diuyrrer.
Diuenwir pob dibryder.

Cann ѵyt kedymdeith a chanon kunlleith.
Trugared duѵ ytheneit.
Pѵy wledych wedy brehyryeit.

Dyrchauaѵt unic o gud.
Nyt achatuo y deurud.
Kynan y kѵn kymry bieinyd.

Kyuarchaf o echlyssur byt.
Ym dywet yn chweryan.
Pѵy wledych wedy kynan.

Gѵr pellennic o dramyr.
Torrant gaereu bierthyr.
Dywedynt brenhin o vrehyr.

Kyuarchaf o echlyssur byt.
Kan g6dost y ystyr.
P6y wledych wedi brehyr.

Disgoganaf seruen wynn.
Kennat g6astat ysg6ydwyn.
Gle6 gadarn garchar gylchwyn.
Treigla6t bro brada6c unbyn.
Ef grynna6t h6nt racda6 hyt ym prydein.

Kyfuarchaf ymbra6t y g6ynn.
Kanys mi ae hamouyn.
P6y wledych wedy seruen wynn.

Deu ysg6ydwyn veli.
A dyvi y uaeth awnant dyuysgi.
Nac eurin hed6ch vi.

Kyuarchaf ym clotleu llalla6c
Annwynna6c yngkymry.
P6y weledych wedy deu. ysg6ydwyn ueli.

'Vnic ar6ynaul. ar wyneb keda6l
Kynghora6t kat diffret.
A wledych kynnor gorminet.

Kyuarchaf ym clotleu llalla6c
Annwyna6c ynlluyd.
P6y yr unic arwynna6l
A darogeny di y uaeth.
P6y y en6 padu pan vyd.

Gruffud y en6 geida6l mirein
G6nawt ef gan argan kyngrein.
A wledych ar dir prydein.

Kyuarchaf ym clotleu
Llallaʊc. anwynnawc ygkadeu.
Neu gʊedy gruffud pieu.

Dywedwyf nyt odrycker
Ormes prydein pryderer.
Gwedy gruffud gʊyn gwarther.

Kyuarchaf ym clotleu llallaʊc.
Annʊynnauc yn ryuel.
Pʊy uledych wedy gʊynn gʊarther.

Ui awendyd wenn maʊr adrasdil gogan.
Chwipleia a chwedleu. atkas
Gwehelieith auyd deu idas.
Am dir etmykaʊr oe gʊir hir alanas.

Kyuarchaf ym clotleu
Llallaʊc. annwynnaʊc yg kadeu.
Pwy wledych uedy ʊynteu.

Disgoganaf nat gʊas beid.
Brenhin llew llaʊdiwreid.
Gyluin geuel gauel bleid.

Kyuarchaf ym ehalaeth
Uraʊt aweleis yn veduaeth.
O dyna pʊy auyd pennaeth.

Kyniuerʊch a rif y ser.
Kynhebycker yniuer.
Ef yʊ ymackʊy deu hanner.

Kyuarchaf ym diuuner
Q

Uraѵt. allwed bydin bud ner.
Pѵy uledych wedy deu hanner.

Kymysc gѵydelieith yn aer
A chymro a chymrud daer.
Ef yѵ arglѵyd ѵyth prifgaer.

Kyuarchaf ymdiagro
Uraѵt a darllewys lyuyr cado.
Pѵy wledych wedy euo.

Mi aedyweit oreget.
Kan amkyueirch ynogonet.
Keneu henri ryuyget.
Byth ynyoes nyt oes waret.

Kyuarchaf y clot ovri
Vraѵt annwynnaѵc ygkymry.
Pѵy wledych wedy mab henri.

Pan uo pont ar dav ac arall ar dywi
Y daѵ ar loegyr dyuysgi.
A mi disgogaf wedy mab henri
Brenhin na vrenhin brithuyt aui.

Kyuarchaf ymbraѵt ygѵyn.
Kanẏs mi ae hamouyn.
Pѵy wledych wedy brenhin na vrenhin.

Letynuyt urenhin a daѵ
A gѵyr lloegyr ynydѵyllaѵ.
Ny byd gѵlatlѵyd y danaѵ.

Myrdin dec daѵnglot gywyt.

Llidyaϭc ymyt.
Beth auyd ynoes ynvyt.

Pan uo lloegyr yn griduan
Achynir. yn drycanyan
Y byd ylluyd bϭhϭman.

Myrdin dec daϭn leueryd.
Na dywet ϭrthyf gelwyd.
Beth auyd wedy lluyd.

Ef a gyfyt un or chwech.
Ary uu ynhir ynllech.
Ar loegyr auyd gortrech.

Myrdin dec daϭnglot wely.
Troyt y gϭynt o vyϭn ty.
Pϭy wledych wedy hynny.

Deuot yϭ dyuot owein.
A goresgyn hyt lundein.
A rodi y gȳmry goeluein.

Myrdin dec daϭnglot bennaf.
Kanys yth eir y credaf.
Owein pahyt y para.

Gϭendyd gwarandaϭ letkynt.
Troyt y gϭynt yrdiffrynt.
Pump mlyned adϭy ualkynt.

Kyuarchaf ym ehalaeth
Uraϭt a weleis yn ueduaeth.
O dyna pϭy auyd pennaeth.

Pan uo owein ym manaᵥ
A chat ymprydyn geirllaᵥ.
Biaᵥt gᵥr ef a gᵥyr idaᵥ.

Kyuarchaf ym ehalaeth
Vraᵥt a weleis yn ueduaeth.
O dyna pᵥy auyd pennaeth.

Pennaeth y uaeth
A oresgyn eluyd.
Gᵥlat wynuyt drᵥy lewenyd.

Kyuarchaf ym chalaeth
Uraᵥt a weleis yn ueduaeth
O dyna pᵥy auyd pennaeth.

Elit lleuein yn dyffrynt.
Beli hir aewyr gorwynt.
Gᵥynn eubyt gymry a gᵥae gynt.

Kyuarchaf ym clotleu
Llallaᵥc annwynnaᵥc yghadeu.
Neu wedy beli pieu.

Elit lleuein yn aber
Beli hir ae wyr llaᵥer.
Gᵥyn eu byt gymry gᵥae wydyl.

Kyuarchaf ym clotleu llallaᵥc
Annwynnaᵥc yn ryuel.
Pa y wae y wydyl.

Disgoganaf un dyssyawc.
Gᵥyned gwedy aᵥch trallaᵥt.
Goruot yᵥch ar bop kiwdaᵥt.

Canon morurynn morunet.
Oedyn myrdin urych vreisc liwet.
Pa da6 yny deu ouunet.

Pan disgynno kadwaladyr
A llu llydan ganta6 kymwed.
Du6 merchyr y a m6yn g6yr g6yned.
Asdeubyd g6yr kaer gamwed.

Nac ysgar yn antrwyadal
A mi o angwarthyr gynnadyl.
Padu ydisgyn kadwaladyr.

Pan disgynno kadwaladyr
Yn dyffryn tywi.
Bia6t tra thrwm ebyr.
G6asgara6t brythot brithwyr.

Kyuarchaf ym ehalaeth
Ura6t a weleis yn ueduaeth.
P6y wledych odynaeth.

Pan uo teir ieithya6c taea6c
Ym mon. ae uab yn gunnacha6c.
Ryglywawr g6yned goluda6c.

P6y g6ascar lloegyr yar diwed
Mor. p6y y g6yn ar deued.
Neu gymry p6y vyd eu g6ared.

Taryf rywyr a th6ryf ryderch.
A bydinoed kadwaladyr.
Yar dardennin auon.
Torrynt allwed g6yr.

Nac ysgar yn aur tywyadyl
A mi o angᴜarthyr gynnadyl.
Paleas a dᴜc kadwaladyr.

As gᴜan gᴜayᴜ o ergrywyd
Llog. a llaᴜ kynndiwedyd.
Dybyd gymry gᴜarth or dyd.

Nac yscar yn antrwyadyl
A mi. o angᴜarth yr gynnadyl.
Pahyt y gᴜledych kadwaladyr.

Tri mis teir blyned teithyon.
A thrychant mlyned kyflaᴜn.
Kadeu gᴜeitheu gᴜledychant.

Nac yscar yn antrᴜyadyl
A mi o angᴜarth yr gynnadyl.
Pᴜy wledych wedy kadwaladyr.

Y wendyd y dywedaf
Oes tragoes disgoganaf.
Wedy kadwaladyr cynda.

Llaᴜ ar gled arall ar groes
Gogelet baᴜp y einyoes.
Gan gÿndaf kymot nyt oes.

Neut a gannaᴜt uudyssyaᴜc
Gᴜyned gᴜedy aᴜch trallaᴜt.
Goruot yᴜch ar bob kiwtaᴜt.

A chiwtaᴜt plant adaf
A henynt ae gᴜaᴜt.
A dioes gᴜaret hyt uraᴜt.

Or pan el kymry heb ganhorthẇy.
Kat heb gadwat eu deurẇd oll
Mal y gallor na pẇy a uyd pennaeth.

Gẇendyd meueneduc virein.
Kyntaf katraf ym prydein.
Arylẇch gymry druein.

Pan dyuo dylat dylyet uchaf.
O uor hyt weryt dylat
Diwed riein orffen byt.

Eu wedy dylat dylyet uchaf.
Pẇy uyd a drefuaẇr
A vi llann a rann periglaẇr.

Na rann periglaur na cherdaẇr
Ny byd nac adreidyaẇ yr allaẇr.
Yny dygẇydho nef ar laẇr.

Llallaẇc kan am hatebyd.
Myrdin uab moruryn geluyd.
Truan a chwedyl a dywedyd.

As dywedaf y wendyd.
Kanys dẇys ym kẏuerchyd.
Dylat diwed riein vyd.

A rydywedeis i hyt hynn
Y wendyd waessaf unbyn.
Diderbyd kymeint timmyn.

Llallaẇc kan am diderbyd.
Neu yr eneit dy urodyr.
Pa bennaeth y uaeth a uyd.

Gẃendyd wenn benn mynogi.
As dywedaf yn difri.
Na byd pennaeth byth wedi.

Och amwylor oer esgar.
Gẃedy dyuot yn drydar.
Gan unben deẃr diarchar.
Dy ylodi y dan dayar.

Gẃasgaraẃt awel awyr
Pẃyll drut adẃyll ot gerdir.
Gẃennffaẃt hÿt vraẃt ys dir.

Och leas di veduaeth.
Neut ym dianmaeth.
Hoet da adoet pan dygir
Clot vrno. pẃy draetho gẃir.

O lochwyt kyuot a thauot
Llyfreu awen heb arsẃyt
A chwdyl bun a hun breudwyt.

Marẃ morgeneu marẃ kyfrennin.
Moryal. marẃ moryen mur trin.
Trymaf hoed am dywoet ti vyrdin.

Digones douyd digued arnaf
Marẃ morgeneu. marẃ mordaf.
Marẃ moryen. marẃ a garaf

Ẃy un braẃt na cheryd arnaf
Yr gẃeith arderyd ẃyf claf
Kyuarẃydyt a geissyaf.
Y duẃ ythorchymynnaf.

Athorchmynnaf ditheu
Y benn y creaduryeu.
Gᵥendyd wenn atlam kerdeu.

Y kerdeu rydrigyassant.
O dyuot clot vodrydant
Och duᵥ ᵥynt a aduant.

Gᵥendyd na vyd anhylar.
Neur roet y llᵥyth yr dayar.
Diofryt o baᵥb agar.

Ym byᵥ nyth diofredaf.
Ahyt vraᵥt yth goffaaf.
Dy ffossaᵥt trallaᵥt trymaf.

Escut gorwyd rᵥyd gᵥynt
Amchyniynaf. vy eirioes
Vraᵥt y ren ryᵥ goreu.
Kymer gymun kynn agheu.

Ny chymmeraf gymun
Gan ysgymun uyneich
Ac eu tᵥygeu ar eu clun.
Am kymuno duᵥ e hun.

Gorchymynnaf vy eiryoes
Vraᵥt. yny gaer wertheuin.
Gogelet duᵥ o vyrdin.

Gorchymynnaf inheu vy eiryoes
Chwaer. yny gaer wertheuin.
Gogelit duᵥ o wendyd. Amen.

II.

GȮASGARDGERD VYRDIN YNY BED.

Col. 584.

ＧWR a leueir yn y bed.
A dysgȯyt, kynn seith mlyned ;
· March marȯ eurdein gogled.

Eryueis i o win o wydyr gȯynn.
Gan rieu ryuel degynn.
Myrdin yȯ vy enȯ uab moruryn.

Erẏueis i owin o gaȯc
Gan rieu ryuel eglȯc.
Myrdin yȯ vy enȯ amheidȯc.

Pan del gȯrthryn yar olwyn
Du. y lad lloegyr llȯybyr wehyn.
Chwerȯ wenȯyn yn amwyn.
Gȯynbrynn wynvrynn eisiwyn erhy.
Hir neuet giwet gymry.

Ny byd diogellaȯr ygkellaȯr ardudȯy
Ar ardalȯy kymry
Rac arderchaȯc tȯrch toryf hy.

Pan dyuo coch nordmandi
Y holi lloegyrwys treul diffȯys.
Treth am bop darogan.
Castell yn aber hodni.

Pan dyuo y brych cadarn
Hyt yn ryt bengarn.
Lliwaȯt gȯyr treuliaȯt karn.
Penndeuic prydein yno penn barn.

Pan dyuo henri y holi
Mur kastell y deruyn eryri.
Galwaꝺt gormes dra gweilgi.

Pan dyuo ygꝺynngꝺann y holi llundein.
Yar veirch nyt kein.
Rygeilꝺ ef deyrnas kaergein.

Teneu y mes teꝺ y hyt.
Pan dyuo yndeissyuyt.
Brenhin guas gꝺae ac cryt.

Mab a uyd maꝺr y urdas.
A orescyn mil dinas.
Hoedel egin brenhin o was

Kadarn ꝺrth wann aduot.
Gꝺann ꝺrth gadarn gordirot.
Pennaeth handes gꝺaeth oc dyuot.

Byt a uyd bryt ꝺrth uaꝺrdes.
Yd bydant gꝺragedeint llaes vuches.
Bydant llu meibyonein eu kyffes.

Byt a uyd bryt ꝺrth ydes.
Yt wnaho taeaꝺc y les.
Disgiwen bun gꝺrthbꝺyth gꝺas.

Byt a uyd a gorffenn oet
Pallant ieueinc rac adwyt.
Mei marꝺ cogeu rac annꝺyt.

Byt a uyd bryt ꝺrth erchꝺys.
Yd adeilaꝺr yn dyrys.
Heb werth maꝺr ni chaffaꝺr crys.

Byt a vyd bryt ỽrthlyeu
Byỽ mall a gỽall ar lanneỽ.
Torredaỽd geir a chreireu.
Eu diuanwaỽt gỽir lletaỽt geu.
Gỽan ffyd bob eildyd dadleu.

Byt a uyd bryt ỽrth dillat.
Kyghaỽs arglỽyd maer chwiniat.
Gwacllaỽ bard hard effeiryat.
Diuannwaỽr gwyr lletaỽr gỽat.

Byt a uyd heb wynt heblaỽ.
Heb ormod eredic heb drathreulyaỽ.
Tir digaỽn uyd un erỽ y naỽ.

Pan dyuo yr gỽyr heb wryt.
Ac ynlle ycoet kael yr yt.
Ympob hed gỽled agyuyt.

Pan uo kyuelin gymyred. gỽyd gỽannỽyn
A ui gỽedy pennaeth gỽenỽyn.
Bydaỽt gỽaeth budelỽ no chrowyn.

Duỽ merchyr dyd kyghor fen.
Ytreulyaỽr llafnaỽr ar benn
Cudyant deu ygkreu kyghenn.

Yn aber sor yt uyd kyghor
Ar wyr gỽedy trin treulitor.
Glyỽ gỽyn llyỽ yn yscor.

Yn aber auon y byd llu mon
Eingyl gỽedy hinwedon.
Hir weryt arwryt uoryon.

Yn aber dúfyr nwy deil duc
Yt vi agnaho gúidic.
A gúedy cat kyuarlluc.

Cat a vi ar hyrri
Auon. a brython dyworpi.
Gnaút gúyr gúhyr gúrhydri.

Yn aber y don peruor cat
A phelydyr anghyuyon.
A gúaet rud ar rud saesson.
Wassaúc dy waed dy wendyd
Am dywaút wylyon.
Mynyd yn aber karaf.

III.*

Col. 1026. LLEWELYN A GÚRNERTH A OEDYNT DEUSEINT BENYDYAÚL YN Y
TRALLÚNG YM POWYS. A DYUOT YGYT AWNEYNT Y TEIR
AÚR DIWETHAF OR NOS. AR TEIR AÚR KYNTAF OR DYD Y
DYWEDUT EU PYLGEINT AC ORYEU Y DYD Y AM HYNNY.
AC Y SEF Y GÚELEI LYWELYN KUDUGYL GÚRNERTH YN
GAEAT. A CHANY WYDYAT PAHAMOED HYNNY. SEF A
WNAETH YNTEU KANU ENGLYN.

EIRY mynyd gwynt am berth.
Kanys creaúdyr nef am nerth.
Ae kysgu awna gúrnerth.

Eiry mynyd duú yn bennaf.
Kanys attaú gwediaf.
Nac ef kysgu nyallaf.

* The remainder of the poems taken from the Red Book of Hergest are in
the same handwriting with another chronicle (Col. 999) which is brought
down to the year 1376.

Eiry mynyd gỽynt am ty.
Kanys llefery uelly :
Beth ỽrnerth awna hynny.

Eiry mynyd gỽynt deheu.
Kanys tracthaf prif eiryeu :
Tebyckaf yỽ mae angheu.

Eiry mynyd gorwyn bro.
Detwyd paỽb ỽrth ae llocho :
Creaỽdyr nef ath diangho.

Eiry mynyd gorwynn prenn.
Kanys llefaraf amgen :
Nyt oes naỽd rac tynghet nen.

Eiry mynyd pob deuaỽt.
Rac gormeil goual dydbraỽt.
A gaffaf i gymun ynghardaỽt.

Eiry mynyd gwynt am ty
Kanys lleuery uelly :
Och vymraỽt ae reit hynny.

Awendrut mi ath garaf.
Hyt ar duỽ y gỽediaf :
Llywelyn rywyr y kaffaf.

Eiry mynyd gỽynt am vrynn.
Kanys creaỽdyr nef am mynn :
Ae kẏsgu y mae llywelyn.

Eiry mynyd gwynt de(heu).
Kanys traethaf prif eiryeu.
Nac ef kanu vy oryeu.

Eiry mynyd godysgeit.
Pan droho góynt yngkylch pleit.
Awdost di póy a dyweit.

Eiry mynyd llafar hy.
Kanys kyrbóylly velly :
Na ónn onys dywedy.

Eiry mynyd pob canherth.
A geiff y voli yn prytuerth :
Mae yma dy vraót gwrnerth.

Blaengerd gymhelri. *ac ynni*
~~Atyma~~ pob drut. ac awen ym peri :
Beth wrnerth oreu ytti.

Blaencat pob deuaót. a llafurnaót
Drut. am vuched hyt dyd braót.
Goreu y keueis gardaót.

Awendrut tec dy gampeu.
Y maer ganon yth eneu :
Dywet py gardaót oreu.

Blaengar awen góynt órth lynn.
Pan ymladho tonn am vrynn.
Goreu yó bóyt rac newyn.

Onyt bwyt nys kyrhaedaf.
Ac am dwylaó nas kaffaf :
Dywet beth awnaf yna.

Blaengerd gymhelri. ac ynni
Pob drut. ac auen ymperi :
Dyro dillat rac noethi.

Vyndillat ṁi ae radaf
Y duỽ y gorchymynnaf :
Py dal yna a gaffaf.

A rodych o da ym pob attrec
Drut ym breint kadỽ dy wyneb ;
Sef y key yn nef ary ganuet.

Kyfliỽ dyd kanyth garaf.
Ardelỽ kerd kanys keissyaf :
Gan duỽ py ỽnpeth gassaf.

Bud ac awen a chyffret.
Pan retto dỽfyr ar anwaeret
Guaethaf tỽyll trỽy ymdiret.

Tỽyll trỽy ymdiret os gỽnaf.
Ac y duỽ naf kyffessaf :
Pa dial a vyd arnaf.

Or gỽney dỽyll ymdiret.
Heb ffyd heb grefyd heb gret :
Key benyt ar dy seithuet.

Kyfliỽ dyd mi ath gredaf.
Ac yr duỽ y govynnaf.
Nef pywed yd henillaf.

Nyt kyffelyỽ da a drỽc.
Pan ymladho gỽynt a mỽc.
Gỽna da yr duỽ sef y diỽc.

Blaengar awen pob achles.
Retuaỽr gorwydaỽr ar tes :
Diwed pob peth yỽ kyffes.

Awnelych obob dirdra.
O dẃyll athreis a thraha :
Yr duẃ kyffessa ynda.

TYSSILYAẃ UAB BROCHUAEL YSCYTHRAẃC AGANT
   YR ENGYLYNYON HYNN Y GAN ẃRNERTH YN
   DYUOT Y GYWIRAẃ Y GRETẃRTH LYWELYN
   SANT Y GYTYMEITH AC A ELWIR YMATREC
   LLYWELYN A GWRNERTH.

IV.

)l. 1028.

EIRY mynyd gẃynn pob tu :
Kynneuin bran a chanu :
Nydaẃ da o drachyscu.

Eiry mynyd gẃynn keunant :
Rac ruthur gẃynt gẃyd gẃyrant :
Llawer deu aymgarant :
Aphyth ny chyfuar uydant.

Eiry mynyd gẃynt ae taẃl.
Llydan lloergan glas tauaẃl.
Odit dyn dirieit dihaẃl.

Eiry mynyd hyd escut :
Gnaẃt ymprydein gynrein drut.
Reit oed deall y alltut.

Eiry mynyd hyd ardes.
Hẃyeit ynllynn gẃynn aches
Hẃyr heu haẃd y ordiwes.

Eiry mynyd hyd ardro

R

Chwerd yt bryt ꝧrth agaro :
Kyt dywetter ꝧrthyf chwedyl.
Mi a atwen venyl lle y bo.

Eiry mynyd graeiniwyn gro :
Pysc ynryt chit y ogo :
Kas vyd a oreilytto.

Eiry mynÿd hyd ar daryf :
Gnaꝧt gan gynran eryan araf :
Ac ysgynnu odu corof :
A disgynnu bar ar araf.

Eiry mynyd hyd kyngrꝩn.
Llawer adywede is os gꝩnn :
An heꝧic y hafdyd hꝩnn.

Eiry mynyd hyd hellaꝧt :
Gochwiban gꝩynt y ꝧch bargaꝧt :
Tꝩr trꝩm aꝧr yꝩ pechaꝧt.

Eiry mynyd hyd ar neit
Gochwiban gꝩynt y ꝧch gꝧenbleit
Uchel gnaꝧt taꝧel yndeleit.

Eiry mynyd hyd ymbro.
Gochwiban gꝩynt yꝧch blaen to.
Nyt ymgel drꝩc ynlle ybo.

Eiry mynyd hyd ar draeth.
Collyt heu y wab olaeth.
Deycorem awna dyn yngaeth.

Eiry mynyd hyd ynllꝩyn :

Purdu bran buan iyrchwyn.
S iachryd ryuedot pag6yn.

Eiry mynyd hyd my6n br6yn
Oer nucued med ygherwyn.
Gna6t gan bob anamis g6yn.

Eiry mynyd brith bronn t6r.
Kyrchyt aniueil glyd6r.
G6aewreic agaffo drycwr.

Eiry mynyd brith bronn kreic.
Krin kalaf alaf dichleic.
G6ae 6r agaffo drycwreic.

Eiry mynyd hyd ynffos :
Kyt uyt lleidyr a hir nos :
Kysgyt g6enyn yndidos.

Eiry mynyd kynglhennyd auon.
H6yrweian 6c yngkynnyd :
Ny moch dieil meuyl meryd.

Eiry mynyd pysc ynllynn.
Balch heba6c bac6ya6c unbynn :
Nyt ef ageiff pa6b auynn

Eiry mynyd coch blaen pyr :
Llidia6c lluossa6c ongyr
Och rac hiraeth vymrodyr.

Eiry mynyd buan bleid :
Ystlys diffeith6ch adreid :
Gna6t pob anaf ardieid

Eiry mynyd hyd nyt hῦyr.
Dygῦydyt glaῦ o awyr
Megyt tristit lleturyt llwyr.

Eiry mynyd eilion ffraeth.
Gowlychyt tonneu glanntraeth :
Keluyd kelet y aruaeth.

Eiry mynyd hyd myῦn glynn :
Gῦastat uyd haf araf lynn :
Baryflῦyt reῦ gleῦ yerchwynn.

Eiry mynyd brith bronn gῦyd :
Kadarn vymreic am ysgῦyd :
Eidunaf nabῦyf ganumlῦyd.

Eiry mynyd llῦmm blaencaῦn :
Crῦm blaen gῦrysc pysc yn eigyaῦn.
Lle nybo dysc nybyd daῦn.

Ery mynyd pysc ynryt.
Kyrchyt caro culgrvm cῦm clyt :
Hiraeth am uarῦ ny weryt.

Eiry mynyd hyd ygkoet.
Ny cherda detwyd ar troet :
Meckyt llῦuyr llawer adoet.

Eiry mynyd hyd ymbronn :
Gochwiban gῦynt yῦch blaen onn :
Trydyd troet y hen y ffonn

Eiry mynyd hyd arnaῦ.
Hwyeit yn llynn gῦynn alaῦ
Diryeit ny mynn gῦarandaῦ.

Eiry mynyd coch traet ieir
Bac dófyr mynyt leueir :
Chwenneckyt meuyl mabreir.

Eiry mynyd hyd esgut :
Odit amdidaór orbyt :
Rybud y dróch ny weryt.

Eiry mynyd góynn y gnu.
Ys odidaóc . . . óbru.
Ogar gyt amynych athreidu

Eiry mynyd góynn to tei.
Beitraethei dąuaót awypei
Geudaót : ny bydei gymydaóc neb rei.

Eiry mynyd dyd aed doeth :
Bitglaf pob trom llóin lletnoeth :
Gnaót pob anaf ar anoeth.

V.

1030. **B**IT goch crib keilyawc. bit annyanaól
Y lef owely budugaól :
Llewenyd dyn duó ae maól.

Bit laóen meichyeit órth ucheneit
Góynt. bit taóel yn deleit :
Bit gnaót aflóyd ar diryeit.

Bit guhudyat keisyat. bit guifiat
Góyd. a bit gyunwys dillat :
A garo bard bit hard rodyat.

Bit avwy unbenn abit leó.

Abit bleid ar ad6y.
Ny cheid6 ywyneb ar ny rodwy.

Bit vuan redeint yn ardal
Mynyd. bit yngheuda6t oual.
Bit anniweir annwadal.

Bit aml6c marcha6c. bit ogela6c
Lleidyr. t6yllit g6reic goluda6c :
Kyueillt bleid bugeil dia6c.

Bit aml6c marcha6c. bit redega6c
Gor6yd. bit uab llen ynch6anna6c :
Bit anniweir deueirya6c.

Bit gr6m bi6. a bit l6yt bleid.
Esgut gor6yd y ar heid.
G6esgyt g6a6n gra6n yny wreid.

Bit gr6m bydar. bit tr6m keu.
Esgut gorwyd ygkadeu :
G6esgyt g6a6n gra6n yny adneu.

Bit haha bydar. bit annwadal
Ehut. bit ynuyt ymladgar :
Detwyd or aeg6yl aekar.

Bit dyf6n llynn bit lynn g6aewa6r.
Bit granclef gle6 6rth a6r :
Bit doeth detwyd du6 ae ma6r.

Bit euein alltut. bit dysgythrin
Drut. bit chwanna6c ynvyt y chwerthin :
Bit wlyb rych. bid uynych mach.

Bit gẁyn claf. bit laẁen iach.
Bit chẁyrnyat colẁyn; bit wenwyn gwrach.

Bit diaspat aeleu. bit ae
Bydin. bit besgittor dyre.
Bit drut gleẁ. a bit reẁ bre.

Bit wenn gẁylyan. bit bann tonn.
Bit hyuagyl gẁyar ar onn :
Bit lẁyt reẁ. bit leẁ callonn.

Bit las lluarth. bit diwarth
Eirchyat. bit reinyat yghyuarth :
Bit wreic drẁc ae mynych warth.

Bit grauangaẁc iar. bit trydar
Ganleẁ. bit ynvyt ym ladgar.
Bit tonn callon ganalar.

Bit wynn tẁr. bit orẁn seirch.
Bit hoffder llaẁer ae heirch :
Bit lẁth chwannaẁc. bit ryngaẁc cleirch.

VI.

Col 1031. Ꙭ NAẁT gẁynt or deheu. gnaẁt atneu
Yn llann. gnaẁt gẁr gẁann godeneu :
Gnaẁt ydyn ofyn chwedleu.
Gnaẁt y vab ar uaeth noetheu.

Gnaẁt gẁynt or dẁyrein. gnaẁt dyn bronrein
Balch. gnaẁt mẁyalch ymplith drein :
Gnaẁt rac traha tralleuein.
Gnaẁt yggwic kael kic ourein.

Gna6t g6ynt or gocled. gna6t rianed
Chwec. gna6t g6r tec yg g6yned :
Gna6t y deyrn arl6y g6led.
Gna6t g6edy llynn lleturyded.

Gna6t g6ynt or mor. gna6t dygynor
Llan6 : gna6t y uan6 uagu hor :
Gna6t y uoch turya6 kylor.

Gna6t g6ynt or mynyd. gna6t meryd
Ymro. gna6t kael to yggwennyd :
Gna6t arlaeth maeth dyn creuyd.
Gna6t deil a g6yeil a g6yd.

*

Gna6t nyth eryr ymblaen dar.
Ac ygkyfyrdy g6yr llauar :
Gol6c vynut ar agar.

Gna6t dyd acanll6yth ygkynnlleith
Gayaf. kynreinyon kynr6ytyeith
Gna6t aelwyt diffyd yn diffeith.

Crin calaf allif yn nant.
Kyfnewit seis ac aryant.
Digu eneit mam geublant.

Y deilen adreuyt g6ynt.
G6ae hi oe thynghet.
Heu hi elein y ganet.

* NOTE. A stanza has here been erased in the Red Book of Hergest, but
there is a copy of the same poem in the MS. of Llywelyn Offeiriad (Jesus Col.),
from which the stanza is thus given :—
           Gna6t o bastardaeth gryunbry aeth
           Awyr a g6ra ged dr6c meduaeth
           Athym ar wyr a gorwyn waeth waeth.

Kyt boet bychan yskeluyd.
Yd adeil adar yggorŏyd
Coet : kyuoet vyd da a detwyd.

Derwlyb mynyd oerlas ia.
Ymdiryet y duŏ nyth dŏylla :
Nyt edeu hirbwyll hir bla.

VII.

Col. 1031.

KALANGAEAF kalet graŏn.
Deil ar gychŏyn llynnwynn llaŏn :
Y bore gynn noe vynet
Gwae a ymdiret y estraŏn.

Kalangayaf kein gyfrin.
Kyfret awel a dryckin :
Gŏeith keluyd yŏ kelurin.

Kalangayaf cul hydot.
Melyn blaen bedŏ gŏedŏ hauot :
Gŏae a haed meuyl yr bychot.

Kalangayaf crŏm blaen gŏrysc.
Gnaŏt o benn dirieit teruysc :
Lle ny bodaŏn ny byd dysc.

Kalangaeaf garŏ hin.
Anhebit y gynteuin :
Namwyn duŏ nyt oes dewin.

Kalangaeaf kein gyfreu
Adar : byrr dyd ban cogeu :
Trugar daffar duŏ goreu.

Kalangayaf kalet cras
Purdu bran buan o vras :
Am góymp hen chwerdit góen góas

Kalangaeaf cul kerwyt
Gwae wann pan syrr byrr vyd byt :
Góir góell hegaróch no phryt.

Kalangayaf llómgodeith.
Aradyr yn rych ych yggweith.
Or kant odit kedymdeith.

VIII.

Col. 1032.

BAGLAóC bydin bagóy onn.
Hwyeit yn llynn graenwynn tonn :
Trech no chant kyssul callon.

Hir nos govdyar morua.
Gnaót teruysc yg kymanua :
Ny chytuyd diryeit ada.

Hir nos gordyar mynyd.
Gochwiban góynt yóch blaen góyd :
Ny thóyll dryc anyan detwyd.

Marchwyeil bedó briclas.
A dynn uyntroet owanas :
Nac adef dy rin y was.

Marchwyeil deró myón llóyn.
A dynn vynntroet o gadwyn :
Nac adef rin y uorwyn.

Marchwyeil derѡ deilyar.
A dynn vyntroet o garchar :
Nac adef rin y lauar.

Marchwyeil dryssi a mѡyar erni.
A mѡyalch ar y nyth :
A chelwydaѡc ny theu vyth

Glaѡ allann gѡlychyt redyn.
Gѡynn gro mor goror ewynn :
Tec agannѡyll pѡyll y dyn.

Glaw allan ygan glydѡr
Melyn eithyn crin euѡr.
Duѡ reen py bereist lyvѡr.

Glaѡ allan gѡlychyt vyggѡallt.
Cѡynuanus gwann diffѡys allt.
Gѡelѡgan gѡeilgi. heli hallt.

Glaѡ allan gѡlychyt ėigyaѡn.
Gochwiban gѡynt yѡch blaen caѡn.
Gѡedy pob camp heb y daѡn. ·

IX.

Col. 1033. ＧORWYN blaen onn. hirwynyon vydant.
Pan dyuant ymblaen neint :
Bron gѡala hiraeth y heint.

Gorwyn blaen neint deweint
Hir keinmygir pob kywreint :
Dyly bun pѡyth hun y heint.

Gorwyn blaen helic eilic pysc

Yn llynn. gochwiban góynt yóch blaen górysc
Man : trech anyan noc adysc.

Gorwyn blaen eithin a chyfrin
A doeth. ac anoeth disgethrin.
Namyn duó nyt oes dewin.

Gorwyn blaen meillyon digallon
Llyfór lludedic eidigyon :
Gnaót ar eidil oualon.

Gorwyn blaen kaón góythlaón
Eidic ysodit ae digaón :
Góeithret call yó carn yn iaón.

Gorwyn blaen mynyded rac anhuned
Gayaf crin kaón tróm :
Rac neóyn nyt oes wyled.

Gorwyn blaen mynyded hydyr oeruel
Gayaf. crin kawn cróybyr arued :
Whefris góall yn alltuded.

Gorwyn blaen deró chweró bric onn.
Rac hóyeit góesgereit tonn :
Pybyr póyll pell oual ymkallon.

Gorwyn blaen deró chweró bric onn
Chec euór chóerthinat tonn :
Ny chel grud kystud kallon.

Gorwyn blaen egroes. nyt moes
Caledi. katwet baóp y eiryoes :
Góaethaf anaf yó annoes.

Gorwyn blaen banadyl. kynnadyl y sercha6c.
Goruelyn kangeu bac6ya6c :
Bas ryd gna6t hyfryt yn huna6c.

Gor6yn blaen auall amgall
Pob dedwyd. wheueryd y arall
A g6edy karu gadu g6all.

Gor6yn blaen auall amgall
Pob dedwyd. hírdyd meryd mall :
Cr6ybyr ar wa6r carchara6r dall.

Gor6yn blaen coll. geir digoll
Bre. diaele uyd pob ffoll :
G6eithret cadarn cad6 aruoll.

Gor6yn blaen corsyd. gna6t meryd
Yn dr6m. a ieuanc dysgedyd :
Ny thyrr namyn ffol yffyd.

Gorwyn blaen elestyr. bit venestyr prob drut.
Geir teulu yn ysg6n
Gna6t gan aghy6ir eir t6nn.

Gorwyn blaen gruc. gna6t seithuc ar
L6fyr. hydyr vyd d6fyr ar dal glan
Gna6t gan gywir eir kyvan.

Gor6yn blaen br6yn kym6yn bi6.
Redega6c vyndeigyr hedi6 :
Amgeled adyn nyt ydi6.

Gor6yn blaen redyn melyn
Kada6arth. mor vyd diwarth deillon :
Redega6c mana6c meibon.

Gor6yn blaen kyra6al. gna6t goual
Ar hen. ag6enyn yn ynyal :
Namyn du6 nyt oes dial.

Gorwyn blaen dar. didar drychin.
G6enyn yn uchel geuvel crin :
Gna6t gan rewyd rych6erthin.

Gor6yn blaen kelli gogyhyt
Yg6yd a deil deri dyg6ydyt :
Awyl agar g6ynn y uyt.

Gorwyn blaen der6. oer uer6
D6fyr. kyrchit bi6 blaen betuerw
G6nelit aeth saeth y syber6.

Gorwyn blaen kelyn kalet ac ereill eur agoret.
Pan gysco pa6b ar gylchet :
Ni ch6sc du6 pan ryd g6aret.

Gorwyn blaen helic hydyr elwic.
Gorwyd hirdyd deilyedic :
A garo y gilyd nys dirmic.

Gorwyn blaen br6yn briga6c vyd.
Pan danner dan obennyd :
Med6l sercha6c syber6 vyd.

Gorwyn blaen yspydat. hydyr wylyat
Gorwyd. gna6t sercha6c erlynnyat :
G6nelit da diwyt gennat.

Gorwyn blaen ber6r. bydina6r
Gorwyd keingyfreu koet y la6r.
Ch6erdyt bryt 6rth agara6r.

Gorwyn blaen perth. hywerth
Gorwyd ys da p6yll gyt a nerth :
G6nelit agheluydyt annerth.

Gorwyn blaen perthi. keingyfreu
Adar. hir dyd da6n goleu :
Trugar daffar du6 goreu.

Gorwyn blaen erwein. ac elein
Yn ll6yn. g6ychyr g6ynt g6yd mi gyein.
Eirya6l ny gara6l ny gyghein.

Gorwyn blaen ysga6 hydyr ana6
Unic. gna6t y dreissic. dreissya6
G6ae a d6c daffar o la6.

X.

1034. GOREISTE ar vrynn aeruyn
Uymbryt : a heuyt nym kych6yn :
Byrr vynteith diffeith vyntydyn.

Llem awel ll6m benydyr by6 :
Pan orwisc coed cogly6
Haf : teryd glaf 6yf hedi6.

Nyt 6yf anhyet : milet
Ny chatwaf ny allaf daryniret :
Tra bo da gan goc canet.

Coc lauar agan gan dyd :
Kyfreu eichya6c yndolyd.
Tua6c g6ell corra6c no chebyd.

Yn aber cua6c yt ganant gogeu.

Ar gangheu blodeuaѱc :
Coc lauar canet yraѱc.

Yn aber cuaѱc yt ganant gogeu.
Ar gangheu blodeuaѱc :
Gѱae glaf ae clyѱ yn vodaѱc.

Yn aber cuaѱc cogeu a ganant :
Ysatuant gan vymbryt :
Ae kigleu nas clyѱ heuyt.

Neus edeweis i goc ar eidorѱc brenn.
Neur laessѱys vygkylchѱy.
Etlit a gereis a gereis neut mѱy.

Yny vann odyѱch llonn dar.
Ydedeweis i leis adar :
Coc uann cof gan baѱp a gar.

Kethlyd kathyl uodaѱc hiraethaѱc
Y llef teith odef. tuth hebaѱc :
Coc vreuer yn aber cuaѱc.

Gordyar adar gѱlyl neint :
Llewychyt lloer oer deweint :
Crei vymbryt rac gofit heint.

Gѱynn gѱarthaf neint deweint :
Hir keinmygir pob kywreint.
Dylyѱn pѱyth hun y heneint.

Gordyar adar gѱlyb gro.
Deil cѱydit divryt dibro.
Ny wadaf ѱyf claf heno.

Gordyar adar gỽlyb traeth.
Eglur nỽybre ehalaeth
Tonn : gỽiỽ callon rac hiraeth.

Gordyar adar gỽlyb traeth
Eglur tonn tuth ehalaeth :
A gret ymabolaeth
Carỽn bei kaffỽn elwaeth.

Gordyar adar ar edryỽyard.
Bann llef cỽn yndiffeith.
Gordyar adar eilweith.

Kynnteuin kein pob amat
Pan vryssyant ketwyr y gat :
Mi nyt af anaf nym gat.

Kynteuin kein ar ystre.
Pan vrys ketwyr y gatle :
Mi nyt af anaf amde.

Llwyt gỽarthaf mynyd breu blaen onn.
O ebyr dyhepkyr tonn :
Peuyr pell chỽerthin om kallon.

Assymy hediỽ penn y mis.
Yny westua yd edeỽis :
Crei vymbryt cryt am dewis.

Amlỽc golỽc gỽylyadur :
Gỽnelit syberỽyt segur :
Crei vymbryt cleuyt am cur.

Alaf yn eil meil am bed.

S

Nyt eidun detwyd dyhed :
Amaerỽy atnabot amyned.

Alaf yn eil meil am lat :
Llithredaỽr llyry llonn caỽat :
A dỽfyn ryt berỽyt brỹt brat.

Berỽyt brat anuat ober.
Bydant dolur pan burer :
Gỽerthu bychot yr llawer.

Pre ator pre ennwir
Pan uarno douyd dyd hir :
Tywyll vyd geu : goleu gỽir.

Perygyl yn dirthiuat kyrchynyat
Kewic : llawen gỽyr odyỽch llat :
Crin calaf alaf yn deilyat.

Kigleu don drom y tholo :
Vann y rỽng gran a gro :
Krei vymbryt rac lletvryt heno.

Osglaỽc blaen derỽ. chỽerỽ chweith onn.
Chỽec evwr chwerthinat tonn :
Ny chel grud kystud callon.

Ymỽng ucheneit : adyuet
Arnaf. yn ol vyggordyfneit :
Ny at duỽ da y diryeit.

Da y dirieit ny atter :
Namyn tristit a phryder :
Nyt atwna duỽ ar awnel.

Oed mackѵy mabklaf : oed goein
Gyuran yn llys vrenhin :
Poet gѵyl duѵ ѵrth y dewin.

Or awneler yn derwd
Ystiryeit yr ae derlly :
Cas dyn yman yѵ cas duѵ vry.

XI.

1036. KYNN bum kein vaglaѵc bum. kyffes
Eiryaѵc. keinmygir ny eres :
Gѵyr ar goet eiryoet am porthes.

Kynn bum kein uaglaѵc bum hy :
Am kynnѵyssit ygkyuyrdy :
Powys paradwys gymiry.

Kynn bum kein vaglaѵc bum eiryan.
Oed kymwaeѵ vympar :
Oed kynnѵyf keuyngrѵm. ѵyf trѵm ѵyf truan.

Baglan brenn neut kynhayaf.
Rud redyn melyn kalaf :
Neur digereis agaraf.

Baglan brenn neut gayaf hynn.
Yt uyd llauar gѵyr ar lynn :
Neut diannerch vy erchѵyn.

Baglan brenn neut gѵannѵyn.
Rud cogeu goleu ewyn :
Wyf di garyat gan uorѵyn.

Baglan brenn neut kynteuin :

Neut rud rych neut crych egin :
Etryt ym edrych yth yluin.

Baglan brenn ganghen uoda6c.
Kynhellych hen hiraetha6c :
Llywarch leueryd uoda6c.

Baglan brenn ganghen galet.
Am kynn6yssy du6 diffret :
Elwir prenn kywir kynniret.

Baglan brenn byd ystywell.
Am kynhelych a uo g6ell :
Neut wyf lywarch lawer pell

Y mae heneint yn kymwed
Ami. om g6allt ymdeint :
Ar cloyn a gerynt yr ieueinc

Y mae heneint yn kymwed
Ami. om g6allt ym damied :
Ar cloyn agerynt y g6raged.

Dyr g6enn g6ynt g6ynn gne. godre
G6yd de6r hyd diwlyd bre :
Eidyl hen h6yr y dyre.

Y deilen honn neus kenniret
G6ynt. g6ae hi oe thynghet :
Hi hen eleni y ganet.

A gereis i yr yn was yssy gas
Gennyf ; merch estra6n a march glas :
Neut nat mi eu kyuadas.

Ym pedwar prif gas eirinoet :
Yngyueruydynt yn vnoet :
Pas a heneint heint a hoet.

Wyf hen wyf unic wyf annelwic
Oer gwedy g6ely keinmic :
6yf truan 6yf tridyblic.

Wyf tridyblic hen wyf ann6adal
Drut : 6yf ehut wyf annwar :
Y sa6l am kara6d. nyn kar.

Nym kar rianed nym kenniret
Neb : ny allaf daryniret :
Wi a agheu nam dygret.

Nym dygret na hun na hoen.
G6edy lleas lla6r a gwen :
Wyf annwar abar 6yf hen.

Truan adynghet a dyngh6yt.
Y lwyarch. yr y nos y ganet.
Hir gnif heb escor lludet.

Na wisc wedy k6yn : na vit vr6yn
Dy vryt. llem awel a chwer6 g6en6yn :
Nam gyhud vy mam mab yt 6yf.

Neut atwen ar vy awen
Yn hamiot : cun achen :
Tri g6yd oric elwic awen.

Llym vympar llachar ygryt.
Armaaf i wylya6 : ryt
Kynnyt anghyf du6 gennyt.

O diegyd ath welwyf.
Oth ryledir ath g6ynn6yf:
Na choll wyneb g6yr ar gnif.

Ny chollaf dy wyneb trin wosep 6r.
Pan wisc gle6 yr ystre:
Porthaf gnif kynn mudif lle.

Redega6c tonn ar hyt traeth.
Echadaf torrit aruaeth:
Kat ac ado gna6t ffo ar ffraeth.

Yssit ym alauar6yf.
Bria6 pelydyr parth y b6yf:
Ny lauaraf na ffowyf.

Medal migned kalet ri6
Rac carn cann tal glann a vri6:
Edewit ni. wnelher nydi6.

G6asgara6t neint am gla6d caer.
A minneu armaaf
Ysg6yt bryt bri6 kynn techaf.

Y corn athrodes di vryen:
Ae arwest eur am y en:
Ch6yth ynda6 oth da6 aghen

Yr ergryt aghen rac aghywyr lloegyr.
Ni lygraf vym ma6red:
Ny duchunaf rianed.

Tra vum i. yn oer y g6as dra6.
A wisc o eur y ottew:
Bydei re y ruthr6n y wae6

Diheu diweir dywaes.
Ti yn vyú ath dyst rylas :
Ny bu eidyl hen yn was.

Gúen úrth lawen ydwelas
Neithwyr. athuc ny techas :
Aer adraúd ar glaúd gorlas.

Gúen úrth lawen yd wylwys neithúyr.
Ar ysgúyt ar y ysgúyd :
A chan bu mab ynn bu hywyd.

Gúen úrth laúen yd wyliis
Neithwyr ar ysgúyt ar ygnis :
Kan bu mab y mi ny diegis.

Gúen gúgyd gochaúd vy mryt.
Dy leas ys maúr casnar.
Nyt car ath lavaúr.

Gúen vordwyt tylluras. a wylyas
Neithwyr. y goror ryt uorlas :
A chan bu mab ynn ny thechas.

Gúen gúydún dy eissillut.
Ruth eryr yn ebyr oedut :
Betún dedwyd dianghut.

Tonn tyruit toit eruit.
Pan ant kyvrein y govit :
Gúen gúae ry hen oth etlit.

Tonn tyruit toit aches.
Pan ant kyfvrin y gnes.
Gúen gúae : ry hen ryth golles.

Oed gỽr vy mab oedisgỽen
Haỽl. ac oed nei y vryen.
Ar ryt vorlas y llas gỽen.

Prennyal dywal gal ysgỽn :
Goruc ar loegyr llu kyndrỽyn :
Bed gỽen uab llywarch hen yỽ hỽnn.

Pedwar meib arhugeint ambu.
Eurdorchaỽc tywyssaỽc llu :
Oed gỽen goreu onadu.

Pedwar meib arhugeint ambwyat.
Eurdorchaỽc tywyssaỽc cat :
Oed gỽen goreu mab oedat.

Pedwar meib arhugeint am bỽyn :
Eurdorchaỽc tywyssaỽc vnbynn :
Y ỽrth wen gỽeissyonein oedyn.

Pedwar meib arhugeint ygkenuein
Lywarch. o wyr gleỽ galỽytheint :
Tỽll eu dyuot clot trameint.

Pedwar meib arhugeint aueithyeint
Vygknaỽt lledeseint
Da dyuot vygcoot coll edeint.

Pan las pyll oed teuyll
Briỽ. a gỽaet ar wallt hyll :
Ac am dỽylann ffraỽ ffrowyll.

Dichonat ystauell oesgyll
Ysgỽydaỽr tra vydat yn seuyll :
A vriwat ar aghat hyll.

Dyn dewis ar vy meibon.
Pan gyrchei ba6p y alon.
Pyll wynn p6yll tan tr6y luuon.

Mat dodes ei uordwyt dros obell
Y orwyd o wug ac obell :
Pyll p6yll tan tr6y sawel.

Oed llary lla6 aergre
Oed aela6 eiluyd oed dinas ar ystre :
Pyll vyn doet perchyll eude.

Pan sauei yndr6s pebyll
Y ar orwyd erewyll.
Ardelwei o wr wreic pyll.

Briwyt rac pyll penngloc ffer
Ys odit llywyr yt llecher :
Yn da6 eidil heb dim digoner.

Pyll wynn pell cunic y glot.
Handwyf n6yf yrot oth dyuot :
Yn vab athara6 atnabot.

Goreu tridyn y dan nef.
A werchetwis y hadef.
Pyll a selyf a sandef.

Ysg6yt a rodeis y byll.
Kynnoe gyscu neu bu doll :
Dimia6 y hada6 ar wall.

Kyt delei gymry ac elyflu
O loeger. a llawer o bell tu.
Dangossei byll b6yll udu.

Na phwyll na mada6c ny bydynt
Hiroedla6c. or dewa6t y getwynt :
Rodyn na rodyn kygreir vyt nyserchynt.

Llyma yma bed di uei
Tringar. i veird ys ei yglot : lle nyt elci
Byll pei pellach parei.

Maeir a mada6c a medel
Dewrwyr di yssic vroder :
Selyf heilin lla6r lliwer.

Bed g6ell yny ri6 velen.
Bed sawyl yn llan gollen
G6ercheid6 llamyr b6ch lloryen.

Bed rud neuscud tywarch
Nys eiryd g6eryt ammarch :
Bed llygedwy uab llywarch.

Pell odyman aber llyw :
Pellach an d6y gyfedli6 :
Talan teleisty deigyr hedi6.

Eryueis i win o ga6c.
Ef aracwan rac reinya6c :
Esgyll g6a6r oed waewa6r d6c.

O diuar gennyf pan ymercheis.
Nat gantu y diewis :
Kynnydyuei hael hoedel mis.

Atwen leueryd kyni.
Pan disgynnei ygkyfyrdy :
Penn g6r pan g6in a dyly.

XII.

1039. ꝹYM kywarwydyat unhwch
Dywal baran ygkyolối :
Gổell yd lad nogyt ydolối .

Dym kyuarwydyat vn hối ch
Dywal : dywedit yn drối s llech.
Dunaối t uab pabo ny tech.

Dym kyfuarwydyat vnhối ch dywal
Chwerối blối ng chwerthin mor ryuel
Dorblodyat. vryen reget greidiaối l gauel.

Eryr gal vnhối ch glew hael :
Ryuel godic budic uael
Vryen greidyaối l. gauael

Eryr gal vnhối ch : berchen enaối r :
Kell llyr kein ebyr gối yr glaối r.

Penn a borthaf auntu :
Bu kyrchynat rối ng deulu :
Mab kynuarch balch bieiuu.

Penn a borthaf ar vyntu :
Penn vryen llary llyw. ei llu :
Ac ar y vronn wennvran du.

Penn a borthaf myối n vygcrys :
Penn vryen llary llywyei llys.
Ac ar y vronn wenvrein ae hys.

Penn a borthaf ym vedeir.

Yr yr echwyd oed nu geil.
Teyrnvron treulyat genniweir.

Penn a borthaf tu mordwyt.
Oed ysgɣyt ar y wlat :
Oed olwyn ygkat :
Oed cledyf cat kywlat rɣyt.

Penn a borthaf ar vygkled.
Gɣell y vyɣ nogyt yued.
Oed dinas y henwred.

Penn a borthaf o godir
Penaɣc pellynnyaɣc y luyd :
Vryen geiryaɣc glotryd.

Penn a borthaf ar vy ysgɣyd.
Nym aruellei waratwyd :
Gɣae vy llaɣ llad vy arglɣyd.

Penn a borthaf ar vymbreich.
Neus goruc o dir bryneich :
Gɣedy gɣaɣr geloraɣr veirch.

Penn a borthaf yn aghat
Vy llaɣ. llary ud llywyei wlat :
Penn post prydein ryallat.

Penn a borthaf am porthes :
Neut atwen nat yr vylles :
Gɣae vy llaɣ llym digones.

Penn a borthaf o du riɣ.
Ac y eneu ewyn riɣ.
Gɣaet gɣae reget o hedi.

Ny thyrvis vymbreich rygardwys vy eis.
Vygcallon neur dorres
Penn a borthaf am porthes.

Y gelein veinwen a oloir hediỼ :
A dan brid a mein
GỼae vy llaỼ llad tat owein.

Y gelein ueinwen a oloir hediỼ.
Ym plith prid a derỼ.
GỼae vy llaỼ llyd vygkeuynderỼ.

Y gelein ueinwen a oloir heno :
A dan vein ae deỼit :
GỼae vy llaỼ llam rym tynghit.

Y gelein veinwen a oloir heno
Ym plith prid a thyweirch :
GỼae vy llaỼ llad mab kynuarch.

Y gelein ueinwenn a oloir hediỼ.
Dan weryt ac arwyd :
GỼae vy llaw llad vy arglỼyd.

Y gelein ueinwen a oloir hediỼ.
A dan brid athywaỼt.
Gwae vy llaỼ llam rym daeraỼt.

Y gelein veinwenn a oloir hediỼ.
A dan brid a dynat :
GỼae vy llaỼ llam rym gallat.

Y gelein veinwenn a oloir hediỼ.
A dan brid a mein glas :
GỼae vy llaỼ llam rym gallas.

Anoeth byd braͼt bͼyn kynnull
Am gyrn buelyn : am drull
Rebyd uilet reget dull.

Anoeth byd braͼt bͼyn kynnwys
Am gyrn buelyn amwys :
Rebyd uilet regethwys.

Handit euyrdyl aflawen
Henoeth. a lluossyd amgen :
Yn aber 'lleu llad vryen.

Ys trist eurdyl or drallot
Heno. ac or llam am daeraͼt :
Yn aber lleu llad eu braͼt.

Duͼ gͼener gͼeleis i diuyd
Maͼr. ar uydinaͼr bedit :
Heit heb uodrydaf hubyd.

Neum rodes i run ryuedliaͼr
Cant heit a chant ysgͼydaͼr :
Ac vn heit oed well pell maͼr.

Neum rodes i run rͼyf yolyd
Cantref : a chant eidyonyd :
Ac vn oed well nogyd.

Ym myͼ run reaͼdyr dyhed.
Dyrein enwir eu byded :
Heyrn ar veirch enwired.

Mor vi gogͼn vy anaf.
Arglyͼ pob un ym hop haf :
Ny wyr neb nebaͼt arnaf.

PỼyllei dunaỼt marchaỼc gỼein.
Erechwyd gỼneuthur kelein :
Yn erbyn cryssed owein.

PỼyllei dunaỼt vd pressen.
Erechwyd gỼneuthur catwen :
Yn erbyn kyfryssed pasgen.

PỼyllei wallaỼc marchaỼc trin.
Erechwyd gỼneuthur dyuin :
Yn erbyn kyfryssed elphin.

PỼyllei vran uab y mellyrn.
Vyndihol i llosgi vy ffyrn :
Bleid a uugei Ỽrth ebyrn.

PỼyllei uorgant ef ae wyr.
Vyndihol llosgi vyntymyr :
Llyc a grauei Ỽrth glegyr.

PỼylleis i pan las elgno :
Ffrowyllei lauyn areidyo :
Pyll a phebyll oe vro.

Eilweith gỼeleis gỼedy gỼeithyen.
AỼr ysgỼyt ar ysgỼyd vryen.
Bueil yno elgno hen.

Ar erechwyd ethyỼ gỼallt
O vraỼ marchaỼc ysgỼeill.
A uyd uyth uryen arall.

Ys moel vy arglỼyd ys euras
GỼrth nys car ketwyr y gas :
LliaỼs gỼledic rydreulyas.

Angerd uryen ys agro.
Gennyf. kyrchynat ympob bro :
Yn wysc llouan laѵ difro.

Taѵel awel tu hirglyѵ.
Odit a uo molediѵ.
Nam vryen ken ny diѵ.

Llawer ki geilic a hebaѵc
Wyrennic a lithiwyt ar y llaѵr :
Kynn bu erlleon llawedraѵr.

Yr aelwyt honn ae goglyt gaѵr.
Mѵy gordyfnassei ar y llaѵr.
Med a meduon eiriaѵl.

Yr aelwyt honn neus kud dyuat.
Tra vu byw y gѵercheitwat :

Yr aelwyt honn neus cud glessin.
Ynu myѵ owein ac elphin
Berwassei y pheir breiddin.

Yr aelwyt honn neus cud kallaѵdyr llѵyt
Mѵy gordyfnassei am y bѵyt :
Cledyfual dyual diarswyt.

Yr aelwyt honn neus cud kein vieri.
Coet : kynneuaѵc oed idi :
Gordyfnassei reget rodi.

Yr aelwyt honn neus cud drein :
Mѵy gordyfnassei y chyngrein :
Kymѵynas kyweithas owein.

Yr aelwyt honn neus cud myr ;
Mύy gordyfnassei babir :
Gloew a chyuedeu kywir.

Yr aelwyt honn neus cud tauaόl
Mύy y gordyfnassei ar y llaόr :
Med a medόon eiryaόl.

Yr aelwyt honn neus clad hύch.
Mύy gordyfnassei elwch :
Gύyr ac am gyrn kyuedόch.

Yr aelwyt honn neus clad kywen.
Nys eidiganei anghen :
Yn myύ owein ac vryen.

Yr ystύffύl hύnn ar hύnn draύ :
Mύy gordyfnassei amdanaύ :
Elύch llu allύybyr anaύ.

XIII.

1041. ⟦M⟧AENWYNN tra vum ythoet :
Ny sethrit vy llenn .i. athraet :
Nyt erdit vyntir .i. heb waet.

Maenwynn tra vum yth erbyn :
Am ieucnctit ym dilyn.
Ny thorei gesseil vynteruyn.

Maenwyn tra vum yth erlit :
Yn dylyn vy ieuenctit :
Ny charei gesseil vyggύythlit.

Maenwynn tra uum .i. efras :

T

Oedŵli dywal galanas :
Gẃnaẃn weithret gŵr kyt bydẃn gẃas.

Maenwynn medyr di yngall :
Anghen kyssueil ar wall :
Keissyet uaelgẃn uaer arall.

Vyndewis y gyfran ac gaeu
Arnaẃ : ym llym megys draen :
Nyt ouer gnif ym hogi maen.

Anrec rym gallat o dyfryn :
Mewyrnyaẃn ygkud yghelẃrn :
Haearn llym llaes o dẃrn.

Boet bendigeit yr aghysbell
Wrach : a dywaẃt o drẃs y chell :
Maenwynn nac adaẃ dy gyllell.

XIV.

Col. 1042.

PANET anet gereint oed agoret
Pyrth nef rodei grist a archet :
Pryt mirein pridein ogonet.
Molet paẃb y rud ereint.
Arglẃyd molaf inneu ereint.

Rac gereint glyn dihat.
Gẃeleis y veirch kymrud o gat :
A gẃedy gaẃr garẃ bẃyllat.

Rac gereint gelyn kythrud.
Gẃeleis y veirch dan gymryd
A gẃedy gaẃr garẃ achlud.

Yn llongborth gỽeleis drydar.
Ac eloraỽr yg gỽyar.
A gỽyr rud rac ruthur esgar.

Yn llongborth gỽeleis i wytheint.
Ac eloraỽr mỽy no meint.
A gỽyr rud rac ruthur gereint.

Yn llongborth gueleis .i. waetfreu.
Ac eloraỽr rac arueu :
A gỽyr rud rac ruthur agheu.

Yn llongborth gỽeleis. i. ottew.
Gỽyr ny gyllynt rac ofyn gỽaeỽ :
Ac yuet gỽiu o wydyr gloew.

Yn llongborth gỽeleis i vygedorth.
A gỽyr yn gode amhorth :
A goruot gỽedy gorborth.

Yn llongborth gỽeleis gymynat :
Porthit gnif bob kyminat.

Yn llongborth gỽeleis drablud.
Er uein brein ar golud :
Ac argrann kynran manrud.

Yn llongborth gỽeleis i brithret.
Gỽyr yggryt a gỽaet am draet.
A vo gỽyr y ereint bryssyet.

Yn llongborth gỽeleis yr ỽydrin.
Gỽyr yggryt a gỽaet hyt deulin :
Rac ruthur maỽr mab erbin.

Lluest gatwalla6n ar wy.
Maranned wedy mord6y :
A diliuat kat kylch6y.

Lluest gatwalla6n ar ffynna6n
Uetwyr. rac milwyr magei da6n :
Dangossei gynon yno haern da6n.

Lluest gatwalla6n ar daf.
Ys lluosa6c y g6elaf.
Kywrennin vreisc naf.

Lluest gatwalla6n ar dawy.
Lleidyat adaf yn ad6y :
Clotryd keissydyd kest6y.

Lluest gatwalla6n tra chaer.
Kaeu bydin a channwr taer :
Kan kat a thorri can kaer.

Lluest gatwalla6n ar gowyn.
Lla6 lludedic ar awyn :
G6yr lloegyr lluosa6c eu k6yn.

Lluest gatwalla6n heno :
Trathir yn tymyr pennvro.
Am na6d ua6r anha6d yffo.

Lluest gatwalla6n ar deiui.
Kymysgei waet a heli :
Angerd g6yned g6y ny gei.

Lluest gatwalla6n ar dufyrd auon.
G6naeth eryron yn lla6n.
G6edy trin dyuineu da6n.

Lluest gatwallaѵn vym braѵt.
Yggѵertheuin bro dunaѵt :
Y uar annwar yn ffossaѵt.

Lluest gatwallaѵn ar uenin.
Lleѵ lluosaѵc y werin.
Tѵrѵf maѵr trachas y ordin.

O gyssul estraѵn ac anghyfyaѵn
Ueneich dillyd dѵfyr offynnaѵn :
Tru trѵm dyd am gatwallaѵn.

Gѵisgѵys coet kein dudet
Haf. dybryssit gѵyth ѵrth dyghet.
Kyueruydoin ny am eluet.

XVI.

1044. SEFѴCH allann vorynnyon a syllѵch werydre
Gyndylan : llys benn gѵern neut tande :
Gѵae ieueinc a eidun brotre.

Vn prenn a gouit
Arnaѵ arno odieinc ys odit :
Ac auynno duѵ derffit.

Kynndylan callon iaen
Gaeaf : awant tѵrch trѵy y benn :
Tu a rodeist yr tѵrѵf trenn.

Kynndylan callon godeith
Wannwyn. o gyflѵyn amgyuyeith.
Yn amѵyn tren tref diffeith.

Kyndylan befyr bost kywlat.

Kadͨynaͨc kildynnyaͨc cat.
Amuscei tren tref y dat.

Kyndylan beuyr bͨyll o vri.
Kadͨynaͨc kynndynnyaͨc llu :
A mucsei tren hyt tra vu.

Kyndylan callon milgi
Pan disgynnei ygkymelri.
Cat : calaned a ladei.

Kynndylan callon hebaͨc
Buteir ennwir gynndeiryaͨc.
Keneu kyndrͨyn kyndynnyaͨc.

Kyndylan callon gͨythhwch.
Pan disgynnei ympriffͨch
Cat. kalaned yn deudrͨch.

Kyndylan gulhͨch gynnifiat
Lleͨ. blei dilin disgynnyat :
Nyt atuer tͨrch tref y dat.

Kyndylan hyt tra attat
Yd adei. y gallon mor wylat :
Gantaͨ mal y gͨrͨf y gat.

Kyndylan powys borffor.
Wych yt : kell esbyt bywyt ior :
Keneu kyndrͨyn kͨynitor.

Kyndylan wynn uab kyndrͨyn :
Ny mat wisc baraf am y drͨyn :
Gͨr ny bo gͨell no morwyn.

Kyndylan kymỽyat ỽyt :
Ar meithyd nabydy lỽyt :
Am drebỽll tỽll dy ysgỽyt.

Kynndylan kae di y riỽ.
Yn y daỽ lloegyrwys hediw :
Amgeled am vu uydiỽ.

Kyndylan kae di y nenn.
Yn y daỽ lloegyrwys drỽy dren :
Ny elwir coet o vu prenn.

Gan vygcallon .i. mor dru.
Kyssylltu ystyllot du :
Gỽynngnaỽt kyndylan kyngran canllu.

Stauell gyndylan ys tywyll
Heno heb dan heb wely :
Wylaf wers. tawaf wedy.

Stauell gyndylan ystywyll
Heno. heb dan heb gannwyll :
Namyn duỽ pỽy am dyry pỽyll.

Stauell gyndylan ystywyll
Heno. heb dan heb oleuat :
Elit amdaỽ am danat.

Stauell gyndylan ystywyll
Y nenn. gỽedy gỽen gyweithyd :
Gỽae ny wna da ae dyuyd.

Stauell gyndylan neut athwyt
Heb wed. mae yn bed dy yscỽyt :
Hyt tra un ny bu doll glỽyt.

Stauell gyndylan ys digaryat
Heno. gẃedy yr neb pieuat :
Owi a anghen byrr ym gat.

Stauell gyndylan nyt esmẃyth
Heno. ar benn carrec hytwyth :
Heb ner. heb niuer. heb amẃyth.

Stauell gyndylan ystywyll
Heno. heb dan heb gerdeu :
Dygystud deurud dagreu.

Stauell gyndylan ystywyll
Heno. heb deulu :
Hidyl meu yt gynnu.

Stauell gyndylan amgẃan
Y gẃelet. heb doet heb dan :
Marẃ vy glyẃ. buẃ mu hunan.

Stauell gyndylan yspeithwac.
Heno. gẃedy ketwyr uodaẃc :
Eluan kyndylan kaeaẃc.

Stauell gyndylan ysoergrei
Heno. gẃedy y parch am buei :
Heb wyr heb wraged ae katwei.

Stauell gyndylan ys araf
Heno. gẃedy colli y hynaf :
Y maẃr drugaẃc duẃ pawnaf.

Stauell gyndylan ystywyll
Y nenn gẃedy dyua o loegyrwys :
Kyndylan ac eluan powys.

Stauell gyndylan ystywyll
Heno. o blant kyndrwyn :
Kynon a g6ia6n a g6yn.

Stauell kyndylan am erwan.
Pob awr g6edy ma6r ymgynyrdan :
A weleis ar dy benntan.

Eryr eli ban y lef.
Llewssei g6yr llynn :
Creu callon kyndylan wynn.

Eryr eli gorelwi
Heno y g6aet g6yr gwynn novi :
Ef y goet tr6m hoet ymi.

Eryr eli a glywaf
Heno. creulyt y6 nys beidyaf :
Ef y goet t6r6m hoet arnaf.

Eryr eli gorthryniet.
Heno. diffrynt meissir myge'da6c
Dir brochuael hir rygodet.

Eryr eli echeid6 myr.
Ny threid pysca6t yn ebyr.
Gel6it g6elit owaet gwyr.

Eryr eli gorymda
Coet. kyuore kinya6a :
Ae lla6ch ll6ydit y draha.

Eryr penng6ern penngarn
Ll6yt. aruchel y atleis.
Eidic amgic.

Eryr .penngẃern penngarn .
Llẃyt. aruchel y euan.
Eidic amgic kyndylan.

Eryr penngẃern pengarn
Llẃyt. aruchel y adaf
Eidic amgic a garaf.

Eryr penngwern pell galwaẃt
Heno. ar waet gẃyr gẃylat :
Rygelwir trenn tref difaẃt.

Eryr penngẃern pell gelwit
Heno. ar waet gẃyr gẃelit :
Rygelwir trenn tref lethrit.

Eglẃysseu bassa y orffowys
Heno. y diwed ymgynnẃys.
Cledyr kat callon argoetwys.

Eglẃysseu bassa ynt ffaeth
Heno. vyntauaẃt ae gẃnaeth :
Rud ynt ẃy rwy vy hiraeth.

Eglẃysseu bassa ynt yng
Heno. y etiued kyndrẃyn :
Tir mablan kyndylan wynn.

Eglẃysseu bassa ynt tirion
Heno. y gẃnaeth eu meillyon :
Rud ynt ẃy. rẃy vyngcallon.

Eglẃysseu bassa collassant
Eu breint. gẃedy y diua o loegyrwys :
Kyndylan ac eluan powys.

Eglỽysseu bassa ynt diua
Heno. y chetwyr ny phara :
Gỽyr awyr ami yma.

Eglỽysseu bassa ynt baruar
Heno. a minneu ỽyf dyar :
Rud ynt ỽy rỽy vyggalar.

Y dref wenn ymbronn y coet.
Ys ef yỽ y hefras eiryoet :
Ar wyneb y gỽellt y gỽaet.

Y dref wenn yn yt hymyr
Y hefras. y glas vyuyr :
Y gwaet a dan draet y gỽyr.

Y dref wenn yn y dyffrynt
Llawen y bydeir. ỽrth gyuanrud.
Kat : ygỽerin neurderynt.

Y dref wenn rỽng trenn athrodwyd.
Oed gnodach ysgỽyt.
Tonn : yn dyuot o gat no gyt ych y echwyd.

Y dref wenn rỽng trenn athraual.
Oed gnodach y gauet : ar
Wyneb gỽellt noc eredic brynar.

Gỽynn y byt freuer mor yỽ diheint.
Heno gỽedy colli keuneint :
O anffaỽt vyntauaỽt yt lesseint.

Gwynn y byt freuer mor yỽ gỽanu
Heno. gỽedy agheu eluan :
Ac eryr kyndrỽyn kyndylan.

Nyt angheu freuer. am de
Heno am damorth brodyrde.
Duhunaf wylaf uore.

Nyt angheu ffreur am góna heint
O dechreu nos hyt deweint :
Duhunaf wylaf bylgeint.

Nyt angheu ffreuer amtremyn
Heno. am góna grydyeu melyn :
A chocheu dagreu dros erchóyn.

Nyt angheu ffreuer aerniwaf
Heno. namyn myhun : ny wanglaf.
Vymbrodyr am tymyr agóynaf.

Ffreuer wenn brodyr athuaeth.
Ny hannoedynt ordiffaeth.
Wyr ny uegynt vygylyaeth.

Ffreuer wenn brodyr athuu.
Pann glywynt gyórenin llu :
Ny echyuydei ffyd ganthu.

Mi affreuer a medlan.
Kyt yt uo cat ympob mann.
Nyn taór ny ladaór an rann.

Y mynyd kyt at uo vch.
Nyt eidigafaf ydóyn vymbuch :
Ys ysgaón gan rei vy ruch.

Amhaual ar auaeróy.
Yda atren yny trydonóy :
Ac yd a atórch ym marchnóy.

Amhaẟl ar eluyden
Ydaa trydonẟy yn tren :
Ac ydaa geirẟ yn alwen.

Kynn bu vygkylchet croen
Gauyr galet. chẟannaẟc y gelein
Rym goruc yn uedw ued bryum.

Kynn bu vygkylchet
Croen neu gauyr galet.
Kelyngar y llillen :
Rymgoruc y uedẟ ued trenn.

Gẟedy vymbrodyr o dymyr hafren.
Y am dẟylan dẟyryẟ :
Gẟae vi duẟ vy mot yn vyẟ.

Gẟedy meirch hywed a chochwed
Dillat. a phlẟaẟr melyn :
Mein uygcoes nymoes du dedyn.

Gwarthec edeirnyaẟn ny buant
Gerdeunin. a cherd neb nyt aethant
Ym buẟ. gorwynnyonn gẟyr o uchuant.

Gwarthec edeirnyaẟn ny buant
Gerdunin. a chant neb ny cherdynt :
Ym byẟ gorẟynnyon gẟr
Eduyn warth gẟarthegyd
Gẟerth gẟyla negyd :
Ar a dyuo dragẟarth ae deubyd.
Mi awydẟn aoed da.
Gẟaet am y gilyd gwrda.

Bei gẟreic gyrthmẟl bydei gẟan

Hediꝺ : bydei bann y dysgyr
Hi gyna diua y gꝺyr.

Tywarchen ercal ar erdywal
Wyr. o etined moryal :
A gꝺedy rys macrysinal.

Heled hꝺyedic ym gelwir.
O duꝺ padiꝺ yth rodir :
Meirch vym bro ac eu tir.

Heled hꝺyedic am kyueirch.
O duꝺ padiꝺ yth rodir gurumseirch.
Kyndylan ae bedwar degmeirch.

Neur sylleis elygon ar dirion
Dir. o orsed orwynnyon :
Hir hꝺyl heul hꝺy vygheuyon.

Neur llysseis o dinlle
Ureconn ffreuer werydre.
Hiraeth amdamorth vrodyrde.

Marchaꝺc o gaer a danaꝺ.
Nyt oed hꝺyr a gꝺynnyon :
Gꝺr o sanneir.

Llas vymbrodyr ar vnweith.
Kynan kynndylan kynnwreith :
Yn amꝺyn tren tref diffeith.

Ny sangei wehelyth ar nyth
Kyndylan. nythechei droetued vyth
Ny uagas y uam uab llyth.

Brodyr amb6yat ny vall.
A dyuynt ual g6yal coll
O vn yun edynt oll.

Brodyr amb6yat aduc
Du6 ragaf. vy anffa6t ae goruc :
Ny obrynynt ffa6 yr ffuc.

Teneu awel tew lletkynt
Pereid y rycheu. ny phara
Ae goreu : ar auu uat ydynt.

As clywo a du6 a dyn.
As clywo y ieueinc a hyn :
Meuyl barueu madeu hedyn.

Ym by6 ehedyn ehedyei.
Dillat yn aros g6aed bei :
Ar glas vereu naf n6yfei.

Ryuedaf dincleir nadi6
Yn ol kilyd keluyd cly6 :
Ygg6all t6rch torri cneu kny6.

Ny 6y ae ny6l ae m6c
Ae ketwyr yn kyuam6c :
Y g6eirgla6d aer yssyd dr6c.

Edeweis y weirgla6d aer ysg6yt.
Digyuyng dinas y gedyrn :
Goreu g6r garanmael.

Karanmael kym6y arnat
U

Atwen dy ystle o gat :
Gnaϭt man ar gran kyniuiat.

Kymϭed ognaϭ llaϭ hael :
Mab kynndylan clot auael :
Dywedϭr kynndrϭynin caranmael.

Oed diheid ac oed.
Oed diholedic. tref tat
A geissywys. caranmael yn ynat.

Karanmael kymwed ognaϭ.
Mab kyndylan clot arllaϭ :
Nyt ynat kyt mynnat o honaϭ.

Pan wisgei garanmael. gatpeis kynndylan
A phyrydyaϭ y onnen.
Ny chaffei ffranc tranc oe benn.

Amser y bum bras vϭyt.
Nydyrchafϭn vy mordϭyt :
Yr gϭr a gϭynei claf gornϭyt.

Brodyr ambϭyat inneu :
Nyscϭynei gleuyt cornnϭydeu :
Vn eluan kyndylan deu.

Ny mat wisc briger. nyw dirper
O ϭr yn diruaϭr gywryssed :
Nyt oed leuaϭr vymbroder.

Onyt rac agheu ac aeleu
Maϭr. a gloes glas uereu :
Ny bydaf leuaϭr inneu.

Maes maodyn neus cud re6.
O diua da y ode6 :
Ar ued eirinued eiry tew.

Tom elwithan neus g6lych gla6.
Maes maodyn y dana6 :
Dylyei gynon y g6yna6.

Pedwar p6nn broder am bu.
Ac y bob un pennteulu :
Ny wyr tren perchen ydu.

Pedwar p6nn broder am buant.
Ac y bop un gor6yf n6yvant :
Ny wyr tren perchen kugant.

Pedwar p6n terwyn o adwyn.
Vrodyr am buant o gyndr6yn :
Nyt oes y drenn berchen m6yn.

Gosgo yghot adot arnat.
Nyt 6yt bylgeint gyuot :
Neum g6ant ysg6r o g6rr dy got.

Gosgo di ẏghot a thech.
Nyt 6yt ymadra6d dibech :
Nyt g6i6 clein yth grein y grech.

XVII.

L. 1049. &OGY gogyfercheis. gogyfarchaf gogyfuerchyd ;
Vrien reget dywallouyet y le6enyd.
Eur ac aryant mor eudiuant eudihenyd.
Kyn noc y da6 r6ng y d6yla6 y g6esgeryd.

Jeuaf awnaeth coll ac alaeth am veirch peunyd.

Keneu y bra6t : kynnindaera6t. ny bugeluyd.

Vrieu awnaeth. dialynaeth. y gewilyd.

Kynin vynnu. kyuarchwelu. eudihenyd.

Deutu aeruen. difföys dilen ; dyda6 luyd.

Seleu delyit. ennynnyessit. or a dybyd.

Dybi y uaeth. aryd achaeth. oceu herwyd.

Cochli6 lafneu. tr6y ualch eiryeu. am ffr6yth eu g6yd.

Wy kynnhalyant. lle pedwar cant. y pedwar g6yr.

D6fyr diyunas. bendig6yf claf clas. oc eu herwyd.

Yr ae kaffo kynuina6l vo. yn dragywyd.

Dyda6 collet. or ymdiryet. yr ardelyd.

Alla6 heb ua6t. allauyn ar gna6t. athla6t luyd.

Oes ueibionein. nyt ymgyghein ymmerweryd.

Nyt ymganret. nyt ymdiret neb oe gilyd.

Dreic o wyned. diffwys dired dirion dreuyd.

Lloegyrwys yd aa. lleta6t yna. y hatchetlyd.

Torrit meinweith. yn anoleith or gyfhergyr.

M6y a gollir. noc a geffir. o wyndodyd.

O gyt gyghor. kyfr6ng escor. mor a mynyd.

Kyuyt ogud. g6r auyd bud. ywyndodyd.

Gorffit brythyon yn atporion ar antyrron gy6ethyd.

Ef ada6 byt. ny byd kerdglyt. ny byd keluyd.

Alaf gar maer. artha6c uyd chwaer. 6rth y gilyd.

Llad a bodi. o eleri. hyt ch6iluynyd.

Vn goruudia6c. antrugara6c. ef a oruyd.

Bychan y lu. yn ymchwelu. or mercherdyd.

Arth or deheu. kyuyt ynteu dychyueruyd.

Lloegyrwys lledi. af riuedi. o bowyssyd.

G6eith cors uochno. o diangho. byda6t detwyd.

Deudeng wraged. ac nyt ryued. am vn g6r vyd.

Oes ieuengtit aghyfyrdelit. y uaeth dybyd.

Ber6 ymdifant. barna6c or cant. nys rywelyd

Vryen o reget. hael ef yssyd ac auyd.

Ac a vu yr adaf.

Lletaf y gled. balch ygkynted

Or tri theyrn ar dec or gogled

A ƀnn eu henƀ. aneirin gƀaƀtryd aƀenyd.

Minneu dalyessin o iaƀn llyn geirionnyd.

Ny dalywyf yn hen.

Ym dygyn aghen.

O ny molƀyf i vryen. Amen.

XVIII.

1050.

ꟼꟼAL rot yn troi tramhƀeilyeu

Trallaƀt meth tra chymell tretheu.

Traƀs arovyn dreic mynnƀyn mynneu ;

Trin engyrth am byrth am borthuaeu.

A gƀenƀyn rieu gan rieu.

Gnaƀt glutuan freinc deuan diuieu.

Ac am gƀyn riein ryueleu

A vyd ; a diffeith eluyd heb a elwydeu.

Ac allwed rufein gan rƀyueu.

Ac allmyn heb allel kyrcheu.

A gƀynvyt gƀyndyt yn gƀan yr deheu.

A gƀander seis oe inseileu.

A llƀgyr meith am gyfreitheu.

A lloegyr yn brydyon brat y rieu.

A gƀth ffreinc ae ffraƀd ar longheu.

A gƀeith dofyr yn dyfvrys agheu.

Eryssi oes uaƀr yr ae kigleu.

Clƀyf am blƀyf amdifflan pleideu.

Dreic didƀyll tywyll a goleu.

Goludaƀc riedaƀc rieu.

An rodo trƀy ryddit adneu.

Y rann oewled oesswed heb eisseu. Amcn.

XIX.

Col. 1050.

Mochdaƿ byt yngryt yngredyf carant.

Mochdaƿ mynych dorr or tƿrneimant.

Mochdaƿ rƿng saesson russyant

Ymdrychu. a dibarch gladu aguassant.

Mochdaƿ gƿyr manaƿ yr mynnu molyant.

Ar gogled dyhed diheu y gƿnant.

Mochuyd ym prydein pryder achwant.

Ac am deutu lloegyr llafar yt gƿynant.

Am lithraƿ mab henri anryuedant.

Meint uyd ygƿascar yr ysgrydyant.

Ysgein dros uoroed rif toruoed taruant.

Tƿrƿf am y teruyn traha ny barchant.

Ami disgoganaf esgut lefant.

Gƿirion ual geuaƿc a gymynant.

Maƿr trachwres llynghes lloegyr a gyrchant.

Lluoed afletneis treis ageissant.

Am gyhoed tyr oed taer ystyngant.

Y tyreu kadarn yn wann y gƿnant.

Am dal tyrua y tƿrneimant.

Am gynghaƿs undyd rif myrd a syrthyant.

Am voroed kyhoed y kymynant.

O honaƿ disgoganaf na hilia plant.

Ac nyt mi ae kel nys treulant.

Oesuot adyuyd douyd ae diuant

Brythyon ae treula penna vydant.

Brithuyt a dybyd o dicter karant.

A seif byd lawen pan ygƿelant.

Dygogan tyfyrru erymes tra bythaƿt.

XX.

Col. 1051.

Llynghes von dirion direidi

Llesteir creu trost rƿyneu trosti.

Llanỽ mỽ ani gonỽy amgyui.

Llithraỽt gỽyr eryr eryri.

Dywres amser teskynn tewi.

Di ryuic kymry rac kammỽri.

Dreic darogan uab henri.

Blỽydyn y eruyn kynn torvi.

Bleid kedyrn kadarn y westi.

Gỽesti byt koel ennyt keli.

Gỽastat gỽlat gỽledic normandi.

Gỽst prydein pryder oe eni.

Gvastatuot ual rot yntroi.

Penn beird pob eluyd oth hen o vynnon.

Mi ath ogyuarchaf ar arỽydon.

Py vynych gymhỽylly vabon.

Mabon karedic y gyweithyas.

Goruchel awen ar weilgi laa.

Mabon oed brython pandelon yỽ hurdas.

Ac owein auyd ryd rỽyf teyrnas.

Gỽr coch ygcochwed gorawen. gỽyned

Gỽreid hyn hil meruyn mur teyrned

Carannaỽc uabon ymbroun gỽaret.

Kyuarwyd yỽ duỽ ymdamunet.

Allmyn argythwyn gochwed dyghet.

Breoled dachwed gyrded gerthet.

Rygas pob rywir bydaỽt dir dyuot.

Gỽyr merweryd am dreuyd yn ymdrauot.

Rudyon galaned lain dyhed heided a diheu eubot.

Pob kof pob kyfnot pob gỽr pob goruot.

Crist amrodes ymlles ym llỽyr wybot.

Lloegyrwys anghymmỽys yn aghyminot.

Llefferthin werin aindrin drauot.

XXI.

Col. 1051.   CRIST iessullwyr uedu lleuuer
Crista⁶n ia⁶n goga⁶n gan ucher.
Crist keli yr peri prudder
Vy marda⁶t traetha⁶t traethatter.
Vy meirdyon bru senhyon synhyer.
Vy marteir eurgadeir catwer.
Vygkerdeu uch llyfreu lleer.
Llⁿrⁿ ganon o gano y pader.
Oret yduⁿ oduu uy omnied.
Cret oe blas nyth gyffro masswed.
Cret ydiodef duⁿ gⁿener.
Ae gyuot y oruot ar niuer.
O gytuon teyrnon tⁿrⁿf glywher.
O gytuot rin animot rosser.
Saesson dyvryssyon kynngⁿander.
Ardaloed llu kyhoed kⁿyner.
Didefuyd maelenyd malucher.
Digyfreith heb gyfreith heb gaer.
Am uael dir y clywir hir aer.
Am lann gⁿyrann ovⁿy ruduer
Am buellt teruyn tⁿrⁿf ucher.
Taryf ar uaryf o uarwaⁿl lyfyrder.
Am aber kammarch y kyfuarcher.
Llyw llewenyd y niuer
Yna yt vyd prydyd heb pryder.
O brydyat gobennyat gloeⁿ der.
O prifieith penyt weith pader.
O bris parch pan yth gyuarcher.
Orchⁿch y douyd o dyuynder.
Ardunyant llⁿydyant uch lleuuer.
Dur ar loegyr a lwgyr y pader.
Ae gar ae vanyar ae vaner.

Gổr o gud paraổchrud wythuer
Adaổ. ytywyaổ y laổer.
Hổ un abeir dechryn pan dechreuer.
Torr terwyn rổyd duổ gổener.
Duổ gổener coeler nat kelwyd.
Kilyaổd seis oedreis dros eluyd.
Am aber kammarch amharch.
Marchdổrổf gaổr llafnaổr alluyd
Allumman aelaổ heb gelwyd.
Alleith dreic dragon y gilyd.
Lloegyrwys ar gổynuan gổann byd.
Gổyr yggryt cổynyt emennyd.
Gổr ar loegyr a lổgyr ygreuyd.
Adaổ y lywyaổ y luyd.
Hổnn abeir dechreu dech vyd.
Ynhir am y tir y deruyd.
Gổaổr peunes aflonyd.
Kyuogyat kymynyat am uedyd.
Byt dydổraổt adro daổn ywaổtryd.
Y weithret yt glywet let eluyd.
Y gyrrif adyrrif ny deruyd.
Y radeu drổy dedueu aderllyd.
Darllydon karổn kaer leriyd.
Rac llef duổ didổyll gerennyd.
Hyt pan vom ynhir ynherổyd.
Gleindit ynrydit rac esplyd.
Aelaổ gan vy reen rodyon bedyd.
Erchổch drugared rac dyhed defuyd.

𝕬M uuell teruyn tổrổf adodi.
Toruoed llu kyhoed kổyn oi yssi.
Ar ellổng redet rodyeu henri
Angklaer. henn* kaer kyuarch trenghi.

* This word is indistinct.

Kynuerth oli* alun teruysgi.
G6as gar ac amhar ac amharch drosti.
Kytlauan dywan ban y hatrodi.
Adra6d y chollet gall gallet uy elli.
O gyfranc bar6n byrr y gyweithi :
Atuyd kelein wenn heb penn heb perthi.
Atuyd meirch g6eilyd g6ael eudiffodi.
Agolwc digu ar wyr tu keri.
A diaspat van ag6an a g6eidi.
Ac och ympob tori* ac atef* tyuoni.*
Escut gymry plant galwant agdewi.*
Agar tagneued trugared tr6ydi.*

G LASSA6N argoedyd kedymdeith.
Gloessedic c6yndic amchweith.
Gloesson cur kefyon kyfarweith.
Kywerlyn hoedyl dyn adiffeith.
Kedyrn loegyr yn llygru kyfreith.
Kyfrych6n g6el6n eu goleith.
Duundeb saesson ysse6 nossweith.
Di boned arwled eu medweith.
Aruollyein heb getwein gytweith.
A dorrirn6rth derwyn dyleith.
Bar6neit byrr hoyd eukyweith.
A llyw pa dyr g6yned g6annareith.
Adra6d lludet ka6d kanhymdeith.
Edrych awelych wael anreith.
Amgyuyrdan kyflauan eilweith.
Dywygir or mynnir milreith.
Bratdyhed o gonimed gobeith.
Dyd6yn dyn att du6 yn vnweith.
Goludant lluoed lla6n ymdeith.
G6rd ha6l6r yn holi affeith.

       * These words are indistinct.

Gÿr alas olesteir dichweith.

Gÿiryon gÿir dileir dyleith.

Gÿaratwyd gan duÿ dÿyn y leith.

Gÿaredaÿr yn yr dewrwyr degweith.

Bodlaÿn duÿ pan deruyn pob ieith.

Iechyt rann penyt poen geith.

Poet ef an rodo rann gobeith.

Diwed trugared trÿy gyfreith. amen.

XXII.

Col. 1053.

ȜȜOR yÿ gvael gÿelet.

Kynnÿryf kynniret.

Bratheu a brythuet.

Brithwyr ar gerdet.

Ac ordaÿt galet.

Ar ardÿy dynghet.

Ac yr duÿ dywet.

Y dywan gollet.

Mab uy mat anet.

Mabineid dynghet.

Anghenaÿd agcret.

Anghenÿri gywet.

Lloegrwys ae dywet.

Och rac anghyffret.

Hyt ympenn y seithuet.

Or kalan kalet.

Gÿir y daÿ gÿaret.

Drÿyrdyn damunet.

Gÿynvryn gÿarthaet.

Gÿyned y drydet.

Kymry vn gyffret.

Eu llu alluchet.

Coeluein eu gÿaret.

Gÿiraÿt keudaÿt ket.

Gѡaranrѡy reget.
Rann gan ogonet.
Gogonet an rann
Am rodes rѡyfuan.
Am bu bard datcann.
At gigleu gamlan.
Atwelir griduan.
Ac amvѡyn kѡynuan.
A chynhen druan.
A chynnyd maban.
Katwer yn vychan.
Kadoed awelan.
Kynnyd kadarnvan.
Cur llauur lluman.
Llumangoch gѡnn vot.
Lleith eu oruot.
Arwyd eu dyuot.
Aerwyr eryrot.
Aweryr eu clot.
Eu cled cleu ragot.
Ragof rinwedeu.
Rann gan gynn angheu.
Dyd gѡeinyd gѡaet creu.
Dyd keryd kaereu.
Ef a daѡ ual diheu.
Aches lyghesseu.
Ar treth na thretheu.
Ny lluyd na sѡydeu.
Gѡann diblan dadleu.
Gan rѡfan rѡyfueu.
Yeir bit greireu.
O von hyt vynneu.
Oret y duѡ buѡ budyeu.
Am byd ryd radeu.

Drѹ eiryaѹl seinheu
A synhwyr llѹyr llyfreu.
An roder rann diuieu.
Gѹenwled gѹal oleu.

XXIII.

Col. 1054. PRIF gyuarch geluyd pan ryleat.
Pѹy kynt ae tywyll ae goleuat.
Neu adaf pan bu pa dyd. y creat.
Neu y dan tytwet. py yr y seilyat.
A uo lleion nys myn pѹyllat.
Est qui peccator am niuereit.
Collant gѹlat nefѹy plѹyf offeireireit.
Boreu eb ni del.
Or ganont teir pel.
Eingyl gallwydel.
Gѹnaont eu ryuel.
Pan daѹ nos adyd.
Pan uyd llѹyd eryr.
Pannyѹ tyuyll nos.
Pan yѹ gѹyrd llinos
Mor. pan dyuerѹyd
Cѹd anys gѹelyd.
Yssit teir ffynnaѹn.
Y mynyd fyawn.
Yssit gaer garthaѹn.
A dan donn eigaѹn.
Gorith gyuarchaѹr.
Pѹy enѹ y porthaѹr.
Pѹy bu periglaѹr.
Y uab meir mѹynuawr.
Pa uessur mѹynaf.
A oruc adaf.
Pѹy vessur uffern.

Pỽy tewet y llenn.

Pỽy llet y geneu.

Pỽy meint enneinheu.

Neu ulaen gỽyd ffaliỽm.

Py estỽng mor grỽm.

Neu pet anat uon.

Yssyd yn eubon.

Neu leu a gỽydyon.

A uuant geluydyon.

Neu awdant lyfyryon.

Pan wnant

Pan daỽ nos a lliant.

Pan vyd y diuant.

Cỽd anos rac dyd.

Pan daỽ naswelyd

Pater noster ambulo.

Gentis tonans in adiuuando.

Sibilem signum

Rogantes fortium.

Am gỽiỽ gỽiỽ am gỽmyd.

Am geissant deu geluyd.

Am kaer kerindan kerindyd.

Ry tynneirch pector dauyd.

Y mwynant ys ewant.

Ym kaffỽynt yn dirdan.

Kymry yggriduan.

Prouator eneit.

Rac lỽyth eissyffleit.

Kymry prif diryeit.

Rann rygoll bỽyeit.

Gỽaed hir ucheneit.

Asgỽyar honneit.

Dydoent gỽarthuor.

Gỽydueirch dy aruor.

Eingyl yghygor.
Gwelattor arbydon.
G6ynyeith ar saesson.
Claudus in syon.
O r6yuannusson.
Bydha6t penn seiron.
Rac ffichit lewon.
Marini brython.
Rydaroganon.
A medi heon.
Am hafren auon.
Lladyr ffadyr kenn amass6y.
Ffis amala. ffur. ffir. sel.
Dyruedi trinet tramoed.
Crea6dyr orohai.
Huai gentil dichmai
Gospell codigni
Cota gosgord mur
Cornu ameni dur.
Neu bum gan wyr keluydon.
Gan uathheu gan gouannon.
Gan eunyd gan elestron.
Ry ganhymdeith achwysson.
Bl6ydyn ygkaer gofannon.
Wyf hen wyf newyd 6yf g6ion.
6yf ll6yr. 6yf synn6yr keinyon.
Dy goui dyhen vrython.
G6ydyl kyl diaerogyon.
Medut medwon.
6yf bard. 6yf ny riuaf y eillyon.
6yf lly6. 6yf sy6 amrysson.
Sihei. arahei nys medy.
Si ffradyr yny ffradri.
Posberdein bronrein a dyui.

Adeuhont vꝺch medlestri.

A ganhont gam uardoni.

A geissent gyfuarꝺs nys deubi.

Heb gyfreith heb reith heb rodi.

Agꝺedy hynny dygovi.

Brithuyt a byt dyuysgi.

Nac eruyn dy hedꝺch nyth vi.

Reen nef rymaꝺyr dywedi.

Rac y gresrym gꝺares dy uoli.

Ri Rex gle amgogyuarch yn geluyd.

A ueleisty dñs fortis.

Darogan dꝺfyn dñi.

Budyant uffern

Hic nemo in por progenie.

Ef dillynghwys y tꝺryf

Dñs uirtutum.

Kaethnaꝺt kynnhullꝺys estis iste est

A chynn buasswn a sunsei.

Arnaf bꝺyf derwin y duꝺ diheu.

A chynn mynnꝺyf deruyn creu.

A chynn del ewynriꝺ ar vynggeneu.

A chynn vyngkyualle ar llatheu preu.

Poet ymheneit yda kyfedeu.

Abreid om dyweit llythyr llyfreu.

Kystud dygyn gꝺedy gꝺely agheu.

Ar saꝺl a gigleu vy mardlyfreu.

Ry bryn hꝺynt wlat nef adef goreu.

XXIV.

GOSSYMDEITH LLEFOET WYNEB CLAꝺR. Yꝺ HYNN.

Col. 1055.   **G**OLUT byt eyt ydaꝺ.

Ket ymgemmycker o honaw

Dychystud aghen dychyfyaꝺ.

Dybyd hinon g6edy gla6.
Ny na6t kyhafal kyvaeth la6.
A gle6 chwerit creu oe dina6.
Pob llyf6r llemittyor arna6.
Pob ffer dyatter heibya6.
Dychymmyd dedwyd ac ana6.
Rihyd ac ef du6 dywalla6.

Golut byt eyt dydo.
Diga6n dovyd darparo.
Hydyr gwaed g6anec 6rth vro.
Pan elwir chwelit acdo.
Dioryuic dyn ny welo.
Ny dida6r ny da6r c6t vo.
Ny wneyd gwir ny ein ymro.
Ny chenir mwyett ar ffo.
Bit vleid beidyat a dwyll.
Chwanna6c vyd llen llwyda6c lla6dino.

Golut byt eyt dybyd.
Atwaed chwant atuant riyd.
Dychynneit ieueinc dychynnyd.
Nyt echwenit clot kelwyd.
Nyt vn aruaeth kaeth a ryd.
Ys g6ac vro ny bo crevyd.
Atuant a da6 ny wnehyd.
Ll6yt ac annwyt ny gymyd.
Ny ob6yll o du6 diffyd.
Ny elwir yngywreint ny gynuyd.
Keinyath6n gofryn6n greuyd.
Hyt pan ynbo gan grist grennyd.

Anghyfaely6r anghyfyrdelit.
Llann. dychystud brun bro lit.

X

G6ell nac no gen edewit.

Ym gweithret g6astra g6eilit.

Chwec yn anwa6s yn odit.

Ch6ery dryc cor wedy trenghit.

Nyt gna6t escussa6t esg6it.

Ny cheffir da heb prit.

Pedryfan d6fyn pedrychwelit.

Areith g6ell goleith no govit.

Dr6c pecha6t oe bell erlit.

Da ynggnif porthi menechtit.

Du6 o nef g6ae drut ny gret it.

Mab meir diweir avenhit.

Da weith yn gobeith 6rthit.

Ath gyrb6yllir yn bronn bit.

Difrys g6anec dycfustit traeth.

Gosgymonn g6yth gordin.

G6yluein hanes gorewin.

P6yll llu. a th6yll tr6y chuerthin.

Bit gynnvidyd gywrenhin.

Bit lesc eidyl bit var6 crin.

Kerennyd fall gall gynnin.

Gan rewyd ny phell vydrin.

Dychyffre gwae6 g6aetlin.

Dychyveruyd tr6ch athrin.

Enghit a vo llyfeithin.

Enwir ef kyll y werin.

Namvyn du6 nyt oes dewin.

Argl6yd g6lat l6yd g6erthevin.

Dyvrys g6anec dyg6rthryn.

Gro. g6st eidyl moch detwyn

R6yfant maon medlyn.

A ordyvyn pa6b oe deruyn.

Trenghyt torrit pob denghyt.
Ry brynỽ nef nyt ef synn
Mor wyt gywrennhin gyrbỽyll.
O nebaỽt. gỽisgaỽt coet kein gowyll.
Nyt eglur edrych yn tywyll.
Rac annwyt ny weryt cannwyll.
Nyt edwyd. nỽy diuo pỽyll.
Kerennyd a dovýd ny dỽyll.

Nỽy dyuo pỽyll prif egỽa.
A gynneu edyn ny wna.
Oer gaeafraỽt tlaỽt morua.
Gỽell rihyd no ryssedha.
Rac drỽc ny diỽc atneir.
Llawer maỽreir a vethla.
Keudaỽt kyt worymdaa.
O ovrýs nywys kỽta
Arythal y drindaỽt traha.
Maỽr duỽ morỽyt wrda.

Redeint gorwyd rwyd pob traeth
Kynnic mynaỽc marchogaeth
Nyt neb aued oe aruaeth
Nyt ef enir paỽb yn doeth.
Nyt ehovyn bryt yn llong dreith.
Ny thangnef gỽynnaỽn a godeith.
Bit vyỽ gỽr heb dryc wryaeth.
Mynaỽc kerd ketwyf eillyaeth.
Ny byd hyvysgỽr neb noeth.
Nyt oes reith nat vo pennaeth.
Breyenhin beidyaỽt anreith
Dywal dir vyd y oleith.
Ny naỽt eing llyfyrder rac lleith.
Enghit gleỽ oe gyfarweith.

Medѵ mutdrut pob anghyfyeith.
Dinas a diffyd diffeith.
Eiryaul a garaѵr haѵdweith.
Ef molir paѵb ѵrth y weith.
Ny char dovyd diobeith.
Goreu kyflwyt yn gyweith.

Gwaeannѵyn goaflѵm tir.
Ot ynt tonnaѵr gaѵr ennwir.
Diwestyl alaf dirmygir.
Gwall arny mynych welir.
Aravo diffyd divennwir.
Y draa kyfa rann rybucher.
Bit wastat gwreic ny erchia.
Mevyl ys gnaѵt o weddaѵt hir.
Ny rydecho rydygir.
O hir dinaѵ dychwynir.
Auo marѵ ny moch welir.
Avo da gan duѵ ys dir.
Avo gleѵ gochlywir.
Y glot o vychot godolir.
Guynn y vyt pydiw y rodir.
Kerennyd duѵ a hoedyl hir.

NOTES AND ILLUSTRATIONS

NOTES AND ILLUSTRATIONS.

I.

TWO POEMS FROM THE CAMBRIDGE JUVENCUS.

Text, Vol. ii. *p.* 1.

THE text of these two poems has been printed after having repeatedly examined the Cambridge *Juvencus* with very great care, and having also had the benefit of a very minute and careful examination of this interesting MS., made by a most competent judge—viz. Henry Bradshaw, Esq. of King's College, Cambridge. Our object was not only to obtain a perfectly correct text of these well-known stanzas, but also to decipher, if possible, another and longer poem written on the first page, in the same character and autograph.

The MS. of *Juvencus* came to the library in 1648, from Dr. Richard Houldsworth, master of Emanuel College, who died in that year, and bequeathed his library to the University. It was first catalogued and put on the shelves in 1663, with the rest of Dr. Houldsworth's books. On the first leaf there is, in the hand-writing of Richard Amadas, who was a clergyman in Essex, and died in 1637, the words " Paraphrasis in Evangelia," with the figures " 1233," and at the end, in the same handwriting, " Juvencus Presbyter in 4 Evangelia, Anno 1233. On the first page is the name " Mr. Price," and in the same hand a reference to *Juvencus* from " James Usher, Bp. of Meathes book, fol. 349." Now Usher was only Bishop of Meath for a few years, from 1624 to 1627, and in a book published by him in 1624, called the *Answer to a Jesuit*, there is a citation of *Juvencus* at p. 349, so that the MS. must have belonged to Mr. Price about that time. There was a John Price, noticed in Williams's *Biography of Eminent Welshmen*, born in

London, of Welsh parents, in 1600, who was elected from Westminster to Christ Church, Oxford, in 1617, afterwards turned
papist and went to Paris. He seems to have made Usher's acquaint-
ance in Ireland, and it is believed there are some of his letters in
Usher's printed correspondence. From him Dr. Houldsworth probably got the MS., with other books, when the troubles began,
while John Price, being a Welshman, probably procured it in
Wales.*

It is a large quarto MS. of 52 leaves of parchment, and is
unquestionably of the ninth century. The text is written in a bold
and free character, and is in the same handwriting throughout. The
colophon at the end, in the same handwriting, is—

> " expliqunt quattuor Evangelia
>   a Juvenco presbytero
>   pene ad verbum translata
>   Araut dinuadu."

i.e., "a prayer for Nuadu." The lines of the text have glosses in
Welsh, written over them in a smaller hand in the Saxon or Irish
character. On the first page, in the same character, is a poem consisting of nine lines, each line forming a triplet, commencing with the
words " *Omnipotens auctor*," and of which the Vicomte de la Villemarqué could only read the last three words, " Molim map Meir." At
the top of pages 48, 49, and 50 are, in the same hand-writing and
character, the celebrated stanzas beginning " Niguorcosam," and on
the last page are, in the same handwriting and character, fifty lines
of Latin hexameters, of which the words " dignissime Fethgna "
can alone be distinguished. We have thus the text of the MS. connected with the name " Nuadu," and the two Welsh poems connected
with the name " Fethgna," to which the epithet of *dignissime* is
attached. Both of these names are Irish in their form, and it is
somewhat remarkable that there was an important person in the
ninth century in Ireland, whose name was Fethgna. This was
Fethgna, who was Bishop of Armagh for twenty-two years, and
died in 874. His death is thus recorded, under that year, in the
Annals of Ulster :—" Fethgna Episcopus haeres Patricii, caput
religionis totius Hiberniæ in Prid. Non. Octobris in pace quievit ;"

---

* I am indebted to Mr. Bradshaw for much of this information.

and it is also remarkable, that one of his predecessors in the bishopric of Armagh, in the same century, was Nuadu, whose death is thus recorded : " A.D. 811 Nuadha of Loch Uamha Bishop, anchorite and abbot of Ardmacha, died."

If Fethgna, Bishop of Armagh, is the " dignissime Fethgna" of the MS., then the two Welsh poems must have been transcribed during his occupation of the bishopric from 852 to 874 ; but how came a MS. containing Welsh glosses and Welsh poems* to be connected with Armagh and their bishops. The probable clue to this is the following. During the time of Fethgna, Armagh was almost totally destroyed by the Danes. In 850, " Armagh was devastated by the foreigners." In 867, " Ardmacha was plundered and burned, with its oratories, by Amhlach. Ten hundred was the number there cut off, both by wounding and suffocation, besides all the property and wealth which they found there was carried off by them." It was restored again by Fethgna. Now, in the *Brut y Tywysogion* of Caradoc of Llancarvan, there is the following passage : 883 a'r un flwyddyn y bu farw Cydifor abad Llanfeithin gwr doeth a dysgedig oedd efe a mawr ei dduwioldeb. Efe a ddanfones chwech o wyr doethion ei gor i ddodi addysc i Wyddelod y Werddon. "And the same year Cydivor Abbot of Llanveithin (or Llancarvan) died a wise and learned man and of great piety. *He sent six learned men of his abbey to Ireland to instruct the Irish.*" Surely they were sent in consequence of the destruction of the seats of learning in Ireland by the Danes, and thus may some learned Welshmen have been brought in contact with the Bishops of Armagh. This would connect the MS. with Llancarvan, and it may have been got from thence on the suppression of the monasteries. I see no reason for connecting it especially with the North. The character is the Saxon or Irish, which was used all over England before the Gothic writing began. The language is of the pure Welsh type of the period, and is opposed to what we know *aliunde* of Pictish forms.† I have always been of opinion that the three well-known stanzas bear evident marks of having been the work of the same author who wrote the Marwnad Cyn-

---

* The principal text of MS. must have been written by a Welshman, as the word "Araut" in the colophon is the Cymric and not the Gaelic form.

† The allusion is to the *gu*, for which Pictish seems to have substituted *f*.

ddyllan. It is written in the same metre, there are the same expressions, it is pervaded by the same sentiment, and in both is the expression of " Franc" used, and I am not aware of its occurrence in any other poem. It would almost seem as if these poems of the ninth century had been preserved for the purpose of refuting Mr. T. Wright. He objects to the metre of " Marwnad Cynddylan," as having been introduced by the Normans, and to the use of the word ' Franc,' as being post-Norman. Yet, here are both in a poem transcribed in the ninth century.

There are only two words in the text of this poem that are doubtful. *Nicanu* in the fourth line may be read *Nicanil ;* and if so, it is probably transposed, and should be placed at the end of the line, so as to correspond in rhyme with the words *nouel* and *patel.* The letter represented by *y* in *discyrr* is a peculiar letter, which may represent one of the Saxon forms for *y,* or the Irish contraction for *ui,* in which case the word will read *discuirr.* I read the third line as " Mi a'm Franc dam an calaur," I and my Franc around (*dam,* so in composition), our (*an,* old form for *ein*), kettle. I think the previous line "my household is not large," refers to there being only two persons. Then, in the last line, I consider the rendering of " Dou" by " God," as inadmissible. I am not aware of any stage in Welsh orthography where Duw could be written Dou. It is the old form of " Dau," two, and seems to refer to the same two persons.

The preceding line I am inclined to read " My song is a lament." " Disgyrr," a wail, a lament ; " Cowyddaid," a song. Cyweithydd would certainly never be written in old Welsh with *d* for *th.* My translation is as follows :—

> I will not sleep, not one hour,
> To-night ; my household is not very great,
> I and my Franc around our kettle.
> I sing not, nor laugh, nor sleep,
> To-night ; though drinking the new mead,
> I and my Franc around our pot.
> No joyousness impresses me,
> To-night ; my song is a lament.
> Two do not talk to me [with] one speaker.

The first poem I do not attempt to translate.—(S.)

315

II.

BLACK BOOK OF CAERMARTHEN.

" Prior to the year 1148," says Tanner, " a priory was founded at Caermarthen for six black canons. It was dedicated to St. John the Evangelist, and received a charter from King Henry the Second, who granted " Deo et ecclesiæ Sancti Joh. Evangelistæ de Kayrmerdyn et canonicis ibidem Deo servientibus veteram Civitatem de Kayrmerdyn." It was granted, 4th July, 33d Henry VIII., to Richard Andrews and Nicholas Temple. Upon the dissolution of the religious houses in the reign of King Henry VIII., Sir John Price, a native of Breconshire, was among others appointed a commissioner for their suppression, and exercised this duty mainly in the county of Brecon, when he received grants of many of the religious houses. In the course of the performance of this duty, he received from the Treasurer of the Church of St. David's a MS. which had belonged to the Priory of Caermarthen, and was known by the name of the *Black Book of Caermarthen*. In his *Historiæ Britannicæ Defensio*, he quotes the concluding verse of the first poem in the MS.

The *Black Book of Caermarthen* is a MS. consisting of fifty-four folios of parchment, in small quarto, and written in the Gothic character with illuminated capitals, but the handwriting varies at intervals. On page ninth there is inserted in the current hand of the sixteenth century the following sentence. It has been read with some difficulty owing to the faintness of the ink, and may not have been quite correctly transcribed.

" Kym henaeth doyth ach ny dwy yr by byf heb wy bod beith wethyn er kym eim ddar henwy dy a llyr llyfyr dy ny dwg
llyfr du
dy allu'r llyfr du nid wiss."

On folio 24 *b* two lines are added in a Gothic hand at the bottom of the page, and the following note is inserted on a separate slip of paper in the handwriting of Dr. H. Humphreys, Bishop of Bangor, who died in the year 1712. "I have an exact copy of this booke writ with ye very same hand with that on the bottom of this leafe. Yᵉ 2d side of the 24th fol. my copy calls this booke y llyfr du o Gaervyrdden." There is now no trace of this copy. There is a complete and accurate copy in the Hengwrt collection, in the handwriting of Mr. Robert Vaughan the celebrated antiquary, from which it might be inferred that Mr. Robert Vaughan was not then in possession of the original MS., but it must have passed into the Hengwrt collection prior to the year 1658, as it appears in the catalogue of the MS. books of Robert Vaughan of Hengwrt, made by Mr. William Maurice in that year. It was examined by Edward Lhuyd, when he was allowed a hurried inspection of the Hengwrt MS. in 1696 ; and it has now passed, with the rest of this valuable collection, into the possession of W. W. E. Wynne, Esq., of Peniarth, M.P. It is a subject of congratulation that these invaluable MSS. should have become the property of a gentleman so well able to appreciate their value as Mr. Wynne, and whose liberality permits them to be used for literary purposes.

The MS. appears thus to have been written in four different handwritings, but they are all of the same period, and the result I have come to, after an attentive study of the MS., is, that the whole of it, with the exception of a few parts, written in a later hand, and evidently inserted at a later period in some blank spaces in the MS., is of the age of Henry II. ; and this is confirmed by the two last pieces but two being laments on the death of Madauc, son of Maredut, Prince of Powys, who died in 1159, in the reign of Henry II.

Are there any indications, then, in the MS. as to the persons by whom it was compiled ? I think there are, though faint and obscure.

The MS., it will be observed, contains copies of the two poems ascribed to Myrdin, called the "Afallenau" and the "Hoianau." Mr. Stephens has, in my opinion, very clearly demonstrated that both of these poems contain passages which could not have been written prior to the time of Henry II. ; and he considers both poems to be compositions of the twelfth and thirteenth centuries. The suspicious passages run through the poem of the Hoianau in such a manner as to indicate that the entire poem is the composition of a later age, and one passage sufficiently indicates its date where it mentions—

" Pump pennaeth o Normandi
  Ar pumed yn myned dros for heli
  I oresgyn Iwerddon."

"Five rulers from Normandy and the fifth going across the salt sea
to conquer Ireland."

Mr. Stephens supposes that this passage refers to four Norman
knights who went to Ireland in 1169 to assist Dermot M'Morrogh
in subjugating Leinster, and that Richard Strongbow was the fifth.
I do not agree with him in this. I do not see what connection
they had with Wales, or why a Welsh bard should thus allude to
them. I think the reference is to the four early Norman kings—
viz. William the Conqueror, William Rufus, Henry I., and Stephen,
and the fifth, Henry II., who conquered Ireland, and points to his
reign as the age of the poem. I do not think Mr. Stephens more
happy in the special events he supposes to be referred to in each
stanza, but I think he has clearly made out the general proposition
that the entire poem is the composition of that age. This is by no
means so clear as to the Afallenau, and the suspicious passages
bear more the marks of being interpolations in an older poem.

Now, on comparing the two poems in the *Black Book* with the
text in the *Myvyrian Archæology,* we find this curious result :—
The text of the Hoianau is the same in both, and the copy in the
Black Book contains all the suspicious passages. The text of the
Afallenau in the *Myvyrian Archæology* consists of twenty-two
stanzas, that in the *Black Book* of only ten stanzas.* The omitted
stanzas are those in which the suspicious passages exist, while the
stanzas found in the *Black Book* contain none of these passages.
In short, the text of the Hoianau contains the whole of the suspicious passages, that of the Afallenau is entirely free from that taint.
The inference I draw is, that the Afallenau, as contained in this
MS., is an older poem, and that the Hoianau is a poem written in
imitation of it, of the same date as the MS. itself—the idea of " Oian
a parchellan," which commences each stanza, being taken from a
stanza in the Afallenau beginning with these words—and that the
latter poem was subsequently doctored by the addition of interpolated stanzas of the same character.

* The stanzas in the poem in the *Black Book,* in the order in which they
occur, are the 21st, 12th, 8th, 3d, 13th, 14th, 15th, 16th, 17th, and 22d.

Is there anything, then, to show by whom the Hoianau was written? It appears to me to contain one reference which cannot be mistaken in stanza eleven :—

> " Oian a parchellan ai byt cyvin
> Ban glyw yn llavar o Gaerfyrddin
> Y ardwyaw deu geneu yn cywrhenin."
>
> Hear, O little pig ; be not open-mouthed
> When thou hearest *my voice from Caermarthen*
> Training two youths skilfully.

I think it clear from this passage that the writer must have been one of the canons of the Priory of Caermarthen.

If the passage

> " A mi a ddisgoganaf cyn fyniwedd
> Brython dros Saeson brithwyr ai medd,"
>
> I will prophesy before my end :
> The Brython over Saxons, the Picts say it,

refers to the writer and not to the supposed author, Myrddin, as a Pict, then, in that age the name was confined to the inhabitants of Galloway, and the author must have come from the south of Scotland.

There is another poem in the *Black Book* which deserves attention with reference to this question.

The following is the text, with a literal translation :—

" Dv dy uarch du dy capan	Black thy horse, black thy cope,*
Du dy pen du duhunan	Black thy head, black thou thyself :
Ia du ae ti yscolan.	Yes, black art thou, Yscolan.
Mi iscolan yscolheic	I am Yscolan the scholar.
Yscawin y puill iscodic.	Fickle his Scottish knowledge.
Guae. ny baut agaut guledic.	Alas ! that there was not to me what the Gwledig had [of a school,†
O losci ecluis. allat buch iscol.	For burning a church and killing the kine

---

* *Capan* is usually translated " cap," but this is a modern use of the word. At that time I believe it represented the Latin *cappa*, which was the ecclesiastical cloak called the cope. In the *Brut y Tywysogion*, Henry II is said to have given to the choir of St. David's " deu gappan cor," translated " two choral caps ;" a strangely small gift for a king. What are choral caps ? In a Catholic choir the two cantors wear copes, and no doubt the gift was that of two copes for the choir.

† Mr. Stephens translates this " hindered school instruction." This is a

Allyvir rod y voti.	And causing a book to be drowned.
Vy penhid. ystrum kynhi.	My penance, very heavy it is to me,
Creaudir y creadurev. perthidev	Creator of creatures, greatest of
Muyhaw. kyrraw de imi vygev.	Supporters. Forgive me my falsehood.
Ath vradaste. am tuyllas ynnev.	He that betrayed thee, deceived me also.
Bluÿtin llaun im rydoded.	A full year I was placed
Ym. bangor ar paul cored.	At Bangor, on the pole of a weir.
Edrich de poen imy gan mor pryued.	Consider thou my sufferings from sea-worms.
Bei yscuypun arvn.	If I knew what I do know,
Mor amluc guint. y vlaen bric guit fallum [aun."	How clearly the wind blows on the sprigs of the falling wood,
Arav vneuthume bith nys gun-	What I did I never would have done.

This poem is usually considered to be a dialogue between Myrddin and Yscolan, but there is nothing in the copy in this MS. to connect it with Myrddin. Davies reads the name as two words, " Ys Colan," which he translates " the Colan," and supposes that the person meant was Columba, the celebrated Missionary from Ireland to the northern Picts of Scotland in 565, and Mr. Stephens adopts the same view and supposes the name Ys Colan to be equivalent to St. Colan or St. Columba. I do not consider this theory to be tenable. Fordun records a conversation between Myrddin and the Apostle of Strathclyde, Kentigern, which bears a remote resemblance to that between Yscolan and his unnamed interlocutor ; but there is no tradition, nor any probability, that Myrddin came in contact with Columba, neither does the construction of the Welsh language justify the separation of the first syllable " Ys" from the rest of the name, and extracting a name " Colan" out of it. There is a class of words in Welsh in which " Ys" may be viewed as a separable prefix, but in most of the words beginning with " Ys" the letter y alone has been prefixed, and the letter s is an essential part of the word, as in " ysbryd" (spirit), " yscol," school, etc., and this is the case in all proper names—thus Ystyffan, Stephen, etc., when the syllable " ys" cannot be thrown off.

good illustration of loose translating. How that meaning can be extracted out of the words " allat buch yscol," I cannot conceive. *Boddi* is to " drown or be drowned." The Irish equivalent is " *bath*, drown ;" but it has also the secondary sense of blot out, suppress, cancel ; and I suspect that this is the meaning of the Welsh word here.

The same name occurs in the lives of St. David, when he is said to have met an Irish ecclesiastic called Scuthyn, at a place called Bed *Yscolan.* Its equivalent in Irish is not Colan or Columba, but Scolan. In another life, in mentioning this Scuthyn or Scutinus, it is added, who had another name Scolanus. The name also occurs in the old Scottish Acts of Parliament, in the reign of Alexander II., when, in the year 1228, " Judicatum est de Gillescop mak*scolane* per diversos judices tam Galwidie quam Scocie," which gives us an instance of the name about the date of our MS., and, strangely enough, connects it with Galloway. It is plain, therefore, that it is impossible to read the name Colam or Columba out of it ; and what renders the supposition still more unlikely, is that while the " Yscolan" of the poem is described as black in dress and appearance, the dress of St. Columba and his monks happens to have been white, as appears from his life by Adomnan.

It has always appeared to me plain that the dress and appearance here described was simply that of the Black Canons of St. Augustine, who wore a black cassock, and over it a black cloak or cope and hood, with a black cap ; and if I am correct in this view, it will bring the composition of this poem likewise, and Yscolan himself, to the period when the *Black Book of Caermarthen* was compiled. The name of Ysgodic, or Scottish, though applicable to Ireland at an early period, was, in the twelfth century, appropriated to Scotland, and we have thus again here the appearance of a Canon of the Priory of Caermarthen of Scottish origin, and apparently from his name connected with Galloway, who is addressed in this poem, and his being contemporaneous with the compilation of the MS. throws additional interest on the allusions contained in it.—(S.)

POEM I.

Translation, Vol. i. p. 368.   Text, Vol. ii. p. 3.

This poem purports to be a dialogue between Myrdin and Taliessin, and the subject of the poem is obviously the battle of Ardderyd, which resulted in the defeat of the Pagan party and their flight into the wood of Celyddon. It has usually been attributed to Taliessin, but it is not contained in the *Book of Taliessin,* and in the poem itself Myrdin claims the authorship.—(S.)

The language of the composition is comparatively easy, and the principal difficulties that meet the translator lie in the obscurity of the allusions, but a certain amount of abstruseness is just what we might expect from the character of the interlocutors—viz. the chief of bards and the chief of enchanters.—(E.)

STANZA I.

Line 2.—' *Deryv* ' = deryw = darvu, from daru, the same as darvu. " Deryw am dano," there is an end of him, he has perished. —(E.)

Line 4.—' *Tryuruyd* ' here is evidently the name of a place. In Poem xxxi. the name occurs twice, and in one of the passages it stands in a connection not very unlike the present :—

" Neus tuc Manauid
Eis tull o trywruid ;"

and in the other we read of " traethev trywruid," a name bearing so strong a resemblance to the " trath treuroit " of Nennius as hardly to leave a doubt of its identity with the scene of the tenth battle of King Arthur.—(E.)

Line 4.—' *Tryuan* ' = trywan.—(E.)

STANZA II.

Line 1.—' *Maelgun.* ' The reference here is to Maelgwn Gwynedd, who appears to have led the host which encountered the Pagan party at Ardderyd.—(S.) ' *Inimnan* ' = inimuan = yn ymwan, combating.—(E.)

STANZA III.

Line 1.—' *Neutur*,' or Nevtur—is probably the same place mentioned by Fiech in his *Life of St. Patrick*, written in the eighth century, as Nemhtur or Nevtur. It is identified by his scholiast with Alclyde or Dumbarton.—(S.)

Line 2.—*Errith* and *Gurrith* = through form and partial form —are probably the same as the " deuur," or two men before whom

Y

the host landed. "*Ar welugan* = Gwelwgan," from "Gwelu," pale, and "can," white. It is evident that a pale white horse is meant, though here, as in many instances, the word "march" or its equivalent is omitted, the colour alone being expressed. Compare the use of "mein winev" (main wineu) in the next line, and of "gwineu" several times in Poem xxvii., where the meaning admits of no doubt.—(E.) The two forms on the pale white horse appear to refer to "Death and Hades on the pale horse" in the Apocalypse, vi. 8.—(S.)

Stanza IV.

Line 1.—'*Rhys*' is both a proper name and an appellation. In the latter case it signifies a rush, a trial, difficulty, or strait; a risk.

> " Dywed Myrddin y dawai
>   Y rhys ar aflwydd ar rai
>   Ieuan Tew."—(E.)

'*Rychvant*' = rhychwant, the ordinary import of which is "a span," may possibly here signify as much as can be compassed with the arms; for the expression seems to convey the idea of a very large shield, which, if only a span in diameter, would not be the case.

> " Duw merchyr medant
>   Rhyodres rychwant.
>   *Gwawd Lludd y Mawr*, p. 207.—(E.)

Stanza V.

Line 3.—'*Dinel*' = Diuel, Dywal or Dywal ab Erbin.—(E.)

Stanza VI.

Line 3.—'*Arywderit*' = Arvderydd = Ardderyd.—(E.)

Stanza VII.

Line 2.—'*Vidan*' = vyddan = vyddant, from "bod" to be.—(E.)

Stanza VIII.

Line 1.—Eliffer = Eliver, and is probably the same as the person generally called Eliver gosgorddvaedr, or large-retinued.—(E.) His name appears in the Gwyr y Gogledd with the following sons : Gurgi and Peredur.—(S.)

STANZA XI.

Line 2.—Celyddon, or wood of Celyddon, seems to have been in the "Gogledd" or Scotland, and included the Ettrick Forest and Tweeddale.—(S.)

POEM II.

Translation, Vol. i. *p.* 497. *Text, Vol.* ii. *p.* 5.

This poem is sometimes attributed to Meigant, a bard and saint supposed to have lived in the sixth century, but on what authority does not appear. With the exception of three lines (the 1st, 2d, and 4th), it is composed entirely of unconnected rhyming adages, most of which will be found in the collection of *Diarebion Cymraeg,* or Welsh proverbs, printed in the *Myvyrian Archæology,* v. 3. The dream seems to refer to the fourth line, which probably ought to stand before the third, for the latter, in its present position, appears to be out of place.—(E.)

Line 3.—'*Meiuret*' = meuedd. "Nid hoffed meuedd bro." *Myv. Arch.*—(E.)

Line 4.—'*Neur,*' written also neud, neus, and neu—is a kind of interrogative to which an affirmative answer is invariably expected, and is often very properly translated simply as an affirmative particle.—(E.)

Line 5.—For '*dinda*' we should read "dim da" (see the proverb in *Myv. Arch.* iii. p. 169.)—(E.)

Line 11.—If, in relating anything, one does not enter minutely into particulars, it is not so easy to contradict him, though his statements may be erroneous.—(E.)

Line 12.—'*Renuet*' = reuuet = rheuvedd. "Ni lwydd rheuvedd i ddiriaid."—*Myv. Arch.* iii. p. 168.—(E.)
'*Buyeid*' (= bwyaid), properly signifies the consecrated wafers

of the Church of Rome (see Poem xxii. p. 44). The word is also written " mwyaid," and in this form we find it in a poem called " Gosymdaith Llevoed wynebglawr" (*Red Book*, p. 305), where, with the exception of the orthographical variation of this word, the same proverb occurs.

> " Ny chenir Mwyett ar ffo."—(E.)

Line 14.—The conclusion is wanting.—(E.)

POEM III.

Translation, Vol. i. *p.* 498.   *Text, Vol.* ii. *p.* 5.

This poem, with the four which follow, is for the most part very obscure. Each line is generally made to consist of three things, with a rhyme in each clause in addition to the principal one at the end, which latter is sometimes a sort of assonance rather than a full rhyme—a peculiarity by no means confined to these compositions.—(E.) The poem is usually attributed to Cuhelyn, a bard of the ninth century, and line 5 appears to imply this. —(S.)

Line 3.—' *Cyridwen*,' Ceridwen, Caridwen, or Cariadwen—is generally considered to be the goddess or personification of Nature in the so-called mythology of the Welsh. She is sometimes represented as the inspirer of poetry, hence " *pair Ceridwen*" or the cauldron of Ceridwen—is often used by the bards for the fountain of poetic inspiration, and in this character she seems to be mentioned in this passage. " *Gogyrven*," the word used here in the original, signifies, according to Pughe (*Welsh Dict.* s. v.) " a spiritual being or form; a personified idea, a prosopopœia." In the following extract from a document on Bardism, probably written about the end of the fifteenth century, the word is unmistakably employed for a symbol, character, or letter:—" Tair elwydden llythyr, /|\ sev o gymmodoldeb y naill neur lall or tri y gwneir llythyr; sev ydynt, tair pelydren goleuni; acor rhai hyn y gwneir yr im *gogyrven* ar bymtheg, sev yr un llythyren ar bymtheg : ac o gelvyddyd amgen y mae saith *gogyrven* a saith [ugain], nid amgen nag arwydd teilyngnod y saith gair a saith ugain yn riaint y Gymraeg, ac o henynt pob gair arall."

The word occurs several times in the poems of Taliessin, and occasionally in some of the later bards ; and in most instances, as in the present case, it is found in connection with, or as a substitute for, Ceridwen.

> " Seith vgein *ogyruen*
> Yssyd yn awen."
>
> *Book of Taliessin*, p. 132.

> " Neut amuc yggkadeir opeir *kerritwen*
> Handit ryd vyn tafawt yn adawt gwawt *ogyrwen*
> Gwawt *ogyrwen* uferen rwy digonis
> Arnunt a llefrith a gwlith a mes."
>
> *Ibid.* p. 154.

> " Ban pan doeth o peir
> *Ogyrwen* awen teir."
>
> *Ibid.* p. 156.

> " Mor wyf gart geinrwyf hyglwyf hagen
> Mor wyf hyglen uart o ueirt *ogyruen*
> Mor wyf gwyn gy gyfrwyf nyd wyf gyfyrwen
> Mor oet gyfrin fyrt kyrt *kyrriduen.*"
>
> *Cynddelw, Myv. Arch.* i.—(E.)

Line 4.—'*Awyrllav*' = " a wyr llaw," alluding to the minstrel's skill as a player on the harp and similar instruments. These two lines are thus translated by Dr. Pughe (*Welsh Dict.* s. v. " Amhad") —" From the venerated song of Ceridwen Ogyrfen's various seeds, concurring with vocal melody, and the flowing speech in the singer's numbers."—(E.)

Line 7.—'*Gathyr*' is probably " geithyr" = either, but, except. —This prosthetic use of the letter *g* may be observed in several other words of the language, as *gaddewid, gagen, galaeth, gallt, genaid,* for *addewid, agen, alaeth, allt, enaid,* and it is very probable that *oddi gerth* is nothing but a modified transposition of *oddi geither,* just as *dierth* is constantly used in the colloquial, and often in the written language, for *dyeithr* or *dieithr.* Compare also *ewyrth* for *ewythr.*—(E.)

Line 8.—' *Cenid cor* ' = cenydd cor, a singer in a choir, or chorister.—(E.)

Line 9.—With "*flamde kywvire vad*" compare the following lines attributed to Taliessin :—

> " Pan ddisgynwys Owain . . .
> Rhag pedrydan *dandde.*
> Rhag cadwn *gyfwyre,*
> Cychwedl am doddyw."

The same bard also says :—

> " Aelen fflam lydan,
> *Cyfwyrain mawr-dan.*"—(E.)

Line 10.—That is, it would seem, the conflagration caused by the nation of the border.—(E.)

Line 11.—' *Waur* ' = " gwawr," a hero.—(E.)

Line 13.—The allusion here probably is to the social qualities of the subject of the poem. The " graid," or heat, was to warm or cheer the bards and others whom the hero entertains.—(E.)

Line 14.—' *Graid.*'—The poet seems to play here on the different meanings of the word *graid*, using it in its physical sense (*heat*) in the first instance, and in its metaphorical sense (*ardent, fierce*) in the second. A similar remark may be applied to the word *ffraw*, which occurs twice in the same line a little further on.—(E.)

Line 18.—' *Mann meidrolaeth,*' a place which has limits or boundaries, an enclosure—that is the " mitlan," or list for combats. —(E.)

Line 22.—' *Nognav,*' is assumed to be the name of a person. —(E.)

Line 23.—' *Anhetauc* ' = "anheddawg," unpeaceful, restless, turbulent. A peaceful disposition formed no part of virtue according to the moral code of those early times.—(E.)

Line 27.—' *Vetvd* ' = meddud from *medd*, mead. See *Book of Taliessin*, p. 169.—(E.)

Line 30.—This line appears to come in parenthetically. The poet, forgetting his theme for a moment, breaks out into a sort of ejaculation suggested by the allusion to "*renuet reen*" at the end of the preceding line, and then resumes his subject in the three lines following.—(E.)

Line 34.—The connection of the three concluding lines with the preceding portion is not apparent.—(E.)

Line 36.—The word "*dac*," here translated "good," I have not met with elsewhere. If a correct form, it is probably the same as the Irish *deagh, dagh*, or *dag*, of which the usual Welsh form is *da*. The two languages afford many other instances of a final guttural being thrown off by the one and retained by the other.—(E.)

POEM IV.

Translation, Vol. i. *p.* 500. *Text, Vol.* ii. *p.* 6.

The authorship of this short composition is by some ascribed to Cuhelyn and by others to Aeddan, a name not found in the lists of Welsh bards; but it appears from line 3 to be by the same author as the preceding poem, and it is probable that it was addressed to a chieftain of the name of Aeddan. The composition has the appearance of being very old.—(E.)

Line 2.—These opening lines are also contained in the preceding poem.—(E.)

Line 9.—The bards contended with one another to sing his praises.—(E.)

POEM V.

Translation, Vol. i. *p.* 504. *Text, Vol.* ii. *p.* 7.

The greater part of this poem appears to be a dialogue between the soul and the body; and the two poems which next follow may be considered as continuations of the same subject.

Line 4.—Taliessin, in the poem called "Anghar Cyvindawd," has a similar allusion to these "pivots or axes"—

" Gogwn py pegor
Yssyd y dan vor."
        Book of Taliessin, p. 135.—(E.)

Line 9.—The reading of the *Black Book*, " Tridawd," seems erroneous, and should be either " Trindawd," Trinity, or " trallawd," tribulation.—(E.) In the orthography of the *Black Book*, *n* before a consonant is frequently omitted, always before *g.*—(S.)

Line 29.—The preceding seven lines, as well as some other portions of the poem, appear to be not in a very correct state, and differ considerably in the *Black Book* and the *Myvyrian Archæology;* such a difference being generally a pretty sure indication that the text has suffered, and that the early transcribers did not fully understand the meaning of what they attempted to copy.—(E.)

Line 30.—A day of fasting.—(E.)

Line 37.—' *Guerth,*' the word used here in the original, should, it is conjectured, be read " gueith" = gwaith.—(E.)

POEM VI.

Translation, Vol. i. *p.* 506.   *Text, Vol.* ii. *p.* 8.

With this short poem and its strange philosophy compare " Cad goddeu," and " Canu y Byt Mawr" in the *Book of Taliessin*, pp. 137, 214.—(E.)

POEM VII.

Translation, Vol. i. *p.* 506.   *Text, Vol.* ii. *p.* 9.

Line 7.—' *Tarian*' for *taran*, thunder.   The same form is occasionally met with in other poets ; as, for instance—

" Trachywyd llechwed lluch a *tharian*
        Casnodyn."

For " *llyaus*" we should probably read *llyas* (= lleas), death. But should " *llyaus*" (= " lluaws," a multitude) be the correct reading, the poet may have intended to connect it with " poploet anylan" of the preceding line, rather than with " lluch a tharian," the words which stand immediately before it.—(E.)

Line 9.—The meaning apparently is, that after peace or silence has been proclaimed, the judgment will sit in a manner similar to what is observed in earthly tribunals.—(E.)

Line 14.—The first host will be all pure, resembling the angels in appearance; the second will be, like " brodorion" (the natives or denizens of a country), of a mixed character, some good and some bad; the third will be thoroughly bad, and will be at once sent to their proper comrades.—(E.)

Line 16.—'*Meillon*' or '*meillion*,' literally clover; but the Welsh word is more poetical than the English, and is used in a more extensive sense, being frequently employed to designate all the sweet flowering herbage that covers a field or lawn.—(E.)

Line 21.—May we be reconciled to the grave, in order to join the company of the blessed.—(E.)

Line 22.—For '*vedit*' I read " venit " = vynydd, mountain. The allusions to Mount Olivet, as the scene of the last judgment, are of frequent occurrence in the works of the mediæval bards.—(E.)

Lines 24 and 25.—The meaning of these two lines is a matter of conjecture rather than certainty. The text is possibly corrupt—a supposition in some degree supported by the fact that the reading in the *Myvyrian Archæology* differs from that in the *Black Book*, where two of the words are written in a way which evidently shows that the copyist did not comprehend the import of what he was transcribing. A similar remark might be made with reference to the opening lines; but the greater portion of the poem is written in language easily understood.—(E.)

POEM VIII.

Translation, Vol. i. *p.* 306. *Text, Vol.* ii. *p.* 10.

This is no poem at all, but a collection of triads respecting celebrated horses, of which similar accounts are given in the triads published in the second volume of the *Myvyrian Archæology*, but the text given in that work embraces several names besides those that are mentioned here. Some difference occurs also in some of the names.

The last triad is incomplete—the name of the horse omitted being Melyngar Mangre, the horse of Llew Llawgyffes.—See *Triads of the Horses*, No. 2.—(E.)

POEM IX.

Translation, Vol. i. *p.* 508.   *Text, Vol.* ii. *p.* 10.

This poem in the *Myvyrian Archæology* is attributed to Gruffydd ab yr Ynad Coch ; but as that poet survived the fall of Prince Llewelyn ab Gruffydd, in the year 1282, no composition of his could have been written sufficiently early to find place in the *Black Book.*—(E.)

Line 3.—' *Modridaw* ' = modrydav, a rallying-point, a standard. —(E.)

Line 5.—This line seems to be out of place here.—(E.)

Line 7.—For the use of ' *caredd* ' in a favourable sense, see Zeuss, *Grammatica Celtica*, ii. 1084.—(E.)

Line 15.—' *Merch* ' (woman) in the *Black Book*, but " meirch " (horses) in the *Myvyrian* copy. The latter appears to be the more correct reading, since we have " graget " (women) again in the next line.—(E.)

Line 24.—He will not attend matins, nor say his prayers, nor sit in a meditative mood, being too much occupied with the things of this world.—(E.)

Line 30.—These would be his tormentors in the regions below, according to the doctrine of the bards. See similar expressions used by Gruffydd ab yr Ynad Coch (*Myv. Arch.* i.) and Dvydd Ddn o Hiraddng.—(E.)

Line 36.—' *Inihagel,*' evidently a clerical or a typographical error for *Mihagel* (= Mihangel, the Welsh form of the name of the Archangel), which in the *Myvyrian* text appears in its modern-ised orthography. With this line, to all appearance, this poem ends, and what immediately follows has no apparent connection with it, and is of a totally different character.—(E.)

Line 41.—'*Llauuridet*' = llawfrydedd, from *llaw* (as in *llaw-en*) and *bryd*, the mind; q. d. *llawenfrydedd.*—(E.)

Line 42.—The interpolation seems to end with this line. The remaining portion may have originally belonged to the poem, but more likely it is part of some other composition, or perhaps different fragments confusedly strung together.—(E.)

POEM X.

Translation, Vol. i. *p.* 510. *Text, Vol.* ii. *p.* 12.

Line 9.—Here the tense changes from the future subjunctive to the past indicative. In the original, after the verb and its object have once been expressed, "A" alone is used for them in both tenses, excepting that four lines further on the past is again given in full. It is therefore possible that, in the instances in which the words are not fully supplied, they should, as in the first portion, be taken in a conjunctive sense, indicating a wish rather than a fact.—(E.)

POEM XI.

Translation, Vol. i. *p.* 511. *Text, Vol.* ii. *p.* 13.

Stanza i.

Line 1.—There can be but little doubt that *Celi*, as an epithet of the Deity, originated in the Latin word *cæli*, the genitive of *cælum*, heaven, and that "Duw *Celi*" is Deus *cæli*, the God *of* heaven; but in process of time, the relation in which it stood to another word having been forgotten or overlooked, it was used independently, and gradually came to be looked on as being derived from *cel*, hidden, concealed, secret, the root of *celu*, to hide or con-ceal. We may therefore, without any impropriety, when *Celi* does not stand as a genitive governed by "Duw," "Crist," or some word of the kind, translate it by the *Mysterious One*, or some equivalent expression. Dr. John Kent, a poet of the early part of the fifteenth century, in his poem on the "Names of God," printed in the *Iolo MSS.* p. 285, mentions *Celi*; not as an independent name or title, but, according to its primary meaning, as an attributive to "Duw."

> " Duw Tri, Duw *Celi*, coeliwn ; Daf, Eli,
>   Dwyv, eilwaith da volwn ;
>   Gwiwner, ei glod a ganwn,
>   Arglwydd Dad mawr ganad, gwn."

The bards, it may be observed, were allowed to introduce *Latin* words into their compositions, but their license in this respect did not extend to other foreign languages.—(E.)

Line 6.—See Mark xv. 34. The same word occurs also at p. 36 in a composition attributed to Elaeth.—(E.)

STANZA II.

Line 6.—*Anhun*, or *Annun*, was a female saint of the fifth century, and the reputed foundress of the church of Trawsvnydd in Merionethshire.—(E.)

STANZA III.

Line 4.—Probably an allusion to the passage of the Red Sea (Exod. xiv.)—(E.)

Line 6.—The word in the original is "*pabuir*" (= pabwyr), which signifies both *rushes* and the *wick* of a candle—the pith of the rush with a small portion of the fibre being formerly used for wicks, and to some degree at the present day in some remote parts of the principality.—(E.)

Line 8.—' *Pimp kaer*,' Pentapolis, or the five cities of the plain (Gen. xix.) ' *Wir* ' (= gwyr), oblique, slanting ; swerving, turning aside, Lot's wife.—(E.)

POEM XII.

Translation, Vol. i. p. 512.   Text, Vol. ii. p. 13.

This poem calls for no remark.

POEM XIII.

Translation, Vol. i. *p.* 513. *Text, Vol.* ii. *p.* 14.

This poem is all through very difficult. In one of the copies printed in the *Myvyrian Archæology* it forms part of Poem XXIX. in the present volume.—(E.)

Line 1.—' *Guirthvin* ' is a word not found in our dictionaries. It may be compounded of *gwyrth*, virtue, grace, a miracle, and *myn*, the will ; or the latter part of it may be *gwyn*, the impulse of the mind, disposition.—(E.)

Line 16.—' *Vn brin.*' Mount Olivet is probably intended, where it was once very generally supposed the last judgment would take place. See note, p. 329.—(E.)

Line 17.—' *Teulv,*' literally a family.—(E.)

Line 18.—The bards divided the heavenly hierarchy into nine degrees or orders.—(E.)

Line 22.—' *Nen* ' should possibly be read " ren " = *Rhên*, one of the names of the Diety, and, as some think, the root of the Latin *parens*.—(E.)

Line 26.—' *Valioff* ' = val Iof—that is, *Iov* or *Iob*.—(E.)

Line 1.—' *Cyllestic* ' should be cyllestric = callestrig, from *callestr*, flint, a word of rather frequent occurrence in the poets, and employed in connections not unlike the present instance :—

" Ergrynaf *kyllestric* kaen
Gan wledic gwlat anorffen."
Book of Taliessin, p. 211.—(E.)

POEM XIV.

Translation, Vol. i. *p.* 303. *Text, Vol.* ii. *p.* 16.

This is simply the last stanza of the poem called " Mic Dinbych," which will be found at length in the *Book of Taliessin*, vol. ii. p. 168.—(E.)

POEM XV.

Translation, Vol. i. *p.* 303.   *Text, Vol.* ii. *p.* 17.

Line 1.—' *Dinas Maon,*' the city of the people.—(E.)

Line 2.—A comparison of this line with others that follow tends to show that "*edar*" should be considered a proper name, though it may possibly stand for "yddar," the oak.—(E.)

Line 7.—' *Merhin*' = merchyn, the diminutive of *March*, a horse.—(E.)

Line 8.—' *Divurn.*'   The rhyme is opposed to " diwurn" (= divurn) being the right reading.   Perhaps *diffyn* may be the form intended, which would rhyme with "maelgyn," and which has been adopted in the translation.—(E.)

POEM XVI.

Translation, Vol. i. *p.* 481.   *Text, Vol.* ii. *p.* 17.

This poem may be called the "Birch-tree," just as the one that follows is named the "Apple-trees."—(E.)   The allusion, however, in stanza 2, line 3, to the Franks in armour, and in stanza 3, line 4, to the bridges over the Tav and Tawy, which likewise occurs in the interpolations in the Cyvoesi Myrddin, seem to indicate that it is one of the spurious poems attributed to Myrddin which were composed in the twelfth century.—(S.)

STANZA I.

Line 2.—' *Sirch,*' a clerical error for *sirth* = *syrth, syrthia,* from *syrthiv,* to fall.—(E.)

Line 4.—' *A chimrevan*' = cymmreuan or cymmrevan, from cym or cyd, together, and breu or brevu, to low.—(E.)

Rhyd Vochuy, as well as Dinwythwy, Edrywy (or Edryvwy), Macbran, Machwy, with some other names mentioned in this and the following poem, are to me unknown.—(E.)

Stanza III.

Line 4.—There are two rivers in the principality bearing the name of Tav—one in Glamorganshire, which enters the sea near Cardiff, and the other in Carmarthenshire, which disembogues into Carmarthen Bay at Langharne.—(E.)

Line 8.—' *Gint* ' = Gynt = *Gaoind*, an old name synonymous with Gaedhel or Gwydhyl. The name occurs also in the Gododin; see p. 92.—(E.)

POEM XVII.

Translation, Vol. i. *p.* 370. *Text, Vol.* ii. *p.* 18.

This seems to be the oldest existing form of the poem attributed to Merlin, termed the Avallenau, before it was interpolated.—(S.)

Stanza I.

Line 8.—' *Cymminawd* ' appears to be here, as elsewhere, used for an imaginary *place of battle*, the word signifying a contact of edges or blades, or, as explained by Pughe, " a striking edges together ; a cutting at each other." Any place, then, where hostile armies met might be denominated " Cymminawd."—(E.)

Line 10.—In a poem attributed to Taliessin a similar expression occurs :—

" A gware pelre â phen Seison."

" And the playing of ball-buffeting with Saxons' heads."—(E.)

Stanza II.

Line 4.—These two lines are, in the original, added at the bottom of the page.—(E.)

Stanza III.

Line 1.—' *Pren melyn*,' a yellow tree, is one of the Welsh names of the barberry.—(E.)

Line 3.—' *Kad im Prydin*.' Prydyn was a name applied to North Britain. The tradition of an invasion of Scotland from

Ireland in seven ships is also to be found in an Irish poem quoted in an ancient tract, called the Dinseanchas, in the *Book of Lecan* :—

> With a fleet of seven ships the king's son sailed
> From Eire to the land of Alba ;
> He fought for the Eastern country
> In battles, in conflicts,
> From Eadain to the wide Lochlann.—(S.)

Line 7.—' *Kenhin.*' Some consider this word to be equivalent to " genddynt," and translate the line thus :—

> "Of those who come, they shall take *with them*."
> Stephens, *Lit. of the Kymry*, p. 227.—(E.)

STANZA IV.

Line 2.—This " fair maid " appears to be Gwendydd, who is said to have supplied her brother with food and drink in his solitary wanderings in the woods.—(E.)

STANZA V.

Line 1.—It has been supposed that " Llanerch," the word used in the original, which signifies a glade, is intended for *Lanark*, in Strath Clyde, the territory of Rhydderch Hael, the patron of Myrddin.—(E.)

Line 11.—The battle of Ardderyd, in which Gwenddoleu fell, occurred, according to the *Annales Cambriæ*, in 573. It was in consequence of the disasters of this memorable battle that Myrddin became insane.—(E.)

STANZA VIII.

Line 3.—' *Hwimleian* ' or " huimleian" (= chwimleian) is the word in the original. It is also written *chwimpleian, chwibleian,* and *chwivleian.* " It is very probable that it is to the present bard, Merlinus Sylvestris, and not to Merlinus Ambrosius, that we ought to look for the origin of much of what is contained in the Brut, as the prophecies of the last mentioned. It also seems evident that it is to his Chwifleian that we are to attribute the origin of the Viviane of the romances of chivalry, and who acts so conspicuous a part in those compositions ; although it is true there is not much resemblance betwixt the two names. But, if we look into the poems of Merlin Sylvestris, we shall find that the female personage of this name, which by the French romancers might easily be modified into Viviane, is repeatedly referred to by the bard in his vaticinations. It also seems probable, as Chwifleian signifies a female who appears and disappears, and also as the word bears some resemblance in sound to Sibylla, that the bard, by a confusion of terms and ideas, not uncommon in early writers, coined this name as an appellation for some imaginary character, and thus furnished the original of Viviane."—Rev. T. Price, *Literary Remains*, i. 144.—(E.)

Line 6.—' *Grat wehin* ' = grad = wehin, from grat or grad = Lat. gratia, grace, favour, and "gwehyn," to shed or diffuse ; the same as "rhadwehyn."—(E.)

Line 8.—By the child here, as in stanza 1, no doubt Cadwaladyr is meant, which indicates its composition before his father's death. —(S.)

STANZA IX.

Line 4.—' *Cadvaon* ' = places of battle.—(E.)

Line 5.—Some of the Scotch rivers seem to have borne the same names in Cymric with rivers in Wales, as the Tay, the Teviot, and the Tweed, which were called Tawy, Teifi, and Tywi. The two latter flowed through Teviotdale and Tweeddale, and may be here meant if the scene was in the north.—(S.)

Line 6.—' *Aranwinion* ' is the same place as Garanwynion, in the battle of Gwenystrad (B. T. 31).—(S.)

STANZA X.

Line 4.—' *Rhyd Rheon*,' the ford of Rheon. Loch Rheon and Caer Rheon are Loch Ryan and Carn Ryan in Wigtonshire, and the ford must be looked for there also.—(S.)

Line 7.—' *Bri Brython*.' " Bri" appears to be redundant here. It probably originated in the first syllable of the word which follows having been written twice. But should it be retained, the line might be thus rendered :—

" All shall have their rights ; in their glory will the Britons rejoice."—(E.)

z

POEM XVIII.

Translation, Vol. i. *p.* 482.   *Text, Vol.* ii. *p.* 21.

This composition is generally called the "Hoianau," from "hoian" or "oian," to listen; is also called "Porchellanau," or "Piglings." "Hoianau" might be translated "Auscultations."—(E.)

STANZA I.

Line 4.—'*Erwis*' = *erchwys,* a pack of hunting-dogs. Dr. Owen Pughe (*Welsh Dict.* s. v. "Erwas") changes this word into *erweis,* which he translates "heroes," and quotes this passage as an authority for that word; but whether such a word as *erwas* (pl. *erweision* or *erweis*) exists in the language or not, it is quite conclu- sive that "erchwys," a word of frequent occurrence in one of the *Mabinogion* (see vol. iii. pp. 4, 5), is intended in this place; and this, it will be seen, is not the only passage in the Hoianau in which reference is made to the *dogs* of Rhydderch Hael. The form "erchwys" itself, it may be added, occurs in another poem which usually goes under the name of Myrddin :—

> "Byt a vyd byt wrth *erchuys*
> Y adeilaur yn dyrys
> Heb werth maur ni chaffaur crys."
> > *Gwasgargerdd Vyrddin,* st. 17.

> "The world shall be when men shall delight in hounds,
> And build in the wilderness ;
> And a shirt without great cost cannot be obtained."—(E.)

STANZA II.

Line 5.—According to the folk-lore of Wales, the ninth wave is larger and stronger than the others, and comes further ashore. The number nine, being a triad of triads, has always been held in esteem by the Welsh. See Stephens, *Literature of the Kymry,* p. 251.—(E.)

STANZA III.

Line 11.—That is, the sod on which I tread.—(E.)

Stanza v.

Line 5.—If '*eneirchiawg*' (from *arch*), the reading in the *Myv. Arch.*, and adopted by Pughe (*Dict.* s. v.), be the correct one, the meaning will be as expressed in the translation; but the *Black Book*, from which we translate, has "*eneichauc*," from *eichiawg*, loud, high-sounding. If we adopt the latter, the passage might be rendered "men of great noise;" the allusion in that case would be to the clang of their arms. Pughe (*s. v.* "Diheddawg") translates "gwyr eneirchiawg" by "hyperborean men."—(E.)

Line 10.—The meaning of this line is not obvious. Mr. Stephens (*Lit. of the Kymry*, p. 254) translates it thus :—"When the horns call men to the squares of conflict;" but unfortunately for this version the word in the original is "guraget" (women), not "gwyr" (men).—(E.)

Stanza vi.

Line 7.—'*Aber Dev.*' For "aber dev" of the *Black Book*, the *Myvyrian* reads "Aber deu gleddeu," which is the Welsh name of Milford Haven in Pembrokeshire.—(E.)

Stanza xi.

Line 3.—'*Ceneu*,' or whelp, for a son or offspring, is often to be taken in a favourable sense. In a well-known passage, Meredydd ab Rhys, by way of compliment, calls Prince Madog "Iawn *geneu* Owain Gwynedd."—(E.)

Stanza xii.

Line 1.—'*Gwys*' (= Lat. *gens*), people; a country.—(E.)

Line 2.—The reading of the *Black Book* is "*prisc*," and that of the copy printed in the *Myv. Arch.* "prysg;" but as neither of these words can properly rhyme with the terminations of the other lines, it may be conjectured that the original reading was "brwys." Should we adopt "brisg" as the correct reading, the meaning of the passage would be to this effect :—"Burrow not in the trodden place."—(E.)

Stanza xiii.

Line 3.—On the margin :—

"Thou shouldst not resort to the desert from the deep lake."—(E.)

STANZA XVI.

Line 10.—' *Deheubarth,*' the word here employed in the original, means any southern region, but in our earlier writings it is almost exclusively used for *South Wales.*—(E.)

STANZA XX.

Line 1.—' *Eilon* ' cannot be reasonably supposed to mean " music " in this place, and " roebucks " near the end of the stanza, as translated in *Literature of the Kymry,* pp. 269, 270, though the word has both these significations.—(E.)

Line 3.—' *Mynydd Maon.*' The Mount of the People.—(E.)

Line 7.—Cors Vochno is an extensive turbary lying in the angle formed by the river Dovey and the sea, in the north-western corner of Cardiganshire. The Welsh Coast Railway between Machynlleth and Aberystwyth skirts its northern and western borders for several miles, and the river Eleri passes through a portion of it. At a little distance from Trev Taliessin, a village lying on its eastern margin, is the Grave of Taliessin, which tradition points out as the final resting-place of the " Chief Bard of the West."—(E.)

' *Minron.*' Other MSS. read " ym mon," in Mona or Anglesey. —(E.)

STANZA XXIII.

Line 6.—' *Itas* ' = Iddas = Judas. Dr. Owen Pughe (*s. v.* " Iddas ") explains the word as a common adjective, adducing this passage as his authority ; but there can be but little doubt that it is a modification of the name of him whose surname was Iscariot ; and the following passages, in which the same person is evidently alluded to in a form which is almost precisely identical, tend to confirm the same view :—

" Llyna mab gowri gobeith.
A dylivas *idas* y leith."
Black Book, p. 46.

" Gogyfarch veird heis
Bath vadawl *idas*
Dofyn eigyawn adas."
Book of Taliessin, p. 152.

" Am eiryoluy Meir ar y mab knaᵡ
Nat eluyf yn llugyr yn lloc *Idas*
Nam gatto reen cyn deg pynnas
An reuin Kayn can Sathanas."

Meilyr.

Mr. Stephens (*Lit. of the Kymry*, p. 273) assumes, but without any probability, that Iddawc Cordd Prydain is the person intended. The ruling passion of Judas was his love of money ; in like manner, the predominant characteristic of these two brothers was their avidity for more territory.—(E.)

Stanza xxv.

Line 5.—See *Red Book*, p. 226.—(E.)

Line 8.—That is, the country.—(E.)

POEM XIX.

Translation, Vol. i. *p.* 309.   *Text, Vol.* ii. *p.* 28.

These " Verses of the Graves " are also called " Verses of the Warriors' Graves," being memorials of the places of sepulture of about two hundred warriors and persons of distinction connected with the early history of Britain.   Many of those whose names are here commemorated are well-known historical characters ; but of some of them no records, excepting these simple verses, have reached us.   Carnhuanawc very plausibly infers that, from the places of sepulture being generally upon the tops of mountains, and but seldom in the churchyards, it is most probable that the verses were composed before that latter mode of burial was adopted, and that the graves here mentioned are the carns and tumuli which are still to be seen upon the mountains, and also sometimes in the cultivated lands.   Whether the mountains were selected in preference to the valleys, or whether the progress of agriculture has caused the disappearing of these carns and tumuli in the cultivated land, is not quite clear ; but it is certain that at the present day these remains are more frequently met with on the mountains than in the valleys.   The same writer adds that these graves are of various dimensions, from such as might be supposed to mark the sepulture of an infant, and might be constructed by one or two persons in half-an-hour, to large mounds that would require the labour of a number of people several days. They generally contain one or more square stone cells, which vary in size from two feet square to such as would afford room for several persons to enter them at once. The smaller cells seem to have been constructed for urns; whilst in the larger it appears that whole-length bodies were deposited.—See *Literary Remains of the Rev. T. Price*, i. 148.—(E.)

STANZA I.

Line 1.—Some of these verses seem to imply a question, though the interrogative, as in the present instance, may be wanting.—(E.)

STANZA XXXV.

Line 3.—'*Gwir.*' Pughe (*s. v.* "Gwir") translates "gwir" in this passage, "justice;" but the allusion is evidently to this noted character's habit of *disguising* himself in his adventures with Gwydion ab Don, as related in the Mabinogi of Math ab Mathonwy. See *Mabinogion*, iii. 336.—(E.)

STANZA XXXVIII.

Line 2.—This place is probably the same as Machawy, mentioned in the Hoianau.—(E.)

STANZA XL.

Line 3.—Vortigern.—(E.)

STANZA XLI.

Line 1.—'*Cian wails.*' A play upon words may have been intended here in the original. "Cian" signifies a little dog; "udo," is, properly, to howl; and "cnud" denotes a pack, as of wolves or foxes. "The little dog howls in the waste of the pack." —(E.)

STANZA XLIII.

Line 1.—'*March*' and '*Gwythur*' are by some considered to be simply appellatives—"the steed" and "the man of conflict;" but it is pretty evident that they are the names of veritable heroes. There was a chieftain of the name of March ab Meirchion (Marcus, the son of Marcianus) living in the fifth century; and Gwythur ab

Greidiol is recorded as one of the warriors who served under Arthur, and was the father of one of his wives.—(E.)

STANZA XLIX.

Line 2.—'*Llanelvy.*' The Welsh name of St. Asaph, in Flintshire.—(E.)

STANZA L.

Line 4.—'*Kein.*' There is a river of this name in Merionethshire, which joins the Mawddach near Dolgelley ; and another in Montgomeryshire, which flows into the Vyrnwy about ten miles above the junction of the latter with the Severn.—(E.)

STANZA LIII.

Line 2.—'*Aber duwir dyar.*' There is a place called Aber Dyar, near Llanybydder, in Caermarthenshire, where the Dyar enters the Teivi.—(E.)

Line 3.—For '*Tavne*' a MS. in the translator's possession reads "Tawe," which is the popular name of the Tawy, which disembogues into the sea at Aber Tawy, or Swansea.—(E.)

STANZA LIV.

Line 2.—'*Rhwyv*' signifies a ruler, chieftain, or governor ; but here it *may* be the proper name of the son of Rhigenau.—(E.)

STANZA LXI.

This stanza is scarcely intelligible, and has the appearance of being corrupt.—(E.)

STANZA LXVI.

Line 3.—For '*brauc*' of the *Black Book*, one MS. has "bradawg," which seems to be the correct reading.—(E.)

STANZA LXVII.

Line 3.—'*Am maelur*' = Amhaelwr = Ab Maelwr. Compare Amhadog, Amheirig, Amheredyd, for Ab Madog, Ab Meirig, and Ab Meredyd.—(E.)

STANZA LXIX.

Line 3.—The *Black Book* text has '*aswy*' in this place, and the *Myvyrian*, "achwy ;" but in a MS. of these verses which once belonged to the Rev. D. Ellis, of Cricieth in Carnarvonshire, of which the translator has a transcript, the word is "avwy," which appears to be the more accurate reading, and has been adopted in the translation.—(E.)

STANZA LXXII.

Line 3.—See Price, *Hanes Cymru*, p. 35 ; *Cambrian Journal*, i. 216.—(E.)

POEM XX.

Translation, Vol. i. *p.* 501.   *Text, Vol.* ii. *p.* 35.

' *Cynghogion,*' from " cynghog," entangled, intricate, or compli-cated.   But why should a composition so simple and inartificial in its construction be so termed, does not appear.   For an account of the Welsh metres called *Cynghogion,* see *Cyfrinach y Beirdd,* p. 152.

Elaeth, to whom the authorship of this and the following poem is attributed, was a bard and saint, who lived in the sixth, or, ac-cording to others, in the seventh century.   He is sometimes called Elaeth Vrenin, or King Elaeth, from his having been, in the earlier part of his life, king or prince of a district in the north of England.   He was driven from his territory by the overpowering attacks of his enemies, in consequence of which he retired to Wales, and spent the remainder of his days in the Bangor or College of Seiriol at Penmon, in Anglesey ; and during his residence in that place, he is stated to have founded the church of Amlwch in that island.   These poetical pieces which bear his name, well accord with the character he assumed towards the close of his life.—(E.)

POEM XXI.

Translation, Vol. i. *p.* 502.   *Text, Vol.* ii. *p.* 36.

Though this poem is stated to be the production of the same author as the preceding, it is considerably more intricate and less intelligible than that composition.—(E.)

Line 28.—This is assumed to be the meaning of the passage.
Of ' *duire y rolre seint*,' it is difficult to make any sense, unless it is
a corruption of some expression like " Duw ar holl saint."—(E.)

POEM XXII.

Translation, Vol. i. *p.* 266. *Text, Vol.* ii. *p.* 37.

This elegy is attributed to Llywarch Hen, and printed among his
compositions in the *Myvyrian Archæology*. It is also printed with
an English translation in Owen Pughe's Heroic Elegies of that bard,
of which considerable use has been made on the present occasion.
The poem, with some variations, occurs also in the *Red Book of
Hergest*.—(E.)

STANZA I.

Line 2.—' *Crimrud* ' = crymrudd, from *crwm*, bent, crooked,
bending or stooping; and *rhudd*, ruddy: the former part of the
word describing the stooping, exhausted appearance of the horses
after the action, and the latter their blood-stains. The other readings are—" cymrud" or " cymryd," and " cymrudd."—(E.)

STANZA II.

Line 1.—' *Dihad* ' = diad, from the privative *di*, and *gad*, the
root of *gadael*, *gadaw*, or *gadu*, to leave, quit, or relinquish.—(E.)

STANZA III.

This stanza is not in the *Red Book*.—(S.)

STANZA VII.

This stanza is not in the *Red Book*.—(S.)

STANZA IX.

Line 2.—' *Dyvnaint* ' (from *dwvn*, deep) implies a country
abounding with deep vales or depressions, and is the ancient
name of that part of England which comprises the present *Devon-
shire;* and it is supposed that from it the modern name of that
county is derived.—(E.)

Stanza x.

Line 1.—For '*rerent,*' or "rereint," here and in the stanzas that follow, we should undoubtedly read "redeint," or "redaint," with the *Red Book, Myvyrian,* and other copies.—(E.)

Stanza xiv.

Line 2.—' *Goteith*' (=goddaith), the word used here in the original, "is a term applied to the burning of furze or heath on the mountains, which is done at seasonable times of the year.— Owen (Pughe), *Llywarch Hen,* p. 9.—(E.)

Stanza xviii.

This is the first stanza in the *Red Book.*—(S.)

POEM XXIII.

Text, Vol. ii. *p.* 39.

This poem is addressed to Hywel, the son of Goronwy and grandson of Edwin, who died in 1103, and does not fall within the scope of this work.—(S.)

POEM XXIV.

Text, Vol. ii. *p.* 40.

This poem is a composition of Cynddelw, a poet who lived at the time the *Black Book* was compiled, and indeed appears to have transcribed the latter part of it. It does not fall within the scope of this work.—(S.)

POEM XXV.

Translation, Vol. i. *p.* 515.   *Text, Vol.* ii. *p.* 41.

This short poem contains nothing to call for remark.

POEM XXVI.

Translation, Vol. i. *p.* 518. *Text, Vol.* ii. *p.* 42.

STANZA I.

Line 3.—*Ja* = ie, yes. The *Myvyrian* has "iad," a scull, which would be a tautology.—(E.)

STANZA II.

Line 38.—Mr. Stephens omits the negative "*ny*" in this place, but on what authority is not stated.—(E.)

STANZA VI.

Line 3.—The fourth stanza is here repeated in a smaller hand, with some few unimportant variations.—(E.)

POEM XXVII.

Translation, Vol. i. *p.* 519. *Text, Vol.* ii. *p.* 43.

This poem resembles, in some of its expressions, the preceding poem, and leads to the supposition that they are by the same hand. —(S.)

STANZA III.

Line 1.—'*Berch*' and '*kerch*' should be "berth" and "certh," as the fact of their rhyming with "nerth" in the following line plainly shows.—(E.)

STANZA XIII.

Line 3.—The following occurs at the bottom of the page in a different hand from that of the body of the poem :—

" White-bellied are the fish ; hastening the swans of the wave ;
Oratory is splendid ; fluent is eloquence ;
God to man will send a companion ;
White the tops of bushes ; tuneful the birds ;
The day long ; the cuckoos loud ;
Mercy is an attribute of the most beneficent God."—(E.)

STANZA XIX.

Line 3.—There appears to be some miscalculation here.—(E.)

STANZA XXI.

Line 1.—' *Deueint*' = Dewaint, denotes properly the time from midnight to cock-crowing, and is often used in a general sense for the dead of night ; but here, in connection with matins, it appears to mean the nocturns, or services held during the night.—(E.)

POEM XXVIII.

Text, Vol. ii. *p.* 45.

This poem is by Cynddelw, and does not fall within the scope of this work. It is printed among his compositions in the *Myvyrian Archæology* (vol. i. p. 264), where it forms the concluding part of the poem called " Marwysgafn Cynddelw."—(S.)

POEM XXIX.

Translation, Vol. i. *p.* 516. *Text, Vol.* ii. *p.* 46.

STANZA II.

Line 9.—' *Cv da. cvd ymda.*' " Da" is the third person singular, present tense, of the obsolete verb *däu*, just as *ä* forms the same person and tense of the obsolete *äu ;* and the past, *daeth*, stands precisely in the same relation to *däu* as *aeth* does to *äu*. In the same line we have an instance of the same word compounded with a prefix, " ymda" (= ymdda) ; and this form is of less rare occurrence.

> " Or *ymdäa* gwraig ei hunan.".
> *Welsh Laws.*

> " Pennpingyon a *ymda* ar y ben yr arbet y draet."
> *Mabinogion,* ii 201.

The word is still further compounded, as *Gworymdda*—

> " Llawer mawreir a vethla.
> Keudawt cyd *worymdaa.*
> O ovrys nywys kwta."
> *Red Book of Heryest,* p. 307.—(E.)

POEM XXX.

Translation, Vol. i. p. 321.   Text, Vol. ii. p. 47.

This poem is printed in the *Myvyrian Archæology*, p. 130, among the poems of Llywarch Hen, as the latter part of a poem called the *Tribanau;* but, while the former part is in the *Red Book of Hergest*, this part is omitted.   They seem, therefore, to be separate poems, but evidently by the same composer.—(S.)

STANZA XI.

Line 1.—That is, hands distributing gold.—(E.)

STANZA XVI.

Line 2.—Gulls leave the sea, and are seen on the cliffs, and often far inland, on the approach of storms.—(E.)

STANZA XVII.

Line 2.—That is, divested of its ornaments of leaves, flowers, and the like.—(E.)

STANZA XXVII.

Line 1.—Aruwl Melyn was the horse of Pasgen ap Urien (see p. 10).   The meaning here and in some other parts of the poem is not very obvious.—(E.)

STANZA XXXI.

Line 2.—' *Mug maur drevydd.*'—"The great burner of towns" is Dr. Owen Pughe's rendering of Mug-mawr-Drevydd ("mug maur heuil"), which more literally signifies the great smoke of towns, or the smoke of great towns ; but the effect may be put for the cause. —(E.)   He is said to have been the son of Ossa Cyllellawr, who fought with Arthur at the battle of Badon.—(S.)

STANZA XXXIII.

Line 1.—' *Cavall,*' except as the name of Arthur's favourite dog, I have met with only in this place and in the last poem in the book, in which this stanza, with some few orthographical varia-tions, is repeated.   Dr. Pughe seems to consider the word to be

the same as *cavell*, a cell or apartment, the chancel of a church ;
and cites the passage thus (*s. v.* " Cafell) :"—

> " Cyfarfan ain *cafell*,"

which he translates "opposite to my reposing cell ;" but, *s. v.*
" Cyfarfan," as well as in his edition of *Llywarch Hen*, his
reading is—

> " Cyfarfan ain *cafall*,"

which he translates in the same way ; but the rhyme plainly shows
that cav*ell* cannot be here intended, and it is doubtful whether we
should read " cyvarvuan," as in the passage before, or " cyvarvan"
as in the concluding poem. " Cyvarvuan," which appears to me
the better reading, it is pretty evident is the modern " cyvarvuant,"
from *cyvarvod*, to meet ; and " Cavall" I take to be the name of
a stream or river on the banks of which the rencontre took place.—
(E.)

STANZA XXXIV.

Line 1.—' *Fonogion*' (from *ffon*, a staff), persons armed with
staves, or similar weapons. ' *Mugc* ' = Mwg-Mawr-Drevydd.—(E.)

Line 2.—The poet apparently means to say that the fate of
Drudwas, who was inadvertently killed by his own birds, was not
so hard as his own.—(E.)

STANZA XXXVI.

Line 1.—Llywarch ab Llywelyn uses a similar expression with
reference to this son of Llywarch Hen :—

> " Mab Llywarch ddihavarch ddyndid."—(E.)

POEM XXXI.

Translation, Vol. i. *p.* 261.   *Text, Vol.* ii. *p.* 50.

This is a very obscure piece.   Many of the names which occur
in it are the same as those mentioned in the Mabinogi of Kulhwch
and Olwen.

Line 11.—The meaning of this couplet, and indeed of many other
passages, is quite problematical.   Davies' translation (*Myth. of the
Druids*, p. 287) is as follows—" Though the birds of wrath should

go forth, and the three attendant ministers should fall asleep."
But we are not informed by what process such a meaning has been
elicited from these five words.—(E.)

Line 21.—' *Trywruid.*' This place is afterwards mentioned as
Traethev Trywruid, and was the scene of Arthur's battle.—(S.)

Line 42.—' *Mynyd Eiddyn,*' or Edinburgh—the same as Mynyd
Agned, the scene of Arthur's battle.—(S.)

Line 80.—The nine maidens or virgins occur frequently in.
Scottish legends. They appear here as nine witches.—(S.)

Line 84.—*Tud* = people, men. Compare the Corn. " tus," Arm.
" tud," and Ir. and Gael. *tuath.* This is the primary meaning of
the word, but in more modern Welsh it denotes land ; as—

> " Chwi drafaelwyr mor a *thud,*
>   Y bydi gyd a'i gyrau.
>
>   *Elis. Wynn,* 1703.
>
>   Ye travellers of sea and land,
>   The world and all its corners."—(E.)

POEM XXXII.

Translation, Vol. i. p. 336. *Text, Vol. ii. p.* 53.

This poem is attributed to Llywarch Hen. It relates to Gwallawg ap Lleenawg, a hero of the north.

POEM XXXIII.

Translation, Vol. i. p. 293. *Text, Vol. ii. p.* 54.

This poem appears to be intended for a dialogue between
Gwynn ap Nudd and Gwyddneu Garanhir. The latter appears
among the Men of the North, and as such has a historic character.
As a mythic person, he was king of *Cantref y Gwaelod,* a region
submerged by the sea in Cardigan Bay. This poem evidently belongs to him in his historic character, as it refers to events in the
north.—(S.)

STANZA IX.

The one Tawy was the river Tay in the north, the other the
Tawy in South Wales.

STANZA X.

Caer Vandwy is also mentioned in the poem called the Preiddeu Annwfn.—(S.)

POEM XXXIV.

Translation, Vol. i. p. 325.   Text, Vol. ii. p. 55.

This is the most confused, and, to me, unintelligible, of all the compositions in the *Black Book.*—(E.) The mention of Mechyd in line 17 seems to connect it with other poems in which Mechyd, the son of Llywarch Hen, is referred to.—(S.)

POEM XXXV.

Translation, Vol. i. p. 288.   Text, Vol. ii. p. 56.

A dialogue between Taliessin and Ugnach.—(E.)

STANZA V.

Line 1.—' *Caer Seon*,' the city of Sion or Jerusalem.   In a passage added to Nennius, Arthur is said to have gone to Jeru-. salem, and returned with a sacred cross.—(S.)

Line 3.—' *Caer Lleu a Gwydyon*,' the city of Llew and Gwy- dyon.   What place is meant it is difficult to say.   It was at a river's mouth, and must have been in or near Manau Guotodin. —(S.)

POEM XXXVI.

Text, Vol. ii. p. 57.

POEM XXXVII.

Text, Vol. ii. p. 58.

These two poems are by Cynddelw, and do not fall within the scope of this work.

POEM XXXVIII.

Translation, Vol. ii. p. 302.   Text, Vol. ii. p. 59.

Line 1.—This poem is attributed to Gwyddneu or Gwyddno Garanhir, a prince and poet, and is said to have been composed by him when the sea burst over the territory called Cantrev y Gwaelod,

or Lowland Hundred, in the latter part of the fifth, or the beginning of the sixth, century of our era. The following judicious remarks of the late Rev. Thomas Price on the subject are worth recording :—
" It is stated that the space now occupied by the Bay of Cardigan was once a fertile and populous plain, the patrimony of Gwyddno Garanhir, but on so low a level as to make it necessary that it should be protected against the sea by an embankment and flood-gates ; and that, in consequence of the latter being left open by *Seithenyn Veddw*, the drunkard, in a moment of intoxication, the sea broke in and entirely overwhelmed the whole country. . . . . Although the Roman Itineraries forbid our adopting this tradition as a correct record of anything that could have occurred to that extent in the fifth or sixth century, yet it is nevertheless possible that some such inundation took place on a minor scale at that time, or else that some more extensive catastrophe occurred at a period anterior to the Roman surveys, and which has erroneously been placed in the fifth century. But, be the historical fact as it may, the lines are certainly old, and possess considerable poetical merit. The opening address to the wretched drunkard, and the call to him to behold the effects of his intemperance ; the twice-uttered maledic-tion, and the cry of distress from the perishing inhabitants, borne on the winds over the heights of the fortress—all combine to pro-duce as striking an effect as perhaps can be found in the same number of lines in any language."—*Literary Remains*, i. 144.—(E.)

Stanza I.

Line 2.—'*Uirde*' = myrdde, from *myr*, the plural of *môr*, the sea, and the affix *de*, as in *tandde*, *creudde*. '*Baranres*' denotes, properly, a rank or file of soldiers ; the poet probably intending to imply that rows of billows were now raging where soldiers formerly used to perform their evolutions.—(E.)

Stanza II.

Line 21.—'*Emendiceid*' = ammendigaid, anvendigaid—that is, non-blessed, accursed. '*Morvin*' = morwyn, a maid, virgin, or damsel. This word has been variously rendered by preceding trans-lators. Lady Charlotte Guest (*Mabinogion*, iii. 398) makes it signify a " sea-guard ;" and Mr. Price (*Lit. Rem.* i. 145) gives " slave " as its equivalent. Dr. Pughe, whose translation of this poem appeared in the *Cambrian Quarterly Magazine*, ii. 17, evades the word altogether. " Morvin," sea-brink or beach, which has sometimes been adopted, is not so probable a reading, and would not properly rhyme with " cvin" (= " cwyn"), and " terruin" (= " terwyn") in the lines which next follow.—(E.)

Line 3.—' *Finaun Wenestir*' = Ffynnon Wenestr, the Fountain of Venus. In the " Triads of Embellishments," published in the *Iolo MSS.*, pp. 88, 480, we are told that this is one of the names given to the sea :—

" Tri enw addurn y Môr ; Maes Gwenhidwy, Llys Neifion, a *Ffynon-Wenestr.*"

" The three embellishing names of the sea : Field of Gwenhidwy, Court of Neivion, and Fountain of Venus."

The origin of the name may probably be referred to the fabulous story which represents Venus (Aphrodite) as having been born from the froth of the ocean, and deriving her name from that circumstance.—See Hesiod, *Theog.* 196.—(E.)

STANZA III.

Line 1.—' *Y vachteith*' = y vachdaith. " Machdaith" is explained by Pughe to signify " a course of security, a dam or embankment ;" but as he gives no other authority for the use of it than this very passage, his explanation is not altogether satisfactory. My impression is that the word is the same as the Cornish *machteth* (written *mahtheia* in the *Cornish Vocabulary*, ap. Zeuss, 1105), a maid or virgin, which in Irish is *moidhidean*, in Gael. *maighdean*, and in Manx, *moidyn*. Compare also the Anglo-Saxon *mägdh*, the German *magd*, *mädchen*, and the English *maid*. Another instance of the use of this word occurs in one of our old proverbs, and is as follows :—" Gorug ei waith a vach y vachdaith ;" which seems to mean, " He that bails the maid has accomplished his work ;" but which Dr. Pughe renders, " He has completed his work that bails the *journey of a surety*."—(*Welsh Dictionary*, s. v. " Merchiaw.")

If my conjecture as to the meaning of " machdaith" is correct, the reading of " morwyn" in the preceding stanza can hardly be wrong ; for it is quite evident that the two verses are addressed to the same or similar objects. However unpoetical the bard may seem in uttering his maledictions on a fair maid, his conduct is certainly more reasonable than if he cursed a dead embankment, as he is generally represented to have done. How the maid in question was instrumental in bringing about the catastrophe so feelingly deplored in the poem, must necessarily remain among the mysteries. —(E.)

STANZA IV.

Line 1.—The import of '*mererid*' is not well ascertained. Dr. Owen Pughe (*Camb. Quart. Mag.* ii. 17) translates it "the western wave," from a supposition, it is presumed, that it is related to "Môr y Werydd" (*Oceanus Verginius*), a name formerly applied to the Irish Sea, including St. George's Channel, but now more generally to the Atlantic. More probably the word is but another form of "merwerydd," or "myrwerydd," which is stated in Dr. Thomas Williams's manuscript *Latin and Welsh Dictionary* (circa 1608), to denote "fremitus maris;" and it is evident that this comes pretty near the meaning in this poem.

> " Prudd vydd ym *merwerydd* môr,
> Y llong a gollo ei hungor."
> *W. Lleyn.*

> " Dismal will be, *in the tumult of the sea*, the ship
> That should lose its anchor."

"Merwerydd" occurs several times in the *Black Book*, but "mererid" in this poem only.—(E.)

STANZA VIII.

Line 3.—"This last verse is not by Gwyddno, but it is attached to the others in the old MS., and taken from the verses on the graves of the warriors, as inserted in the *Welsh Archæology*, vol. i. p. 79." *Owen Pughe.*—(E.)

POEM XXXIX.

Translation, Vol. i. *p.* 319. *Text, Vol.* ii. *p.* 60.

STANZA I.

Line 3.—By some error, the name "Llywarch" is here omitted in the text of the *Black Book ;* but it must at one time have been part of it. The omission is supplied from the *Myvyrian.*—(E.)

Stanza iii.

Line 3.—' *Llew and Arawn and Urien.*'   These have been included among the sons of Llywarch, but surely they can be no other
than Llew, Arawn, and Urien, the sons of Cynvarch.   The rhyme
shows that this line, usually considered the first line of this stanza,
really belongs to the preceding stanza.—(S.)

Stanza vii.

This stanza, as well as stanzas viii. x. and xi. also occurs in
poem xxx.—(S.)

III.

THE BOOK OF ANEURIN.

AMONG the Hengwrt MSS. there existed formerly a MS. termed in the catalogues the "Book of Aneurin." In the catalogue of these MSS. by Mr. William Maurice, in 1685, it is thus described : " ı Caniad y Gododin o waith Aneurin Wawdrydd. It 2d Caniad a elwir Gwarchan Adebon, Gwarchan Cynfelin o Gwarchan Maelderw. Hwn o law hen gwedi ei gaeadu yn Lundain gan Robert Vaughan, Esq., in 8vo, un fodfedd odew." And the catalogue adds : "This is perhaps the most ancient copy now extant of that truly venerable and illustrious relic of Welsh poetry called the 'Gododin,'" etc. Lluyd, who examined the Hengwrt MSS. in 1696, thus describes it : "46 Gododyn o waith Aneurin. Gwarchan Adebon. Gwarchan Kynvelyn. Gwarchan Maelderw o waith Taliessin. Membr. Antiq. 4to."

A MS. containing the same poems was purchased in Aberdar by Mr. Thomas Bacon, and given by him to Mr. Theophilus Jones, the historian of Brecknock. While in his possession it was transcribed by Edward Davies, the author of the *Celtic Researches.* The MS. was afterwards given by Mr. Jones to the late Rev. T. Price, rector of Cwmddu ; and after his death passed into the possession of his executrix, Mrs. Powell of Abergavenny. It was purchased from her by Sir Thomas Phillipps, of Middle Hill, Baronet. This MS. is a small 4to MS. consisting of nineteen folios of parchment, and contains first the "Gododin," and secondly the four "Gorchanau" in the following order :—the "Gorchan Tudwulch," "Gorchan Adebon," "Gorchan Kynvelin," and "Gorchan Maelderw." On p. 20 the names of Gwilym Tew and Rhys Nan- mor appear in a more modern hand. Gwilym Tew presided at the Glamorgan Gorsedd in 1460. The text of the "Gododin," printed by Mr. Williams ab Ithel in his edition of that poem, was taken from a transcript of this MS., and is very nearly correct. The whole of it, with the exception of the stanzas marked 92, 93, 94, 95, 96, and 97, in Mr. Williams's edition, are in the same handwriting ; and the capitals which mark the beginning of the stanzas are coloured alternately red and green. This part of the

MS. is certainly of the early part of the thirteenth century. Stanzas 92 to 97 inclusive, are written in a different hand, and the capitals are plain. The part of the MS. containing the "Gorchanau" has the first page rubbed and turned, as if the MS. had been sometimes folded so as to place them first, and at other times with the "Gododin" first; and the first four "Gorchanau" are written in the same hand with the main part of the "Gododin," with the capitals coloured alternately red and green. The "Gorchan Maelderw" is written in the same hand with the two last stanzas of the "Gododin," and the capitals are plain. It is followed by a number of lines in the same hand, which appear not to be parts of the "Gorchan Maelderw," but additional stanzas of the "Gododin."

The "Gododin" is declared to be the work of Aneurin, and the "Gorchan Maelderw" the work of Taliessin.

The opinion I have formed is, that this MS. is the same MS. which once belonged to the Hengwrt Collection, and disappeared after Lhuyd examined them in 1696.

In a letter which appeared in the *Cambrian Quarterly Magazine* (vol. v. p. 123), Mr. Price maintains that it could not have been the Hengwrt MS. on two grounds—1st, that the Hengwrt MS. is said, in the catalogue of 1658, to have been 8vo, while this MS. is small 4to; 2dly, that this MS. contains the "Gorchan Tudwulch," which is omitted in the list of contents in the Hengwrt MS. The first objection is of no weight; for the same catalogue terms the "Book of Taliessin" likewise an 8vo; and this MS., which is still extant, is in reality a small 4to, and of exactly the same size and shape as the "Book of Aneurin;" and Lhuyd, who saw it among the Hengwrt MSS., expressly calls it a 4to. It is plain, therefore, that William Maurice applied the term 8vo to MSS. of this size and shape. And the second objection is alone insufficient to lead to the conclusion that the MSS. are different; for it is unlikely that the "Book of Aneurin" in the Hengwrt Collection should have omitted one of the "Gorchanau" attributed to that bard, while it contained the "Gorchan Maelderw," which, as we have seen, was attributed to Taliessin, and written in a different hand; and as the page on which the "Gorchan Tudwulch" appears is much rubbed and bruised, and so less distinct, the title might have escaped the cataloguer. The appearance and binding of the MS.

so much resemble that of the "Book of Taliessin" still in the Hengwrt Collection, that the probability seems greater that this was the MS. which once existed in that collection, and bore the title of the "Book of Aneurin."—(S.)

POEM I.

THE GODODIN.

Translation, Vol. i. p. 374.   Text, Vol. ii. p. 62.

The great poem of the "Gododin" has attracted much attention, from its striking character, its apparent historic value, and the general impression that, of all the poems, it has the greatest claims to be considered the genuine work of the bard in whose name it appears.   It was at first supposed to contain the record of a war between the tribe termed by Ptolemy the Ottadeni and the Saxons, in the sixth century, when Aneurin lived, till Edward Davies announced the theory that the event really celebrated in this poem was the traditional slaughter of the British chiefs at Stonehenge by Hengist, usually termed "the plot of the long knives;" and this theory was adopted by that ingenious theorist, Algernon Herbert. In the whole history of Welsh literature there is, perhaps, not a more curious specimen of perverted ingenuity than the elaboration of this theory by Davies and Herbert; but it has failed to commend itself to the judgment and conviction of others; and the opposite view, that it recorded a battle or series of battles in the north in the sixth century, in which the Ottadeni bore a part, has been generally accepted.   By both the poem was considered as one entire poem, an authentic production of the sixth century.

The first to cast doubt upon this was the writer of a letter in the *Cambrian Quarterly Magazine* (vol. i. p. 354), who is generally supposed to have been Mr. Price himself, the then possessor of the MS.   This writer was the first to point out the line—

"A phen dyvynwal vrych brein ae cnoyn,"

which he thus translates, "And the head of Donald Brec, the ravens gnawed it;" and to suggest that the person here meant was Donald Brec, king of Dalriada, who was slain in 642; which leads to the necessary inference that the author who witnessed his slaughter in

that year could not have been Aneurin. He also objects to the
line—

> " Er pan aett daear ar Aneurin,"

(" Since the time that earth went on Aneurin "), as referring to the
death and sepulture of Aneurin, which had already taken place, and
that the poem could not have been composed by him.

With regard to the first objection, he points out that there are
obvious inaccuracies in the *Irish Annals* with regard to this event,
the death of Donald being likewise entered under 678 and 686,
and therefore it may have really belonged to a still earlier date ;
but this explanation is not tenable, for there is no event in that
early period the real date of which can be more certainly ascertained ; and there is no doubt that it really took place in the year
642.

The second objection he does not attempt to obviate ; but the
usual explanation is that it refers to his imprisonment in a chamber
under ground, supposed to be described in stanza 45, where he
says—

> " I am not headstrong and petulant.
> I will not avenge myself on him who drives me.
> I will not laugh in derision.
> Under foot for a while
> My knee is stretched,
> My hands are bound,
> In the earthen house,
> With an iron chain
> Around my two knees.
> Yet of the mead from the horn,
> And of the men of Catraeth,
> I, Aneurin, will compose,
> As Taliessin knows,
> An elaborate song
> Or a strain to Gododin,
> Before the dawn of the bright day."

But this explanation is not satisfactory ; for the language of the
" Gododin " clearly implies that the chamber under ground was the
tomb in which he was confined by death. Thus in the next stanza
it is called " the chamber of death ;" and in the same way it is said of

Gwair, who is described in the *Preiddeu Annwn* as similarly imprisoned—

> "And for the spoils of Annwn gloriously he sings,
> And *till doom* shall continue his lay."

The explanation seems to me to be this :—These old poems are frequently added to and continued by later hands ; and when the continuation is written in the person of the original author, the machinery is introduced of his being called from his tomb for the purpose. The poem of the " Gododin " is very clearly divided into two parts by the remarkable stanza 45, which Aneurin speaks in his own person :—

> " I am not headstrong and petulant," etc.

He then describes the imprisonment under ground ; and this is followed by the following lines :—

> " Yet of the mead and of the horn,
> I, Aneurin, will sing
> What is known to Taliessin,
> Who communicates to me his thoughts,
> Or a strain of the ' Gododin,'
> Before the dawn of the bright day."

The first part of the " Gododin," before stanza 45, is one consistent poem, connected together, treating evidently of the same war, and with the same characters appearing in it. The second part, after stanza 45, begins with the line—

> " The chief exploit of the north did
> The hero accomplish ;"

and this exploit was

> " From the cruel, subterraneous
> Prison he brought me out ;
> From the chamber of death,"

And we are then introduced to a different set of incidents, and to different characters, not mentioned in the first part, intermixed with stanzas relating to the incidents of the first. The two divisions of the poem are very different in their character. It is in this second division that Dyfynwal Vrych is introduced. In the first part there is no allusion to him whatever ; and, moreover, the passages in the second part, which allude to the battle of Catraeth, correspond, to a large extent, with similar passages in the "Gorchan Maelderw." I consider, therefore, that the first part is the original poem of the "Gododin ;" and that the second part is a later continuation, made up partly of passages from the "Gorchan Maelderw," which was attributed to Taliessin, and to which allusion seems to be made in the line in which Aneurin says of the rest of the poem

>   "Taliessin communicates to me his thoughts ;"

and partly of later events, including the death of Dyfynwal Vrych, which may have been so far connected with the battle of Catraeth that the district called Gododin may have been the scene of both.

For this later continuation, the machinery was devised of Aneurin being called up from his chamber of death under ground ; and we find the same machinery in a poem to which a continuation has been manifestly added by a later hand—I mean the "Cyvoesi Myrdin," which seems to consist of three parts—an original poem terminating with Cadwallader, a continuation to the time of Howel Dda, and a still later interpolation of the reign of Henry II., and in which we find the same machinery of Myrdin being called from the dead :—

St. 117. " Alas, dearest ! the cold separation
>   When comes the day of tumult,
>   Thy imprisonment beneath the earth
>   By a monarch valiant and fearless."

St. 121. " Arise from thy prison, and unfold the books
>   Of the awen without fear,
>   And the speech of Bun and the visions of sleep."

I consider, therefore, that in the continuation, or second part, there is a clear allusion to the death of Dyfynwal Brych in 642, as having happened before that part of the poem was written ; but the first part may, notwithstanding, relate to different and earlier events ; and in endeavouring to ascertain the historical events which really form the subject of this poem, it is necessary to distinguish between the statements made in the first and in the second division of it.

Looking, then, to the first division of the poem, we can see that the parties to the struggle were, on the one side—*first*, the Bedin

Gododin, or host of Gododin. Thus in stanza 3, "He retreated not before the Bedin Gododin ;" and in stanza 12, "Exceedingly great were the bloodshed and death, of which they were the cause, before the Bedin Gododin." *Secondly*, the men of Deifr and Brynaich, as in stanza 5, "Before his blades fell five battalions of the men of Deifr and Brynach, uttering groans ; and stanza 9, "If I had judged me to be on the side of the tribe of Brynaich, not a phantom of a man would I have left alive." These were the enemies, and a part of them were Saxons, as in stanza 13, Tudvwlch Hir, near his lands and towns, slaughtered the Saxons for seven days.

On the other side there were—*first*, the Gosgord, or retinue of Mynyddawg, as in stanza 11, "Their blades were white as lime, their helmets split into four parts before the Gosgord of Mynyddawg Mwynvawr." The Gosgord usually consisted of three hundred men with their three leaders. Thus in stanza 18, "Three chiefs and three hundred." These were cut off to a man, as appears from stanza 31 :—

> "The Gosgord of Mynyddawg, renowned in a trial,
> Their life was the price of their banquet of mead.
> When they were slain they also slaughtered :
> Not one to his native home returned."

And in "Gorchan Maelderw :"—

> "Three chiefs and three hundred :
> Alas ! none returned."

Secondly, the Brython, as in stanza 18, "Three sovereigns of the people came from the Brython—Cywri and Cynon and Cynrain, from Aeron." Of this body it is said in stanza 21, "Three heroes and three score and three hundred, wearing the golden torques of those who hurried forth after the revelry. But three escaped by the prowess of the gushing sword—the two war-dogs of Aeron and Cynon the dauntless."

Besides these bodies especially mentioned, were the followers of numerous other leaders mentioned in the poem. These were : *first*, Caeawg. He is the hero of stanzas 2, 3, 4, and 5. This name, like that of Mynyddawg, is obviously an epithet, *caeawg* being an adjective formed from *cae*, "an enclosure ;" just as Mynyddawg is from *mynydd*, "a mountain ;" and the one signifies the man of the enclosure ; as the other does the mountaineer. Who Caeawg was we know from stanza 5, where his name is given as Hyvaidd Hir. The first stanza of the poem is usually supposed to be addressed to a person called Owen, from one of the lines generally translated, "Alas, Owain, my beloved friend !" But this translation is incorrect. The words are, "Ku kyueillt ewein ;" and the natural construction is, "Thou beloved friend of Owen." The person meant is evidently the same who is celebrated in the four following stanzas under the epithet "Caeawg"—viz. Hyfeidd Hir, who is mentioned in a poem in the *Book of Taliessin* in close connection with an Owain of Mona : " Haerndur and Hyfeidd and Gwallawg and Owain of Mona ;" *second*, Tudwulch Hir and Cyvwlch, said to be of the clan of Godebawg ; *third*, Cydywall from Gwynedd, in stanza 19 ; *fourth*, Buddvan, son of Bluddvan ; *fifth*, Gwenabwy, son of Gwen ; *sixth*, Caredeg ; *seventh*, Caradawg ; *eighth*, Rhiwawn Hir.

The scene of the struggle was Catraeth and Gododin. These were not two names for the same place ; but two districts evidently adjoining each other. Stanzas 6 and 7 begin with the expression, " warriors went to Gododin ;" and stanzas 8, 9, 10, 11, 12, 13, 14, which follow, with that of "warriors went to Catraeth ;" and as a part of the enemy were called "the host of Gododin," it is plain that stanzas 6 and 7 describe the march of the enemy to Gododin ; and the stanzas which follow, that of the British army to Catraeth ; and this latter army proceeded from Eidyn Ysgor, or the fort of Eidyn, as in stanza 13 :—

> " There hastened not to Catraeth
> A chief so magnificent ;
> Never was there such a host
> From the fort of Eidyn ;"

The country about this fort seems to be called the Mordei, as in stanza 20, " I drank of the wine and the mead of the Mordei ;" and in connection with Catraeth there is repeated allusion to a rampart with a ditch, as in stanzas 21, 27, 39, as separating the armies.

Mr. Williams supposes that the Catraeth was the Catrail in Roxburghshire, and that this was the rampart meant ; and that the battle was fought between the Cymry and the Saxons in the year 570.

Villemarqué, in his *Poemes des Bardes Bretons*, places the battle on the banks of the river Calder in Lanarkshire, from which it was called Kaldrtraez or Kaltraez, the name which he gives the battle, and fixes its date at 578.

Stephens, in his *Literature of the Cymry*, considers that the subject of the poem is an expedition of the Ottadeni against the town of Cataracton, which he considers to be the place meant by Catraeth ; but I believe he has abandoned this idea, and now considers it to refer to the battle mentioned by Bede as having been fought between Aidan, king of the Scots of Dalriada, and Ethelfrid, king of Northumbria, at Degsanstane, in 603.

Mr. Nash, in a very ingenious paper in the *Cambrian Journal* (1861), identifies it with the battle fought between Oswy and Penda, where the latter was slain at Winwedfield, which battle is called by Nennius and the *Annales Cambriæ* " strages Gai Campi ;" and he seems to identify it likewise with the battle in which Donald Brec was slain, which he calls Vraith Cairvin.

Mr. Vere Irving, in several papers, adopts Villemarqué's name for this battle, Kaltraez, and considers that it relates to a seven years' struggle, from the year 642, where he finds in the *Irish Annals*, in the same year with the death of Donald Brec, " Cath Oswei et Britones, to the year 650, when he finds the entry, " Cath Ossei fra Pante." The latter, however, is an erroneous entry. It refers to the battle of Winwedfield, and the same entry is repeated under the year 656.

The objection to the first three suppositions is, that they place the site of the battle far inland, while the poem clearly implies that both Gododin and Catraeth were washed by the sea. A poem in the *Book of Taliessin* refers to the Morhoedd Gododin, or seas of Gododin ; and the term " Mordei" certainly implies that it was on the sea-shore. The theory of Mr. Nash has certainly one feature to recommend it—viz. that the name " Gaus Campus" does certainly greatly resemble Catraeth. This word is ordinarily spelt " Cat-traeth," and translated the " battle-strand ;" but in every poem in which it is mentioned it is uniformly spelt "Catraeth ;" and the syllables which compose it are not " Cat-traeth," but " Ca-traeth." *Traeth*, meaning a shore, may be translated *campus ;* and the resemblance of *ca* and *ga*, forming *gaus*, is very striking. There is, how-

ever, in the poem no allusion to either Oswy or Penda; and the battle
where Donald Brec was slain was fought in 642, while the battle
of Winwedfield was fought in 654. Moreover, the battle in
which Donald Brec was killed is in no chronicle called "Fraith
Cairvin;" and it is much to be regretted that historians will still
continue to confuse matters by quoting at second hand, while good
editions of the original chronicles are accessible to them. This
quotation is taken from Ritson's *Annals*, which were compiled from
the *Annals of Tighernac* and the *Annals of Ulster*, and are full of
typographical blunders. The account is more correctly given in
the edition of these Irish *Annals* by O'Connor; and in the original
MSS. the name is given in *Tighernac* as Strathcauin, and in the
Annals of Ulster Strath Cairinn.

For the name of Kaeltraez, given to it by Villemarqué, and
adopted by Mr. Vere Irving, there is no authority whatever. Some
editions of the *Gododin* read "Galtraeth" instead of "Catraeth;"
but this does not warrant such a transformation of the word, and
there is a certain affectation in using Cymric words in their Breton
form. The same observations apply to Mr. Irving's dates as to
Mr. Nash's.

It is plain from the poem that two districts, called respectively
Gododin and Catraeth, met at or near a great rampart; that both
were washed by the sea, and that in connection with the latter was
a fort called "Eyddin." Nennius mentions Manau Guotodin as a
"regio in sinistrali parte insulæ," an expression equivalent in Welsh
to "y gogled," or the north; that is, that part of the island north of
the Humber. The name Guotodin is plainly the same as the Gododin
of Aneurin. On the other hand, Manau is the same name as that
of the Island of Man. There was, therefore, an island called Ynys
Manau, and there was a district "yn y Gogled," called "Manau Guotodin," or Manau of Gododin, to distinguish it. The Cymric word
"Manau" has its equivalent in old Gaelic in the word "Manand."
And here, too, we find both an island and a district; for the Isle of
Man is called "Innis" or "Eilean Manand;" and *Tighernac* has in
581 "Cath Manand in quo victor erat Aedan mac Gabran;" and
again, in 711, "Strages Pictorum in Campo Manand a Saxonis."
Now the *Saxon Chronicle*, in describing the same event, has
"Beorhtfrith eoldorman fought with the Peohtas between Haefe

and Caere ;" and Henry of Huntingdon has " Tunc etiam Berfrid consul restitit superbiæ Pictorum, dimicans inter Heue et Cere ; ubi multitudine magna Pictorum strata, ultor extitit regis Egfridi et consulis Berti ;" and by Gaimar they are called " dous ewes," or two rivers.

There was, therefore, a " Campus Manand," which lay between Haefe or Heve and Caere or Cere, and which seems to have been occupied by Picts.

The name of Eyddin takes us at once to Lothian, where we have Dunedin or Edinburgh, and Caredin on the shore, called by Gildas " antiquissima civitas Britonum." That the Edin in these two names is the Eyddin of the poem is clear from a poem in the *Black Book of Caermarthen*, where Edinburgh is called " Mynyd Eiddin ;" and in a poem in the *Book of Taliessin* there is the expression, " Rhuing Dineiddyn ac Dineiddwg," where Dineiddyn can hardly be anything but Dunedin. At Caredin the Roman wall terminated ; and here there was a headland and a promontory jutting out into the Firth, on which was a royal castle called Blackness, where probably was the "Ynys Eiddin yn y Gogled" mentioned in the *Bonedd y Saint.* Caredin is not far from the river Avon, and parallel to it flows the river Carron ; the two rivers enclosing a district at the west end of which is a great moor still called Slamannan ; in old Gaelic, " Sliabh Manand," or the moor or plain of Manand. This is " Campus Manand," and the Avon and Carron are meant by Haefe and Caere. Gododin, which contained it, was therefore equivalent to the north part of Lothian, and was washed by the Firth of Forth. The *Irish Annals* frequently mention a district called Calathros, as in *Tighernac,* " Cath i Calathros in quo victus est Domnal Brec ;" and in 736, " Bellum Cnuice Cairpre i Calathros uc etar linn du ;" which latter place can be identified as Carriber on the Avon, near Linlithgow. Calathros, therefore, adjoined this district. Its Latin form was Calatria. In a charter in the chartulary of Glasgow, Duffodir de Calatria is a witness ; and Walter L'Espec, in his address at the Battle of the Standard in 1130, as reported by Ailred, in alluding to William the Conqueror's expedition to Abernethy, says, " Cum Angliæ victor Willielmus Laodoniam *Calatriam* Scotiam usque ad Abernaeth penetravit ;" where Calatria is placed between Lothian and Scotland proper north of the Firths. Calatria is surely

the Cymric Galtraeth, which we know was the same place as Catraeth. The requirements of the site seem, therefore, satisfied in that
part of Scotland where Lothian meets Stirlingshire, in the two districts of Gododin and Catraeth, both washed by the sea of the Firth
of Forth ; and where the great Roman wall terminates at Caredin,
or the fort of Eidinn.

As to the date of the battle, we are not without indications. The
poem opens with several stanzas devoted to two heroes disguised
under the epithets of Caeawg and Mynydawg. Caeawg is derived
from *cae*, meaning in its primary sense " an enclosure ;" in its secondary, "a necklace." Mr. Williams has understood it in its latter
sense, when he translates it "adorned with his wreath ;" but as the
true signification of Catraeth seems to be " the strand of the *cae*, or
enclosure," I am inclined to think that it is here used in its primary
sense, and that Caeawg signifies " the man of the enclosure," in con-
tradistinction to Mynydawg, " the man of the mountains," or the
mountaineer. Caeawg, the poem tells us, was Hyfaidd Hir, of
whom it is said in one of the *Triads*, " Three kings, who were of
the sons of strangers—Gwryat, son of Gwryan yn y Gogled ; and
Cadafel, son of Cynfedw in Gwynedd ; and Hyfeidd Hir, son of
Bleidic in Deheubarth." Cadafael, however, is mentioned in another
Triad as having killed Jago vab Beli, king of Gwynedd, who was
succeeded by his son Cadvan in 603, who ruled over Gwynedd and
all Wales. The period when these three interlopers reigned was
apparently prior to 603 ; and this is the exact period when, in the
line of monarchs, the direct line is interrupted, and Caredig is inter-
posed between Maelgwn and Cadfan—a period extending, according
to Matthew of Westminster, from 586 to 603.

Now, there seems to be an allusion to Hyfaedd having been
contemporary with two plebeian kings in Gwynedd, and the Gogled
in stanza 4, where it is said of Caeawg—

   " He repelled the violence of *ignoble men*, and blood trickled down,
     For *Gwynedd* and *the Gogledd* would have come to his share
     By the advice of the son of Ysgyran,
     Who wore the broken shield."

Again, in stanza 19 Cydywal is mentioned in connection with
Gwynedd. In stanza 30 Gwrien is mentioned among the enemies ;

and in stanzas 28 and 29 Caredig is celebrated as the amiable leader. This would place the battle between 586 and 603.

But who was Mynydawg, or the mountaineer, of whom we know that his *gosgord*, or retinue, consisted of three hundred and three warriors, and that they were slain to a man, while he escaped and was ultimately victorious? Now Adomnan, in his Life of St. Columba, has the following heading to one of his chapters, " De Bello Miathorum," and proceeds thus: " Alio in tempore, hoc est post multos a supra memorato bello" (Culdrebene, fought in 561) annorum transcursus, cum esset vir sanctus in Ioua insula, subito ad suum dicit ministratorem Diormitium, Cloccam pulsa. Cujus sonitu fratres incitati ad ecclesiam, ipso sancto præsule præeunte, ocius currunt. Ad quos ibidem flexis genibus infit: Nunc intente pro hoc populo et Aidano rege Dominum oremus; hac enim hora ineunt bellum. Et post modicam intervallum egressus oratorium, respiciens in cœlum inquit, Nunc barbari in fugam vertuntur; Aidanoque, quamlibet infelix, tamen concessa victoria est. Sed et de numero de exercitu Aidani *interfectorum, trecentorum et trium virorum,* vir beatus prophetice enarravit." The allusion to the three chiefs and three hundred slain at Cattraeth seems unmistakable; and if so, Mynyddawg was Aidan, king of Dalriada. The combatants were therefore, on the one side the Britons and the Scots under Aidan; the enemy or " Barbari" were the pagan Saxons and the half-pagan Picts of Manau Guotodin, here called the " bedin" or host of Gododin. The identity of the battle of Catraeth with the " bellum Miathorum" of Adomnan enables us to fix its date; for in another chapter, in giving the fate of the sons of Aidan, he says: " Nam Arturius et Eochodius Find non longo post temporis intervallo Miathorum superius memorato in bello trucidati sunt;" and *Tighernac*, in 596, has " Iugulatio filiorum Aidan—*i.e.* Bran et Domanquet et Eochaidh Find et Artur i cath Chirchind in quo victus est Aidan." The history of Caeawg, therefore, places the battle between 586 and 603, and that of Mynyddawg fixes it at 596.

The first part of the poem alone relates to this battle; the second part, or continuation, contains in it an allusion to the death of Dyfynwal Vrych, or Domnal Breck, which the bard saw from the heights of Adoyn. The date of this event is known to be in 642. The site is not difficult to fix. Tighernac calls it Strathcauin; the

Annals of Ulster, Strathcairinn. The upper part of the vale of the Carron, through which the river, after rising in the Fintry Hills, flows, is called Strathcarron ; but it also bore the name of Strath-cawin. Thus in the Morton chartulary there is a charter by Alexander II. which mentions " Dundaf et Strathkawan quæ fuerunt foresta nostra ;" and Dundaff adjoins Strathcarron. In the Statistical Account of the parish of Fintry there is the following notice : " At the foot of the rock which encircles the western brow of the Fintry Hills there is a considerable extent of table-land, and on the descent below this starts out a knoll, *commonly known by the name of the Dun or Down*, of a singular appearance. Its front is a perpendicular rock fifty feet high. The western extremity of this rock is one solid mass." This is surely the height of Adoyn.—(S.)

Stanza i.

Line 1.—That ' *Gredyf*,' the first word in the Gododin, is a common, not a proper name, admits of but little doubt, though Sharon Turner and Probert take it in the latter sense. The same view is adopted also by Zeuss, who remarks (*Grammatica Celtica*, 951) : " Primum inter bellatores Cambrorum contra Anglos poëta celebrat juvenem, cujus nomen est *Gredyf* (Gretimus = ibus ? cf. adj. hod. *graid*, ardens, verb. *griediaw*, flagrare), sed in luctum mox vertitur de interitu ejus in proelio." The modern form of the word is " greddv," *disposition*, *habit*, or *instinct*, which is in common use at the present day.—(E.)

Line 17.—' *Ku kyueillt Ewein*' is generally translated as if the bard addressed Owain as his friend or companion. This view may be correct, but the more natural construction is to consider the friend of Owain, and not Owain himself, as the person whose death is here deplored.—(E.)

Stanza ii.

Line 1.—It is not quite obvious whether ' *Caeawg*' in this and the three following stanzas should be regarded as the name of a person, or simply as an appellative. The word, which is properly an adjective, means *one having* or *wearing a wreath* or *torque*. It will be noticed that the fifth stanza begins with " Caeawg," and ends with " Hyvaidd Hir" as its hero.—(E.) " Caeawg" is an adjective, formed from " cae," an enclosure, a necklace, a wreath. It may therefore mean the man of the enclosure, in contrast to " Mynyd-dawg," the man of the mountains.—(S.)

Line 2.—'*Diffun ;*' various explanations of this word have been suggested, but few of them are satisfactory. I translate it quite literally, taking it to be compounded of the privative prefix " di" and " ffun," breath. The hero being represented as standing "breathless" in the presence of a lady may be intended to show that, bold and courageous as he was in the face of the enemy, he was gentle even to diffidence in the social circle ; and this contrast between the warrior in the field and in the hall is in several instances brought under our notice in this poem.

As " ffun" bears also the signification of *a bundle*, as in the following line of Bedo Brwynllys—

" A phan oedd ym ffunoedd yd,"—

Mr. Williams ab Ithel translates " diffun" by " troops unattended." But I am not aware that " ffun" (allied to the Latin *funis*) is ever used for a band or troop. Zeuss, fancying that " diffun" is derived from " pun," a word used by Llywarch Hen in the sense of *equal* or *equivalent*, renders the passage as follows :—

Caeauc antecessor ubicunque veniebat
Partem a femina principe mulsi tenebat.
(*Celt. Gram.* 953.)

The Rev. Evan Evans, who translates portions of the Gododin in his *De Bardis Dissertatio*, leaves this part of the stanza blank, being evidently unable to satisfy himself as to the meaning. The Rev. T. Price's rendering, though not quite literal, seems to come pretty near the sense intended—

" Honourably in the presence of the maiden he distributed
the mead."—(E.)

STANZA III.

Line 1.—'*Kynnivyat*' (from " cynniv," *conflict*), one accustomed to the conflict. Zeuss, who, contrary to the MSS., writes the word " cynnyviat," and translates it " condomitor," as if derived from " dov " or " dovi ;" but the root is obviously " gniv," *toil, conflict*, a word of comparatively common occurrence in our ancient writers. Cyndelw applies "cynniviad" as well as "cynnivwr" to the Lord Rhys :—

> "*Cynnivwr* cynniv nid diover,
> *Cynnivyad* cynneddv Alecsander."

Llywarch ab Llewelyn calls Meredydd ab Cynan

> "Mur graid *cynniviaid* Cynan ;"

And Gruffyd ab Cynan

> "Mab mad *cynniviad* Cynan."—(E.)

Line 2.—' *Ebyr*,' the places where rivers enter the sea.—(E.)

Line 6.—' *Manawyt*,' according to Dr. W. O. Pughe, means, "the staff of a banner or standard." Accordingly, he translates this passage thus :—

> "There was a confident impelling forward of the *shaft* of the varie-gated standard."

Zeuss regards it as a verb formed from "ban," high ; and Ab Ithel adopts it as the name of a person. The probability, how-ever, is, that it is the name of the *place* where the "breithell" or battle occurred.—(E.) It is another form of Manau, and is, no doubt, the Cath Manand of Tighernac, and the Bellum contra Euboniam of the old Welsh Chronicle, fought by Aedan in 583.—(S.)

Stanza IV.

Line 2.—For ' *godiwawr*,' we should, with several of the copies, probably read "godrwyawr," from "godrwy," *a wreath or chain.* —(E.)

Line 10.—' *Hyfaidd hir*.' No other name is mentioned in con-nection with the epithet Caeawg, and I believe it applies to ' Hy-faidd hir' throughout.—(S.)

Stanza V.

Line 1.—' *Men went to Gododin*.' This and the next stanza describe the Bedin Gododin marching to battle.—(S.)

Line 4.—' *Bodgad*.' The same as Badcat, or Bathcat, now Bathgate. The heroes are often described as " son of '" the place of their birth.—(S.)

STANZA VI.

Line 5.—' *Ket elwynt e lanneu e benydyaw'* is generally rendered " They should have gone to churches to do penance;" but the original can hardly be made to bear such a meaning. "Ket" (= cyd) as an adverbial particle, signifies *though, since, seeing that, because that, forasmuch, while,* and has no negative force whatever. Compare Stanza 44, line 1. What the poet seems to imply is, that *though* they went to churches to do penance, they did not escape the inevitable fate of death ; in other words, their having done penance did not avail them in the day of battle, since they entered the field in a state of intoxication.—(E.)

STANZA VII.

Line 1.—' *Gwanar.'* Dr. Pughe, in his *Welsh Dictionary,* as is often the case with that elaborate work, gives us two different renderings of this line, neither of which seems to supply the true meaning. Thus, *s. v.* " Gwanar," the translation is :—

" Heroes went to Gododin, a laughing course."

But, *s. v.* " Diachar," the couplet is rendered in this manner :—

" To Gododin warriors hied ; the leader
    Smiles at the uplifting of his jewel
    By the host of terrific toil."—(E.)

Line 2.—' *Em bedin,'* rendered " jewelled army" in Ab Ithel's translation, is nothing more than *ym mydden,* in, or " on the army," the preposition *yn* here changing into *ym* before a labial.—(E.)

STANZA VIII.

In this and the six following stanzas, the forces on the side. of the Britons are described as marching to Catraeth.—(S.)

STANZA IX.

Line 6—' *Dilyw'* I take to be " diliw," *a phantom ;* but it may be " diluw," *deluge,* as understood by the Rev. G. Evans, who renders the line :—

" Aeque ac diluvium omnes una strage prostrarem."—(E.)

STANZA X.

Line 4.—' *Gwynnodi,*' from " gwynnod," *a white mark, a butt.*

Line 6.—' *Mwynvawr,*' *of great courtesy or kindness, courteous.*
—(E.) The three hundred mentioned in this and the 8th stanza
were the retinue of Mynyddawg.—(S.)

STANZA XI.

Line 5.—' *Phurawr.*' The Book of Aneurin has " phurawr ;"
but as " pluawr," *plumes,* which is the reading of some copies,
appears to make better sense, I adopt it. " Pluawr," in connection
with military matters, occurs also in another writer contemporary
with Aneurin :—

> " Gwedy meirch hywedd, a chochwedd ddillad
> A phluawr melyn
> Main vy nghoes, ried oes ym dremyn."
>
> *Llywarch Hen.*

" Coch," in the same line, should apparently be " cochad ;" for
" na phurawr " (or phluawr) implies that a comparison is intended.
—(E.)

STANZA XII.

Line 4.—' *Bedydd.*' *Baptism* is constantly used by the early
bards synonymously with Christianity.—(E.)

STANZA XIII.

This stanza describes a single hero going to Catraeth, and names
him Tudvwlch Hir.—(S.)

Line 2.—' *Ne*' (= neu, neud, or neus) is probably here to be
taken in an affirmative sense, as we are repeatedly told in other
parts of the poem that all the warriors who went to Catraeth had
partaken too freely of mead and wine before entering the field.—
(E.)

Line 3.—The meaning apparently is, that he was unlucky on
this occasion, though his previous career had been remarkably
fortunate.—(E.)

Line 9.—' *Eidyn ysgor.*' The fort of Eiddyn or Caredin on the
Firth of Forth, where the Roman wall terminated.—(S.)

Line 11.—Some suppose that the word '*ech*,' here translated *near*, is equivalent to the Greek *εκ* or Latin *ex*, and accordingly translate the passage—

" Tudvwlch Hir deprived of his lands and towns."

But it is more probable that it is simply a mutation of " ach," *near*, *close by*, as " ach eilaw," *by his hand.* Similar mutations are by no means uncommon in the productions of the early bards. Dr. Pughe's translation of the passage is curious :—

" Tudvwlch the Tall, a *spot* of earth reduces him to corruption."—(E.)

Line 13.—'*En wrvyd*.' It is not very easy to ascertain the right reading here. Some of the copies read "yn wr rhydd" and others "yn wrryd." I regard "wrvyd" as equivalent to "orvydd," from "gorvod," to *conquer, subdue*, or *overpower*.—(E.)

STANZA XV.

Line 4.—'*Meibyon Godebawc*' were the descendants of Coel Godebawc or Coel Hen, who formed the main portion of the Men of the North.—(S.) '*Enwir*.' Though the prefix *en* has generally an intensive force, we find " enwir " very commonly used by our older writers, and even in the Welsh translation of the Bible, in a negative sense, convertibly with " anwir," of which in this case it must be considered a mutation. But as the sons of Godebog appear to be represented here as fighting on the side of the Britons, we may assume that the epithet is intended to be taken in its proper and honourable acceptation. " Enwir " occurs again in the 62d stanza, where its relation to " cywir," *true, right, faithful*, is clearly indicated.—(E.)

STANZA XVI.

Line 2.—'*Bludue*' appears to be a proper name, probably of a river. A similar word occurs in an early poem attributed to Meigant :—

" *Plwde* y danav hyd ym mhen vy nghlun."

Ab Ithel affirms that " it is certain that Meigant uses the word " in the sense of *blood*, and conformably to this view he thus translates the passage—

" Under me was *blood* to the top of my knee."

But to me this does not seem so clear, as a person may be knee-deep in water as well as in blood.—(E.)

Line 9.—That is, in the number of the enemy.—(E.)

STANZA XVII.

Line 14.—'*Arued.*' The rhyme, supposing the stanza to be complete, would, instead of "arued," require "aruel" (arvel), the form found in several copies.—(E.)

Line 20.—"No shield was unexpanded" is Ab Ithel's version. Dr. Pughe's is as follows :—

"There was not the want of forwardness of shield."

One copy, instead of "diryf" has "eiryf" (= eiriv) number :—

"There were shields without number."—(E.)

Line 28.—For '*vreisc*' we should in all probability read "vras," to suit the rhyme. Both words as used here are nearly synonymous. —(E.)

STANZA XVIII.

Line 3.—'*Pymwnt*' = pummwnt, pum mwnt. "Mwnt," used in a strictly numerical sense, stands for one hundred thousand ; but here, as elsewhere in this poem, it seems to be employed in a general sense to signify a large number.—(E.)

Line 5.—Ab Ithel translates this line—"three *hundred* knights of battle ;" but there is no *hundred* in the original. "Tri si chatvarchawc." "Si" = sy, sydd, *is, there is.*—(E.)

Line 3.—'*Tri eur deyrn dorchawc*' = three golden kings wearing a wreath ; a sort of tmesis for "tri theyrn eurdorchawg," *three golden-wreathed kings.*—(E.)

Line 14.—'*Llew,*' a lion, is possibly a clerical error for "llewod," *lions.* The line as it now stands is a syllable too short for the metre, and the verb ("ledynt") being in the plural, requires a plural noun for its subject. But supposing "llew" to be the right reading, the line might be rendered—

"Like a lion they would kill dead as lead."—(E.)

Line 1.—' *Deivyr diuerogyon*' is rendered by Davies "the men who dropped into Deira;" and by Ab Ithel, "the men who dropped from Deira;" both apparently forgetting that " diveru" (now generally written "dyveru"), unlike the English *to drop*, is never used but in its proper physical sense, and that it invariably refers to some liquid. Even if men actually *dropped* from the region of the clouds, no Welshman would ever employ "dyveru" to describe that act.

"Deivyr," besides being the name of the district called *Deira*, forms also the irregular plural of "dwvr," *water;* so "deivyr diuerogyon" may mean *distillers of waters*. "Deivr" for "dyvroedd," is very frequently met with both in old and comparatively modern writers. With "deivyr diuerogyon" of the Gododin, compare "Gwydyl diefyl diuerogyon" and "Gwydyl kyl diuerogyon" of the Book of Talieasin.—(E.)

STANZA XIX.

Line 1.—' *E Mordei*' = ym Mordai, in Mordai.—(E.)

Line 14.—' *Athrwys ac affrei.*' The meaning here is by no means obvious. The version adopted is partly that of my predecessors, which is based on readings different from what we find in the Book of Aneurin.—(E.)

STANZA XX.

Line 2.—The meaning of "*fawt ut*" is doubtful; but taking it as equivalent to "ffawd hud," the import would be that the fact to which the bard alludes was the necessary consequence of giving way to the allurements of mead and wine.—(E.)

Line 3.—' *Colwedd*' is to all appearance a proper name. The various readings of the word show that the ancient transcribers were much puzzled by it. —(E.)

Line 6.—This line in Gorchan Maelderw (p. 100) stands thus—

"Pressent kyuadraud oed breichyaul glut ;"

which Dr. Pughe (*Welsh Dict. s. v.* "Breichiawl") translates—

"Present, ere he spoke, was carried with the arms."—(E.)

STANZA XXI.

Line 1.—The stanzas opening ' *Men went to Catraeth*' seem to indicate different events in the war, and the fate of different portions of the combatants. This stanza commemorates a body consisting of 363 heroes, who were different from the 300 who formed the retinue of Mynyddawg.—(S.)

Line 6.—' *O wrhydri fossawt*,' Ab Ithel converts into, " by valour from the funeral fosse ;" but the import seems to be that given by Evans (*De Bard. Diss.* p. 73) :—

" Non evasere nisi tres, qui sibi gladiis viam muniebant."—(E.)

Line 8.—' *Om gwaetfieu*,' must mean either " from the spilling of *my* blood," or " from my spilling of blood ;" and the passage cannot be rendered, as Ab Ithel does, " from the spilling of blood," in a general sense. Davies is here more correct : " through my streams of blood."—(E.)

STANZA XXII.

Line 2.—' *Gwyn Dragon* ' must have been a Saxon commander. —(S.)

Line 5.—' *Aelawd* ' is a *limb* or *member ;* but it is here translated *hearth*, on the supposition that the word is used in this place in the sense of " aelwyd," the term now in common use for hearth or fireside. Davies translates the line thus—

" Base is he in the field, who is base to his own relatives."
And Ab Ithel—

" He crept into the martial field, he crept into our families."
It is hardly necessary to add that " aelawd " signifies neither " relatives " nor " families."—(E.)

Line 7.—' *Llivyeu.*' The form of this name in Gorchan Maelderw is " Llif."—(E.)

STANZA XXIII.

Line 7.—' *Hoewgir*' in the Book of Aneurin ; but the Myvyrian copy has " Hoewgi ;" and the rhyme shows that this must be the correct reading.—(E.)

STANZA XXIV.

Line 1.—Unless ' *adan*,' which meant a *wing*, be a proper name in this place, it is difficult to make sense of the passage. We find further on in the poem (st. 86 and 92) mention made of a person bearing this name.—(E.)

Line 2.—' *Orwydan*' (= gorwyddan) appears to be a diminutive of " gorwyd," a *war-horse.*

Ab Ithel finds in this word the name of *Prydwen*, King Arthur's shield ; but the copy from which we translate has not the slightest allusion to anything of the kind, nor does the name occur in any of the various readings in Ab Ithel's edition, the nearest approach to it being " prwydan," or " prydan." The name *prydwen*, as applied to Arthur's shield, it is almost superfluous to add, is a creation of mediæval romance.

The opening lines of this stanza, according to the *Myvyrian* text, are thus versified by Dr. Owen Pughe (*s. v.* " Talfrith") :—

> " His painted front on ample shoulders soars,
>   Which marks the hero, swifter in his course
> Than Prwydan, when the sound of war he hears,
>   And sees the thick incessant gleam of spears."—(E.)

Line 4.—More literally, " there was sun," which Davies amplifies into " the rays of the blazing sun."—(E.)

Line 12.—' *Eleirch*,' probably an error of some scribe for " efeirch = ei veirch, *his horses ;* but it should be noticed that all the copies read " eleirch," and that it is not unlikely that a sort of alliteration may be intended between this word and " olo" in the same line.—(E.)

STANZA XXV.

Line 1.—' *Camb*' = camm = cam, *crooked, bent ; wrong, false.* The form " camb " will be recognised in *Morecambe, Cambodunum,* and other ancient names. See Zeuss, *Gram. Celt.* 75, 96, 825.—(E.)

STANZA XXVI.

Line 5.—That is, probably, to bring slaughter on the enemy, and support to his countrymen.—(E.)

Line 8.—' *Meinnyell*,' a word which I have not met with elsewhere, may be from " main," the plural of " maen," *a stone ;* or from " main," *slender, small, narrow.*—(E.)

Stanza XXVII.

Line 7.—The achievements of his sword were talked of and admired by mothers.—(E.)

Stanza XXX.

Line 1.—'*Gwrien.*' It is doubtful what name is here intended. Our text has "vrun;" and other copies exhibit the following readings :—"Fron," "unun," "uron," and "vrun" *vel* "uryen." It is pretty evident that a person is intended, not "bryn," *a hill*, as some are disposed to translate it. A monosyllable, it may be added, will not suit the metre.—(E.)

Stanza XXXI.

This stanza begins "Men marched with speed," and describes the fate of the retinue of Mynyddawg, which consisted of 300 men, of whom not one returned.—(S.)

Stanza XXXIV.

Line 8.—'*Wit uap Peithan.*'—Gwit or Gwid is obviously a Pictish name, and the Picts are called Peithwyr in one of the most authentic poems in the Book of Taliessin. Three sons of Wid were kings of the Picts from A.D. 631 to 653.—(S.)

Stanza XXXV.

Line 1.—'*Anvonawc*' (from "anvon," *to send*), so full of persons *sent* thither from different places to take part in the conflict. —(E.)

Stanza XXXVII.

Line 5.—I consider '*Eithinyn*' (the masculine form of "eithinen," *a furze*) to be the proper name of the hero celebrated in this stanza, and "volaid" an epithet qualifying it. '*Molaid*' here appears to be from "moli," *to praise*; but "molaid" (from "mol") signifies also, *spotted, dappled;* and in this latter sense the word appears to be used by Llywarch ab Llewelyn in the following passage :—

> "Meirch . . . .
> Ymmhole lliw ceinwiw can ryvygaid dyn ;
> Yn velyn, yn *volaid.*"

In support of the supposition that "Eithinyn" is a proper name, it may be remarked that this is not the only name of the kind taken from botanical nomenclature. Compare *Collen, Onen* Greg *Ysbyd-daden,* Bencawr, etc.—(E.)

STANZA XXXIX.

Line 1.—'*Nar,*' which signifies *a dwarf* or *pigmy,* may be a proper name, for we find "Neddig *Nar*" introduced in a subsequent stanza.—(E.)

STANZA XL.

Line 4.—'*Wyr*' (= wyr) means *grandson;* and "wyr," the plural of "gwr," signifies *men.* If the bard intended "wyr" to rhyme with "eryr," in accordance with what we find in some of the other lines, the latter form must be the correct one.—(E.)

Line 9.—'*Hen,*' the quantity of which is long, can hardly be the correct reading in this place. I conjecture that the original form of "am hen" was "ymben" or "unben," *a chieftain, monarch,* or *sovereign,* which latter occurs in the following stanza :—"Rac trychant unben."—(E.)

Line 11.—'*Deudec*' (= deuddeg). This line occurs at the end of stanzas 93 and 94, with "deheuec," *a sigh,* substituted for "deudec," *twelve.* Which is the correct reading, if either, I will not undertake to decide ; but it is pretty evident that "deudec" and "deheuec" are intended for one and the same word.—(E.)

STANZA XLI.

Line 1.—This is identical, to the very letter, with the opening line of the preceding stanza. There is, therefore, no ground for translating, as Ab Ithel does, the one "the most learned *man,* and the other, "the most learned *woman.*"—(E.)

Line 5.—The hero alluded to had probably had some adventure with a wolf. This couplet, with some variations, occurs again in the last stanza.—(E.)

STANZA XLV.

Line 4.—'*A dan droet ronin.*' "Gronyn," literally *a grain* or *particle,* signifies also *a while* or *short space.* Should we take the word in its primary acceptation, the line might be rendered—

> " Under foot there is grain" (or gravel).

Ab Ithel gives us a somewhat strange translation of this passage—

> " This particle shall go under foot ;"

and illustrates it by this quotation :—

> " Nid â gwaew yn ronyn ;"

of which he gives a still stranger translation—

> " Pain will not become a particle."

This adage will be found in the collection of Welsh proverbs printed in the third volume of the *Myvyrian Archæology,* and the meaning is intelligible enough : " A lance will not go into a particle," implying that the smaller of two objects connot contain the larger.—(E.)

Line 6.—This line is evidently imperfect. Of '*bundat*' I know not the meaning, having never met with the word except in this passage. Ab Ithel says, as if the matter admitted of no doubt, that it is from "pwn," *a load.* I am inclined to think that the first syllable "bun," may be allied to "mun," *a hand ;* and it is not at all improbable that the bard's *hands,* as well as his legs or knees, were confined, and that that is the particular part of his person that is here intended. Of course the translation of such a line can only be conjectural.—(E.)

STANZA XLVII.

Line 7.—' *Vythmeirch* ' = myth = veirch, meirch mwth or mythion, *fleet horses.*—(E.)

STANZA XLVIII.

Line 10.—' *Wyt yn dywovu* ' is not very intelligible. The whole stanza is confessedly difficult, and in many places probably corrupt.—(E.)

STANZA LI.

Line 2.—' *Heli bratwen.* ' For "heli," *brine,* I read "heb," *without;* the similarity of the words being sufficient to account for the supposed error.—(E.)

STANZA LII.

Line 2.—The ridges of Drum Essyd may refer to the Kilsyth hills; the old form of the word was Kilvesyth.—(S.)

STANZA LVIII.

Ab Ithel very appropriately remarks that the first lines of this stanza may be translated in divers ways. A similar remark might apply to the whole of the stanza, and indeed to several other stanzas in the poem.—(E.)

Line 6.—' *Buddugre*' is stated by Dr. Pughe (*Welsh Dict.* s. v.) to mean—" the impeller, or hastener to victory; the demon of war;" and he adduces the following couplet from Marwnad Corroi vab Dairy, a poem ascribed to Taliessin, in support of his explanation :—

" Tra vu *vuddugre* vore ddygrawr,
    Chwedlan am gwyddir owir hyd lawr."

" While the *demon of war* was in the morning heaping carnage,
    Rumours fell to me down from the air."

Dr. Fr. Carl Meyer (*Die noch Lebenden Keltischen Völkerschaften,* p. 45) sees in " Buddugre" the name of a goddess, and gives " *Schlachtgeschrei*" (war-cry) as its German equivalent.—(E.)

Line 10.—' *Heit*' = haid, *swarm.* If " haidd," *barley,* were intended, as some suppose, the form probably would be " heid."—(E.)

Line 17.—They had been awake, drinking mead and wine, the night before the battle, when they ought to have been asleep; and now the bereaved mother of Rheiddun is, in consequence, sleepless from sorrow for the fall of her son.—(E.)

STANZA LX.

Line 4.—' *Mal*,' which probably is the right reading, anything ground, meal.—(E.)

STANZA LXI.

Line 2.—' *E hu*,' most likely, stands for echu = echw, *a horse.* —(E.)

Stanza LXII.

Line 1.—'*Angor*' means *an anchor*. It is here taken as a proper name; and "Angar," a name found in other writers, may be but a slight variation of the same word.—(E.)

Line 13.—See stanza xv.—(E.)

Stanza LXIII.

Line 4.—That is, the courage inspired by intoxicating drink. —(E.)

Line 6.—'*Cibno*' is said to signify *a cup*, but here it has the appearance of a proper name.—(E.)

Stanza LXV.

Line 2.—'*Aeron*.' Other MSS. read '*Auon*.' The Avon, which falls into the Firth of Forth, near Careden, is the river probably meant, and the name "Aeron" seems preserved in the *Iron*-gath hills, past which it flows.—(S.)

Stanza LXVI.

Line 4.—That is, as it would appear, he spared none of these things, if by means of them he could procure a minstrel.—(E.)

Stanza LXVII.

Line 3.—'*Gwahanhon*' occurs in the 73d stanza. Davies and Ab Ithel translate it as an appellative.—(E.)

Stanza LXVIII.

Line 1.—It is not quite clear whether "Nyved" in this passage is a common or a proper noun. Dr. Pughe renders it "sanctity;" Davies, "holy ones;" and Ab Ithel, "holy one." I prefer leaving it in its original form.—(E.)

Stanza LXX.

Line 7.—'*Dynin*' = dynyn, *a little man*.—(E.)

Stanza LXXI.

Line 2.—'*Kywyt*' = cywydd (from *cy* and *gwydd*) may perhaps signify a collection of trees, or grove, as well as a song; and this view seems to receive some support from the next line—"E lad ar *gangen*"—unless the latter stands here for "gagen," *a cleft or breach*. But we are not justified in taking "cangen" in the third line, as Ab Ithel does, to signify *a breach*, and in the fifth to mean *a branch*, the word being precisely the same in both places.—(E.)

Stanza LXXII.

Line 2.—'*Reapers*,' warriors that carry all before them. See stanza lxiv.—(E.)

Line 4.—Alluding to the chief or leader mentioned in the first line.—(E.)

Stanza LXXIII.

Line 1.—'*Dina*,' apparently an error for "diva," *to destroy*.—(E.)

Stanza LXIV.

Line 1.—For '*agerw*,' *vapour*, I read "agarw" (from "garw"), *rough, harsh, severe*. If "agerw" be the right reading, it may still be a modification of "agarw."—(E.)

Line 10.—'*Sychyn*' (diminutive of "swch), *a small plough-share;* here possibly the iron head of some weapon resembling a ploughshare.—(E.)

Stanza LXXV.

Line 3.—'*Dinus*.' I cannot understand how "dinus" can be a compound of "din" and "ysu," as stated by Ab Ithel. If not a proper name, it may be an epithet derived from "din," *a fort*. In that case "bedin dinys" would mean the army of a fort or city. —(E.)

Stanza LXXVI.

Line 9.—'*Aryf*' in ancient writings constantly stands for "arv," *a weapon*, and not for "arav," *slow*, the sense in which Davies and Ab Ithel seem to understand it in this passage. For the oddity of the expression here employed, Aneurin, not his translator, must be held responsible. "Aryf" may be used for the person that bore it. —(E.)

Stanza LXXVII.

Line 4.—Being somewhat doubtful as to the import of "preig-

2 c

lyn," I follow my predecessors in translating it *crozier*. The probability is, however, that "preiglyn" is a corruption of " periglyn " (= peryglynt, from "peryglin," *to endanger*) ; and, if this view be correct, the line might be translated thus :—

> " His heavy shafts endangered the priest's head."—(E.)

STANZA LXXVIII.

Line 6.—This line—

> " A phenn dyvynwal a breych brein ae cnoyn,"

is generally translated in the same way as the last line of stanza lxxxix.

> " A phenn dynynwal vrych brein ae knoyn "—
> " And the head of Dyvynwal Vrych, ravens devoured it."

But the two lines are not identical, and this difference exists not only in the Book of Aneurin, but in all the other copies except the transcript of the Rev. Evan Evans, made about a century ago.—(E.)

STANZA LXXIX.

Line 8.—'*Kenhan*' is probably a mistake of some early transcriber for "kenhau" = ceneu, cenaw, *a whelp*. Some copies read " Cynon."—(E.)

STANZA LXXXII.

Line 8.—The readings of this line vary considerably, but none of them gives us much assistance to arrive at the meaning. For "llew" I read "llain" with the Myvyrian and three other copies ; and by "gwelir" I understand "gwylir" (from "gwylio," *to watch*). But should we adopt "llew," the reading found in the Book of Aneurin, the passage might be rendered in this way :—

> " The utterance of the lion was carefully watched."—(E.)

STANZA LXXXIV.

Line 2.—'*Fun*' = bun, *a woman, a maid, a fair one.* Some take this word to stand for "ffun," which does not appear probable. See note on "ffun" in stanza ii. The multitude of cares ("lliaws pryder "), of which the poet here complains, seems to have been caused by his anxiety on account of a certain maid, as well as on account of the army.—(E.)

Line 8.—'*Kelleic*' (= cellaig or cyllaig), the dweller in the *celli* or grove, is one of the old Welsh names for the stag ; and " kelleic ffaw " might here be translated " illustrious stag." The name appears to be applied to the leader of the Argoedwys.—(E.)

STANZA LXXXVI.

Line 4.—See stanza xcii.

Line 6.—' *Gelwideint*' is evidently the same with " gwelydeint " of the 92d stanza ; but which is the more correct reading it is not easy to decide.—(E.)

Line 15.—The *words* employed in this line are intelligible enough ; but what the bard intended to predicate of the " damsel, and maid, and hero," it is difficult to conjecture. Ab Ithel thus renders the passage :—

> " Even he, who was like a dame, a virgin, and a hero."

That is, according to him, " in domestic life he was as refined as a lady, modest as a virgin, whilst in war he was brave and high-minded." This may be all true, but the poet does not say so. The meaning may be that the lady, the servant-maid (for " morwyn " has that import), and the hero, all shared the same fate.—(E.)

STANZA LXXXVII.

The bard, in this stanza, which affords an apt illustration of the bathos, appears to be deploring the degeneracy of the days of the son compared with those of the father.—(E.)

Line 3.—' *Chwit*' is one of the Welsh words for a *whistle;* and " chwit chwit " is commonly used to imitate a person whistling or calling on dogs.—(E.)

Line 16.—' *Llewyn a llwyvein.*' It is difficult to ascertain the particular animals which these words respectively represent. The former might denote a young lion, a white lion, or any beast in general to whose eating faculties the word *lleva* would be applicable. The latter might signify any animal whose haunts were the elm-forests, or whose property was to *llyvu*, or to lick, as does a dog. The fox being named *llwynog*, from *llwyn*, a forest (a grove or bush), and the forests in the north being chiefly of elm, it is not unlikely but that the said animal was frequently called *llwyvain* in that part of the country when the bard wrote, though it is not known now by that name. It is remarkable that both terms also signify certain kinds of wood; the former the herb orach, the latter the elm.—*J. W. ab Ithel*.

In addition, it may be remarked that "llewa" is applicable to any animal, the word signifying simply *to eat, devour,* or *consume ;* and we find it employed even in reference to drinking :—

> " Llewais wirawd,
> Gwin, a bragawd."
> *Taliessin.*

As regards the "llwyvain," it is evident that it cannot by any legitimate process be deduced from *llyvu*. Were it not that "gwytewch" occurs in a preceding line in connection with "ywrch" and "hyd," we might infer that that word, as well as "llewyn" and "llwyein," represented the name of some celebrated hunting-grounds.—(E.)

Stanza LXXXVIII.

Line 7.—' *Gwair Hir* ' here may be a proper name. Taking it as such, we might render the line thus—

> " Before Gwair Hir was covered under the sod."—(E.)

Line 8.—' *Ffervarch.*' Ab Ithel, unsupported by a single MS., reads "Morarch," apparently for no other reason than that the name "Morarch" occurs in some of the later bards.—(E.)

Stanza LXXXIX.

Line 1.—This line may be rendered also :—

> " I saw the men who with the dawn dug the deep pit ;"

Or,

> " I saw at dawn a great breach made in the wall at Adoyn ;"

Or,

> " I saw the men who had made a great breach, approaching with the dawn."—(E.)

Stanza XC.

Line 2.—' *En emwyd* ' is perhaps a corruption of " er enwyd " (= yr enwyd). If " en emwyd " be the correct reading, the passage appears inexplicable, unless we take " emwyd " as the name of a place.—(E.)

Stanza XCI.

Line 1.—Such is Ab Ithel's version. "Gardith tith ragon" is to me unintelligible. The passage is in all probability corrupt, as appears to be the case with the greater part of what follows to the end of the poem.—(E.)

Stanza XCII.

Line 4.—'*Cas ohir.*' This expression Ab Ithel converts into a proper name, "Caso Hir," but none of the copies present that form. This stanza, which is a repetition of the 86th, appears to be made of different fragments. The difference in many of the forms which evidently stand for one and the same word shows that the text is in a very corrupt state.—(E.)

Stanza XCIII.

Line 1.—Compare stanzas xl. xli. and xciv.

Line 3.—That is, supposing " plec hen " to stand for " plygain." —(E.)

Line 5.—'*Urag*' = " gwrag " or "gwyrag," a bow. "Hancai " = " angai," from " angu " or " engu," to loosen, to set free or at large.—(E.)

Line 6.—'*Gwyr,*' which, as an appellative, signifies men (Lat. *viri*), I leave untranslated, having an impression that, like " Gynt " in the following stanza, it is a proper name, though I am not able to say to what people it may refer. '*Prydein*' in this place must be equivalent to Pryden = Prydyn, here probably the inhabitants of Scotland, or of a part of it, though the term is generally applied to the country rather than to the people.—(E.)

Line 7.—The '*kelein*' (celain) referred to was perhaps killed by mischance. For '*rein*' some copies have "vein " (= main), a much preferable reading.—(E.)

Stanza XCIV.

Line 8.—This couplet, with some variations, occurs in the 41st stanza.—(E.)

Line 9.—This line appears to have no connection with the preceding portion of the stanza, and it is evident that it does not belong to this place.—(E.)

POEM II.

GORCHAN TUDVWLCH.

Translation, Vol. i. *p.* 410. *Text, Vol.* ii. *p.* 93.

Gorchan (from the intensive prefix *gor,* and *can,* a piece of poetry, a song, or poem) has generally been translated *incantation;* but apparently without sufficient reason; for the word does not necessarily nor primarily convey that meaning. The term is of frequent occurrence in Welsh prosody, in which it signifies, as correctly explained by Pughe, " the canon, or fundamental part of song;" that is, one of the primary or principal metres, as distinguished from the secondaries or derivatives, which are called *adlawiaid.* The following passage from *Cyvrinach y Beirdd,* p. 72, exemplifies this usage of the word :—

Yr adlawiaid a ddawant oll o golofnaur *Naw Gorchan;* ag am hynny y gelwir y *gorchanau* ynddyledogion gogyfurdd; am fod yr *adlawiaid* fal gweision dyled iddynt.

" The derivatives all come from the verses of the nine *canons;* and therefore the *canons* are called superiors coequal in rank, on account of the derivatives being like servants dependent upon them."

The reason why these compositions were termed *gorchanau* was not because they were supposed to contain any incantation or enchantment, but because they were considered to be a species of poetry of the highest order, as may be inferred from the argument prefixed to Gorchan Maelderw.

Gwarchan is merely a different orthography of *gorchan,* and both forms are used indiscriminately.

As far as I am able to understand these ancient and very difficult documents, there is nothing in them that would justify their being called *Incantations,* in the usual meaning of that term. With the exception of Gorchan Adebon, they appear to be much on the same subject as the *Gododin*, and are probably no more than fragments of that work; for there are not wanting indications that that poem, as it has come down to us, is far from complete; and the fragmentary character of these gorchanau must, it is presumed, strike every reader. It is possible, also, that fragments of some other early poems may have become mixed up with them.

Tudvwlch, the hero who forms the subject of this gorchan, is in the *Gododin* called "Tudvwlch Hir," or the Tall. He is also celebrated in Gorchan Maelderw. He is mentioned nowhere except in these early poems.—(E.)

POEM III.

GORCHAN ADEBON.

Translation, Vol. i. p. 522. Text, Vol. ii. p. 94.

This gorchan consists of a few proverbs, of which some may be seen in the collection in the Myvyrian. The opening ones are plain enough, but the meaning of the remaining portion is not so obvious. The metre, which consists of three lines rhyming together, would lead to the inference that some of the lines have been lost.

Adebon, whose name is prefixed to it, but who cannot be regarded in any way as its subject, appears to have been a warrior of the sixth century. He is also mentioned by Taliessin.—(E.)

Line 8.—The reading of the *Myv. Arch.* is different:—" Ny cheri y gyneuin gyvieith " = Thou wilt not love the common mother-tongue.—(E.)

Line 9.—That is, an effeminate person (*mwythwas, anwychwas,* or *gwas mwythan*) delights in dainties and voluptuous pleasures, rather than in horses (*emys*) and manly achievements.—(E.)

Line 11.—For '*collit,*' we should possibly read " colit " = *coledd,* to cultivate or cherish—" Cultivate peace at home."—(E.)

Line 14.—The signification of this line is not very intelligible, especially as we are not certain whether we should take "medel" in its usual meaning of—" a reaping, a company of reapers," which has been assumed in the translation ; or read "methe," "a foil, or defeat ; an embarrassment or perplexity." In the latter case, the passage might be rendered, "High stones are barriers to the foe." Llywarch Hen had a son whose name was *Medel,* and who is mentioned by the venerable bard in the "Elegy on his Old Age" (p. 266) :—

> " Maen a madawe a *medel*
> Dewrwyr di yssic vioder :
> Selyf heilin llawr lliwer."

Should the allusion be to that hero, the meaning would be, "Like a high rock (a 'Stonewall') was Medel to his foes."

Dr. Pughe (*Welsh Dict. s. v.* "Dywenu"), taking *Maen* ("Mein") as a personal name, gives the following version of the concluding couplet :—

> "Maen, his slain heap of foes is high ; he smiles on the incantation of Adebon."—(E.)

Line 15.—'Dyben' (= end, or conclusion), is here conjecturally substituted for "dy ven" of the *Book of Aueurin,* and "dyuen" of the *Myv. Arch.,* under the impression that such was the original reading. The substitution of *v* or *u* for *b* having occurred through the inadvertence of some early scribe, the meaning of the last line was overlooked, and another line of similar was added to show the conclusion of the piece. The signification, according to the received reading, is given in the extract from Pughe's *Dictionary* in the preceding note.—(E.)

POEM IV.

GORCHAN CYNVELYN.

Translation, Vol. i. *p.* 412.   *Text, Vol.* ii. *p.* 94.

That the allusion here is to the romantic story of Twrch Trwyth, which constitutes the principal portion of the Mabinogi of Kilhwch and Olwen, there can scarcely be a doubt. This story in the original Welsh, with an English translation and highly interesting notes, will be found in the second volume of Lady Charlotte Guest's *Mabinogion.* This curious tale, Lady Guest remarks, "appears to be purely British. The characters and events which it celebrates

are altogether of native origin, nor has any parallel or counterpart
been discovered in any other language. It abounds in allusions to
traditions of personages and incidents belonging to a remote period ;
and though it is true that some few of these have now become
obscure or unintelligible, yet many are, even to the present day,
current in the principality. Of a much greater number, though all
distinct recollection has ceased to exist, yet the frequent references
made to them in Bardic and other remains, prove that, to our
ancestors at least, they were well known ; and so numerous are the
instances we meet with of this class, that we may safely infer that
all the allusions this Mabinogi contains were generally familiar to
those for whom it was designed."—*Mabinogion,* ii. 319.—(E.)

Line 3.—More literally, " If I were to poetise, if I were to sing,
my superior lay would cause luxuriant buds to spring up."—(E.)

Line 4.—The name is sometimes written *Twrc Trwyd,* or the
Bursting Boar, as may be seen in the following instances taken
from two of the most eminent bards of their day :—

> " Keffid eu ceinllith kwn kunllwyd
> Keffynt veryon voreuwyd
> Keffitor ymdwr am *drwyd*—heuelyt,
> *Twrch* teryt y ar vwyd.
>
> *Cynddelw : Myv. Arch.* i. 261.

> " Y tro a aeth ir *Twrch Trwyd,*
> I Ddavydd a addevwyd."
>
> *L. G. Cothi.*

With *Trwyth* or *Trwyd* compare the Irish *triath,* a hog.—(E.)

Line 5.—For *trychinfwrth* (which I take to be from *trychu,* to
cut, lop, or mangle, and *burthio* (burth), to thrust or repel), the Rev.
Edward Davies (*Mythology,* p. 618) reads *trychinfwrch* (from *trychu,*
and *ffwrch*) ; but as he sees a close connection between this gorchan
and the figures on the coins of Cunobelinus, this is possibly a conjectural emendation resorted to in order to make the description in
the poem refer more pointedly to the figure of a horse " cut off at
the haunches" as represented on these coins. *Burth,* it is observable, appears again in the composition of the word " govurthyach" a
little further on in the poem.—(E.)

Line 6.—The allusion appears to be to the river Severn, in which the encounter took place between Twrch Trwyth and Arthur and his warriors, at which he lost two of the "tlysau"—the "ceinion," or precious things, mentioned in the next line, which were the comb, scissors, and razor, which Twrch had between his ears, and for the purpose of obtaining which the hunt was undertaken. The comb with which he escaped from the Severn was taken from him in Cornwall.—*Mabinogion,* ii. 314, 316.—(E)

Line 48.—The allusion to the Fort of Eiddyn in this line connects this poem with the events of the Gododin, to which the subsequent lines more or less refer.—(S.)

POEM V.

GORCHAN MAELDERW.

Translation, Vol. i. *p.* 414.   *Text, Vol.* ii. *p.* 97.

Line 21.—Dinas Ffaraon is the same as Dinas Emmrys in Snowdown. It is a rocky detached eminence, or a small insulated hill situated in a most romantic valley in the parish of Beddgelert, Caernarvonshire.—(E.)

Line 25.—' *Gosgordd mavr mur,*' the great retinue of the wall. Probably the body of 900 often alluded to.—(S.)

Line 30.—The mention of Eiddyn connects this poem with the scene of the Gododin.—(S.)

Line 47.—The expression of ' *Dremrudd,*' in line 53, shows that this was ' Rhun Dremrudd,' son of Brychan.—(S.)

Line 50.—The three lines beginning

" Am rwyd am ry ystofllit "

I do not pretend to understand. The following is Davies' rendering of the passage :—

" In the network which surrounds the sovereign, dispose thou the threads of wrath, dispose wrath in the flowing streamer. Irksome in front be the glance of the radiant presence."—(E.)

Line 67.—Here, according to Davies, Gorchan Maelderw concludes. " What follows consists of various fragments of the Gododin and other pieces of the sixth century. In the ancient MS. from which I copy, these detached scraps are properly separated from the preceding poem and from each other by large capital initials."— *Myth.* p. 588.—(E.)

STANZA I.

Compare with the Gododin, stanza li.

STANZA VI.

Compare with the last six lines of stanza xxiii. of the Gododin.

STANZA VII.

Line 4.—This line occurs in the Gododin, stanza xx.

Lines 9 *and* 10.—These lines occur in the same stanza of the Gododin.

STANZA VIII.

Lines 7 *and* 8 occur in stanza xxii. of the Gododin.

STANZA IX.

The first two lines of this stanza occur in stanza lxii. of the Gododin.

STANZA X.

Compare the last four lines of this stanza with part of stanza lxii. of the Gododin.

STANZA XIII.

Compare this stanza with stanza xxvi. of the Gododin.

STANZA XIX.

Compare this stanza with stanza xlviii. of the Gododin.

STANZA XX.

Compare this stanza with stanza xlii. of the Gododin.

STANZA XXIV.

Compare this stanza with stanza lxviii. of the Gododin.

Stanza xxv.

Line 1.—Compare this line with the first line of stanza xxxix. of the Gododin.

Stanza xxvii.

Compare this stanza with stanza lxx. of the Gododin.

Stanza xxviii.

Compare this stanza with stanza lxix. of the Gododin.

Stanza xxxiv.

Compare the first five lines of this stanza with the first six lines of stanza lxv. of the Gododin; and the last two lines of this stanza with lines 8 and 9 of the other.

Stanza xxxv.

Compare this stanza with stanza lxiii. of the Gododin.

Stanza xxxvii.

Compare the fragment of this stanza here contained with stanza lxvi. of the Gododin.

The lines not here noticed have no corresponding lines in the Gododin.—(S.)

The conclusion is wanting in the original, and a few of the closing lines are scarcely intelligible.—(E.)

IV.

THE BOOK OF TALIESSIN.

THE MS. called the Book of Taliessin is a small quarto MS. written on vellum, in one hand throughout, of the early part of the fourteenth century, and has always been in the Hengwrt collection. It consists now of thirty-eight leaves of vellum, and at the bottom of one of the pages is the name of Robert Vychan or Vaughan, which shows that it was one of the MSS. collected by him. The outer page both at the beginning and at the end is wanting, and the MS. now begins in the middle of the poem known by the name of "Prif gyfarch Taliessin," and ends in the middle of a poem called "Darogan Katwaladyr."

One of the poems in this book mentions the Books of Beda, and another the line of Anaraut, who died in A.D. 913, so that these poems cannot have been brought together into one collection till the tenth century. On the other hand, none of the poems attributed to Jonas Athraw, and none of those which refer to Henri, are to be found in it.

POEM I.

Translation, Vol. i. p. 284.   *Text, Vol. ii. p.* 108.

The Book of Taliessin being defective both at the beginning and the end, commences in the middle of a poem. It is the poem usually termed " Prif gyfarch Taliessin," and a complete copy will be found in the Red Book of Hergest, No. xxiii. p. 301, which see.

POEM II.

MARUNAT Y VIL VEIB.

Translation, Vol. i. p. 545.   *Text, Vol. ii. p.* 109.

This poem, and the poems Nos. v. and xvii., are the only two contained in the Book of Taliessin which are of the class of religious poems, and do not contain historical allusions. The second last stanza appears to be a fragment of a Latin hymn.

POEM III.

BUARCH BEIRD.

Translation, Vol. i. *p.* 523.   *Text, Vol.* ii. *p.* 115.

This is one of a class of poems in which Taliessin, or the pseudo Taliessin, applies a number of epithets to himself.   It is of no historical value, and is classed with others of the same character.

POEM IV.

ADUVYNEU TALIESSIN.

Translation, Vol. i. *p.* 550.   *Text, Vol.* ii. *p.* 116.

This poem likewise contains no historical allusions.   It is classed with the religious poems.

POEM V.

Translation, Vol. i. *p.* 552.   *Text, Vol.* ii. *p.* 118.

This poem is also of a religious character.

POEM VI.

ARYMES PRYDEIN VAWR.

Translation, Vol. i. *p.* 436.   *Text, Vol.* ii. *p.* 123.

This poem is in the *Myvyrian Archæology* attributed to Golyddan, a bard said by the Triads to be the bard of Cadwaladyr, but there is nothing in the poem itself to show that it was written by him, and it seems to be merely a conjecture arising from the frequent mention of Cadwaladyr in the poem, which places it at a period subsequent to that in which Taliessin flourished.   It is contained, however, in the Book of Taliessin, and belongs to a class of poems in the same book in which Cadwaladyr is likewise mentioned.   The opening lines are the same as those of another poem, No. xlvii.

Line 7.—' *Caer Weir,*' probably Durham on the Wear.

Line 9.—' *Dulyn.*' The Gaelic equivalent is *Dubhlinne,* or Dublin.

Line 10.—The whole Gaelic race is here comprehended under the Gael of Ireland, Anglesea, and Prydyn or Scotland.

Line 11.—' *Chludwys.*' The men of the Clyde, or Strathclyde Britons.

Line 15.—'*Gwyr Gogled.*' The Men of the North, a term used for the Cumbrian and Strathclyde Britons.

POEM VII.

ANGAR KYFYNDAWT.

Translation, Vol. i. *p.* 525. *Text, Vol.* ii. *p.* 129.

This poem contains no historical allusions. It is of the same class as poem No. iii.

POEM VIII.

KAT´ GODEU.

Translation, Vol. i. *p.* 276. *Text, Vol.* ii. *p.* 137.

This poem has been considered in Chapter xi. It is classed with the poems relating to the Gwyddyl of Gwydyon ap Don. They are described in lines 28 to 38 under various figures. The reference in lines 32 and 34 to a combat at the root of the tongue, and to another in the *occiput,* I cannot help suspecting refers to the most striking difference between the Cymric and Gaelic—viz. the interchange of gutturals and labials, which might be called a combat at the root of the tongue ; and it is remarkable that in the *crania* found within the limits of ancient Manau there is an artificial compression in the *occiput.* Godeu was certainly the name of a district, but the word also means trees, and the subject of the poem soon passes over into a symbolical battle of trees. It seems also to have a philological meaning, as in lines 51, 52, 53, 54—

> " The Lord answered them
> Through language and elements :
> Take the forms of the principal trees,
> Arranging yourselves in battle-array."

And in lines 199 and 200—

> " He will compose, he will decompose,
> He will form languages."

POEM IX.

MAB GYFREU TALIESSIN.

Translation, Vol. i. *p.* 542.   *Text, Vol.* ii. *p.* 144.

This poem contains no historical allusions.   It may be classed with Nos. iii. and vii.

POEM X.

DARONWY.

Translation, Vol. i. *p.* 269.   *Text, Vol.* ii. *p.* 147.

This is a very curious poem.   Daronwy belongs to the tradition of the Gwyddyl in Gwynedd.   According to the pedigrees connected with them, he was the son of Brynach, or Urnach Wyddel, by Corth, daughter of Brychan, and the grandfather of Gwydyon.   It is classed with poems containing allusions to the same traditions, and placed first as relating probably to the earliest events.   The scene of the poem is, however, in the north.

Lines 3 *and* 4.—The power of Daronwy seems here compared to the billows rolling over the beach.

Line 19.—The same figure is here used.   Four sovereigns, and a fifth mentioned in the two following lines, are here represented as coming over the strand.   They are probably the five chiefs of the Gwyddel Ffichti mentioned in another poem (xlix.), as preceding the Norddmyn in Bernicia.

Line 28.—The two dames, one single and the other a widow, surely refer to Monenna, who founded a church at Duneden, or Edinburgh, a place mentioned in line 51, and was accompanied by "una vidua."

Line 42. The princes from Rome were no doubt the ecclesiastics of the Christian church.

Line 43.—'*Dineidyn*' is Edinburgh. '*Dineiduc*,' probably another name for *Magedauc* or Mugdock. These two places indicate a district between Edinburgh and Mugdock—that is, Manau.

Line 50.—'*Kaer Rian*'—the city of Ryan, or Loch Ryan. "*Kaer Rywc*" probably refers to Sanquhar or Senchaer, the old city, which is on the Crawick, a name formed from Caer Rawick, as Cramond is from Caeramond. These two places indicate a district between Loch Ryan and the Nith, or Galloway, and in these lines the two regions peopled by the Picts appear as the scene of Daronwy's power.

POEM XI.

Translation, Vol. i. *p.* 337. *Text, Vol.* ii. *p.* 149.

Mr. Stephens places this poem in his first class of *Historical Poems of the Sixth Century;* but in his attempt, in an article in the *Archæologia Cambrensis*, to identify the places mentioned in the poem with localities in Wales, he entirely fails. They are easily found in the north.

Line 9.—'*From the bush of Maw and Eiddyn.*' The Moss of Maw is on the borders of the counties of Edinburgh and Peebles, in the parish of Pennicuik, and Eiddyn is Edinburgh.

Line 17.—'*Agathes*' is probably Irongath Hill near Linlithgow. It is on the east side of the river Avon, which we learn from the Gododin was also called the Aeron, and probably appears in the first part of the name "Iron." Sir R. Sibbald, in his History of Linlithgowshire, says—"The tradition is current that there was a fight between the Romans and the natives under Argadus in this hill, and that it had its name from Argad." Argad was the name of a son of Llywarch Hen.

Line 19.—'*The Region of Bretrwn*' is that part of Ayrshire where the promontory of Troon is situated.

Line 22.—'*Aeron*' is the Avon.

Line 23.—'*Arddunion*' is Ardinning, near Mugdock, in the parish of Strathblane.

Line 25.—'*The Wood of Beid*' is the moor at Beith in Ayrshire, where there was formerly a wood.

Line 27.—'*Mabon*' appears to have been a name applied to the district about Lochmaben in Dumfriesshire.

Line 29.—'*Gwensteri.*' There is a river which separates Cumberland and Westmorland, and another in Derbyshire, called the Winster. As this battle was against the spearmen of Lloegr, it was probably in the south.

Line 31.—'*The Marsh of Terra.*' The Statistical Account of Inch, in the county of Wigton, contains the following :—" What are called 'the stepping-stones of Glenterra' are not a little curious. About three feet deep, in a peat-moss, there is a regular file of stepping-stones extending about a quarter of a mile. These must have been placed to form a passage through a swamp previous to the growth of the peat-moss."

There seems to be a record of the battle in "four large unpolished stones placed erect, and forming a circle. At a distance of some yards stands a single stone. They are called by the country people 'The Standing Stones of Glenterra.'"

Line 39.—'*Pencoet Cledyfein.*' This seems to be the same event mentioned in poem **xxxvi.**, line 25, as " *Kat glutvein gueith pen coet*"—the battle of Clutvein or Cledyfein, at the head of the wood. As Clut is the Clyde, Clutvein is probably the Cluden, and in the parish of Holywood, on the north bank of the Cluden, where it falls into the Nith, the author of the *Statistical Account* says,— " The lower part of this parish was unquestionably at an early period a *quercetum* or oak-forest, extending most probably to Snaid, a distance of eight miles." It was termed the Holywood, and a monastery was afterwards founded here, called " Abbatia Sacri nemoris."

The writer adds—" Not more than a quarter of a mile south-west of the church eleven large stones are placed in an oval form. They are situated near the lower termination of the Sacred Grove," a record of the battle at *Pencoed*, the end of the wood. As the enemies are termed the Peithwyr, this name must have been applied to the Picts of Galloway.

Line 43.—' *Gafran*' is either intended for Girvan in Ayrshire, or for the country of Gavran, father of Aedan, or Dalriada. " *Breccheinawg*" is here probably applied to the district about " Eiddyn " mentioned in the preceding line, which was inhabited by the Catbregion. The scene of the poem is thus entirely in the north.

In the Verses of the Graves, stanza vii., the grave of Gwallawg is thus mentioned :—" In Carawg the grave of Gwallawg Hir." Carawg is Carrick in Ayrshire.

POEM XII.

GLASWAWT TALIESSIN.

Translation, Vol. i. *p.* 300. *Text, Vol.* ii. *p.* 150.

The reference in line 26 to the line of Anarawd shows that this poem refers to events subsequent to Anarawd, the son of Rodri Mawr, who died in 913.

POEM XIII.

KADEIR TALIESSIN.

Translation, Vol. i. *p.* 533. *Text, Vol.* ii. *p.* 151.

This poem is of the same class with Nos. iii. and vii., and is ranged with them accordingly.

POEM XIV.

Translation, Vol. i. *p.* 274. *Text, Vol.* ii. *p.* 153.

This poem is connected by its title with the legends of the sons of Llyr, and is full of allusions to the heroes of that Mabinogi.

There is only one reference to a later historical event—viz. in lines 7 and 8, to the war between Brochwel of Powis and Ethelfrith, which indicates the year 613 as a date before which it cannot have been composed.

Line 12.—' Ogyrwen.'   See note, p. 324.

Line 33.—' Gerdolyon,' for Cerddorion, singers or bards.

Line 34.—' Diferogyon,' distillers. These are the same Gwyddyl termed in the Gododin " Deifr diferogyon," and in poem No. i. " Kyl diferogyon."   The union between the bardic or pagan party of the Brython and the Gwyddyl is here alluded to.

Line 35.—' Penryn Wleth' is Glasgow, for Joceline describes Kentigern as proceeding from the Clyde, and sitting "super lapidem in supercilio montis vocabulo Gwleth" (c. xiv.) Gwleth, forming in combination Wleth, signifies dew, and this hill was afterwards known as the Dew or Dowhill in Glasgow. Lwch Reon is Loch Ryan, and this passage shows a Cymric population extending from Loch Ryan to Glasgow.

Line 45.—' Caer Sidi.' This place is also mentioned in poem No. xxx., and is there said to be the prison of Gweir, where he was confined through the spite of Pwyll and Pryderi. Here it is mentioned in connection with Manawyd and Pryderi, and is described in line 49 as surrounded by the sea. It is probable that this island Caer is the " Urbs Giudi " of Bede, which was in the Firth of Forth, and the " Urbs Iudeu " of Nennius, which is mentioned by him in connection with Manau.

POEM XV.

KADEIR TEYRNON.

Translation, Vol. i. *p.* 259.   *Text, Vol.* ii. *p.* 155.

This poem is placed by Stephens in his third class, but apparently for no other reason than because Arthur is mentioned in it. Its true place is indicated in chapter xiii. It is a very curious poem. The man of two authors, or sprung from two sources, is the Guledig, and the two sources are indicated in lines 65 to 69.

Line 4.—' *Aladwr.'* Ala was the name of a troop of horse in the Roman army. ' *Dwr,'* steel.

Line 12.—' *Gosgordd Mur.'* The Gosgordd, or company of the wall.

Line 13.—' *Gawrnur.'* The *Myvyrian Archæology* reads ' Gawr mur,' the Giant Wall. If Gawrnur is the correct reading, it must be a proper name.—(W.)

Line 23.—' *Chynweissat,'* chief ministers. The Triads of Arthur have "Three chief ministers (Chynweissat) of ynys Prydain —Caradawc son of Bran, and Caurdaf son of Caradawc, and Owen son of Macsen Guledig.

Line 37.—' *Mynawg,'* willing. It may be, however, a proper name.—(W.)

Line 44.—The expression " between the flood and the ebb" pro bably implies a Caer on a rock connected by a low neck of land with the shore, which was dry at ebb-tide and covered with water at flood-tide.

POEM XVI.

CADEIR KERRITUEN.

Translation, Vol. i. *p.* 296. *Text, Vol.* ii. *p.* 158.

This poem is not classed with the other poems relating to Gwydyon, as it is obviously of much later date, and refers to events in the Mabinogi which none of the others do.

Line 14 refers to the incident, in the prose tale, of Gwydyon producing a woman from flowers.

Line 28.—Nantffrancon is a valley in Snowdon.

Line 38 mentions the Book of Beda, and shows that its composition must be placed later than his death in 735.

POEM XVII.

CANU Y GWYNT.

Translation, Vol. i. p. 535. *Text, Vol.* ii. *p.* 159.

This belongs to a class of poems attributed to Taliessin, in which he deals with the natural phenomena of the earth. The subject is the wind.

POEM XVIII.

Translation, Vol. i. *p.* 363. *Text, Vol.* ii. *p.* 162.

This poem refers to the battles in which Owen, the son of Urien, fought. Stephens, in his *Literature of the Kymry,* places it in his fifth class, and supposes that it refers to Owen Gwynedd, but he retracts that opinion in the *Archæologia Cambrensis.*

The scene of the poem is in the north.

Line 1.—'*Calchvynyd*' is Kelso in Roxburghshire. See vol. i. p. 172.

Line 13.—'*Tir Gwyddno,*' the land of Gwyddno. Gwyddno appears in the *Bonhed Gwyr y Gogled* as one of the thirteen kings of the North.   There seems to have been a historic Gwyddno and a mythic king of that name, whose land, called *Cantref y Gwaelod,* is supposed to have been in the Bay of Cardigan and to have been submerged by the sea. I cannot help suspecting that Gwaelod was the real name of his country, and that the word, also signifying "sunk, or gone to the bottom," gave rise to the fable. It may be a mere transposition of letters from "Gwaedol," or Wedale, the vale of woe.

Line 15.—The land of the Cludwys was Strathclyde.

Line 19.—We have here a battle at the ford of Alclut or Dumbarton, and Gwen may be Gwenystrad.

Line 23.—As these battles are connected with Mabon, Man-Llachar is probably Lochar Moss on the shore of the Solway Firth.

Line 30.—The country of Mabon is the vale of the Nith, in which lies Lochmaben.

POEM XIX.

KANU Y MED.

Translation, Vol. i. *p.* 538.   *Text, Vol.* ii. *p.* 164.

This poem is classed with those containing allusions to the personal history of Taliessin.

POEM XX.

KANU Y CWRWF.

Translation, Vol. i. *p.* 427.   *Text, Vol.* ii. *p.* 165.

Mr. Stephens considers that this poem consists of two poems artificially put together, which have no natural connection. The latter part, commencing with the line " Teithi etmygant," he calls "Dyffryn Gwarand," and places in his first class as a genuine poem, and the first part he places in his third class. The metrical construction of both parts is, however, the same, and the first part begins with a very similar line, "Teithi Etmynt." Both resemble the beginning of a stanza in the Gododin, "Teithi Etmygant," and this poem is, from the allusions in the second part, classed along with the Gododin poems.

STANZA II.

Line 2. — ' *Tryffin Garant,*' the boundary of Carant. The Myvyrian reads ' *Dyffryn* ' valley. There are two rivers called Carron—the one in Stirlingshire, which flows into the Firth of Forth ; the other, in Dumfriesshire, flows into the Nith. The latter is probably the river here meant.

Line 17. — ' *Carawg,*' taken in combination with Coel and Canauon in line 28, shows that the three provinces of Ayrshire— Carrick, Cyle, and Cuningham—are meant.

Line 19. — " Carawg of the Cymry abounding in cities," is here called the father of Caradawg, as, according to Boece, he was born in Carrick.

Line 23. — The mention of the Gwentians with that of Ynyr in subsequent lines shows that Ynyr Gwent is meant. As he was a descendant of Dyfynwal Hen, and closely allied to the princes of the north of that race, his intervention in this war, the scene of which is in the north, was natural.

Line 30.—The seas of Gododin show that this district was bounded by the sea.

POEM XXI.

Translation, Vol. i. *p.* 303.   *Text, Vol.* ii. *p.* 168.

Mr. Stephens places this poem in his fifth class, and considers that it refers entirely to Tenby. He founds mainly upon the title usually assigned to this poem, of *Mic Dinbych,* which he translates the " Prospect of Tenby," but these titles are generally modern additions, and the poem has no title in the Book of Taliessin. It describes eight cities, and they seem to be different, and to range from north to south.

STANZA I.

This city is described as on the surface of the ocean, and the billows roll to it from the region of the Picts. It must therefore have been on an island in the Firth of Forth, and is probably Bede's *Urbs Giudi.*

STANZA II.

This city is described as on an island in a lake.

STANZA III.

The allusion in the sixth line to the tenants of Deudraeth, or the two strands, in contrast to the serfs of Dyfed, seems to point to the Traeth Mawr and Traeth Bychan in North Wales, and the city may be Caernarvon.

STANZA V.

The mention of Dinbych in the third line shows that the city celebrated in this stanza was Tenby; and this being the only known name appearing in the poem, has led to the title of *Mic Dinbych* having been given to it.

STANZA VIII.

This stanza also appears in the Black Book of Caermarthen ; and being the only stanza of the poem there given, it was probably understood to refer to the town of Caermarthen. The differences between the two texts of this stanza are not great, and the older version has been followed. Instead of Gwyned, in lines 3 and 8, the Book of Taliessin reads *vyned = myned,* " going," and in line 5, *kyfnovant,* " mutual enjoyment," instead of *cwinovant,* " distress."

POEM XXII.

PLAEU YR EIFFT.

Translation, Vol. i. *p.* 559. *Text, Vol.* ii. *p.* 170.

This is the first of a class of poems attributed to Taliessin relating to Jewish history.

POEM XXIII.

TRAWSGANU KYNAN GARWYN M. BROCH.

Translation, Vol. i. *p.* 447. *Text, Vol.* ii. *p.* 172.

Kynan Garwyn being the son of Brochwel Powis, who fought with the Angles in 613, this poem belongs to a later date.

POEM XXIV.

LLATH MOESEN.

Translation, Vol. i. *p.* 561. *Text, Vol.* ii. *p.* 173.

This poem is of the same class as No. xxii.

POEM XXV.

Translation, Vol. i. *p.* 307. *Text, Vol.* ii. *p.* 175.

This poem has been placed along with the Triads of the Horses. It contains allusions to various heroes of the Welsh romance, but does not seem to call for remark.

POEM XXVI.

Y Gofeisswys Byt.

Translation, Vol. i. *p.* 566.   *Text, Vol.* ii. *p.* 177.

This poem bears the title of " *Y Gofeisswys Byt*," the Contrived World, but it relates entirely to the legends connected with Alexander the Great, and is classed with poem No. xxviii.

That these legends had early entered into Celtic tradition we see from their likewise forming the subject of Gaelic poetry (Dean of Lismore's book, p. 110).

POEM XXVII.

Translation, Vol. i. *p.* 557.   *Text, Vol.* ii. *p.* 178.

This poem, though termed in the *Myvyrian Archæology* " Luryg Alexander," seems to have no reference to Alexander, but is one of those religious poems which show the Christian character of most of these poems.   It is classed with poems ii. iii. and v.

POEM XXVIII.

Translation, Vol. i. *p.* 567.   *Text, Vol.* ii. *p.* 179.

This poem refers also to Alexander.

POEM XXIX.

Translation, Vol. i. *p.* 563.   *Text, Vol.* ii. *p.* 179.

This poem belongs to the same class with Nos. xxii. and xxiv.

POEM XXX.

Translation, Vol. i. *p.* 264.   *Text, Vol.* ii. *p.* 181.

This poem is usually termed " Preiddeu Annwfn," or the " Spoils of Annwn."   It appears to relate to an expedition of Arthur's to the unknown region of Annwfn, but whether the cities mentioned were different places, or different names for the same place, it is difficult to say.

STANZA I.

Caer Sidi is also mentioned in the poem No. xiv. of this book, usually termed *Cerdd am Veib Llyr.* It appears from that poem to have been upon an island, and is probably Bede's island city of Giudi in the Firth of Forth.

STANZA II.

Caer Pedryvan, or the quadrangular Caer, must have been a Roman camp. The legend of the " Tuatha de Danann" describes them as bringing to Alban four precious things from four cities. The second was the sword of Lughaidh from the city of Gorias. The fourth was the Cauldron of Dagda from the city of Murias. The " Nine Maidens " also belong to an old Scottish legend. The name " Murias " seems connected with *mur*, the wall ; and the village where the Roman camp called Camelon is situated is still called Carmuirs. According to tradition, Camelon had twelve gates of brass, and in the next stanza this Caer is called the Isle or Inch of the strong door. Camelon is immediately north of the wall, and seems to be the place meant.

STANZA IV.

Line 2—' *Caer wydyr,*' or the fort of glass, seems to point to a vitrified fort.

Line 3.—This line shows the connection of the poem with the country beyond the Roman wall. *Canhwr*, as appears from the *Bonhed Gwyr y Gogled*, was a body of 100 men, or a *centuria ;* and thrice twenty or sixty centuries composed the Roman legion, here placed at the *mur* or wall.

STANZA V.

' *Caer Vandwy*' is also mentioned in the dialogue between Gwyddno Garanhir and Gwynn ap Nudd in the Black Book of Caermarthen, No. xxxii. It may have been Cramond, a corruption of Caeramond.

STANZA VII.

This stanza seems to be a later addition to the poem, with the subject of which it has no connection.

POEM XXXI

Translation, Vol. i. p. 343.   *Text, Vol.* ii. *p.* 183.

This is the well-known poem on the battle of Gwenystrad, and its antiquity has hardly been called in question.   The mention in line 20 of Garan*wynyon*, and of the cross, points to the same scene as Arthur's battle " in Castello *Guinion*,"—that is, at Wedale, where the sacred cross was preserved.   Gwenystrad, or the White Strath, seems therefore the valley of the Gala Water; and the white stone of Galystem, in which word the name Gala seems contained, is probably the stone mentioned in the *Statistical Account.*   "A little above it (St. Mary's Church of Stow) is a very fine perennial spring, known by the name of the Lady's Well, and a huge stone, recently removed in forming the new road, but now broken to pieces, used to be pointed out as impressed with the print of the Virgin Mary's foot."   In the Verses of the Graves, stanza xx., the grave of three persons is said to be on an elevated hill in the " Pant Gwynn Gwynionawg."   Pant is a valley, and being masculine, takes Gwynn in its masculine form, as Ystrad, being feminine, takes Gwen; both mean the white valley, and the epithet Gwynionawg connects it here also with Gwynion.

Some of the passages in this poem are very obscure, and are left blank in Evans' translation in the *Myvyrian Archæology.* Lines 21 and 22 seem to imply that the enemy took refuge on the sea.

POEM XXXII.

Translation, Vol. i. *p.* 344.   *Text, Vol.* ii. *p.* 184.

This poem Stephens places in his first class.   It does not call for remark, as no localities are mentioned in it.

POEM XXXIII.

Translation, Vol. i. *p.* 346.   *Text, Vol.* ii. *p.* 185.

This poem is also admitted to be genuine.

Line 41 mentions Llwyfenydd as having been given to the

bard, and in line 35 it is the reward of Taliessin's song. Llwy-fenydd is formed from Llwyfain, the elm-tree. From Leamhain, the elm-tree in Gaelic, comes Leamhanach, corrupted into Leven-achs or Lennox. Llwyfenydd is the Welsh equivalent of Leam-hanach. It is the district between Loch Lomond and Loch Long, and therefore adjoined Reged.

POEM XXXIV.

Translation, Vol. i. p. 348. *Text, Vol. ii. p.* 187.

It is hardly possible to doubt that this and the two preceding poems are by the same author.

Line 12.—'*Gwaith Mynaw.*' Mynaw seems to be the same word as Mynyw, the Irish equivalent of which was Emain or Muine. What place is meant there is nothing to show.

The lines 36 to 49 of the poem are highly poetical. Lines 50 and 51 contain a Welsh proverb.

POEM XXXV.

GWEITH ARGOET LLWYFEIN. KANU VRYEN.

Translation, Vol. i. p. 365. *Text, Vol. ii. p.* 189.

The word Llwyfain or Leven is the Cymric equivalent of Leam-han, which places the scene at the end of a wood on the river Leven. It describes Urien and Owain his son as fighting against Flam-ddwyn, or the Flame-bearer; and as Urien and his son are recorded to have fought against Theodric, king of Bernicia, he, and not his father Ida, as is usually supposed, must be meant by the name of Flamddwyn, or the Flame-bearer.

Line 3.—Goden and Reged are here placed together, and, in order to surround these districts, Flamddwyn had to extend his forces from Argoed to Arfynydd, their northern and southern terminations.

Line 11.—Ceneu, son of Coel, was the ancestor of the race from which Urien and other northern kings derived their descent. This line has usually been supposed to indicate that Ceneu was present at the battle, and Stephens founds upon this a charge of anachronism. but this is a mistaken meaning. The idea intended to be expressed is that Owen would not give hostages, and that his ancestor Ceneu, son of Coel, would in similar circumstances have been an irritated lion before he would have given a hostage to any one.

POEM XXXVI.

Translation, Vol. i. p. 350.   Text, Vol. ii. p. 190.

This poem Stephens admits to be genuine. It describes a war between Urien and Ulph with the Angles. Ulph is probably Friodulph, the king of Bernicia, who reigned between Ussa and Theodric, against both of whom Urien is recorded by Nennius to have fought.

Line 12.—Urien goes to Aeron or the Avon.

Line 14 probably refers to Urien's expedition to Wales, alluded to in the poem called Anrhec Urien.

Line 16.—' *Hyfaid.*' This is one of the leading heroes of the Gododin.

Line 19.—' *Llwyfenyd*' is here mentioned evidently in connection with the battle which follows.

Line 21.—' *Alclut* ' is Dumbarton, and the battle at the ford and at the *ynver* must have been at the junction of the Leven with the Clyde. Places beginning with Aber are usually at a ford over a river near its mouth, and those with Inver at the actual junction.

Lines 22 *and* 23.—These localities cannot be identified.

Line 25.—' *Cat Glutvein gweith pen coed.*' This is obviously the same locality which appears in poem xi. See Notes, p. 402.

Line 43. — ' *Godeu a Reget.*' These two districts are frequently mentioned together, and must have been adjacent. Reged is Dumbartonshire, and Godeu probably the middle ward of Lanarkshire, and the same as Cadyow.

POEM XXXVII.

YSPEIL TALIESSIN. KANU I URIEN.

Translation, Vol. i. *p.* 353. *Text, Vol.* ii. *p.* 192.

This poem Stephens also admits to be genuine.

Line 9.—Urien is here called the ruler of Catraeth ; and in line 21, a protector in Aeron.

Line 26.—This line shows that Llwyfenydd was on the sea-shore.

Line 44.—Ceneu was the son of Coel, and the ancestor of many of these northern kings. Nudd Hael, a descendant of Dyfynwal Hen.

Line 47.—' *Gwyden* ' is here put probably for Gwydyon, whose Gwyddyl the bard wishes exterminated.

POEM XXXVIII.

Translation, Vol. i. *p.* 338. *Text, Vol.* ii. *p.* 193.

This poem is placed by Stephens in his second class of doubtful poems ; but in the *Archæologia Cambrensis* he seems to admit it as genuine.

Line 45.—' *Caer Clut* ' is the city on the Clyde, or Glasgow. " *Caer Caradawc*," probably the traditionary city in Carrick, mentioned by Boece as " Caractonium." The region between these two cities comprised the shires of Renfrew and Ayr, and is much the same as that indicated in another poem as possessed by the Cymry from Loch Ryan to Penrhyn Wleth.

POEM XXXIX.

DUDOLWCH URIEN.

Translation, Vol. i. *p.* 352. *Text, Vol.* ii. *p.* 195.

Stephens admits this poem to be genuine.

Line 12.—' *Gogled*' connects this poem with the north.

Line 18.—' *Llwyfenydd*,' the district given to the bard, is the same word as Lennox.

Line 28.—The kings of every language are said to be subject to Urien, which shows the mixed population of these northern districts.

POEM XL.

Marwnat Erof.

Translation, Vol. i. *p.* 255.   *Text, Vol.* ii. *p.* 196.

The title of "Marwnat Erof," or the Death-song of Erof, is pre-fixed to this poem, which, however, relates exclusively to Ercwlf, while Erof is mentioned in the next poem. The two poems, how-ever, are closely connected. The poetic structure is the same in both, and they are obviously by the same bard. They are placed by Mr. Stephens among the poems forming portions of the Mabinogi of Taliessin ; but no reason is given, and they neither have any analogy to that tale, nor do they appear in any copy of it. Who is intended here by Ercwlf it is difficult to say. The name is the same as Hercules, as appears from the allusions to the columns in the line ; but he is called Chief of Baptism and the Piercer of the *Mur* or Roman wall, which connects it with the post-Roman period. As the Picts were said to be descended from Gileoin Mac Ercail, or son of Hercules, it is probable that a Pict was intended under the name of his mythic ancestor.

POEM XLI.

Translation, Vol. i. *p.* 256.   *Text, Vol.* ii. *p.* 197.

This poem bears no title in the Book of Taliessin. The title in the *Myvyrian Archæology* is " Marwnad Mad. ddrud ac Erof," or the Death-song of Madawg the valiant and Erof. Madawg is called the son of Uthyr, which connects him with Arthur, and the epithet *Mur Menwyd*, or joy of the *mur* or wall, with the post-Roman period. Erof is considered by Nash to be intended for Herod, but in order to support this he is obliged to suppose that two different fragments having no connection with each other have been united in one poem, and to alter his text. The character intended seems that of a Christian who had apostatised, and he is probably one of the Southern Picts.

POEM XLII.

MARWNAT CORROI MAP DAYRY.

Translation, Vol. i. *p.* 254. *Text, Vol.* ii. *p.* 198.

This poem is the solitary specimen of a Welsh Ossianic poem which has come down to us. It relates to the Irish tale of Curoi, son of Dairi of Munster, and Cuchullin, the celebrated Ossianic hero of Ulster. A full notice of it will be found in the Dean of Lismore's book, p. 141. Mr. Stephens has so completely misapprehended its meaning, that his arguments have no bearing upon its date.

POEM XLIII.

MARWNAT DYLAN EIL TON.

Translation, Vol. i. *p.* 288. *Text, Vol.* ii. *p.* 198.

This short poem has been classed with those relating to Gwydyon, from the name of Dylan eil Ton occurring in the Mabinogi of Math, son of Mathonwy, but there is nothing in the poem to indicate any other connection.

Lines 6 *and* 7 class the inhabitants of the British Isles under four heads :—*Iwerdon,* or Ireland ; *Manau,* or Man ; *Y Gogledd* or *Prydyn,* which is Scotland ; and Prydain, or South Britain. It may be remarked that *Prydain* in its feminine form seems used in these poems for South Britain, and in its masculine form of *Prydyn* for North Britain.

POEM XLIV.

MARWNAT OWEIN.

Translation, Vol. i. *p.* 366. *Text, Vol.* ii. *p.* 199.

This poem is called the Death-song of Owain, son of Urien, and is admitted to be genuine by Stephens.

2 E

Line 6.—This line has been read as if it narrated the death of Flamddwyn by Owain, but the other is the natural construction, and the poem being the Death-song of Owain leaves no doubt that the true meaning is that Flamddwyn slew Owain. He was Theodric, king of Bernicia, who reigned from 580 to 587, against whom Owen is said by Nennius to have fought.

POEM XLV.

Translation, Vol. i. *p.* 299.   *Text, Vol.* ii. *p.* 199.

This poem consists of two parts, each beginning with the words *Echrys Ynys*, "disturbed is the Isle." It appears to me to be a late composition, and to emanate from South Wales. North Wales is here called the Land of Gwydyon, and the mention of Hu shows that it belongs to the school alluded to by Sion Kent, who lived from about 1380 to 1420, when he says—

> "Two kinds of Awen truly
>   There are in the world, and manifest their course.
>   The Awen from Christ of joyful discourse
>   Of the right tendency, a sprightly muse.
>   There is another Awen not wisely sung,
>   And they make false and filthy predictions.
>   This one has been taken by the men of Hu."

POEM XLVI.

Translation, Vol. i. *p.* 257.   *Text, Vol.* ii. *p.* 200.

This poem obviously relates to Cunedda, whose sons conquered North Wales from the Gwyddyl, as in line 43 he is called son of Edeyrn. Mr. Stephens, in his *Lit. of the Kymry*, places it as doubtful ; but in a paper in the *Arch. Camb.* vol. iii. p. 47, he argues that Cunedda and Taliessin must have been contemporary from the expressions in several of the lines. He endeavours to show that Cunedda must be placed a century later, but his arguments are very inconclusive ; and to alter chronology on account of such expressions, is to exact too definite a meaning from mere poetic licence, which permitted the bard to use language as if he had personally known the hero whom he celebrates.

Line 6.—' *Caer Weir'* and '*Caer Lliwelydd'* seem intended for Durham on the Wear and Carlisle.

Line 21.—'*Furrow'*—*i.e.* the grave.

Line 24.—The Men of Bryneich here were probably the Picts who preceded the Angles in Bernicia.

POEM XLVII.

Translation, Vol. i. *p.* 443.   *Text, Vol.* ii. *p.* 202.

The first four lines of this poem are the same as those in poem vi. The three following lines mention seven sons of Beli, but it does not appear to be meant that they were all sons of the same Beli. Caswallawn and Llud were sons of Beli mawr. Iago, son of Beli, was father of Cadvan and grandfather of Cadwallawn, He is said to be from the land of *Prydyn*, or the north, from whence Cunedda and his sons, from whom he was descended, came. The other names are unknown.

POEM XLVIII.

MARWNAT UTHYR PEN.

Translation, Vol. i. *p.* 297.   *Text, Vol.* ii. *p.* 203.

This poem has the title attached to it of the *Marwnat*, or Death-song of Uthyr Pendragon, the father, according to the Arthurian romance, of King Arthur; but the mention of Hu, in line 35, connects it with poem xlv., with which it has been classed. These two poems, with the one called Kadeir Kerritwen, I believe to be poems written in imitation of those which really belong to that class of ancient poetry to which the name of Taliessin has been attached, and to have emanated from South Wales.

POEM XLIX.

Translation, Vol. i. *p.* 431.   *Text, Vol.* ii. *p.* 204.

This very curious poem has been noticed in vol. i. chapter xiii.

The two lochs or lakes mentioned in line 2 probably refer to the Firths of Forth and Clyde.

In lines 18 and 19 Beli, son of Manogan, is mentioned, but he is likewise referred to in the *Historia Britonum,* a work of the same century in which I place this poem :—" Ipse (Julius Cæsar) pugnabat apud Dolabellum, qui erat proconsul regi Britannico, qui et ipse *Bellinus* vocabatur et *filius* erat *Minocanni."*

The last part of the poem has been commented on in chapter xiii.

POEM L.

Translation, Vol. i. *p.* 432.   *Text, Vol.* ii. *p.* 205.

This poem is classed with the preceding poem, as referring to Cadwallawn, from lines 17 and 18 mentioning his return from Ireland.

Line 22.—' *Aranwynyon,*' also mentioned in the Avallenau, is probably the same place as *Garanwynyon* in Gwenystrad.

Line 24.—' *Cat Vreith* ' are the same people mentioned in the *Historia Britonum* as " Catbregion," who dwelt near *Mynyd Agned,* or Edinburgh.

Line 25.—' *Ryt ar taradyr* ' is the Ford of Torrator, on the Carron, near Falkirk.   The Carron was the northern boundary of the Picts.

POEM LI.

Translation, Vol. i. *p.* 564.   *Text, Vol.* ii. *p.* 206.

This poem belongs to the same class with poems xxii. xxiv. and xxix.

POEM LII.

Gwawd Llud y Vawr.

Translation, Vol. i. p. 271.   Text, Vol. ii. p. 207.

This poem seems likewise to refer to the Gwyddyl of Gwydyon ap Don, and has been classed with them.

Line 16 refers to an expedition of five hundred warriors in five ships, and they sing a song contained in lines 18, 19, 20, and 21. This song appears to be in old Irish.   Many years ago I sent these lines to Archdeacon Williams and to Professor O'Curry.   The former could make nothing of them.   The latter, in a letter dated 19th December 1856, says—" Whether the words of the Rann which you have sent me were intended to be Irish or not, I have no hesitation in saying that they make good and very ancient Irish. *Brit, Brith, Bretanaigh*, are legitimate Irish forms of Briton and Britons.   The few words besides this name in your lines are *nuoes*, co-occupancy of land ; *nu*, or ; *edi*, battle ; *sych*, in preference to, before ; *eu*, a spear ; *roi*, a battlefield."

Line 73.—' *Cyllellawr*,' the knife-man.   This was probably Ossa Cyllellawr, who fought with Arthur at the battle of Badon Hill.

Line 77 shows that the poem relates to events connected with the population of Prydyn or Scotland.   The three races of the Cymry, Angles, and Gwyddyl are described in the lines that follow. Lines 78 and 79 refer to the Cymry ; lines 80, 81, and 82 to the Angles ; and the third race or the Gwyddyl are described in lines 83, 84, and 85.

POEM LIII.

Translation, Vol. i. p. 444.   Text, Vol. ii. p. 211.

This poem is classed along with the two prophecies, termed " Arymes," relating to Cadwaladyr and his times.

POEM LIV.

YMARWAR LLUD BYOHAN.

Translation, Vol. i. p. 253.   Text, Vol. ii. p. 213.

This poem is placed by Mr. Stephens in the class of Predictive Poems of the twelfth century, probably from the allusion to the Mabinogi, called " Kyfranc Lludd and Llefelys " in line 11, but there is nothing predictive about it, and the name given has been shown to be inconclusive.

It is a curious poem, giving an account of an early colonisation or invasion of Britain. It has been supposed that the Coraniaid are alluded to, as they are said to have come in the reign of Ludd, but lines 13 and 17 show that the Romans are meant. Caswallawn, in whose reign, according to the Bruts, Julius Cæsar landed in Britain, was brother and successor to Ludd.

POEM LV.

KANU Y BYT MAWR.

Translation, Vol. i. p. 539.   Text, Vol. ii. p. 214.

This poem relates likewise to natural phenomena, and must be classed with the poems, Nos. iii. vii. xiii. xvii. and xxix.

The last four lines contain a formula which occurs twice in the poem No. vii.

POEM LVI.

KANU Y BYT BYCHAN.

Translation, Vol. i. p. 541.   Text, Vol. ii. p. 216.

This poem belongs to the same class with the preceding.—(S.)

V.

THE RED BOOK OF HERGEST.

This very valuable MS., in which so much of the ancient literature of Wales has been preserved, is now the property of Jesus College, Oxford, and is well known from the Mabinogion published by Lady Charlotte Guest having been taken from it.

This MS. was given to Jesus College in 1701 by Thomas Wilkins of Llanblethian, to whom it had been left by Dr. John Davies. Dr. John Davies obtained it in Glamorgan in 1634 from Louis Mansel of Margam, and it appears then to have belonged to the Margam family. The MS., however, takes its name from Hergest Court, a seat of the Vaughans, near Knighton, Radnor, and was probably compiled for them. A complete table of its contents will be found in the *Cambro-Briton*, vol. ii. p. 75.

It is a thick folio MS. consisting of 360 leaves of vellum, and has been written at different times, extending from the early part of the fourteenth to the middle of the fifteenth century.

It is written in double columns, and apparently in three different handwritings.

The first handwriting extends to column 999, and in this part of the MS. there is a chronology terminating with the year 1318. The second handwriting commences at column 999 with the "Brut y Saeson," terminating with the year 1376; and the same handwriting continues to column 1143, where a more modern hand begins.

In the first handwriting are the two poems "Kyvoessi Myrdin" and "Gwasgardgerd Vyrdin." In the second, all the other poems here printed; and the MS. contains, in the more modern hand, poems by bards who flourished from the eleventh to the middle of the fifteenth centuries. Among them is a poem beginning (column 1154) "Goruchel duw gylo," attributed to Taliessin, but which is the work of Jonas Athraw.—(S.)

POEM I.

KYVOESSI MYRDIN.

Translation, Vol. i. *p.* 462. *Text, Vol.* ii. *p.* 218.

This dialogue appears to have been called *Cyvocsi* (from *ocs*, an

age), or synchronism, from the chronological character of the compositions.—(E.)

STANZA II.

Line 3.—That is, supposing *eneichiad*, the word used here in
the original, to be from *anach*, one that is dull or slow.—(E.)

STANZA III.

Line 1.—" It is worthy of notice that Gwenddydd in this dialogue addresses Myrddin by the appellation of Llallogan, twin-
brother. . . ." Now this will explain a passage in the Life of St.
Kentigern, in which it is said that there was at the court of
Rydderch Hael a certain idiot, named *Laloicen*, who uttered pre-
dictions :—" In curia ejus quidam homo fatuus vacabulo Laloicen ;"
and in the *Scotochronicon* it is stated that this Laloicen was
Myrddin Wyllt. By connecting these several particulars, we find
an air of truth cast over the history of this bard, as regards the
principal incidents of his life, and there can be no reason to doubt
that some of the poetry attributed to him was actually his composition."—Rev. T. Price, *Literary Remains*, i. 143.—(E.)

STANZA IV.

Line 3.—In the opening verses it is pretty clear that a certain
amount of confusion has crept into the text, and this will appear
the more evident if we compare the readings of the Red Book with
those of the *Myvyrian Archæology*.—(E.)

STANZA VI.

Line 3.—Tawy is here the name of the river Tay. The old
name of the Tay was Tava, which comes from Gaelic *Tamh*, smooth,
of which *Taw* is the Cymric equivalent.—(S.)

STANZA VII.

Line 2.—Clyd is probably the Clyde. According to some of
the readings of the Myvyrian, this line may be rendered—

" The fosterer of song about the waters of Clyde."—(E.)

STANZA XXIX..

Line 1.—' *Gwledychawt* ' = Gwledychawd. The verbal termination *awd, awdd,* must, in many passages of this poem, have a future rather than a past meaning.—(E.)

Line 3.—' *Ysgwydwyn*,' from " Ysgwyd " (= Latin, *scutum*), a shield, and " gwyn," white. Some read it " Ysgwyddwyn," white-shouldered, from " Ysgwydd," the shoulder. In the Bruts we find this epithet applied to Æneas, the son of Anchises, and it is generally translated *white-shield* or *white-shielded*, but Mr. Taliessin Williams (*Iolo MSS.,* note, p. 332) says, that " after mature consideration " he is " induced to reject this hypothesis, conceiving that the word is ' Ysgwyddwyn,' or rather ' Ysgwydd-ddwyn,' being compounded of ' Ysgwydd,' *a shoulder,* and ' dwyn,' *to bear* or *carry away,* and that hence Æneas Ysgwyddwyn, signifies Æneas of *bearing-shoulder,* in allusion to his filial devotion in bearing away his father Anchises on his shoulders from the flames of Troy." To this explanation he supplements another, in which he proposes to give the latter part of the compound a metaphorical signification. " But if a figurative etymology be admitted (and it is certainly sustained by classic authority), we shall conclude that the last syllable of *Ysgwyddwyn* is radically *gwynn,* white, but signifying, metaphorically, *blessed* (as in the phrase " Gwynn ei fyd," blessed is he), and hence *pious,* an epithet so frequently applied to Æneas by Virgil, " Pius Æneas." But, unfortunately for these theories, Mr. Williams has overlooked the important fact that, in the case before us and in other instances, the epithet is applied to others who did not distinguish themselves in the way the Trojan hero is represented to have done.—(E.)

Stanza XXXIII.

Line 1.—' *Byd*,' which often means a state or condition ; the circumstances of a being or thing at a given time. Compare the compounds *advyd, blinvyd, gwynvyd, hawddvyd,* etc.—(E.)

Stanza XXXVI.

Line 2.—The Panton MS. has " armes," a presage or omen, for " ormes," oppression.—(E.)

Stanza XLI.

Line 6.—' *Bargotyein*,' from " Bargod," a border. The word

does not occur in existing Welsh dictionaries, but this is not the
only place in which it is found in Welsh writings.   In a work on
bardism, written about the beginning of the sixteenth century,
Bargodiain is explained to mean " a civil convention for the purpose of renewing and revising old statutes and forming new ones,
for reviewing old institutions and establishing new ones."   The
word has the appearance of a plural, but in the text before us the
verb is in the singular number.   ' *Bisswys*,' a word not found elsewhere.   The translator supposes it to be related to or possibly a
transcript for *buwys*, a form of the perfect tense of *bod* occasionally
met with.—(E.)

STANZA LI.

Line 3.—According to the Panton MS., as given in the various
readings of the Myvyrian—

" Seek no peace—it will not be to thee."—(E.)

STANZA LVII.

Line 3.—The white or blessed cavalier.—(E.)

STANZA LIX.

Line 1.—The meaning of ' *Adrasdil*,' here rendered " prognos-
tication," is not very obvious.   Dr. Owen Pughe (*Welsh Dict.*)
explains it by " the thought of the foe," and in this passage, which
he subjoins " the infernal thought," but, *s. v.* " Gogan," his
rendering is " promised ills."   In both places he reads "Andrasdyl,"
or "Andrasdl," as if derived from "Andras ;" but both in the
text before us and that printed in the Myvyrian, the word is spelt
" Adrasdil " without any *n.*—(E.)

STANZA LXII.

Line 1.—' *Ehelaeth*,' extensive, spacious, large, abundant—an
epithet not commonly applied to persons.—(E.)

Line 2.—Literally, mead-nourished.—(E.)

STANZA LXIII.

Line 3.—Two-halved youth.—(E.)

Stanza LXXXI.

Line 3.—" Gwynedd will be men to him."—*Panton MS.*—(E.)

Stanza LXXXIII.

Line 3.—There is evidently a gap in this line as it stands in the Red Book, but the deficiency is supplied by the Myvyrian, which reads—

" Penaeth da ei faeth ada fydd."—(E.)

Stanza LXXXV.

Line 2.—If '*gorwynt*' here is = *gorvynt*, then the translation would be—

" Beli Hir and his men of Ambition."—(E.)

Line 3.—' *Gynt ;* ' see note, p. 335.

Stanza LXXXIX.

I can hardly pretend to understand this stanza, and it is evident from the confused state of the text, that some of the earlier transcribers must have felt its difficulties.—(E.)

Stanza XCI.

Line 4.—The city of iniquity. According to another reading, " Caer Ganwedd," the city of bright aspect.—(E.)

Stanza XCIII.

Line 3.—Or, " He will disperse the tumult of the Brithwyr :" Myvyrian readings.—(E.)

Stanza XCVII.

Line 4.—Or, " Broke all the order of men," according to the Myvyrian copy. Probably " torrynt " here should be read " torrant," will break.—(E.)

Stanza XCIX.

Line 2.—The Myvyrian marginal reading has—

" And the hand of an unbaptized person."—(E.)

Stanza CIII.

Line 3.—In the Panton MS. " Cyneddaf."—(E.)

Stanza cvii.

This stanza has the appearance of having suffered greatly at the hands of transcribers, and the preceding one does not seem to be in a much better state.—(E.)

Stanza cxxviii.

The first line appears to have no connection with the remainder of the stanza, and is altogether out of character with the rest of the Cyvoesi. In the Myvyrian it forms the beginning of a stanza not found in the Red Book.—(E.)

POEM II.

Gwasgardgerd Vyrdin yny Bed.

Translation, Vol. i. *p.* 478. *Text, Vol.* ii. *p.* 234.

' *Gwasgargerdd*,' from " gwasgar," to scatter, spread, or disperse, meaning either a song of scattering or dispersing, or, which is more probable, a song composed of scattered or unconnected subjects. The term has generally been rendered " a song of prediction," " a predictive poem." The composition under consideration is certainly of a predictive or prognosticating character ; but there does not appear to be anything in the *name*, apart from other considerations, that could suggest that translation.

This poem, as printed in the first volume of the *Myvyrian Archæology*, contains several stanzas not found in the Red Book copy ; and these were probably added to it after the compilation of that volume.—(E.)

Stanza i.

Line 3.—' *Eurdein*.' This name, in the marginal copy of the *Myvyrian Archæology*, appears as " Eurdeyrn," the golden sovereign. —(E.)

Stanza iv.

Line 1.—Compare the following couplet of Llywarch Hen :—

> " Penn a borthaf tu mordwyt,
> Oed ysgywt ar y wlat, oed olwyn ygkat."

> " A head I bear by the side of my thigh, that was a shield over his country, and a wheel in battle."—(E.)

STANZA VI.

Line 4.—'*Aber Hodni*,' now Aber Honddu, the Welsh name of Brecon, situated on the confluence of the rivers Honddu and Usk, in a beautiful open valley. The castle was built A.D. 1094 by Bernard Newmarch, who wrested the country from the hands of the Welsh princes. It was afterwards considerably increased and improved by the last Humphrey de Bohun, Earl of Hereford and governor of Brecon.—(E.)

STANZA VII.

Line 2.—'*Pengarn*,' sometimes called "Nant Pengarn," is a river in Monmouthshire. "Here Henry II., passing the ford of Nant Pengarn, discouraged the Britons, who relied too much on their oracle Merlinus Sylvester, who had said that when a strong prince with a freckled face should pass that ford the British forces should be vanquished."—*Lewis Morris (MS.)*—(E.)

STANZA VIII.

Line 2.—'*Mur Castell*,' called also Tomen y Mur, is supposed to be the *Mons Heriri* of the Romans, the site of which is situated in the western extremity of the parish of Maentwrog, in Ardudwy, Merionethshire. In the year 1111, according to *Brut y Tywsogion*, Henry I., with the combined forces of England and Scotland, marched as far as this place against Gruffydd ab Cynan; and, though the king cannot be said to have gained the victory, the expedition resulted in a peace concluded between him and the prince.—(E.)

STANZA IX.

Line 3.—By '*Cargein*' Canterbury is probably intended, which in Welsh is called Caergaint. According to another reading—"Ni cheidw ev dinas Kaergein" = "he will not keep the city of Caergain."—(E.)

STANZA XIII.

Line 1.—'*Byd*,' the word used here in the original, though it primarily and generally means the *world*, not unfrequently signifies a state or condition, a particular mode of being—as in the common expression, "gwyn ei vyd"—*i.e.* happy in his state or condition; blessed or happy is he.—(E.)

Stanza xxi.

Line 1.—Instead of '*Kyuelin*,' we should perhaps read " Kyn-velyn," the personal name Cynvelyn.   The whole verse is obscure.
—(E.)

Line 11.—There is a proverb to the same effect :—

"Gwell im crywyn no dan fuddelw."

" One coulter is better than two cowhouse posts."—(E.)

Stanza xxiv.

Line 1. Aber Avon, or Aber Avan, in Glamorganshire.

Line 2.—'*Hinwedon.*' Where or what this is I know not. The text has "hinwedon," but the Myvyrian copy has the forms "hinuedon" and "hynfyddon" besides.—(E.)

Stanza xxv.

Line 1.—'*Aber Dwfr*' = the confluence of water.   Here it stands for the name of some particular place.—(E.)

Stanza xxvi.

Line 1.—For '*hyrri*' we should here undoubtedly read "byrri," which is the reading in the Rev. E. Davies's MS., as it is evident the Burry, which contributes to form the estuary of the Burry, sometimes called Aber Llychwyr, between the counties of Glamorgan and Caermarthen, is the river intended.   It rises in Gower, and is but a small stream compared with the Llychwyr.   On this estuary the town of *Leucarum* once stood.—(E.)

Stanza xxvii.

Line 1.—For '*Aber y don*' the Rev. E. Davies's copy has "Aber *Peryddon*," which is one of the old names of the river Dee.

"Mae brenddwyd am *Beryddon*.
Yr ai gaer hir ar gwr hon."—*Indur. Aled.*—(E.)

Line 6.—It is observable that "Carav" or "Caraw" does not rhyme with "wylyon" in the preceding line ; and this peculiarity leads to the supposition that we should read "Caron" instead, which is possibly the same river as the *Carawn* mentioned by Nennius, which has by some been identified with the Carron in Scotland.—(E.)

POEM III.

Translation, Vol. i. *p. 590. Text, Vol.* ii. *p. 237.*

This poem concludes with the following sentence :—

"Tyssilio, the son of Brochwael Ysgythrog, composed these verses concerning Gwrnerth's coming to perform his devotions with Llewelyn the saint, his companion ; and they are called the colloquy of Llewelyn and Gwrnerth."

Tyssilio, or Tysilio, was an eminent saint and writer who flourished about the middle of the seventh century, being the son of Brochwael Ysgythrog ab Cyngen ab Cadell Deyrnllwg, Prince of Powys. He is said to have been Bishop of Llanellwy or St. Asaph, and is supposed to have been the immediate successor of St. Asaph, to whom he was cousin in the first degree. He was a bard, and is reported to have written an ecclesiastical history of Britain, which, if it ever existed, appears to be now lost. St. Tysilio is the founder and patron saint of the following churches :—Meivod and Llandysilio in Montgomeryshire, Llandysilio and Bryn Eglwys in Denbighshire, Llandysilio in Anglesey, Llandysilio yn Nyved in Caermarthenshire, Llandysilio Gogor in Cardiganshire, Sellack and Llansilio in Herefordshire. He was commemorated November 8."—Williams' *Eminent Welshman, s. v.* "Tysilso."

The only remnant of poetry attributed to Tyssilio is the preceding dialogue, which, in its present form at least, cannot be much older than the MS. in which it is preserved.

Llewelyn, the son of Tegonwy ab Teon ab Gwineu da i Freuddwyd, was one of the many Welsh saints that lived in the sixth century. He founded a religious house at Trallwng or Welshpool, in Montgomeryshire, and ended his days at the monastery of Bardsey. Gurnerth is stated by some authorities to be his son, and by others his brother, which is more probable. Both saints were commemorated April 7. See "Achau y Saint" in *Iolo MSS.*—(E.)

POEM IV.

Translation, Vol. i. *p.* 586.   *Text, Vol.* ii. *p.* 241.

This poem resembles the previous poem, and is ranged with it.

POEM V.

Translation, Vol. i. *p.* 569.   *Text, Vol.* ii. *p.* 245.

The proverbial triplets of which this composition consists are sometimes called *Bidiau* (from *bid*, the imperative form of the substantive verb *bod*), and may be translated "fiats." They are so called from *bid* being the first word in almost every line.—(E.)

STANZA II.

Line 1.—" Because then the swine would have acorns without his being at any trouble."—*Pughe.*

Swine are known to be very sleepy in windy weather; and this might be viewed as another cause of joy to swineherds.—(E.)

STANZA IV.

Line 2.—' *Bleid* ' of the original is generally read ' blaidd,' which signifies a wolf; but I take it to be " plaid " (*dim.* pleiden), that which separates, a partition, a wall, a hurdle or wattle. The softening of the initial *p* into *b* is in unison with the rest of the composition, and the only thing that militates against taking it in this sense is, that the final letter is *d* not *t;* but this may be an error of a transcriber taking it to be the same word as ' bleid ' in the sixth and eighth verses.—(E.)

STANZA VIII.

Line 3.—Alluding, I suppose, to the lightness of the steed's tread. Compare also stanza ii. line 3. Pughe very appropriately remarks that these two lines seem very obscure. His translation of them is as follows :—

" Let the tender grain be pressed at the roots,
    The tender grain be pressed when deposited in the ground."

But for "gwawn," gossamer, the ground, he evidently reads "gwan," weak or tender.—(E.)

STANZA XIV.

A line is here omitted in the Red Book, but is supplied by the Myvyrian copy :—

"Bid llym eithin."

"Let the furze be prickly."—(E.)

POEM VI.

Translation, Vol. i. *p.* 571. *Text, Vol.* ii. *p.* 247.

STANZA I.

Line 1.—' *Gnawd* ' (from *nawd*, nature, and allied to the Latin *natus* or *gnatus*), natural, congenial, usual, customary, habitual, common ; what is generally seen or observed in the ordinary course of events. It is sometimes written *cnawd*, and *nawd* without the prosthesis is met with in the same sense.—(E.)

POEM VII.

Translation, Vol. i. *p.* 573. *Text, Vol.* ii. *p.* 249.

STANZA I.

Line 1.—' *Calangauaf*,' the calends of winter, or the first day of November. *Calanmai*, the calends of May, is the first day of summer.—(E.)

STANZA VI.

The characteristics of winter and summer are curiously jumbled together in this triplet. It should be, as we find it elsewhere :—

"Calan Mai cain gyfrau adar,
Hir ddydd, ban cogau."

"On the first of May, gay the plumage of birds,
Song the day, loud the cuckoos."—(E.)

2 F

POEM VIII.

Translation, Vol. i. *p.* 574. *Text, Vol.* ii. *p.* 250.

STANZA IV.

Line 3.—' *To a youth,*' or to a servant.—(E.)

POEM IX.

Translation, Vol. i. *p.* 576. *Text, Vol.* ii. *p.* 251.

STANZA VIII.

Line 2.—' *Crwybr* ' is used in many parts of Wales for rime or hoar-frosting, not recorded in the Dictionaries.—(E.)

STANZA XXV.

Line 2.—' *Geuvel* ' = " gvevel " (*Black Book,* p. 30), = *gwywel* from *gwyw,* withered.—(E.)

POEM X.

Translation, Vol. i. *p.* 580. *Text, Vol.* ii. *p.* 255.

STANZA IV.

Line 2.—' *Tuawc* ' here must be a misscript for " Cuawc."—(E.)

STANZA XXIII.

This and the preceding stanza are very obscure, and possibly corrupted by transcribers.

STANZA XXVI.

Line 1.—' *Cewig,*' from *Caw,* a band—a badge or distinction. Bardd *Caw* = a graduated bard, or one that won the band of his order. " Cyrchyniad Cewig," = cyrchynvardel Caw, a graduated itinerant bard or minstrel. The text of this verse is not in a satisfactory state.—(E.)

STANZA XXIX.

Line 1.—*The son of sickness.*' " There is a doubt whether this is an epithet for the bards, or a proper name ; it has been taken for the latter.   The original (mackwy mabklaf), if written a compound word, as mabglav, or *sick for a son ;* if uncompounded, as *mab claf,* it implies the sick son, sick man, or the man of sickness.   According to some MSS., Llywarch had a son called *Mabclav ;* but perhaps it is making the epithet a proper name by mistake."— *Dr. Pughe.*—(E.)

POEM XI.

Translation, Vol. i. p. 326.   *Text, Vol. ii. p.* 259.

STANZA 1.

Line 1.—Owen Pughe translates the opening line as follows :—

" Before I appeared with crutches I was eloquent in my complaint ;"

and Carnhuanavc, thus :—

" Before I became hoary-headed and crutch-supported I was expert in speech."

It is difficult to conceive how " cain faglawg " of the original can possibly bear the meaning here given to it.   " Cain " signifies fair or beautiful, and " cain faglawg " (if we derive " baglawg " from " bagl " in the sense of a crutch) would mean beautifully or elegantly crutched, words implying a compliment which the bard is by no means disposed to pay to his appearance in his helpless old age.   Though not so stated in our dictionaries, the word " bagl " (pl. baglau) is frequently used for one of the human limbs ; as, for instance, in the phrase " cerdded ar ei bedair bagl " = to go on all fours ; and the adjective " baglawg " or " baglog," in the sense of limbed or membered, is equally common.   Assuming, then, that " cyn " is = cynn = cynt, and that " baglawg " is used in the acceptation just indicated, the rather perplexing expression " cain faglawg " will bear the translation which is above given it, and which has the appearance of being quite in accordance with the spirit of the poem.   The often-repeated expression—" baglan bren " —wooden crook or crutch, with which several of the verses begin, does not seem inconsistent with this view, it being not unnatural for the bard to contrast his agile limbs in his youthful days with his wooden crutch, by which he is now supported.—(E.)

STANZA II.

Line 3.—A portion of the old principality of Powys was called Powys Wynva, or Powys the Paradise.—(E.)

STANZA XXIV.

Line 3.—This line has many different readings, but none of them can be considered satisfactory.—(E.)

STANZA XXIX.

Line 2.—The word here translated *hart* is *cann* in the original, but *carw*, hart, a stag, is intended, as is evident from the following passage in the Black Book, p. 49 :—

> " Briuhid taglan gan
> Garn *carw* culgrum cam."—(E.)

STANZA XXXIV.

Line 1.—For '*Dywaes*' we should evidently read " Dywas" (gwas), to rhyme with " Rylas" and " Nas."—(E.)

STANZA XXXV.

Line 2.—For '*Athuc*,' the reading in the Red Book, some MSS. have " Arthur," and the line has generally been rendered

> " Arthur did not retreat."—(E.)

STANZA XXXIX.

Line 1.—' *Tyllwras* ' = tyllbras. Possibly " longshanks " may give the meaning which the bard intended.—(E.)

STANZA XL.

Line 2.—A similar comparison is used by Aneurin, p. 263—

> " Ruthyr eryr en ebyr pan llythywit."—(E.)

STANZA XLIV.

Line 2.—The Red Book has " llu kyndrwyn," but in the verses of the Warriors' Graves, p. 30, where the grave of Gwen ap Llywarch is recorded, the corresponding expression is " lv kegrun = llu cyngryn " of the Myvyrian copy in this place. The rhyme is conclusive against " kyndrwyn " being the right reading.—(E.)

Stanza lii.

Line 3.—That the word as it originally stood must have been *llumon*, though in the text before us it is corrupted into *luuon*, is evident from the succeeding stanza, in which the concluding line is the same, except that the epithet *wynn* bestowed on Pyll and Sawell, a word of the same import with *llumon*, is used instead of it. —(E.)

Stanza lix.

Line 3.—The meaning is obscure.—(E.)

Stanza lxv.

Line 1.—'*Rhudd*' (ruddy) is here taken for a personal name. '*Eiryd.*' This word is possibly an error for *arhudd* (arhuddo) to cover or conceal, which is here adopted. Some copies have "ni seirudd," and others "ny sevryd."—(E.)

Stanza lxvii.

Line 3.—For '*Dwc*' of the Red Book we should undoubtedly read "Duawg" with the Myvyrian copy. Duawg was, according to Pughe, one of the sons of Llywarch Hen.—(E.)

POEM XII.

Translation, Vol. i. *p.* **355.** *Text, Vol.* ii. *p.* **267.**

Stanza i.

Line 1.—"In the original '*Ynhwch*,' or the *Ashen Thruster ;* and which is also a proper name of men ; and it has been taken by some to be so in this poem ; but by taking into consideration all the passages wherein the word occurs, it seems most natural to take it in the sense as if the bard was addressing his spear, and bent on revenging the death of his friend."—*Owen Pughe.*

In accordance with this view Pughe renders the opening couplet to this effect :—

"Let me be guided onward, thou ashen spear of death, fierce
Thy look in the mutual conflict."

That *Unhwch* (for the form *Ynhwch* is not supported by any authority) is a personal name can admit of little doubt, the word

being nowhere found as an appellative. Unhwch Unarchen is recorded (*Iolo MSS.* p. 73) as one of three chief bards of Maelgwn
Gwynedd in the sixth century, the other two being Mynach ab
Nywmon (or Mydnaw) and Maeldav ab Unhwch. And the memory
of a person bearing the same name, whether identical or not with
the contemporary of Llywarch Hen, or with the son of Unarchen,
is preserved in Caer *Unhwch,* or Caer *Unwch,* near Dolgelley in
Merionethshire.

"This elegy has suffered by transcribing, as may be seen by the
various readings ; but whether the reading adopted is the best must
be left to the Welsh critics."—*Owen Pughe.*

Pughe translated not from the Red Book, but from a more
modern transcript, which is printed in the *Myvyrian Archæology.*
—(E.)

Stanza IV.

Line 1.—' *Eryr Gâl*' in the original. *Gâl* signifies a *Gaul,* and
also an enemy (hence *galon, gelyn, gelynion*) ; thus it seems that the
Belgic Gauls were the earliest and greatest molesters of the *Cymry ;*
hence a *Gaul* and an enemy were considered as synonymous."—
Owen Pughe.

Gâl is likewise the Welsh form of *Gallia,* the country of the
Gauls or Galli. It also signifies an open or champaign country, a
plain ; and in this sense it appears to be related to, as well as synonymous with, *ial.* See Owen Pughe's *Dictionary, s. v.* " Gal."—(E.)

Stanza V.

This stanza is seemingly incomplete in the middle line, and is
altogether very obscure.—(E.)

Stanza XI.

Line 1.—The original " cledd" signifies the left hand or side
as well as a sword.

"Argledd y canghellawr," on the left of the chancellor.—*Welsh
Laws.*—(E.)

Stanza XIII.

Line 3.—"A common exclamation amongst the Britons."—
Pughe.

STANZA XXIII.

Line 2.—'*Arwydd*,' a sign or token ; any memorial to mark the spot.—(E.)

STANZA XXVIII.

Line 1.—" Or, perhaps, more literally *the hidden or mysterious thing of the world;* any great exploit a warrior was to accomplish to establish his character. In the age of chivalry the *Anoethau* came to signify the impossibilities that were enjoined to be performed by knights of romance."—*Pughe.* A long train of these Anoethau will be found detailed in the Mabinogi of Kilhwch and Olwen.—*Guest's Mab.* vol. ii. pp. 197-318. This is an obscure stanza, as might be suspected from the number of the various readings. Pughe says that the brother alluded to is Urien, as he was the brother of Eurddyl, whom the bard addresses here.—(E.)

STANZA XXIX.

Line 2.—" Alluding to the two uses made of the horn—to sound the alarm of war, and to drink the mead at feasts."—*Pughe.*

STANZA XL.

Line 1.—" This probably is the Morgant by whose instigation Urien was murdered."—*Pughe.*

STANZA XLV.

Line 3.—'*Llovan Llawdivro*,' otherwise called Llovan Llawdino or Llawdivo, is recorded in the Triads as the author of one of the three " anvad gyflavar," or detested assassinations of the island of Britain, in killing Urien, the deed alluded to in this place.—(E.)

STANZA XLIX.

Line 3.—This line is omitted in the Red Book. It is supplied from the *Myvyrian Archæology.*—(E.)

STANZA LII.

Line 3.—" The original of this passage is rather equivocal, as it might be rendered, the gifts bestowed by Urien ; however, it is intended to signify the contrary ; or the gifts and contributions of the country of Reged to their prince."—*Pughe.*

Something equivalent to "firebote" given to the prince is probably intended.—(E.)

POEM XIII.

Translation, Vol. i. p. 584.   *Text, Vol. ii. p.* 273.

" An exhortation to Maenwyn, a young warrior, who, it seems, had been commanded to capitulate and deliver up his arms. Llywarch endeavours to encourage him to resist the offer, and show his fidelity to Maelgwn."—*Pughe.*

STANZA II.

Line 1.—' *Yth erbyn,*' the expression in the original, may signify " to receive " or " entertain thee," as well as " to meet " or " oppose thee ; " but the use of " yth erlit," " to pursue thee," in the next verse, seems to determine the sense in which " yth erbyn " should be taken here.—(E.)

Line 2.—' *Jeuenctid,*' like its English equivalent, *youth,* denotes both the early part of life and young persons considered collectively. —(E.)

Line 3.—The original here, and in the following stanza, is " gesseil," the import of which is not clear in this connection. " Cesail," in its usual acceptation, signifies the armpit ; and, metaphorically, the region under the arm, the bosom, and also a nook or corner ; hence " ceseilio," to take under the arm, to take to the bosom ; to shelter or harbour.   The various readings in the Myvyrian, which give " gasseil " in one place, and " gossail " in the other, afford us no assistance to arrive at the right meaning.   The word is rendered " foe," on the supposition that it is a mistake for " gassawl " (casawl), hateful, odious ; from " cas," hatred ; hateful, odious ; a hateful one, an enemy.

> " *Casawl* yw'r gwr a'i ceisiai,
>   A dannod ei bod mewn bai."
>   *D. ab Darydd Llwyd.*

" Odious is the man that would seek her, and insinuate that she is in error."

"Casai," especially in its plural form "caseion," is in common use for a hater or an enemy.

"Kyssueil," in the fifth stanza, is assumed to be a transcriber's mistake for *cyssyl*, advice or counsel.—(E.)

STANZA V.

Line 3.—"The original is *maer;* of the same import as the English bailiff; the head officer of a town, district, or farm."— *Pughe.*

STANZA VI.

Line 3.—"This seems intended as a pun upon the name of the youth. *Maenwyn* implies *having the nature* or *hardness of a stone;* and still the poet thought that the *stone* that he was speaking of wanted a little more hardening."—*Pughe.*

STANZA VII.

Line 2.—'*Celwrn*' is a pail or bucket; but may possibly signify here a case or cover.—(E.)

Line 3.—"A sword is here described; but the name designedly omitted."—*Pughe.*

POEM XIV.

Translation, Vol. i. *p.* 266. *Text, Vol.* ii. *p.* 274.

This poem appears also in the Black Book, No. xvii.

POEM XV.

Translation, Vol. i. *p.* 433. *Text, Vol.* ii. *p.* 277.

The fourteen principal battles ("pedair prif gad ar ddeg") of Cadwallawn are enumerated in this elegy; but it is remarkable that it contains no undoubted allusion to the important battles which he fought in the north of England, unless they are reckoned among the sixty skirmishes ("cyfarfodydd"), a supposition hardly supported by probability. All the places mentioned by the bard, except one or two the situations of which are doubtful, are within the present limits of the Principality.

Stanza I.

Line 1.—Before he came to *his end* or *death* appears to be meant. The stanza is seemingly incomplete, a whole line being wanting.—(E.)

Stanza II.

Line 1.—The original has no verb expressed in this and similar instances, and a more strictly literal translation would be—"The camp (or encampment) of Cadwallawn on Caint," etc.—(E.)

Line 4.—'*Caint*' is the Welsh form, or rather origin, of *Kent* (cantium); but as the preposition *ar*, on, not *yn*, in, is used, it is highly probable that a *river* is intended, and by some it has been supposed that the Kent in the north of England is the one referred to. It may, however, be stated that there is a Caint in Anglesey, which, after joing the Cevni nearly opposite Llangristiolis, falls into Malldraeth Bay on the southern side of the island. The name has also been compared with *Cain*, an appellation borne by two rivers in the Principality—the one in Merioneth and the other in Montgomeryshire.—(E.)

Stanza III.

Line 1.—'*Ar ydon*.' Some transcripts have "ar y don"—that is, on the wave, or near the sea. What river, if any, is intended, it is difficult to ascertain. As far as the mere name is concerned, it may be identified with the *Ithon*, Eithon, or Ieithon, which falls into the Wye about seven miles above the town of Builth, Breconshire.—(E.)

Stanza IV.

Line 2.—'*Digoll Vynydd*,' or "Mynydd Digoll," Long Mountain in Montgomeryshire. This battle was fought between Cadwallawn and Edwin of Northumbria, and is recorded in the Triads one of the "three discolourings of the Severn," which was occasioned by the flow of the blood of the slain into it.

"On this mountain may be said to have expired the liberties of Wales, for here was the last contest against the power of our conqueror. After the death of Llewelyn the northern Welshmen set up Madoc, cousin to our slain prince; who assembled a great army, and after several eminent victories at Carnarvon, near Denbigh, Knockin, and again on the marches, was here overthrown, in

1294, by the collected power of the Lord Marchers, after a well-fought and long-contested engagement."—Pennant, *Tours*, iii. 208.

The mention of " Digoll Vynydd" in this early poem, proves the erroneousness of Pennant, who states that the mountain derived its appellation from the following circumstance :—" On this mountain Henry VII. mustered the friends who promised to join him from North Wales and Shropshire, and did not find one who had failed of his appointment. On which account the Welsh call it *Digoll*, or *Without Loss;* the English name it the Long Mountain."

The number of daily skirmishes, as given here, is an instance of poetic embellishment.—(E.)

Stanza v.

Line 1.—The Severn. The battle of the Severn and on the further side of Dygen, and the burning of Meigen, should be reckoned as forming but one action, being the fourth in the catalogue..—(E.)

Line 8.—'*Dygen*' is, in all probability, Dygen Freiddin, a conical and picturesque mountain in the valley of the Severn, below Welshpool in Montgomeryshire. Some are of opinion that this mountain was the site of the last battle which Caractacus fought against the Romans under Ostorius.—(E.)

Line 3.—The battle of Meigen, in which Edwin fell, is mentioned by Nennius, and in the *Annales Cambriæ;* but Bede (*Hist. Eccles.* ii. 20) gives Haethfelth (supposed to be Hatfield in Yorkshire) as the place of his death ; hence it has been assumed that Meigen and Haethfelth are one and the same place, but it is sufficiently evident that the Meigen of Llywarch Hen must be somewhere in Powys, and at no great distance from the Severn.—(E.)

Stanza vi.

Line 1.—' *Gwy*,' the Wye.—(E.)

Stanza vii.

Line 1.—" In the upper part of Gwaen Llwg, Monmouth shire."—*Pughe.*

STANZA VIII.

Line 1.—There are two rivers of this name—the one for a considerable part of its course divides the county of Caermarthen from that of Pembroke, and falls into Caermarthen Bay at Langharn; and the other, after draining a portion of Glamorganshire, disembogues into the Bristol Channel at Cardiff. Dr. Owen Pughe remarks on this passage, that "nearly opposite Llandaff, on the other side of the Tav, there are the ruins of a British camp in a place called Gwaen y Trodau. The tradition of the neighbourhood is that the Saxons suffered a great defeat there."—(E.)

STANZA IX.

Line 1.—A river in Glamorganshire, on which the town of Swansea, or Aber Tawy, is situated.—(E.)

STANZA X.

Line 1.—' Caew,' ' Caeo,' or ' Caio,' a hundred in the upper part of Caermarthenshire; and also a parish in that hundred sometimes called "Cynwyl Gaeo," from the church being dedicated to St. Cynwyl. The church is seven miles west-north-west from Llandovery. "Caer Gaeo" is now a mere village, but it appears to have been formerly a place of importance, and many Roman remains have been found in the neighbourhood. The name occurs as "Cair Caiau" and "Kaircaiau" in the *Liber Landavensis.*—(E.)

STANZA XI.

Line 1.—' Cowyn,' or ' Cywyn,' a river that falls into the Tav at Aber Cowyn, near St. Clare's, Caermarthenshire. —(E.)

STANZA XII.

Line 2.—' Penvro,' the county of *Pembroke;* that is, Land's End or headland. The encampments on the Cowyn and in Penvro are to be regarded as one battle, being the tenth in the bard's enumeration.—(E.)

STANZA XIII.

Line 1.—The Teivi, for the greater part of its course, forms the boundary between Cardiganshire and Caermarthenshire, and enters the sea a little below the town of Cardigan, which, from this circumstance, is called in Welsh, Aber Teivi.—(E.)

Stanza xiv.

Line 1.—'*Duffyrd.*' This river is unknown. Pughe suggests that it may be a mistake for the Dyvi or Dovey, between the counties of Cardigan and Merioneth.—(E.)

Stanza xv.

Line 2.—'*Bro Dunawd,*' or Cantrev Dunodig, a district comprehending the sea-coast of Merioneth, and part of Carnarvonshire.

Stanza xvi.

Line 21.—Or *Meinin*, as some copies have it. Pughe says, "perhaps where the abbey of *Maenen* [Maenan] stood, near Llanrwst," but more probably it denotes some river, no longer recognised under that name.—(E.)

Stanza xviii.

Line 3.—'*Elved.*' There is a hundred of this name in the lower part of Caermarthenshire.—(E.)

POEM XVI.

Translation, Vol. i. p. 448. *Text, Vol. ii. p.* 279.

The first fifty-seven stanzas of this poem have been carefully translated by Dr. Guest in the *Archæologia Cambrensis*, ix. p. 142, and the translation has been, with his permission, adopted. The reader is referred to the notes by Dr. Guest on this part of the poem. The remaining stanzas have been translated by Mr. Silvan Evans.

Stanza lxvi.

Line 3.—'*Rei*' (apparently from the Latin *res, rei*) is sometimes used for riches, wealth, or treasure, as in the following passage of Gwalchmai's Ode to Owain Gwynedd :—

> " Teyrnain ni grain
> Ni grawn *rei.*"

That is, " A sovereign is he, who will neither cringe
nor hoard up *wealth.*"

The mediæval poets used their license to borrow words from the

Latin with great freedom. The bard no longer wore his gorgeous dress and golden torques ; but now, in the days of his misfortune, he has only a rude goatskin to shield him from cold. It was hardly worth his while to seek refuge in the mountains, as he had nothing valuable of which he might be deprived.—(E.)

Stanza LXVII.

Line 1.—'*Amhafal*,' which may here imply, similar, in like manner, after the same manner or fashion, just as. '*Avaerwy*.'—This river has not, as far as I am aware, been identified with any known stream.—(E.)

Line 2.—According to Lhuyd, the Trydonwy may be identical with the Roden in Shropshire.—(E.)

Line 3.—'*Twrch*.' There are many rivers in Wales called by this name. '*Marchnwy* :' the Marchnwy and the Elwydden are unknown.—(E.)

Stanza LXVIII.

Line 3.—"The Alwen, or very foamy water, falls into the Dee a little above Corwen."—*Owen Pughe.*

Stanza LXIX.

Line 3.—This can scarcely be a correct form. There are various readings, but none satisfactory.—(E.)

Stanza LXX.

This appears to be only a different reading of the preceding stanza.—(E.)

Stanza LXXI.

Line 2.—'*Dwyryw*,' the Dee, according to Owen Pughe, but this is very questionable. There is *Dwyriw* in Montgomeryshire, which falls into the Severn at Berriw, about five miles from Welshpool.—(E.)

Stanza LXXIII.

Line 1.—'*Edeyrnion*,' a district in Merionethshire watered by the Dee.—(E.)

Line 3.—'*Uchant*,' a district in the upper part of Montgomeryshire. This stanza and portion of what follows appear to be interpolations, having, as far as I can see, no reference to Cynddylan. —(E.)

STANZA LXXIV.

This stanza, which consists of eight instead of three lines, seems to have been made up by the huddling together of three or more imperfect stanzas. Any consecutive sense is, therefore, hardly to be expected from such a jumble.—(E.)

STANZA LXXVI.

Line 1.—' *Ercal*,' now called High Ercal, near Shrewsbury.— (E.)

Line 3.—Unless ' *Macrysinal* ' is intended for Mae rhysonial," or " Mawr y sonial," I know not what it means.—(E.)

STANZA LXXVII.

Line 1.—' *Heledd* ' implies a brine or salt pit ; and it is also the name of several places ; and there were women of this name. " One of the daughters of Cyndrwyn was so called."—*Owen Pughe.*

Yn Heledd Wen and *Yn Heledd Ddu* are respectively the Welsh names of Nantwich and Northwich in Cheshire. The meaning of " Heled hwyedic ym gelwir," the expression in the original, which I have rendered as above, is not obvious. Lhwyd (*Arch. Brit.* p. 258, col. 3) supposes that the poet here speaks in the name of Heledd, one of the sisters of Cynddylan, which, if granted, does not remove the difficulty. Owen Pughe translates the passage (Llywarch Hen, p. 95) :—" Heledd henceforth shall I be called ; but in the *Welsh Dictionary* (*s. v.* " Hwyedec "), it is construed thus :— " I am called a filling brine-pit." Assuming that " hwyedec " (hwyedĭg) is the past participle of hwyhau, to lengthen, it cannot, without very considerable violence, be rendered " henceforth." In the Welsh Laws, the term *hwyedig* occurs several times for the male hawk, as in these instances :—

" Ef adele *huyedyc* hebawc y kan epenhebogyt pop guyl Uhyhaghel"—" He is to have a male hawk from the chief falconer every feast of St. Michael."—(Vol. i. p. 22.)

" Pedeir ar ugeint yw gwerth hwyedic "—" Twenty-four pence is the worth of a male hawk."—(Vol. i. p. 738.)

I have therefore construed " Heled hwyedic," the hawk of

Heledd, an expression which may be compared with "Eryr Eli" in other parts of the poem.—(E.)

STANZA LXXXVII.

Line 3.—'*Mevyl baryw*,' or disgrace of the beard, was a heinous crime; but of what nature has not been expressly defined.—*Owen Pughe.*

This and the three following stanzas are very obscure; a remark applicable to many other stanzas in this portion of this ancient poem.—(E.)

STANZA XCVI.

Line 2.—'*Pyrydyaw*' or "pyryrdyau" (which appears to be the more correct reading) = *pyrhyrddiaw*, from *pyr*, forward, and *hyrddiaw*, to push, thrust, or drive.—(E.)

Line 3.—Instead of '*tranc*,' dissolution, death, some MSS. have "tanc," peace, tranquillity. "A Frank would have no peace from his mouth."—(E.)

STANZA CI.

Line 2.—"The portion, most likely, of Maoddyn, the brother of Cynddylan, as it seems the share of each was called after its owner. So *Dyffryn Meisyr* and *Dyffryn Ffreuer* were the shares of the two daughters of *Cyndrwyn*."—*Owen Pughe.*

Lhwyd thinks that *Maoddyn* may possibly be identical with *Mwythig* or *Amwythig*, the modern Welsh appellation of Shrewsbury. Maes Maoddyn is probably the same as Maes Meueddawg, mentioned in "Englynion Beddau Milwyr," in the vicinity of which Elchwith is said to be interred.—(E.)

POEM XVII.

Translation, Vol. i. *p.* 341. *Text, Vol.* ii. *p.* 291.

Line 1.—'*Gogyfuerchyd*' (= *gogyverchydd*, from "cyvarch," to greet or salute freely) appears to be put in opposition to the person implied in the verbs preceding it, and not as the objects governed by them.—(E.)

Line 3.—How perishable gold and silver are, even when they do not fall into the hands of the spendthrift, compared with the lasting eulogy of the bard!—(E.)

Line 5.—'*Ieuaf*' (sometimes written *Ievav*), which signifies *youngest*, was not an uncommon name in former times.—(E.)

Line 6.—'*Kynnin*' I take to be a misscript for "kynniu" = *cynniv*, a conflict. '*Celuyd*' or '*keluyd*,' may be read either "celwydd," falsehood, or "celvydd," skilful, expert. The latter I believe is intended here, as well as in a subsequent passage of the poem, in which the form "kelwyd" occurs.—(E.)

Line 8.—There does not appear any reason why '*Kynin*' here should not be taken as a personal name.—(E.)

Line 9.—'*Aerven*' is an old name for the river Dee, which in Welsh is generally called *Dyvrdwy*. In an account of "The Principal Territories of Britain," printed in the *Iolo MSS.*, p. 86, and translated p. 476, it is stated that Gwynedd extends "from Cantrev Orddwyv to Menai, including also *Aerven* and Teyrnllwg;" and Teyrnllwg, from *Aerven* to Argoed Derwennydd." Madog ab Gronwy Gethin, in a poem on the sudden overflow of the Dee in the time of Owen Glyndwr (1404), applies the same name to the river:—

> "Garw distrych llwyth-wrych llaeth-wawr
> *Aerven* bengrech felen vawr."—(E.)

Line 10.—'*Seleu*' = Selev or Selyv, which is the Welsh form of *Solomon*, *Salomon*, or *Shalomo*. Selev or Selyv Ddoeth = Solomon the Wise. The name is common amongst the Welsh as early at least as the sixth century, at which period we find Selyv, son of Cynan Garwyn, mentioned among the chieftains; and Selyv, son of Geraint ab Erbin, among the saints.

> "Deu-lyvr a ddaeth i'm dwylaw,
> Llawn ddoeth, a dan well ni ddaw,—
> Syw-lyvr y Brerin *Selev*,
> A Llyfr pur Benadur nev."
> *Gronwy Owen.*—(E.)

Selev and Ceneu were sons of Llywarch Hen.—(S.)

2 G

Line 11.—That is, on account of the army (*llüyld*) mentioned in a preceding line.—(E.)

Line 22.—For '*torrit*,' I read "torrir," the future instead of the past.—(E.)

Line 24.—'*Mor a mynyd*' (= môr a mynydd), literally "sea and mountain ;" but the expression is often used simply for "sea and land."—(E.)

Line 29.—'*Eleri*,' a river in the upper part of Cardiganshire, which, after passing through the village of Tal y Bont, winds its course through Cors Vochno, and falls into the estuary of the Dovey opposite the town of Aberdovey. Where '*Chwilfynydd*' is I have not been able to ascertain.—(E.)

Line 37.—For '*Barnawc*' I read "Baruawc" (= barvawg, bearded), assuming that the middle letter was originally *u* and not *n ;* and the passage seems to imply that in consequence of the devastations of war, grown-up men would be so scarce, that the lines would have to be filled up almost entirely with beardless youth.—(E.)

Line 39.—The meaning apparently is, that Urien was the most generous man since Adam.—(E.)

Line 42.—'*Eu*' (their), the word used here in the original appears to be erroneously employed for "ei" (his). Some early transcriber, we may conjecture, finding the word commonly written *enw*, beginning with an *h*, assumed that the prosthetic letter owed its introduction to the influence of the preceding word, which he knew would be *eu* rather than *ei*, altered the pronoun accordingly, forgetting that *henw* is about as old and independent a form as *enw*. —(E.)

POEM XVIII.

Translation, Vol. i. *p.* 595.   *Text, Vol.* ii. *p.* 293.

No remarks occur upon this poem.

POEM XIX.

Translation, Vol. i. *p.* 492. *Text, Vol,* ii. *p.* 294.

Line 28.—The meaning of this line is not clear.—(E.)

POEM XX.

Translation, Vol. i. *p.* 490. *Text, Vol.* ii. *p.* 294.

Dr. Owen Pughe (*Welsh Dict. s. v.* "Mabon") attributes this poem to Golyddan, the bard of Prince Cadwallon ab Cadvan in the seventh century, but on what grounds does not appear.—(E.)

POEM XXI.

Translation, Vol. i. *p.* 493. *Text, Vol.* ii. *p.* 296.

Dr. Owen Pughe (*Welsh Dict. s. v.* "Cyweithi") attributes this poem to Adda Vras, a bard of the early part of the thirteenth century; but, *s. v.* "Cynferth," to Gwylym Ddu o Arvon, who flourished in the time of King Edward II., but it is not found among his compositions printed in the first volume of the *Myvyrian Archæology.* No portion of the genuine works of Adda Vras is known to be extant. Some of the words in this poem being illegible, it is impossible to give a full translation of every line.—(E.)

POEM XXII.

Translation, Vol. i. *p.* 290. *Text, Vol.* ii. *p.* 299.

Line 4.—'*Brithwyr*,' the speckled men or the Picts.—(S.)

POEM XXIII.

Translation, Vol. i. *p.* 284. *Text, Vol.* ii. *p.* 301.

This poem is interspersed with Latin lines, which seem to be fragments of Latin hymns.—(S.)

Line 10.—' *Gallwydel.*' Galloway was called in Gaelic *Gall-gaidel*, of which this is the Cymric equivalent. From Gallwyddel comes the Latin form Galweithia. This poem must have been written before Galloway became a part of the Anglic kingdom of Northumbria.—(S.)

Line 36.—The allusion to Lleu and Gwydion connects this poem with the alliance between the Brython and Gwyddyl alluded to in lines 89 and 90.—(S.)

Line 82.—The Myvyrian text reads "Gwyr Kelydon," men of Celyddon.—(S.)

The last part of this poem, from line 84, is contained in the Book of Taliessin. The variations between the two texts of this part of the poem are very trifling.—(S.)

Line 86.—' *Caer Govannon.*' In an old list of the churches of Linlithgow, printed by Theiner, appears "Vicaria de Gumanyn." The place meant is probably Dalmeny, on the Firth of Forth, formerly called Dumanyn.—(S.)

Line 90.—' *Diaerogyon,*' unwarlike, from *aer*, battle. The Book of Taliessin reads "*Diverogyon*," distillers, which is preferable. The Gwyddyl are called in the Cerdd y Veib Llyr "Diefyl diverogyon," in the Gododin "Deifr diverogyon," and here "Kyl diverogyon." Kyl may be translated furnace or kiln.—(S.)

POEM XXIV.

GOSYMDEITH LLEFOET WYNEBCLAWR.

Translation, Vol. i. *p.* 596. *Text, Vol.* ii. *p.* 304.

This composition, which is a versified collection of aphorisms or proverbs, is ascribed to Llevoed, surnamed "Wynebglawr," the flat or broad-faced, who is said to have flourished about the beginning of the tenth century. It is called *Gosymdaith*, or Viaticum, being the bard's stock of provisions for the journey through life. It is the only poem extant which bears the name of this poet.—(E.)

I.

MS. HENGWRT 536.

BONHED GWYR Y GOGLED YW HYN.

Vryen uab Kynuarch mab Meirchaѵn mab Gorust
Ledlѵm mab Keneu mab Coel.

Llywarch Hen mab Elidyr Lydanwyn mab Meirchaѵn mab
Gorust Ledlѵm mab Keneu mab Coel.

Clydno Eidin a Chynan Genhir a Chynuelyn Drѵsgyl a
Chatraѵt Calchuynyd meibon Kynnѵyt Kynnѵydyon mab
Kynuelyn mab Arthwys mab Mar mab Keneu mab Coel.

Dunaѵt a Cherwyd a Sawyl Penuchel meibyon Pabo
Post Prydein mab Arthwys mab Mar mab Keneu mab Coel.

Gѵrgi a Pheredur meibon Eliffer Gosgorduaѵr mab Arthwys
mab Keneu mab Coel.

Gwendoleu a Nud a Chof meibyon Keidyaѵ mab Arthwys
mab Mar mab Keneu mab Coel. ·

Trychan cledyf kynuerchyn a ttrychan ysgѵyt kynnѵdyon
.a ttrychan wayѵ coeling pa neges bynhac yd elynt iddi yn
duun.   Nyt amethei hon honno.

Ryderch Hael mab Tutwal Tutclyt mab Kedic mab
Dyuynwal Hen.

Mordaf mab Seruan mab Kedic mab Dyfynwal Hen.

Elffin mab Gѵydno mab Caѵrdaf mab Garmonyaѵn mab
Dyfynwal Hen.

Gauran mab Aedan Uradaѵc mab Dyuynwal Hen mab
Idnyuet mab Maxen Wledic amhcraѵdyr Ruuein.

Elidyr Mѵynuaѵr mab Gorust Priodaѵr mab Dyfynwal
Hen.

Huallu mab Tutuѵlch Corneu tywyssaѵc o Kernyѵ a
Dywana merch Amlaѵt Wledic y uam.

I.

TRANSLATION.

DESCENT OF THE MEN OF THE NORTH IS THIS.

I. Uryen son of Kynvarch son of Meirchawn son of Gorust Ledlum son of Keneu son of Coel.

II. Llywarch Hen son of Elidyr Lydanwyn son of Meirchawn son of Gorust Ledlum son of Keneu son of Coel.

III. Clydno of Eidyn and Chynan Genhir and Cynvelyn Drwsgl and Catrawt Calchvynyd, sons of Kynwyt Kynwydyon son of Kynvelyn son of Arthwys son of Mar son of Keneu son of Coel.

IV. Dunawt and Cerwyd and Sawyl Penuchel, sons of Pabo, the pillar of Prydein, son of Arthwys son of Mar son of Keneu son of Coel.

V. Gwrgi and Peredur, sons of Eliffer of the great retinue, son of Arthwys son of Keneu son of Coel.

VI. Gwendoleu and Nud and Cof, sons of Keidyaw son of Arthwys son of Mar son of Keneu son of Coel.

Three hundred swords (of the tribe) of Kynvarch, and three hundred shields of Kynwydyon, and three hundred spears of the tribe of Coel. Whatever object they entered into deeply—that never failed.

VII. Rydderch Hael son of Tutwal Tutclyt son of Kedic son of Dyfnwal Hen.

VIII. Mordaf son of Serfan son of Kedic son of Dyfnwal Hen.

IX. Elffin son of Gwydno son of Caurdaf son of Garmonyawn son of Dyfnwal Hen.

X. Gavran son of Aedan the treacherous, son of Dyfnwal Hen son of Idnyvet son of Maxen Guledic, Emperor of Rome.

XI. Elidyr Mwynfawr son of Gorust Priodawr son of Dyfnwal Hen.

XII. Huallu son of Tutvwlch of Cornwall, prince of Cornwall, and Dywana daughter of Amlawt Guledic was his mother.

II.

MS. HENGWRT 536.

TRIOED ARTHUR AE WYR.

Teir Lleithiclỽyth Ynys Prydein. Arthur yu pen teyrned ym Mynyỽ a Dewi yn pen ysgyb a Maelgỽn Gỽyned yn pen hyneif. Arthur yn pen teyrned yg Kelliwic yg Kerneỽ a Betwini esgob yn pen esgyb a Charadaỽc ureichuras yn pen hyneif. Arthur yn pen teyrned ym Pen Rionyd yny gogled a Chyndeyrn Garthwys yn pen esgyb a Gỽrthmỽl Wledic yn pen hyneif.

Tri Hael Ynys Prydein. Nudd Hael mab Senyllt; Mordaf Hael mab Seruan ; Ryderch Hael mab Tutwal Tutclyt.

Tri Gwyndeyrn Ynys Prydein. Run mab Maelgỽn; Ywein map Uryen a Ruaỽn Peuyr mab Deorath Wledic.

Tri Deifniaỽc Ynys Prydein. Gwalchmei mab Gỽyar a Llecheu mab Arthur a Rhiwallaỽn wallt Banadleṅ.

Tri Phost Cad Ynys Prydein. Dunaỽt mab Pabo Post Prydein a Gwallaỽc mab Leenaỽc a Chynfelyn Drỽsgyl.

Tri Tharỽ Caduc Ynys Prydein. Kynuarch Cat Caduc mab Kynnỽyt Kynỽytyon a Gwendoleu mab Keidyaỽ a Vryen mab Kynuarch.

Tri Tharỽ Unben Ynys Prydein. Elmỽr mab Cadeir a Chynhaual mab Argat ac Auaon mab Taliessin. Tri meib beird oedynt eu tri.

Tri Lledyf Unben Ynys Prydein. Llywarch Hen mab Elidyr Lydanwyn a Manawydan mab Llyr Lledyeith a Gỽgaỽn Gỽraỽn mab Peredur mab Eliffer Gosgorduaỽr.

Tri Unben Llys Arthur. Goronỽy mab Echell Uordỽytỽn a Chadreith mab Porthuaỽrgadu a Phleidur fflam.

Tri Unben Deiuyr a Brynych. Gall mab Disgyuedaỽt ac Ysgafnell mab Disgyuedaỽt a Diffydell mab Disgyfedaỽt. Tri meib Beird oedynt ell tri.

II.

TRIADS OF ARTHUR AND HIS WARRIORS.

I. Three tribe thrones of the Island of Prydain. Arthur the chief lord at Menevia, and David the chief bishop, and Maelgwyn Gwyned the chief elder. Arthur the chief lord at Kelliwic in Cornwall, and Bishop Betwini the chief bishop, and Caradawc Vreichvras the chief elder. Arthur the chief lord at Penrionyd in the north, and Cyndeyrn Garthwys the chief bishop, and Gurthmwl Guledic the chief elder.

II. Three generous ones of the Island of Prydain. Nud Hael son of Senyllt; Mordaf Hael son of Servan; and Ryderch Hael son of Tutwal Tutclyt.

III. Three fair lords of the Island of Prydain. Run son of Maelgwyn; Owen son of Urien; and Ruawn Pefyr son of Deorath Guledic.

IV. Three naturalists of the Island of Prydain. Gwalchmei son of Gwyar; and Llecheu son of Arthur; and Rhiwallon Gwallt Banadlen.

V. Three pillars of battle of the Island of Prydain. Dunawd son of Pabo, pillar of Britain; and Gwallawc son of Lleenawc; and Cynfelyn Drwsgl.

VI. Three bulls of battle of the Island of Prydain. Kynvarch Cat Caduc son of Kynnwyt Kynwytyon; and Gwendoleu son of Ceidyaw; and Uryen son of Kynvarch.

VII. Three bull princes of the Island of Prydain. Elmwr son of Cadeir; and Cynhafal son of Argat; and Afaon son of Taliessin. Three sons of bards were these three.

VIII. Three humble princes of the Island of Prydain. Llywarch Hen son of Elidyr Lydanwyn; and Manawydan son of Llyr Lledyeith; and Gwgawn Gwrawn son of Peredur son of Eliffer Gosgordvaur.

IX. Three princes of the Court of Arthur. Goronwy son of Echell Fordwyten; and Cadreith son of Porthfaurgaddu; and Fleidur Flam.

X. Three princes of Deira and Bernicia. Gall son of Desgyfedawt; and Ysgafnell son of Disgyfedawt; and Diffydell son of Disgyfedawt. Three sons of bards were these three.

Tri Gway6rud Beird Ynys Prydein. Tristuard Bard Vryen a Dygynel6 Bard Ywein a Mianuerdic Bard Cadwalla6n mab Catuan a ryha6t eil Morgant.

Tri Chynweissat Ynys Prydein. Carada6c mab Bran a Cha6rdaf mab Carada6c ac Owein mab Maxen Wledic.

Teir Llyghessa6c Ynys Prydein. Gereint mab Erbin ; Gwen6ynwyn mab Naf a March mab Meirchia6n.

Tri G6rduagla6c Ynys Prydein. Rineri mab Tang6n a Dinwaed Uagla6c a Phryder mab Dolor Deiuyr a Brynych.

Tri Huala6c Ynys Prydein. Catwaladyr Uendigeit a Run mab Maelg6n a Riwalla6n wallt Banadlen.

Tri Chaduarcha6c Ynys Prydein. Carada6c Ureichuras ; Menwaed o Arllechwed a Llyr Lluydda6c.

Tri Gallouyd Ynys Prydein. Greidia6l Galouyd mab Enuael Adran a Gweir G6rhyt Ua6r a Drystan Tall6ch.

Tri Ruduoa6c Ynys Prydein. Arthur a Run mab Beli a Morgant M6ynnua6r.

Tri Thaleicha6c Cad Ynys Prydein. Trystan mab Tall6ch a Huil mab Ca6 a Chei mab Kynyr Kynuarua6c ac un oed taleitha6c arnadunt wynteu ell tri, Bed6yr mab Pedra6t oed h6nn6.

Tri Gle6 Ynys Prydein. Tri meib Hayarnwed Urada6c ; Grudnei a Henpen ac Edena6c.

Tri Thraha6c Ynys Prydein. Sawyl ben uchel a Phasken mab Uryen a Run mab Eina6n.

Tri Ysgymyd Aereu Ynys Prydein. Gilbert mab Catgyf-fro ; Moruran eil Tegit a G6ga6n Cledyfrud.

Tri G6rdueichat Ynys Prydein. Trystan mab Tall6ch a getwis moch March mab Meircha6n tra aeth y meichat y erchi y Essyllt dyfot y gynadyl ac ef ; ac Arthur yn keissa6 unh6ch ae y t6yll, ae y treis, ac nys cauas a Phryderi mab P6yll am6yn a getwis moch Pendaran Dyued yn Glyn Cu6ch yn Emlyn a Choll mab Collurewy a getwis henwen h6ch Dallweir Dallben a aeth yg gordodo hyt ym penryn A6stin

XI. Three ruddy-speared bards of the Island of Prydain. Trist-vard bard of Urien; and Dygynelw bard of Owen; and Mainferdic, bard of Cadwallawn, son of Catfan; and they were sons of Morgant.

XII. Three supreme servants of the Island of Prydain. Caradawc son of Bran; and Caurdaf son of Caradawc; and Owen son of Maxen Guledic.

XIII. Three fleet owners of the Island of Prydain. Gereint son of Erbin; and Gwenwywnwyn son of Naf; and March son of Mer-chiaun.

XIV. Three strong-crutched ones of the Island of Prydain. Rineri son of Tangwn; and Tinwaed faglawc; and Pryder son of Dolor of Deira and Bernicia.

XV. Three fettered ones of the Island of Prydain. Cadwaladyr the blessed; and Run son of Maelgwyn; and Riwallan wallt Banadlen.

XVI. Three cavaliers of battle of the Island of Prydain. Cara-dawc freichfras; Menwaed of Arllechwed; and Llyr Lluydauc.

XVII. Three hostile ovates of the Island of Prydain. Greidiawl Galovyd, son of Enfael Adran; and Gweyr of great manliness; and Trystan son of Tallwch.

XVIII. Three red-spotted ones of the Island of Prydain. Arthur; and Run son of Beli; and Morgant Mwynfawr.

XIX. Three front leaders of battle of the Island of Prydain. Trystan son of Tallwch; and Huil son of Caw; and Cei son of Cynyr Cynfarfawc and one person was supreme over these three: Bedwyr son of Pedrawt was that one.

XX. Three heroes of the Island of Prydain. The three sons of Hayarnwed the treacherous: Grudnei and Henpen and Edenawc.

XXI. Three arrogant ones of the Island of Prydain. Sawyl penuchel; and Pasgen son of Uryen; and Run son of Einaun.

XXII. Three obstructors of slaughter of the Island of Prydain. Gilbert son of Catgyffro; Morfran son of Tegid; and Gwgun of the ruddy sword.

XXIII. Three powerful swineherds of the Island of Prydain. Trystan son of Tallwch, who kept the swine of March, son of Meir-chawn, while the swineherd went on a message to Essylt to desire a meeting with her, and Arthur desired one pig by deceit or by theft, and could not get it; and Pryderi, son of Pwyll, who kept the swine of Pendaran Dyfed in Glencuwch in Emlyn; and Coll son of Collfrewy, who kept the ancient sow of Dallweir Dalben, who went burrowing

yg Kerny6 ac yna ydaeth yny mor, ac yn Aber Torogi yg
Gwent iscoet ẏ doeth yr tir, a Choll mab Collurewy ac la6
yny gwrych pa fford bynhac ẏ kerdhei nac ar uor nac ar tir,
ac yn Maes Gwenith yg Gwent ẏ dodwes gwenithen a
gwenenen, ac er hynny y mae goreu lle y wenith y lle h6nn6,
ac odyna yd aeth hyt y Llonwen ym Penuro ac yno y dotwes
ar heiden a gwenenen, ac er hynny y mae goreu lle y heid
Llonwen, ac odyna y kerd6ys hyt yn Ri6 Gyuerth6ch yn
Eryri, ac y dotwes ar keneu bleid ac ar ky6 eryr, ar eryr a
rodes Coll mab Collurewy i Urynach Vydel or Gogled, ar bleid
a rodes i Uenwaed o Arllechwed, ar rei hynny uu uleid Menwaed, ac Eryr Brynach.   Ac odyna yd aeth hyt y Maendu
yn Llanueir yn Aruon ; ac yno y dodwes ar keneu cath, ar
keneu h6nn6 a uyry6ys Coll mab Collurewy ym Menei ; a
honno wedẏ hynny uu Cath Paluc.

Tri Phrif Lleturitha6c Ynys Prydein.   Coll mab Collurewy
a Meny6 mab Teirgwaed a Drych eil Ki6dar.

Teir Prif Hut Ynys Prydein.   Hut Math mab Maton6y a
Hut Uthyr Pendragon a˙Hut G6ydelyn Gor.

Tri Diweir Teulu Ynys Prydein.   Teulu Catwalla6n mab
Catuan auuant seith mlyned yn Iwerdon y gyt ac ef ; ac yn
hynny o yspeit ny ouynassant dim ida6 rac goruot arnadunt
y ada6 ; a Theulu Gauran mab Aedan a aethant yr mor dros eu
hargl6yd ; ar tryded Teulu Gendoleu mab Keidya6 yn Arderyd
a gynnalassant y ur6ydyr pythe6nos a mis wedẏ llad eu
hargl6yd sef oed riuedi teuluoed pob un or gwyr hynny un
Canh6r ar ugeint.

Tri Aniweir Teulu Ynys Prydein.   Teulu Goron6 Pefyr o
Penllyn a omedassant eu hargl6yd o erbynneit y gwen-
6ynway6 y gan Leu Lla6 Gyffes yn Llechoron6y yn blaen
Kynuael ; a Theulu G6rgi a Pheredur a ada6ssant eu hargl6yd
yg Caer Greu, ac a oed ymllad trannoeth udunt ac Eda Glin-
wa6r ; ac yna y llas ell deu.   Ar trydyd Teulu Alan Fyrgan
a ymchoelasant y 6rth eu hargl6yd ar y ford hyt nos ae ell6ng
ynteu ae weisson Kamlan ac yno y llas.

as far as Penryn Awstin in Cornwall, and there going to sea, landed at Abertorogi in Gwent Iscoed, and Coll son of Collfrewy having his hand on the bristles, whenever she went on the sea or on the land, and at Maes Gwenith in Gwent she dropped wheat and bees, and from henceforth there is the best wheat there, and from thence she went to Lonwen in Penbro, and there she dropped barley and bees, and from thence there is the best barley in Lonwen, and from thence she proceeded to the Riw Cyferthwch in Eryri, and there she dropped a wolf-cub and an eagle, and Coll son of Collfreuy gave the eagle to Brynach Gwyddel of the north, and the wolf he gave to Menwaed of Arllechwedd, and these are the wolf of Menwaed and the eagle of Brynach, and thence going to Maendu in Llanfare, in Arvon, and there she dropped a kitten, and Coll son of Collfrewy threw the kitten into the Menai, and she became afterwards the Paluc cat.

XXIV. Three chief-gleaming ones of the Island of Prydain. Coll son of Collfrewy ; and Meniw son of Teirgwaed ; and Drych son of Kiwdar.

XXV. Three primary illusions of the Island of Prydain. The illusion of Math son of Matonwy ; and the illusion of Uthyr Pendragon ; and the illusion of Gwydelen Gor.

XXVI. Three loyal households of the Island of Prydain. The household of Catwallaun son of Cadfan, who were seven years in Ywerdon with him, and in that time demanded no pay nor compensation from him ; and the household of Gafran son of Aedan, who went to sea with their lord ; and the third the household of Gwendoleu son of Ceidyaw at Arderyd, who maintained the contest forty-six days after their lord was slain. The number of the households each one of their warriors one hundred men and a score.

XXVII. Three disloyal households of the Island of Prydain. The household of Goronw Pebyr of Penllyn who refused to stand in place of their lord to receive the poisoned darts from Low Law Gyffes in Lech Goronwy in Blaen Cynfael ; and the household of Gwrgi and Peredur, who deserted their lords in Caer Greu, when there was appointment for battle next morning against Eda Glinmaur, and they were both slain ; and the third, the household of Alan Fyrgan, who returned back by stealth from their lord, on the road at night with his servants at Camlan, and there he was slain.

Teir Gosgord Adѵy Ynys Prydein. Gosgord Mynydaѵc
Eidyn a Gosgord Melyn mab Kynuelyn a Gosgord Dryan
mab Nud.

Trywyr a wnaeth y teir Mat Gyflauan. Gall mab Disgyfedaѵt a ladeid deu ederyn Gwendoleu, a ieu o eur oed
arnadunt a dwy kelein or Kymry a yssynt ar eu kinyaѵ, a
dѵy ar eu cѵynos, ac Ysgafnell mab Disgyfedaѵt a ladeid
Edelfflet urenhin Lloegyr a Diffedell mab Disgyfedaѵt a ladaѵd
Gѵrgi Garѵlѵyt, ar Gѵrgi honnѵ ladei kelein beunyd or Kymry
a dѵy pob sadѵrn rac llad y sul yr un.

Teir Anuat Gyulauan Ynys Prydein . Eidyn mab Einygan
a ladaѵd Aneirȳn Gwaѵdrud methdeyrn beird ; a Llaѵgat trѵm
bargaѵt a ladaѵd Auaon mab Taliessin ; a Llouan Llaѵdino a
ladaѵd Vryen mab Kynuarch.

Teir Anuat Uѵyellaѵt Ynys Prydein . Bѵyellaѵt Eidyn ym
pen Aneiryn ; ar uѵyellaѵt ym pen Godlan bard ; ar uѵyellaѵt
ym pen Iago mab Beli.

Tri Chyuor a aeth or Ynys hon, ac ny doeth yr un
dracheuyn o nadunt. Un a aeth gan Helen Luydaѵc a Chynan
y braѵt. Eil a aeth gan Yrp Luydaѵc yn oes Cadyal mab
Erynt ; a doeth yma y erchi kymorth ; ac nyt archei o bob
prifgaer namyn deu kymeint ac a delhei gantaѵ idi ; ac ny
doeth gantaѵ yr gyntaf namyn ef ae was, ac ardustru uu
rodi hynny idaѵ. A hѵnn essoes llѵyraf lluyd a aeth or ynys
honn, ac ny doeth dracheuyn neb o nadunt. Sef lle y
trigyѵys y gwyr hynny yn dѵy ynys yn ymyl mor Groec. Sef
ynt y dѵy ynys Gals ac Avena . Trydyd kyudu a aeth
gan Caswallaѵn mab Beli a Gwenwynwyn a Gwanar meibon
Lliaѵs mab Nѵyure ac Aranrot uerch Beli eu mam ; ac o
Arllechwed yd hanoet y gwyr hynny ; ac yd aethant y gyt a
Chaswallaѵn eu hewythyr yn ol y Cesaryeit trѵy uor. Sef lle
y mae y gwyr hynny yg Gwasgwin. Sef eiryf a aeth ym pob
un or lluoed hynny un mil ar ugeint ; ar rei hynny oed y tri
aryant llu . Sef y gelwit y uelly ; ѵrth uynet eur ac aryant
yr ynys gantunt ae hethol wynteu o oreu y oreu.

XXVIII. Three pass retinues of the Island of Prydain. The retinue of Mynydawg of Eidyn; the retinue of Melyn son of Cynvelyn; and the retinue of Dryan son of Nud.

XXIX. Three warriors who made the three good assassinations of the Island of Prydain. Gall son of Disgyfedawt, who slew the two birds of Gwendoleu, who had a yoke of gold about them, and devoured two bodies of Cymry at their dinner and two at their supper; and Ysgafnell son of Disgyfedawt, who slew Edelflet, king of Lloegyr; and Diffedel son of Disgyfedawt, who slew Gwrgi Garwlwyt, and this Gwrgi killed a male and female of the Cymry, and two on Saturday that he might not kill one on Sunday.

XXX. Three atrocious assassinators of the Island of Prydain. Eidyn, son of Einygan, who slew Aneiryn Gwawdrud, the supreme of bards; and Llawgat Trumbargawt, who slew Afaon son of Taliessin; and Llovan Llawdino, who slew Urien son of Kynvarch.

XXXI. Three atrocious axe-strokes of the island of Prydain. The axe-stroke of Eidyn on the head of Aneiryn; and the axe-stroke on the head of Godlan the bard; and the axe-stroke on the head of Iago son of Beli.

XXXII. Three combined expeditions that went from this island and never returned. One went with Helen Luydawg and Cynan her brother. Another went with Yrp Luydawc, in the time of Cadyal son of Erynt, he came to ask assistance, and he asked not from each city, but the same number he should bring with him, and there came with him to the first only one youth, and he obtained one given him. He was the greatest levier of an expedition that went from this island, and none of the warriors returned. They went on an invasive expedition, these warriors, to two islands in the sea of Greece. These are the two islands, Gals and Avena. The third host went with Caswallaun son of Beli, and Gwenwynwyn, and Gwanar sons of Lliaws son of Nwyure, and Aranrot daughter of Beli, was their mother, and from Arllechwed were these warriors, and they went with Caswallawn, their uncle, against the Cesariot over the sea, and these warriors are now in Gwasgwyn. There went with each of these hosts one thousand and twenty. These are the three silver hosts. They were thus called, for they took the gold and silver of the island with them, as much as they could.

Teir Gormes a doeth yr Ynys hon ac nyt aeth yr un dracheuyn · Kyƀdaƀt y Korannyeit a doethant yma yn oes Llud mab Beli ac nyt aeth yr un dracheuyn.   A gormes y Gƀydyl Fichti ; ac nyt aeth yr un drachefyn · Trydyd gormes y Saesson ac nyt aethant dracheuyn.

Tri Chud a Thri Datgud Ynys Prydein · Pen bendigeit Uran uab Llyr a cladƀyt yny Gwynfryn yu Llundein a hyt tra vei y penn ynyr ansaƀdyd oed yno ; ny doy ormes byth yr ynys hon.   Eil, Esgyrn Gƀercheuyr Vendigeit a a gladwyt ym pryf byrth yr ynys hon.   Trydyd, y dreigieu a gladwys Llud mab Beli yn dinas Emreis yn Eryri.

Three oppressions came to this Island, and did not go out of it. The nation of the Coranyeit, who came in the time of Llud son of Beli, and did not go out of it; and the oppression of the Gwydyl Fichti, and they did not again go out of it. The third, the oppression of the Saxons, and they did not again go out of it.

Three closures and disclosures of the Island of Prydain. The blessed head of Bran son of Llyr, which was buried in the Gwynfryn in London, and while the head remained in that state, no invasion would come to this island. The second, the bones of Gwerthefyr the blessed, which are buried in the principal ports of the island; and the third, the dragons which Llud son of Beli buried in Dinas Emreis in Eryri.

2 I

THE END.

Printed by R. CLARK, *Edinburgh.*

In one Vol. 8vo, price 12s., uniform with

"THE FOUR ANCIENT BOOKS OF WALES."

THE DEAN OF LISMORE'S BOOK:

SPECIMENS OF ANCIENT GAELIC POETRY

Collected between the years 1512 and 1529 by Sir JAMES M'GREGOR, Dean of Lismore—illustrative of the Language and Literature of the Scottish Highlands prior to the Sixteenth Century. Edited, with a Translation and Notes, by the Rev. THOMAS MACLAUCHLAN. The Introduction and additional Notes by WILLIAM F. SKENE. 8vo, price 12s.

U·7

CPSIA information can be obtained
at www.ICGtesting.com
Printed in the USA
BVHW072319171120
593490BV00008B/139